PETER COLE
(Lead Editor)

BRIAN MCQUINN
(*Editor*)

The Libyan Revolution and its Aftermath

OXFORD
UNIVERSITY PRESS

OXFORD

UNIVERSITY PRESS

Oxford University Press is a department of the
University of Oxford. It furthers the University's objective
of excellence in research, scholarship, and education
by publishing worldwide.

Oxford   New York

Auckland   Cape Town   Dar es Salaam   Hong Kong   Karachi
Kuala Lumpur   Madrid   Melbourne   Mexico City   Nairobi
New Delhi   Shanghai   Taipei   Toronto

With offices in

Argentina   Austria   Brazil   Chile   Czech Republic   France   Greece
Guatemala   Hungary   Italy   Japan   Poland   Portugal   Singapore
South Korea   Switzerland   Thailand   Turkey   Ukraine   Vietnam

Oxford is a registered trade mark of Oxford University Press
in the UK and certain other countries.

Published in the United States of America by
Oxford University Press
198 Madison Avenue, New York, NY 10016

Library of Congress Cataloging-in-Publication Data is available
Cole, Peter and McQuinn, Brian.
The Libyan Revolution and its Aftermath

ISBN 978-0-19-021096-0

Printed in India on acid-free paper

CONTENTS

CONTENTS

NOTE ON TRANSLITERATION

This volume employs the transliteration system used by the *International Journal of Middle Eastern Studies* (IJMES) (available online at: http://ijmes.ws.gc.cuny.edu/authorresources/#transliteration).

Some simplifications have been made to promote readability and a clean text. Long vowels—*alif*, *yaa'*, and *waw* (و ي ا) are rendered with 'a', 'i' or 'u', and not with the macron as in IJMES. Thus قذافي is rendered 'Qadhafi'. Similarly the consonants *saad* and *taal* (ط ص) are rendered as 's' and 't' respectively; *daad* (ض) as 'd', and *dhaal* (ظ) as dh without macron. The *yaa* preceded by a *hamza* ـئ is transliterated 'ai': thus شيخ is rendered *shaikh*, not *sheikh*. *Ain* ع and *hamza* ا are transliterated with', but dropped entirely when appearing as the first letter. Thus أوباري is Awbari, not 'Awbari. Letters with the *shadda* are doubled; thus بلحاج is 'Bilhajj', not 'Bilhaj' or 'Belhaj'.

The definite article ال is transliterated lower case 'al', and attached to the word it governs by hyphen ('Saif al-Islam'). For readability, 'moon' letters, (which elide the *lam* with the first consonant of the next word), are not rendered; thus الشمس ('the sun') is written *al-shams*, not *ash-shams*; the name عبد الرحمان is written Abd al-Rahman, not Abd ar-Rahman.

Names are written in full on first usage (Abd al-Fattah Yunis) and subsequently with reference to their last name ('Yunis'). For last names employing 'al-', the name is spelt in full on first usage (Mu'ammar al-Qadhafi) but references to the last name drop the 'al' ('Qadhafi'). The definite article is also dropped for place names; al-Iraq is rendered 'Iraq', al-Khums as 'Khums'. Names employing 'Abd al-', however, always include that phrase for religious reasons. Thus مصطفى عبد الجليل

vii

is rendered Mustafa Abd al-Jalil and subsequently 'Abd al-Jalil'. The name عبد الله is written as Abdullah, not Abdallah or Abd Allah.

Libyan Dialects and Other Exceptions

The standard IJMES 'exceptions' list is used for Arabic names in English that when rendered formally would be hard to recognise; for example, جمال عبد الناصر is written Gamal Abdel Nasser, not Jamal Abd al-Nasir. For similar reasons, بنغازي is written 'Benghazi' not 'Binghazi'. Place names that are completely different in English and Arabic use the English variant; طرابلس is written Tripoli, not 'Tarablus', القاهرة Cairo, not 'al-Qahira', and ليبيا 'Libya', not 'Libia'.

Libyan dialects sometimes elide the first two consonants or radicals in a word, and occasionally transliteration reflects this. For example, we have chosen to render أبو سليم as Abu Slim, not Abu Salim. Likewise some Libyan dialects elide the initial *mim* م in a word with the following radical, particularly in names, and sometimes render this with an initial *alef*, reflected here with an initial 'I'. Thus امحمد is transliterated 'Imhammad', امضخم is Imdakhum and محمد مغريف, is rendered Imhammad Imgharyif.

Tuareg and non-Arabised Tebu and Amazigh names, reflecting both a different language and sometimes the French phonetic system, have been transliterated according to authors' own systems.

Frequently Used Terminology[1]

Revolution/Civil War

The book adopts the term 'revolution' to refer to the events of 15 February 2011–23 October 2011 in Libya, which Libyans named the '17 February Revolution'. This recognises that these events ended not only Mu'ammar al-Qadhafi's rule, but his conception of Libya as a decentralised 'state of the masses' (*jamahiriyya*) and the institutions he invented to administer and enforce that order, such as the General People's Congress, Revolutionary Committees, Popular Social Leadership Committees, and many others. It also follows the definition of 'revolution' employed by historian Charles Tilly.[2] Some contributors employ the term 'civil war' to describe the fighting that took place over this period; here, the formulation devised by Kalyvas[3] of 'armed combat within the boundaries of a recognised sovereign entity between parties subject to a common authority at the outset of the hostilities' is understood. Furthermore, the minimum threshold of violence for civil wars devised by the Uppsala Conflict Data Program and International Peace Research Institute, Oslo, which describes conflicts with 25 battle deaths per year as 'civil conflicts' and those with 1000 battle deaths per year as 'civil wars', applies to the Libyan conflict.[4]

Regime/Government. The term 'government' in this volume refers to official organs of the Libyan state, including its ministries and office of the prime minister, judiciary, and armed forces. Qadhafi's philosophy of government included successive attempts to dismantle this state. In the process, he created a large, finely-tuned system of non-governmental 'revolutionary', tribal or security institutions, headed by loyal individuals who were often rotated between posts. The word 'regime' applies to this system. Examples of 'regime' bodies found in this volume include the Revolutionary Committees and their Revolutionary Guard, People's Social Leadership Committees, the Central Intelligence Bureau and its subsidiary internal and external security apparatus (al-Amn al-Dakihli/ al-Khariji), and the security brigades (see below). While the 'regime' was swept away by the 17 February Revolution, the National Transitional Council (NTC) turned to the remains of the government for governance and security during the transition. The phrases 'interim government' and 'transitional government' apply to the post-revolutionary administrations of Abd al-Rahim al-Kib (24 November 2011–14 November 2012) and Ali Zaidan (14 November 2012–11 March 2014).

Katiba/'Revolutionary battalion'. Revolutionary fighters adopted military terminology to describe their armed groups; the most commonly used term was *katiba*, (pl. *kata'ib*). An army *katiba* denotes a force of anything from several hundred to around a thousand soldiers; in the Libyan army, it denoted a unit headed by a colonel.[5] In that sense, this volume uses 'battalion' as a more appropriate translation for *katiba* than the oft-used 'brigade', which denotes a far larger force. It differentiates revolutionary forces as 'revolutionary battalions' as opposed to Qadhafi's 'security brigades'. Nonetheless, 'revolutionary battalions' were often far smaller and less organised than their military equivalents; the term *katiba* became used to describe any group regardless of size.

Security brigades. Qadhafi's military-security apparatus employed a variety of 'security brigades' that worked in parallel to the armed forces. The former were recruited explicitly tribally and represented on the 'permanent security committee' which was based in Qadhafi's head-quarters in Bab al-Aziziyya alongside other state security organs; the internal security (*al-Amn al-Dakhili*), and strategic installations security bodies. Two of the most prominent—the 32 Reinforced Brigade and the Imhammad Imgharyif Brigade—were considered 'rapid intervention forces'. Other brigades that are prominent actors in this volume are the Fadil, Faris, Sahban, Hamza and Maghawir Brigades. 'Security brigades' possessed lines of command and communication to the armed forces and its chief of staff, from which they recruited, but unlike the armed forces, were sworn to protect Qadhafi's regime and revolution rather than the Libyan state. Two other forces—the People's Guard and People's Resistance Forces—were comprised of reservists and volunteers from loyal tribes mobilised to fight alongside the security brigades. While the armed forces persisted beyond the revolution, the 'security brigades' did not. (Another key actor in this volume, the *Sa'iqa* Special Forces Battalion, was part of the regular armed forces.)

LIST OF ACRONYMS

GNC   General National Congress, Libya's interim government
          elected 7 July 2012.
LIFG   Libyan Islamic Fighting Group (now defunct).
LYD   Libyan Dinars
NATO   North Atlantic Treaty Organisation
NFSL   National Front for the Salvation of Libya (now defunct)
NTC   National Transitional Council
UNSCR   United Nations Security Council Resolution
UNSMIL   United Nations Support Mission in Libya
US   United States (of America)

ABOUT THE CONTRIBUTORS

Peter Bartu teaches political transitions in the Middle East at the University of California, Berkeley and was present in Benghazi during the Libyan revolution as a member of the UN's Standby Mediation Support Unit. He has previously worked in Iraq (2008–2009), Israel-Palestine (2001–2003), East Timor (1999) and Cambodia (1991–1993), among other countries.

Peter Cole was Senior Analyst for International Crisis Group in Libya (July 2011–July 2012). He has consulted for the United Nations Support Mission in Libya, the Carnegie Endowment for International Peace and Small Arms Survey. He read Modern Middle Eastern Studies at the University of Oxford.

Mary Fitzgerald is an Irish journalist and analyst specialising in post-Gaddafi Libya. She has reported from Libya since February 2011 for media including the Economist, the BBC, *Foreign Policy, the New Yorker, the Financial Times and the Guardian*. She spent 2014 living in Tripoli after taking a sabbatical from her post as Irish Times foreign affairs correspondent.

Yvan Guichaoua is a lecturer in International Politics at the University of East Anglia. He is a former teaching fellow at Yale University and research officer at the University of Oxford. He studies irregular armed groups in Nigeria, Côte d'Ivoire, Mali and Niger and the rise of jihadism in West Africa.

Sean Kane served as the Benghazi representative for the Centre for Humanitarian Dialogue. He has worked for the United Nations and the United States Institute of Peace in Iraq and Afghanistan. He has published on Iraqi and Libyan politics, natural resource negotiations and political transitions during the Arab Spring.

Ahmed Labnouj has a B.A. in Political Science from the University of California Berkeley, an M.A. in Law and Diplomacy from the Fletcher School, Tufts University, and a Certificate from the Graduate Institute in Geneva. He has worked extensively in the MENA region and has been based in Libya since early 2011.

Wolfram Lacher is a researcher on Libya and the Sahel/Sahara region at Stiftung Wissenschaft und Politik in Berlin. Previously, he worked as a North Africa analyst at Control Risks in London. He studied Arabic, Politics, as well as Conflict and Development Studies in Leipzig, Paris, Cairo and London.

Ian Martin was Special Representative of the United Nations Secretary-General and head of the UN Support Mission in Libya from September 2011 to October 2012. Previous, Ian was Special Adviser coordinating post-conflict planning for Libya from April 2011; headed UN peace operations in Nepal and East Timor and served as Secretary General of Amnesty International (1986–92).

Brian McQuinn is currently completing a PhD in anthropology as a Guggenheim Foundation Dissertation Fellow at the University of Oxford on the 2011 uprising in Libya. He was previously the assistant director of the Carter Centre Conflict Resolution Program and a conflict prevention adviser for the United Nations Development Programme.

Rebecca Murray writes regularly from the Middle East and Africa for publications like Al Jazeera English and Inter Press Service. Murray was based in Libya in 2012, and returned in the Spring of 2013, visiting the country's south Sahara desert several times. There she talked to Libya's Tebu community about their history, their integral role in the 2011 revolution, and their place in the country's future.

Dirk Vandewalle teaches at Dartmouth College. He is the author of *Libya Since Independence* and *A History of Modern Libya* and is currently the field office director for the Carter Center in Tripoli.

Vandewalle has been one of the only western academics to have worked consistently in Libya during the Qadhafi period and is currently working on a new book, *Libya: The Uncertain Revolution*.

Frederic Wehrey is a senior associate in the Middle East Program at the Carnegie Endowment for International Peace. His writing on Libya has appeared in the *New York Times*, the *Washington Post*, the *Atlantic Monthly*, *Foreign Affairs*, and the *Financial Times*. He holds a doctorate in International Relations from Oxford University.

Marieke Wierda is a Dutch lawyer, born and raised in Yemen and educated in the UK and the US; specialising in international criminal law, transitional justice, international investigations and prosecutions in the MENA region, sub-Saharan Africa and Afghanistan. She joined the United Nations Support Mission in Libya in October 2011.

INTRODUCTION

Peter Cole and *Brian McQuinn*

The essays in this volume provide a granular account of the period beginning in Benghazi, Libya on 15 February 2011, when protests over the arrest of Fathi Tirbil, a legal advocate for families of victims of the 1996 Abu Slim prison massacre, precipitated what is now called the '17 February Revolution'. Focusing primarily on the military conflict spanning 15 February–23 October 2011, and the first year of the transition that followed, its chapters recount events from the perspective of its key geographic, tribal/communal and political players, networks and constituencies. The chapters in this volume argue, as a whole, that these communities' narratives are stronger, more distinct and self-contained than one single 'Libyan' narrative. Yet those narrative strands, read together, weave into a single thread that, while discordant, is uniquely 'Libyan'.

The volume was conceived through a series of conversations among field practitioners in Libya to address many of the myths and analytic shorthands that had become commonplace concerning both the Libyan revolution and its aftermath, and the international intervention that accompanied it. The editors sought contributors with deep relationships to the communities they studied, based on at least three months' field experience in Libya. Some conducted specific research for this volume, drawing on interviews with senior fighters, politicians and civil society leaders. Each followed their own methodology. Three chapters—those covering the National Transitional Council (NTC), UN, and transitional justice sector—were penned by senior diplomatic officials. Two, covering Islamist networks and the Tebu, were contributed by journalists. The remaining chapters employ varying methodologies drawn from political science and anthropology.

Taken together, the chapters illustrate how, firstly, Libya's revolution, and the intervention, not only toppled Mu'ammar al-Qadhafi, but removed key decision makers and ended Libya's modality of government—Qadhafi's 'state of the masses'—creating profound issues surrounding national identity. Consequently, the multiple military and political actors that arose to fight or support Qadhafi acted on parochial logics and historical narratives, which determined their desire to co-opt, support or oppose the transitional authorities or Qadhafi's state. The result was a revolution disconnected beyond the shared goal of Qadhafi's defeat, resulting in unique political and military structures and relationships in every major city and sub-region. Accordingly, the chapters in the first part of this volume discuss Libyan transitional authorities' attempts to direct the revolution and transition, and the resultant political discord, while the second part focuses individually on the major geographic, tribal and political networks that emerged to shape events.

The volume also discusses the policy implications faced by the international intervention; the military intervention, framed by United Nations Security Council resolutions (UNSCR) 1970 and 1973, and enforced primarily through NATO air power, and the political and civilian support requested by the NTC and transitional authorities in the form of a UN mission and multiple forms of bilateral assistance. It demonstrates how both political and military planners were influenced by the desire to maintain an international 'light footprint', to cede ultimate decisions on national self-determination to Libyan authority, and to avoid mistakes made with the rapid dissolution of the Iraqi state in 2003–4. Yet the Libyan political divides discussed above presented no institutional or charismatic authority, but rather a rump state, surrounded by sub-national identities and communities older than itself. The ensuing debates and power struggles over who had the authority to take decisions provoked discord and drift. Policies and plans that may have enabled a more stable transition, therefore, necessarily gave way to these debates, while military support during and after the intervention could not prevent—and sometimes encouraged—a fragmented security sector.

Special mention must be made of the role women and youth played in the events herein. Though most named political and military actors in this collection are male (a fact reflecting Libya's gender politics), the vast network of safe houses, aid, weaponry, medical and food distribution networks that supported them speak for the critical role of women. Women were also present as fighters, medics, diplomats, journalists, politicians and professionals, and staffed NTC and Libyan government offices. Similarly, most of these networks, and the vast majority of protestors and fighters, were males and females under thirty years old, who, as can be seen below, challenged the views and politics of their elders continually.

Part 1: The Revolution and its Governance

In 2011 an unprecedented wave of social protest, now known as the 'Arab Spring', surged through the Arab world, sparked by the self-immolation of the Tunisian street vendor Muhammad Bouazizi. Activists throughout the region sought to replicate the Tunisian example in their own countries, but the governments that proved most vulnerable were republics created by military coups:[1] Syria (whose first coup was in 1949) and Egypt (1952), which sparked imitative examples in Yemen (1962) and Libya (1969). These military-led states originally legitimised themselves by appealing to a republican and 'pan-Arab' nationalism, but by 2011 these narratives were defunct. As their populations swelled, their social support base shrank, while competing narratives, identities and political movements emerged based on sub-state communities (city, tribe), supra-state loyalties (political Islam, religious sects or cross-border kinships) or nationalism. 'Unable to marginalize these rival identities, state leaders … pursued authoritarian strategies', either manipulating or repressing them.[2] None could do so well enough when faced with the mass socio-economic protests of the Arab Spring, causing leadership changes and transitions in Egypt, Yemen and Libya, and protracted civil war in Syria. While Egypt and Tunisia's revolutions did not overturn state institutions and symbols—flags, constitutions, militaries and modes of governance—Libya's did.

Chapter 1, by Dirk Vandewalle, frames the 17 February Revolution—and this book—in this context. Elsewhere, Vandewalle has charted how Qadhafi's 1 September 1969 revolution undid an 'accidental' state created in 1951 by the UN General Assembly 'at the behest of the

Great Powers ... without a unifying ideology or movement'.[3] 'Here, Vandewalle argues that Qadhafi's 'Green Revolution' further disrupted this nascent state by bypassing state institutions. This distrust of central authority, 'taken to a logical extreme under the *diktats* of his *Green Book*, was itself a symptom of ... the tension between a hinterland culture and the culture represented by the country's urban areas' (page 22). Vandewalle posits that the revolution, like Libya's history and national identity, were contested by these long-repressed sub-national interests and identities, which 'as both Qadhafi and the NTC came to realize ... were powerfully attractive and divisive' (page 19), concluding that 'today, as in 1951, there remain competing visions of what Libya should look like as a state' (page 27).

Subsequent chapters focus on the Libyan and international political actors seeking to guide the revolution and transition. In Chapter 2, Peter Bartu describes how the 'Provisional National Transitional Council', formed in Benghazi on 5 March 2011, endeavored to articulate the political direction of the revolution. Bartu argues that the NTC began as an extension of the temporary local councils that coalesced, in the wake of the collapse of Qadhafi's state, 'without a strategic imperative or vision' beyond calling for Qadhafi's removal and, to distance themselves from his authoritanarism, with 'a shared anxiety... to show they had not seized or assumed power'. Bartu charts the attempt of a dominant current of lawyers and political veterans within the NTC to delineate a political vision for the transition; initially the '5 May Roadmap', which was predicated on a negotiated ceasefire agreement with Qadhafi, followed by an inclusive transitional government in which senior armed forces and security services officials would 'avoid chaos during the transitional phase' (page 40). Bartu notes how this current's political imperatives were entwined with their need to gain early international cooperation 'to pay salaries and otherwise run a wartime economy' (page 43). This was facilitated by the creation of a Contact Group that included staunch support from Qatar, France, the UK and US in setting up creative extra-legal mechanisms to allow the NTC to receive oil products on credit, access Libyan sovereign assets abroad to pay salaries and to source Libyan currency printed offshore to deal with a liquidity crisis. This support, Bartu argues, was critical in allowing the NTC to meet 'a minimum threshold of legitimacy' (page 53).

Bartu notes, however, that the NTC's vision was successfully challenged by Islamist and Tripoli-centric elements within it. They sought to dissolve the NTC and embark on a riskier, albeit more legitimate and democratic, transition, by electing an interim government—the General National Congress (GNC)—only 240 days after the end of the revolution was declared.

In Chapters 3 and 4, Peter Cole and Umar Khan expand on this factional discord within the NTC and its entwinement with international support by charting the competing planning and military networks that sought to influence the fall of Tripoli, both of which engendered diverging visions of Libya after Qadhafi. The architects of the '5 May Roadmap' sponsored a network of security service defectors in Tripoli, negotiating with community leaders from Qadhafi's support base with the hope that surgical strikes from NATO and a benign popular uprising could force capitulation from Qadhafi. Meanwhile, Tripoli-centric and 'Islamist' networks sought to empower frontline fighters to surround Tripoli's access routes and take on Qadhafi's security brigades by force. Both sides tried to manipulate regional hubs and actors, particularly Misrata and Zintan, to see their vision fulfilled. They also manipulated, and were manipulated by, partnerships with NATO member states, particularly the UK, US and France, as well as Qatar and the UAE, which offered both coordination with NATO's air campaign and political cover for weapons and ammunition supplies. However, 'parts of both plans succeeded, but much of both failed when confronted by a more chaotic reality', namely the rapid growth of Tripolitanian armed groups, and the rapid influx of fighters into the capital. Those who hoped the NTC would helm a stable transition atop remaining security institutions and ministries found that they struggled to cope. Those who wished to empower the new 'revolutionary' forces, and reelect a transitional government after Qadhafi's fall, faced an ensuing struggle for power in the security sector. The contours of Libya's new politics forged in 'Tripoli's haphazard fall... created competing visions over... who should and shouldn't be empowered'; the surviving institutions of the Libyan state, the new 'revolutionaries', or the NTC's executive. The balancing of these interests fell primarily to Mustafa Abd al-Jalil, whose role in doing so is still not perhaps fully appreciated or understood.

These internal Libyan struggles were shaped in the context of international intervention, the legal and military framework for which was UNSCR 1970 and 1973, and the 'no-fly zone' imposed by French, US and UK, and then NATO, forces. UNSCR 1973, which allowed 'all necessary means' excepting a 'foreign occupation force' to protect civilians from harm,[4] was justified by a new doctrine named 'Right to Protect' (R2P), developed following UN failures to prevent massacres in Rwanda (1994), Srebrenica (1995) and Kosovo (1998–9). It culminated in a 2005 UN General Assembly document which said that 'should peaceful means be inadequate', the UN was entitled 'to take collective action' under Chapter VII of its Charter, which authorised military force 'to help protect populations from genocide, war crimes, ethnic cleansing and crimes against humanity.'[5] The doctrine was invoked to prevent an apparently imminent massacre in Benghazi following Qadhafi's threat to cleanse Libya 'inch by inch, house by house, street by street', and as its first explicit application, Libya became a case study for its use.[6] In doing so it protected an already-armed uprising that had little clear political direction.

Chapters 5 and 6 examine NATO and the United Nations' engagement with Libyan opposition forces—later its transitional authorities. Both sought a 'light footprint' in Libya following lessons learned from previous interventions in the greater Middle East and beyond, and this in part determined their successes and challenges. The UN, after some setbacks in directly administered interventions in Somalia (1992–4) and Kosovo (1998), convened a panel chaired by Lakhdar Brahimi to review UN peacekeeping operations which advocated smaller, politically-led missions, and called light footprint, that minimised international staff, working instead through national staff, NGOs and coordinated international assistance.[7] Likewise, those in military circles had learned from the 2001 NATO intervention in Afghanistan and 2003 US-led invasion of Iraq, which resulted in repeated deployments and indefinite end goals of 'nationbuilding'. Domestic insurgencies and other asymmetric security challenges were countered with modern COIN (counter-insurgency) doctrines focused on special operations and intelligence agents building relationships with local partners, supported by air power, also called 'light footprint',[8] subsequently employed by NATO powers in Libya in 2011.

In Chapter 5, Frederic Wehrey evaluates NATO's 'light footprint' air campaign in Libya—the 'so-called Afghan model' based on 'the combination of precision airpower, ground advisers, supplies, and training' (page 125) and the delicate partnership that therefore evolved between NATO, its member states, and the Libyan opposition fighters. Charting how the no-fly zone 'shifted the tide of battle at crucial stages of the revolution' (page 106), from the eastern frontline at Brega, to keeping Misrata's port open, and backing up the rapid advance of Nafusa Mountain fighters into Tripoli, Wehrey notes the challenges this type of mission posed: difficulties in target assessment and intelligence; political and operational disunity between rebel fighters; and a UNSCR mandate that the NTC stipulated forbade 'boots on the ground'. To overcome these challenges NATO and member states sent 'ground advisers' to partner with Libyans, setting up communications and operations rooms that routed directly to NATO, AFRICOM, and other externally-based central commands. Wehrey concludes that the success of the NATO campaign was dependent on this 'political and operational unity' between Libyan fighters and NATO member states. Yet Wehrey also notes that this model invited competition between them and their local partners, which was particularly prominent in Benghazi and the Nafusa Mountains.

In Chapter 6, Ian Martin, who led the UN mission in Libya, reviews the issues facing the first year of the transition, including the 7 July 2012 elections, the political and managerial issues in the security sector and transitional justice. In all three, Martin notes, 'Libyans... were determined to be in control of the transition, and were wary of post-conflict situations dominated by external actors' (page 129). Martin argues that this 'Libyan-led' approach matched the UN's evolving thinking on designing peacekeeping missions with a 'light footprint'.[9] The NTC, 'firm in its desire to avoid "boots on the ground"' ... articulated the parameters of the support it wished to receive', meaning that where Libyan authorities were decisive, as with the swift and smooth election of the GNC on 7 July 2012, the international community could successfully support the transition.

Martin also highlights limits of the mandate and 'light footprint' design, including the inability of the UN to intervene 'at key moments of internal disarray', or where the NTC did not request support or was otherwise constrained by its short timeframe and limited legitimacy, which saw decisions postponed 'before a stronger government with a basis of democratic legitimacy was in place'. Martin argues that 'the greatest failure' of the transition, for these reasons, was in Libyan attempts to command its security sector, where 'an ideological divide that emerged between some who preferred a managed transition with the participation of elements of the former regime's security forces, and those revolutionaries—particularly Misratans, civilian fighters from the east and former members of the Libyan Islamic Fighting Group—who wanted to exclude these elements'. Martin discusses how the consequent government paralysis over the issue, and the severely limited capacities of the police and armed forces, hampered international support efforts, and instead led to the rise of parallel security forces—the Supreme Security Committees, Libya Shield Forces, Border Guard and others—staffed by salaried, but untrained, civilian fighters.

Chapter 7, by Marieke Wierda, who led the UN's Transitional Justice support team, outlines the transitional justice challenges facing Libyans. Wierda examines the NTC's initial 'relatively modest process' of excluding 'only those with, in Abd al-Jalil's formulation, "blood on their hands"', which was inspired by the lessons of Debaathification in Iraq. Wierda concludes, however, that even these efforts were quickly sidelined by other political currents in and outside the NTC, including the local revolutionary fighters or *thuwwar* who demanded a wide-ranging 'political isolation law' and the powers to arrest, detain and interrogate those they deemed political criminals. These fighters' command of prisons and prisoners in illegal detention prevented the processing of detainees and trials of senior Qadhafi-era figures, while granting amnesties to the *thuwwar* themselves. Wierda pays particular attention to the disparity between Libyans' desire to deal internally with their transitional justice issues and the international best practice of the International Criminal Court, to which the UN Security Council referred Libya on 25 February 2011, but which Libyan authorities and armed groups rebuffed. Wierda's chapter, as with Ian Martin's, highlights the challenges of the early transmission of powers to state institutions that lacked capacity to address their extraordinary circumstances, and how this has dictated governance after the 17 February Revolution.

Thus the original questions posed by Libya's 'statelessness'—the lack of a head of state, constitution, charismatic authority or state institution to guide the 17 February Revolution and its transition dominated Libyan politics well into 2013. Later events such as the death of US Ambassador Chris Stephens on 11 September 2012, or Prime Minister Zaidan's formal request for NATO assistance in the security sector in May 2013, unaddressed in this volume, compelled new international engagement to grapple with the questions that the 'light footprint' military and UN interventions left unaddressed. All the while, Libya's subnational political forces—the *thuwwar*, political Islam, tribes and insistent eastern regionalism sought to make their voices heard.

Part 2: Sub-national Identities and Narratives

Part 2 of this volume examines these sub-national social forces and identities shaping Libya's revolution, which frequently challenged or worked independently of the transitional authorities and their international supporters. In Chapter 1, Vandewalle notes 'both Qadhafi and the NTC came to realise during the revolution … long-submerged sub-national interests and identities were powerfully attractive and divisive.' Those sub-national interests and identities were older than, and transcended, the state; for them, the 17 February Revolution was but the most recent event in their own far older narratives. Communities fighting or defending Qadhafi or the state retold and reappropriated their historic resistances during the Ottoman and Italian colonial enterprises, creating new icons like Misrata's Ramadan Suwaihli, Nalut's Khalifa bin Askar, and eastern Libya's Umar al-Mukhtar.[10]

'Sub-national identities' is a term used in international relations theory to refer to concepts such as 'tribe'. The English word 'tribe' is imperfect, being an artifact of early anthropological efforts to translate social and kinship networks into discrete units of analysis.[11] In modern anthropology the concept of 'tribe'—segmentary genealogy—includes multiple signifiers: social narratives projected into the past justifying present interpersonal and intergroup relationships; value systems of honour and group reputation; received oral histories.[12] These all apply to the way the word 'tribe' is used in this volume. The Libyan political scientist Amal Obeidi also employed a definition of 'tribe' as invoking either solidarity based on common descent, long, close contact between members of a social or economic group, or a combination of these and other factors such as common geography.[13] If foreign observers risked misinterpreting 'tribal' loyalties in Libya, Libyans did too. The chapters of this section illustrate how Libyan actors took time to understand when and how 'tribes' were relevant. Qadhafi's governance attempted to manipulate and control the same 'tribalism' that had led to internal conflict when fighting against the Ottomans and Italians, yet ultimately failed with respect to Zintan and the Tebu. Likewise, the eastern federalist project tried to mobilise an eastern identity based around tribes, but failed.

The events of 2011 also created, or reinvigorated, political networks and identities that supported the revolution, but challenged the status quo during the transition in various ways. One, discussed in Chapters

5–7, are the 'revolutionaries' or *thuwwar*, who, barring some personal and communal rivalries, were closely knit by the experience of fighting together against Qadhafi, and the NATO operations rooms, shipping, humanitarian aid, arms and money networks that connected them. They did not challenge the democratic transition in Libya, but sought to join it, voting in (and some providing 'security' for) the 7 July elections; others ran as candidates, creating a political bloc in the GNC. All the while they challenged the assumption that the rump state and its armed forces, which the NTC executive inherited, were the sole legitimate actors in Libya, and sought political alliances among ministers and the GNC to constrain them.

Chapter 8, by Mary Fitzgerald, examines Islamist movements that alternatively supported and challenged the status quo created by Libya's transitional authorities. Taking a practical definition[14] of Islamism as 'support for the introduction of Islamic tenets into political life through the implementation of *sharia*'[15] (page 177), Fitzgerald delineates the various ideological trends of political Islam active in Libya in 2011, from the Muslim Brotherhood, to Salafism, to the spectrum of political *jihadism*, whilst also emphasising how a shared history of political persecution bonded them as a community. All the while, they 'contended with more radical elements both critical of their engagement in politics and determined to disrupt the country's democratic trajectory' (page 204). Fitzgerald sees Libya's Islamists as entering a crisis of identity in Libya's transition, as their primary unifying factor—opposition to Qadhafi, and the experience of his repression—ceased to hold currency. Fitzgerald traces the attempts of Libya's various Islamic movements to unite under 'a national umbrella movement' (page 184) aiming to challenge the NTC's 'secular' orientation through civil society work and political lobbying. As with tribalism, however, being 'Islamist' or 'Islamic' was not enough to command a unified point of view, and Libya's Islamic groups failed to create a united political front post-revolution. Yet 'the failure of Libya's self-described "Islamic current" to unite,' Fitzgerald argues, 'did not mean they were a spent force' (page 204). Islamists turned to either influencing the security structures of the new Libya, or else 'rallying' and building 'alliances ... in the General National Congress' (page 204).

In Chapter 9, Sean Kane describes a more existential challenge to the Libyan transition: an attempt by some easterners to reject the NTC and revert to the Libyan constitution of 1951, granting them autonomy under a 'federal' state. Kane details how the resurgence of 'federalism' grew as the NTC, originally heavily eastern in its makeup, moved to Tripoli and took over the rump of Qadhafi's state apparatus. Kane argues that 'federalists' did not reject the 17 February Revolution, noting that some federalist leaders were founders of the NTC. Nevertheless, they feared that the NTC, by moving to Tripoli and governing through Qadhafi's ministries, was succumbing to 'a stealthy return to the *status quo ante*' (page 214) wherein all administrative functions were centralised in Tripoli. Eastern federalists, Kane argues, reverted to, and tried to exploit, a 'tribal' and regional identity based on 'common shared lineage', and shared memories of traditional influence during the monarchy of King Idris. Kane argues, however, that federalists failed to promote a boycott of the 7 July 2012 elections, partly because the 'tribalism' it appealed to ultimately limited it. A variety of alternatives to tribal organisation existed in 2012 that did not exist in 1951, including political parties, Islamist movements, civil society and youth groups. Likewise, within the tribal families and houses that potentially could have gained from federalism a wide variety of political opinions emerged, some supporting its members in the NTC, others going on an even more militant path. Eastern identity, Kane argues, was a rich mix of heritage and influences that was beyond the ability of any one 'tribal leader' or political family to embody or command. In this way, perhaps, the federalists attempted to appeal to the same tribal dynamics as Qadhafi, and failed for the same reasons.

In Chapter 10, Brian McQuinn offers an anthropological account of how sub-national narratives and close-knit social networks underpinned the formation of the 236 armed groups to emerge from Misrata. McQuinn reconstructs the events of the siege of Misrata from February to July 2011—one of the most pivotal battles of the uprising—demonstrating how the goals, identity and discipline of Misratan fighters was driven partly by their sense of destiny, embodied in the historical figure of Ramadan Suwaihli and the history of the Tripolitanian Republic, which saw Misrata become temporarily independent. McQuinn argues that, while this 'sense of historical destiny was mythologised' (page 231), its revival defined Misrata's political direction and identity. The chapter likewise illustrates how Misratan fighting units shaped that direction, undergoing organisational transformation from urban warfare to frontline combat fighting, aided by neighbourhood executive committees, military suppliers and NATO ground advisers.

Chapter 11 discusses the Arab and Amazigh Nafusa Mountains uprisings as embedded in the same micro-politics of communities and 'their historic local struggles against each other' (page 258). Wolfram Lacher and Ahmed Labnouj explain how both loyalist and revolutionary communities 'activated historical allegiances with other regions' (page ???), including the Tebu, Tuareg and littoral, which surpassed any one cohering national identity. The authors describe how Zintan and Nalut's critical defections in February 2011 were marked by Qadhafi's failure to manipulate its communal allegiances and financial interests, with elders' struggling and failing to balance those considerations against their pro-revolutionary youth. The chapter echoes themes expressed elsewhere in the volume by noting the role of military defectors in armed group formation and political liaison, and how the arrival of NATO ground advisers in summer 2011 'fomented discord among mountain towns' (page 273). The chapter also traces how, in the year following Qadhafi's death, the reactivation of local identities in Nafusa led to communities prioritising their interests in the transition, either with or against the state. An 'expansionary' Zintan took control of a tract stretching from Tripoli to Sabha and the Algerian border, formalising its control of western borders and southern oil fields through the defence minister, Usama Juwaili, while Amazigh towns asserted their linguistic and cultural identity through political activism.

Chapter 12 charts how the same tribal micropolitics of the west and south spurred loyalism to Qadhafi, focusing on one specific community, Bani Walid. Peter Cole traces how these communities' political views, like those of Misrata, were rooted in a history beginning with the tribal confederations against the Ottomans and Italians. On independence, they 'formed part of the bedrock of the Libyan state in the west' (page 288) and their identity was based around the belief they were the 'protectors of independent Libyan statehood' against foreign incursions (page 289). Cole argues that the key to understanding Bani Walid's loyalism was Qadhafi's manipulation of tribal and social leadership in the town following a failed coup by Bani Walid officers in 1993. This coup also saw Qadhafi further sideline the armed forces and rapidly expand his security brigades, which he staffed with loyal tribes and communities, thus creating the security landscape faced by Libyans

1

LIBYA'S UNCERTAIN REVOLUTION

Dirk Vandewalle

All revolutions experience what Leonard Binder, writing about Gamal Abdul Nasser's Egypt after 1952, characterised as a 'moment of enthusiasm': the euphoria that an old regime has been replaced; the temporary unity before age-old divisions and cleavages reassert themselves; and the moment before old state structures—fragmentary or whole-sale—reappear.[1] It marks the time before the need to create new state institutions introduces the wrenching choices the country's new rulers must make—often, as in Libya, while possessing very little capacity to do so. Invariably, revolutions contain their own legitimating rhetoric. And inevitably, this moment of enthusiasm wanes—to use Weber's often-cited dictum, the charismatic must yield to the bureaucratic. Post-revolutionary rulers throughout the history of the modern Middle East and North Africa have found themselves weighing what of the past should be salvaged, refashioned or jettisoned, and how revolutionary rhetoric serves post-revolutionary reality.

In some revolutions the institutions and social structures left by previous governments and regimes can be adapted into new statebuilding elements. But oil exporters like Algeria, Indonesia or Nigeria that have undergone revolutions or civil wars have tended to exhibit lagging

17

institutional development influenced by extensive patronage, creating inequalities, distrust and entitlements that inhibit reform and reconstruction. In Libya, where state institutions had been ignored, neglected or outright destroyed for decades, and where oil flowed into the national economy before any real institutional development took place, uncertain and extended post-revolutionary adjustments were inevitably needed to endow state institutions with the legitimacy required to function. Marx's observation that men create their own history within the structural constraints of the past weighed perhaps nowhere as heavily as during the Arab Spring as in Libya.

Libya's own moment of enthusiasm arguably lasted eight months: from the death of Mu'ammar al-Qadhafi on 20 October 2011 until the elections of 7 July 2012. It was generated not only by the rebels' victory, but also by the emerging institutional symbols of democracy—an elected government, free press and vibrant civil society. Yet the country's institutions had neither the capacity nor mechanisms to support this new political system. Some observers hoped that the institutional tabula rasa left by Qadhafi meant that the new state would not, as in other Arab Spring countries, have to remove the barnacles of the 'deep state' that had slowed down or even reversed political reconstruction.[2] Disillusion set in, however, as the country's militias formed an insurmountable obstacle, leaving the National Transitional Council (NTC) without the coercive power to affect decisions.

The removal of Libya's dictatorship raised significant worries over how its new rulers would create, virtually *ex nihilo*, new governing institutions and a sense of identity and community out of the ashes of a history that, since 1969, had glorified the very destruction of those institutions. The challenge was turning the subjects of a former dictator, in an oil state where economic hand-outs substituted for policy, into citizens with a sense of political responsibilities, duties and obligations towards the state. How could the country's new rulers prevent individuals or groups pursuing their own interests at the nation's expense? In sum, how heavily would the shadow of past legacies weigh on the new Libya—and how would those legacies also become a shadow of the country's future?

* * *

The chapters in this book illuminate those dilemmas by focusing on different aspects of Libya's revolution and its aftermath. They accentuate the way Libya's historical problems with central authority—immeasurably exacerbated by Qadhafi's political experimentation—persisted despite new, contemporary and discontinuous post-revolutionary events. They describe how the revolution unleashed social and political groups—tribes, old and new elites, Salafi and jihadist movements, militias, returned exiles, cities and regions, old government supporters—that reinvigorated the social structures Qadhafi declared archaic and obsolete. But they also indicate where, in important and unexpected ways, the Libyan revolution has been and remains *sui generis*.

Whether some of these groups in Libya have acquired real power remains contentious, as illustrated in this volume. Some argue, for example, that tribes constituted a powerful force in Libyan society during the civil war. Certainly, both sides' assiduous attempts to cultivate their loyalty—even Qadhafi who had once declared them useless before reinvigorating the tribal elder system in the 1990s—contributes to the impression that they were political actors in the revolution and then beyond. Others, however, have argued that beyond their social purpose tribes retained little relevance in Libya's current political system, that both sides needed to cultivate their support during the revolution but that the tribes, in a traditional pattern, carefully stayed on the sidelines, and weighed their options.[3]

The *jamahiriyya*[4] had always appeared so immobile, held in check by the late dictator's repressive security services, that meaningful political opposition movements no longer existed when the revolution started. Below this chimera of placidity, however, were a large number of social, economic, political, tribal, regional and ethnic problems that had been held in abeyance, or declared no longer existent, for over four decades. Much as both Qadhafi and the NTC came to realise in their wooing of Islamic sentiments and tribal loyalties, these long-submerged sub-national interests and identities were powerfully attractive and divisive, posing critical issues for the country's way forward. Above all, balancing the needs of western, southern and eastern Libya constituted a baseline for all major political developments in Libya.

It would have been utterly unrealistic, of course, to expect on 20 October 2011, when the *jamahiriyya* became a political bygone, that these tensions would not resurface. Inadvertently, the revolution reexposed differences between Tripolitania and Cyrenaica, by Benghazi's considering itself the cradle of the revolution and founding place of the NTC. The euphoria following the end of the war, and in part because of the legitimacy of the national elections in July 2012, suspended these competing claims and expectations—even though the killing of Abd al-Fattah Yunis in late July 2011 indicated the fragility of a society riven by traditional historical fractures.

While post-revolutionary countries always present a tabula rasa—and Qadhafi's *jamahiriyya* particularly so—this vacuum is often seized upon by competing factions whose fates were affected by the revolution. In Libya, the ability to shape the political landscape and fill this vacuum was a race against time: a window of opportunity to restructure and refashion political and social institutions and economic arrangements before the disintegrative, centrifugal forces of subnational or supra-national loyalties—whether tribal or geographical, linked to circles of patronage or to Islamic movements—could assert and consolidate themselves.

During the administrations of the NTC and General National Congress (GNC) this window of opportunity narrowed considerably, and valuable opportunities were lost. What one observer noted in the political arena—that 'for now ... the institutional void forms a major obstacle to democratisation'—appeared true of virtually all major aspects of public life in Libya during the transition.[5] In the remainder of this introductory chapter, I detail the difficulties in creating this new state, the obstacles its new rulers faced in implementing national policies and what these portend for Libya's future as a unified nation.

* * *

History provides particularly meaningful clues to Libya's difficulties in consolidating its revolution and refashioning the state. Throughout 2011, observers noted that its tumultuous history since independence in 1951 had created disturbing social, political and economic legacies that would impact the country's rebuilding after Qadhafi.[6] The political disenfranchisement of the population during the monarchy and the Qadhafi years had left an especially heavy legacy of distrust of national institutions, a lack of interpersonal trust, and the absence of personal initiative. These were exacerbated by Qadhafi's extensive security organisations and manipulation of oil revenues within a carefully calibrated patronage system that immobilised Libyans politically, socially and economically. The NTC inherited these legacies as it tried to develop organisational and policy coherence during the revolution.

This challenge was enormous, irrespective of the widespread international support and expertise it garnered and was willing to accept.

Although some Libyan state institutions existed, they were put to the purpose of preserving Qadhafi and his family, not the state. Those who embodied the state had failed to regulate its institutions; instead, Qadhafi had intervened in a wholesale fashion, arbitrarily determining how Libyans should be governed, to the extent that arguably '[t]he only encompassing "institution" in Libya was [Qadhafi] himself and his clutch of advisers. Subordinate institutions were entangled in overlapping and contradictory networks with no common ordering principle or chain of authority beyond Qadhafi's presence at the top of every heap.'[7]

The only real exception was the country's well-provided-for coercive institutions—a coterie of Revolutionary Committees and security organisations that reported directly to Qadhafi's residences at Bab al-Aziziyya, the nerve centre of government. Libya during the monarchical and Qadhafi years never developed a truly national, professional army that could act as a buffer and intermediary when popular uprisings erupted. Instead, a system of security brigades, headed and often staffed by Qadhafi confidants and loyalist groups, formed the core of Qadhafi's protective umbrella. Both the Revolutionary Committee system and the brigades disappeared with Qadhafi, leaving a security vacuum, into which stepped a multiplicity of militias, empowered both by their role in the revolution and by the massive amounts of Qadhafi-era arms left unattended during the conflict.

Libya also had no effective political intermediaries or leadership figures that enjoyed national visibility or a high level of legitimacy. Some in the NTC's top leadership had held high-level positions in Libya after 2003 when the government, under Saif al-Islam al-Qadhafi's guidance, attempted a desultory series of economic and political reforms. Their coalescence and ability to act under the difficult circumstances of February 2011 was partly because the NTC's core consisted of a group of lawyers from eastern Libya who knew and trusted each other. None, however, enjoyed high political standing or a nationwide following that cut across the country's sub-national, regional or local loyalties. Many would prove unable to build strong ties with those who fought against Qadhafi, exposing the division between those who experienced the fighting first hand, and the political leadership initially in charge of its direction. Even those outside Libya—such as Dr Muhammad Mugharyif, who had faithfully guided the country's main opposition movement to Qadhafi during decades in exile, proved to have little political traction inside Libya when they returned.

This collective amnesia and distrust of those who had not been active participants in the revolution quickly became and remained a dividing point in the postwar period. The central dilemma for Libya was that those who fought the revolution—the '*thuwwar*', or revolutionaries—refused to disarm until they felt they trusted those representing the state, while those in charge of the state argued that the continued presence of the *thuwwar* prevented them from building that state. This bifurcation into two camps, described as the 'revolutionary sector' versus a sector that wanted to create or resuscitate institutions at the expense of the *thuwwar*—became one of the enduring characteristics of post-revolutionary Libya,[8] though in practice different groups for their own purposes navigated back and forth between the two sides, and the *thuwwar* themselves often splintered into sub-groups with their own agendas and goals.

This distrust and opportunism partly resulted from two aspects of Qadhafi's rule that destroyed any sense of cooperation and left many Libyans with a profound dislike of national institutions and those who represented them. Firstly, almost by osmosis, many of the political ideas Qadhafi once espoused about the evils of political representation and political parties had been inculcated in many Libyans, leaving them with few mechanisms for cooperation between different political currents during and after the revolution. A popular quip in Libya noted 'there is a little Qadhafi in all of us.' Although Qadhafi had insisted that his system of popular committees and congresses embodied a perfect and decentralised democracy, this experimentation had systematically destroyed not only the necessary institutions of a modern democratic polity, but also the supporting norms and arrangements—trust in the system, interpersonal trust, the willingness to provide guarantees to those who lose out in political contestations—that sustain democratic systems. Qadhafi's nullification of all forms of affiliation—the country's tribal system, labour unions, civil society organisations, and organised Islam—that had traditionally provided alternative forms of identity and allegiance to citizenship meant that the NTC and its backers encountered a low sense of political community and a *sauve-qui-peut* attitude among Libya's citizens.

Even so, Qadhafi's distrust of central authority, though taken to a logical extreme in his *Green Book*, was itself a symptom of a profounder and older Libyan phenomenon. This was the tension between a hinterland culture and the culture represented by the country's urban areas that precedes even the country's independence in 1951. Libya's modern history in part reflects the contestation of these cultures over power and national identity.[9] In the power vacuum and with the incapacitated government left in the wake of the revolution, this contest—also the contest of central-versus-decentralised power—surfaced again. Tripoli's new rulers were faced with new revolutionary battalions whose power they could not control, cities and towns largely running their own affairs and a longstanding desire for greater autonomy in Cyrenaica that harkened back to Libya's original 1951 constitution.[10]

The second aspect contributing to Libyans' lack of cooperation, and distrust of national institutions, was the Qadhafi regime's systematic use of economic patronage, ranging from simple economic goods to jobs and education, which had become a tool to divide and rule individuals and make them dependent on government largesse. Noncompliance with Qadhafi's directives simply meant the end of access to patronage.[11] Patronage therefore politically and economically immobilised most Libyans, made cooperation on communal goals problematic, and created an enormous sense of entitlement that lingered on after 2011, when, in the absence of state capacity, individuals and groups often grabbed what they could at the expense of the public interest.[12] Oil revenues were crucial in allowing Qadhafi to use distributive largesse to keep Libya politically immobile, rather than creating modern state institutions with bonds of reciprocal duties and obligations between the state and its citizens.

* * *

Some chapters in this volume make clear that the NTC understood that they stood at the beginning of a long, difficult process of national consolidation and integration that would witness a struggle for power once Qadhafi was removed. Even so, few anticipated what the impact would be when a closed society, unable to contemplate or express any ideas beyond those espoused by Qadhafi, suddenly saw those restraints removed. The NTC arguably underestimated the extent to which the country would be subjected to the centrifugal forces of Libya's battalions, tribes, and regional and Islamist movements. As the chapters by Frederic Wehrey and Mary Fitzgerald testify, they could not have predicted how the dynamics of the revolution created a political landscape in which previously unknown actors—most notably the country's militias but also Islamist groups of various political inclinations—would contest the NTC's vision of a new Libya with central, transparent institutions.

The NTC's main problem was that its transitional executive branches did not possess the basic state capacities needed to implement their vision, nor a monopoly on coercive power. Qadhafi's deliberate monopoly on decision making left Libya's governing institutions unable to defend themselves, ideologically or physically, against actors whose own vision of what Libya's new state should look like stood in stark contrast to theirs. The executive branch was thus reduced to convincing different militias and opposition groups to incorporate under the aegis of national institutions (such as the army, police force, different bureaucracies and ministries). Despite some limited success, lingering incoherence in these institutions made these attempts arduous and slow, and left basic authority and capacity in essential areas like tax collection, border control, and law enforcement, lacking.

This dim picture contrasted with the country's emergent political life. With only a slight delay, following the guidelines laid down by the NTC in its Constitutional Declaration of August 2011, the national elections of 7 July 2012 were hailed by Libyans as a major achievement. Having barely emerged from the highly exclusionary *jamahiriyya*, which forbade political parties, Libya's elections were indeed remarkable—with much of the credit due not only to Libyans themselves but also to the international community, especially the United Nations Support Mission in Libya (UNSMIL). The NTC's ability to fulfil its own roadmap for national elections and hand over power to the elected GNC in August 2013 indicated that Libyan institutions could meet important political thresholds.

The July elections were also considered, by Libyans and the international community alike, as harbingers of the kind of political community Libya could create. An important question was whether this first attempt at national political institutionalisation would prove resilient and inclusive enough to rein in the divisive forces the country faced: tribalism and regionalism; federalism in eastern Libya; different forms of Islamism; and the country's militias. The NTC's leadership debated this very question, and with it, whether the new political system (institutionalised around the GNC) could prevent the abuse of oil revenues to recreate the powerful patronage mechanisms that had immobilised politics and the country's population during Qadhafi's *jamahiriyya*— but also kept the country stabilised.

In the event, the elections demonstrated Libya's inexperience of political organisation. Party platforms were hardly articulated, and revolved around individuals rather than representing clear presentations of political views. The population's understanding of the country's political process and procedures often seemed rudimentary. None of this was helped by a somewhat awkward electoral system that combined proportional and majoritarian representation for GNC seats, designed purposely to ascertain that no political group would dominate the elections. Libyans' expectations that the July 2012 elections would effortlessly lead to a democratic system, despite Libya's lack of institutions and historical references that could underpin it, proved unrealistic. Few saw that the creation of truly national political institutions inevitably takes years to accomplish.

Libya also embarked on its transition with little unified national identity or consolidation of political interests. Instead, the country's elections were only a prelude to the challenge of constructing a national identity that both the monarchy and Qadhafi after 1969 had discouraged. The GNC and the transitional executive administration purported to govern in the name of a nation that had little prior identity, and, unsurprisingly a good amount of confusion arose over its purpose and legitimacy. The political infighting and the pressure from revolutionary battalions it suffered showed that it became valued for what it could deliver to different groups—for example by assigning important ministerial positions to powerful groups from Misrata and Zintan—rather than as an institution where national policies were forged through compromise and dialogue. While the institutions that held the national elections succeeded, therefore, the country's political institutions fared less well.

But Libya's lack of national identity was perhaps most dramatically expressed by the debate over federalism and decentralisation that punctuated the transitional era. These debates, though obscured during the war, originated with the creation of Libya in 1951. Though during the 2011 conflict, eastern Libyans voiced strong, palpably shared feelings that 'Libya is free' and indivisible, debates over autonomy for Cyrenaica and special privileges for the different provinces continued soon after the NTC's move to Tripoli. But they did not threaten the NTC's

Constitutional Declaration, which envisaged the continuation of a unified and centralised state until at least the drawing up of a constitution. At first, the federalist movement in Cyrenaica, consolidated around Ahmad Zubair al-Sanusi, attracted few supporters and the exigencies of marketing the country's oil to sustain the transition was largely unchallenged. As in the country's earlier history, oil tied Libya closer together rather than pushing its constituencies apart.

Over time, these dynamics changed dramatically as some easterners grew disillusioned with the NTC and GNC, whose administrations met demands for decentralisation with periodic handouts and subventions and announcements (unimplemented) of their intention to relocate national companies and institutions to Benghazi. But over time the uneasy relationship between Cyrenaica (Barqa) and Tripolitania, and also between southern Libya (where long neglected minorities raised citizenship, identity, and cultural rights issues) and the two northern provinces, made these debates over federalism and decentralisation more intransigent.

This deteriorating relationship culminated in the unilateral announcement by Sanusi of a Transitional Council of Barqa on 1 June 2013, outfitted with its own congress, senate and provincial government. By itself it was not necessarily a turning point in Libya's fortunes, but rather part of a continuum of actions taken by the federalists that started before the national elections. The occupation of Cyrenaican oilfields and installations that followed Sanusi's announcement in summer 2013, however, indicated that the tactics of those arguing for greater political and economic power had shifted considerably. A psychological threshold had seemingly been crossed. For the first time, Sanusi's essentially tame federalist rhetoric had been superseded by groups willing to take direct action against national assets.

A similar line was crossed during debates surrounding the country's Political Isolation Law, summarily settled in summer 2013 when the *thuwwar* physically surrounded several ministries and the GNC to intimidate the latter into passing it. The law, meant to remove former Qadhafi personnel from the country's political, economic, educational and security institutions, represented a purely punitive instrument, without any of the conciliatory measures that have proved instrumental in reconstructing several other states after civil wars. Although Marieke Wierda's chapter in this volume pinpoints efforts at constructing a legislative groundwork for aspects of transitional justice, its pursuit has remained haphazard until today.

Given these two fundamental challenges, the NTC relied—much like Qadhafi—on doling out financial resources through direct handouts and a wide variety of subsidies to keep different interests in the country balanced.[13] These have been portrayed by several of the country's leaders as stopgap measures—and can be defended as such—and the current government has attempted to phase out some of these by-now-customary entitlements. But they remain an engrained legacy of Qadhafi's era and one of the few levers available to a weak central government.

As many Libyans have gradually realised, statebuilding and fostering national identity takes time, compromise, and good ideas by leaders with a common vision for the country. Understandably Libyans' impatience with their government has been heightened by high expectations and the rhetoric of the revolution. Libya has also been marked by a lack of political compromise, resulting both from the overwhelming military power of the *thuwwar* versus the government, but also from a historical experience of authoritarian politics where compromise was never required or demanded.

* * *

Libya's difficulties in statebuilding and national identity were exacerbated by its unique history that overshadowed the country's political way forward. The country's lingering difficulties flowed partly from a conflict that kept military and political power fragmented, pitting a revolutionary sector against the oil-based government. But the conflict also reawakened more structural dilemmas of Libya's identity, state, and concept of citizenship within the country's political system, which the transitional government could not resolve or address.

Yet unlike during the monarchy and Qadhafi's dictatorship, Libyans are participating in creating their state for the first time. No matter how chaotic, disorganised and undisciplined that effort, it is a singular step forward that Libyans can now consider themselves state citizens and no longer simply the subjects of their rulers. They have truly owned their most recent revolution. And for all its inevitable ebb and flow, this singular achievement will indelibly mark Libya's future. Ironically the new Libya has become to some extent the kind of decentralised polity Qadhafi pursued so assiduously in his *jamahiriyya*.

In 2011–13, as in 1951, there remained competing visions of what Libya should look like as a state, and of central government's role in the daily affairs of its citizens' lives.[14] As always, the creation of a centralised state is a race against time, against a closing window of opportunity to construct viable state institutions and implement agreed-upon rules of the game before the centrifugal forces that dispute those rules overwhelm the forces of centralised control.

Although the government is gaining some traction as the routinisation and further bureaucratisation of the central state continues, the difficulties of accomplishing greater integration, and of creating functioning national institutions—whether in a centralised or decentralised political system—have grown substantially since the end of the civil war. But the state- and nationbuilding process Libya has engaged upon relies on complex long-term sociopolitical changes. Even in what are now considered models of democratic governance in western Europe, this process took decades—or centuries—to achieve, and was often marred by violence and temporary setbacks as countries constructed social contracts between governments and citizens.[15]

* * *

If Libya's difficulties of central control indicate much deeper structural problems, this would indicate an inability by Libya's leaders to construct centralised and functioning state institutions that are based on a national consensus and whose reach is nationwide. If so, then Libya would indeed be, as many observers have noted, in danger of becoming a 'failed state', with sustained intergroup conflicts targeting and challenging the state directly. Certainly events in the summer of 2013—the occupation of the oil fields, the hardening of the federalist agenda—indicate that certain groups were willing to target national symbols that had once been sacrosanct and central to the vision of a unified Libya.

But a different scenario, unstable but not catastrophic, is possible. The year following the national elections of July 2012 clearly showed how nonstate actors filled the power vacuum created amidst the GNC's political bickering, taking leading roles toward whatever new form of state was taking shape. Municipalities and local councils took on the burdens normally preserved for the central government. This scenario, then, is of a weak state in a form of mild and perpetual anarchy, with a relatively weak centre offset by a revolutionary sector that keeps its privileges intact, guided by a decentralised political and bureaucratic system, and with all sides coexisting while sharing ample oil revenues. The political process becomes a fig leaf for a patronage-fuelled system in the interest of all sides.

The final scenario seems, for the time being, the most difficult to achieve: where Libya's central institutions over time slowly gain the monopoly of power over the revolutionary sector through a variety of political and economic inducements that shift their preferences to national rather than personal or group interests. This scenario certainly represents enormous challenges for Libya's future rulers, but they are not impossible to overcome. In modern history, state- and nationbuilding have often been long drawn-out processes where a central monopoly of power is achieved relatively late, and where expanding bureaucratic reach and regulatory ability prove as powerful as coercive capacity. And certainly, the resilience of Libya's civil society and its resistance to the unfettered power of certain armed groups at the expense of a centralised coercive institution is an important variable for what the future may hold.

* * *

Libya's age-old dilemma—of pitting the hinterland with its echoes of decentralisation versus a centralised government—resurfaced after the country's civil war. The challenges the country faces at the time of writing, two years later, remain enormous: creating an institutionalised state in a country where state institutions were deliberately neglected for several decades and are still subject to suspicion; incorporating citizens further into a national identity that has not been clearly defined beyond some references to Islam; the need to make Libyans meaningful participants in the country's political and economic life and to wean them away from a patronage system that had, in return for some of the riches of an oil state, demanded political quiescence. All of this must occur in an atmosphere where interpersonal trust, and trust in centralised power, remains minimal. Out of these unpromising remnants of the Qadhafi regime Libya has moved forward, haltingly, uncertain, subject to the power of the gun.

Finally, adding to the challenges Libya faces, fuelled by its lingering power vacuum, are a number of nonstate transnational actors, most specifically a number of radical Islamist movements. Much in Libya's history suggests an antipathy to these more radical groups. But in an environment where many actors seek to bolster or maintain their power at the state's expense, tactical alliances with such groups become attractive opportunities. Whether the ideology of these radical groups will become inculcated and result in more local extremism presents another problem for Libya's weak government. Some argue that their influence is already visible within the weak formal structures of government in Libya, particularly the GNC, and that incidents such as the kidnapping of Abu Anas al-Libi in October 2013 has allowed them to further propagate their agenda in Libya.[16] Clearly Libya provides a permissive environment for these movements, and their presence has added immeasurably to the burden of the national government.

Qadhafi's self-styled revolution was once described by one of its most insightful early observers as 'enigmatic': full of contradictions and unexpected developments that took unprecedented turns in Qadhafi's creation of a highly idiosyncratic political system.[17] Libya's revolution since 2011 has perhaps been less enigmatic. As many chapters in this volume testify, it is perhaps appropriate, and most accurate, to describe Libya's tortuous path since 2011 as an 'uncertain revolution': a revolution still in search of its identity, torn between different visions, with historically few ideological references that can provide a clear path for the country's future, with little notion of national rather than group or personal interests, and with the preponderance of power still held by nonstate actors. The chapters that follow highlight different aspects of this process as Libya proceeds on its difficult transition toward a new state and nation.

2

THE CORRIDOR OF UNCERTAINTY[1]

THE NATIONAL TRANSITIONAL COUNCIL'S BATTLE FOR LEGITIMACY AND RECOGNITION

Peter Bartu

Introduction

Within days of the first protests in mid-February in east Libya, an unlikely leadership and structure fitfully cohered in organic fashion in Benghazi around the idea of a National Transitional Council (NTC). This citizens' movement brought together an eclectic mix of notable families, lawyers, academics, young activists, serving diplomats, former ministers and security chiefs, government reformers, and diaspora leaders, some of whom had long opposed Mu'ammar al-Qadhafi.

From its inception in emergency circumstances until the fall of the capital Tripoli, the NTC was often derided within and without Libya. Nonetheless, it met a critical threshold of legitimacy for the Libyan revolutionary moment. Significantly, no one ever challenged the NTC for leadership of the revolution despite often severe criticisms as to how it organised itself, the opaque manner in which it took decisions, and the way it engaged with external patrons and managed domestic affairs.

One factor critical to the legitimacy of the NTC was the speed of the events surrounding its formation. This was enabled by the erratic public responses of Qadhafi and his son Saif al-Islam and the early defection of Qadhafi's interior minister, General Abd al-Fattah Yunis, and his troops, which allowed the rebels to create a safe haven in Libya's east. Suddenly, almost one third of Libya's land mass was outside government control and pockets of resistance in the western areas of Nafusa, Nalut and Zintan quickly threw in their lot with the NTC.

A second factor was that these domestic imperatives converged with unprecedented regional and international support for the protests. The United Nations Security Council rapidly agreed to sanctions targeting Qadhafi and his family, and a referral to the International Criminal Court (ICC) later authorised a no-flight zone policed by NATO, on the recommendation of the Arab League. Arguably, this was done with scant knowledge of circumstances on the ground and ignorance of who the rebels were and what they stood for. A final factor was luck: the cadence and tempo of action and reaction, inside and outside Libya, occurred in a context of revolutionary change in neighbouring Tunisia and Egypt and elsewhere, without which Qadhafi may well have prevailed.

This chapter traces the NTC's transformation from a committee to a political entity and how it struggled to finance the revolution and win international recognition. It discusses the crisis of the 28 July 2011 slaying of Yunis, by then the NTC's 'commander-in-chief' and chief of staff, which led to the wholesale firing of the NTC's executive board. It looks at how the NTC argued and negotiated internally over the 3 August 2011 Constitutional Declaration (CD), the political framework by which Libya would restore constitutional government, including a transparent path to the NTC's own dissolution.

Despite near solvency and increased international recognition, the NTC was essentially a bystander in the drama of the fall of Tripoli on 20 August, which was being orchestrated by emerging political forces over which it had marginal authority. But it had nonetheless deliberated a pathway to the return of constitutional government with those same forces, with whom it shared the common goal of removing Qadhafi and his family. Arguably, having finally secured international recognition for the revolution and a bankroll for the transition against Libya's sovereign assets by the end of July, the NTC and its leaders had achieved the limited goals they articulated at the outset.

Early days

One of the first demonstrations calling for the removal of Qadhafi was in the eastern city of Baida on 15 February 2011, at which two demonstrators were shot dead by the security forces. On the same day in Benghazi the arrest of Fathi Tirbil, a lawyer for families of Abu Slim prisoners, sparked a daily cycle of protests calling for his release. Two days later in Baida another fifteen demonstrators were shot dead in chaotic circumstances where the police joined the revolution, the courthouse was burned, and all prisoners were set free. A local committee was formed and chaired by Mustafa Abd al-Jalil, a diminutive, fez-wearing, quietly-spoken man who had served four years as the secretary general of the General People's Committee of Justice in Qadhafi's Libyan Arab Jamahiriyya.[2] Abd al-Jalil had just publicly resigned his post and in a telephone call he received from Qadhafi's prime minister, Umar al-Baghdadi al-Mahmudi, explained that the protesters sought 'a ceasefire, removal of the mercenaries, and a space to express their aspirations'.[3] By 18 February all international calls had been cut. The Libyan diplomat Ahmad Gebreel began uploading information to the internet and helped Abd al-Jalil do his first media interviews. Once the internet ceased working a network of runners carried images to Egypt daily.[4]

With little knowledge of each other, communities in eastern Libya who freed themselves in similar circumstances debated how to organise. In Benghazi discussions began at the courthouse on 17 February among a group of lawyers and academics who initially called themselves the 17 February Coalition (*al-I'tilaf Sab'at Ashr Fibrayir*), namely: Fathi al-Ba'ja, Abdullah Shamia, Abd al-Hafiz Ghugha, Abu Gharghis, Mahdi Kashbur, Hana al-Jalal, Jamal Bannur, Kamal Hudhaifa, Zahi Mugharbi and Abd al-Salam al-Mismari. In the initial chaos there was no obvious leader, though Qadhafi's internal security apparatus took Ghugha to Tripoli on 18 February 2011 and held him in a cell for two days before returning him to Benghazi after demonstrations in Tripoli demanding his release.[5]

The Coalition and other Benghazi notables made several attempts to reach out to Yunis, who was in Benghazi to put down the revolt with Sa'adi al-Qadhafi and the *Sa'iqa* ('Thunderbolt') Special Forces Battalion. Yunis and the *Sa'iqa* initially waited over an agonising few days while the demonstrations and attacks increased outside the

Central Security compound in Benghazi. Perhaps Yunis understood from the demonstrations in Zintan and Tubruq on 16 February, in Misrata on 19 February, and Tripoli the next day, that Libya's psychological moment had arrived. Perhaps Saif al-Islam's televised speech on 20 February may have played a role in Yunis's decision,[6] as with Qadhafi's promise on 22 February to eradicate the 'drug addicts', 'jihadists', and 'rats' who dared oppose him.[7]

On Sunday, 20 February, Mahdi Ziu, a manager at the Arabian Gulf Oil Company, loaded his black Kia sedan with gas canisters and drove into the security compound gate, killing himself in the explosion but allowing others in bulldozers to enter the compound. At some point that afternoon Yunis appeared with the Special Forces. Charged by Qadhafi with relieving the besieged barracks, Yunis instead promised the soldiers safe passage if they would leave eastern Libya.[8] Yunis, according to one source, was still undecided on 20 February, but had convinced Abdullah al-Sanusi, director of military intelligence, and Sa'adi al-Qadhafi, technically commander of the *Sa'iqa*, to evacuate the barracks but to allow him to continue holding the *Sa'iqa* base in Benghazi. According to one source, Yunis also on 20 February gave Libyan police in Tripoli orders to stand down against protestors.[9] A 'fraught' meeting occurred at 7.30pm that evening between Special Forces commanders Abd al-Salam al-Hasi and Coalition representative Abd al-Karim Bazama. Yunis begged for time to think, protesting that he did not want to be pushed and that he 'was between obeying Qadhafi, pointing to the phone that was the hotline to his office—and suicide'.[10] There were three or four delegations besides the two men, all pressing the same thing on him.[11] These included Mustafa Saqizli, a prominent businessman, and the lawyer Mismari. Later that night one of Yunis's bodyguards was shot dead and a house in Benghazi owned by Yunis was torched. Yunis was advised to flee to Egypt, but he held his ground and finally defected to the rebel side on 22 February, the day after the rebel flag was hoisted above the Benghazi courthouse.[12] Within days Yunis was appointed chief of staff of the rebels' 'military', which in reality resembled a ramshackle coalition of militias and defectors.

Yunis' defection, whatever its motivation, was the primary reason why Libya's revolutionaries won the initial space in which to organise and ultimately create the NTC. The fighters pushed west of Benghazi, initially gaining ground in Ajdabiya and the oil centres of Brega and

Ra's Lanuf. Then, overextended and under-experienced, they fell back in a harried retreat in the first week of March.

Creating the NTC

Responding to the initial need for emergency governance, the 17 February Coalition formed a Benghazi local council on 22 February. As similar entities formed elsewhere, this group saw the need for a national body to represent all Libyans and invited representatives from other cities in the east to come to Benghazi to discuss this.[13] These initial meetings were held at the state university in Benghazi at Ard Bal'un and also at the Libyan International Medical University. One observer recalled: 'The lawyers say everything was decided at the court house; others say that everything was decided in the private university.'[14] On 26 February an agreement was reached to bring the local councils under a national council to run the liberated areas in the east.[15] Abd al-Jalil was a part of those discussions and his leadership emerged through consensus at those meetings. In Benghazi, several former members of Qadhafi's original network of revolutionary officers had been sounded out to take command of a potential rebel military council. Others thought that surviving scions of the 1951–69 monarchy such as Ahmad Zubair al-Sanusi, or even Yunis, would lead the national council. But according to one attendee there was a general consensus that Abd al-Jalil should lead the council rather than Yunis—that a judge who had integrity and respect was preferable to a military leader. In this the Benghazi group consciously followed Misrata's lead, where a respected judge, Khalifa al-Zawawi, had been chosen to lead the local council.

Meanwhile the defection of significant numbers of diplomats who began to argue the protesters' cause was an important boost to this new council. Critical here were the defections of Libya's permanent representative to the UN, Abd al-Rahman Shalgham, and his deputy, Ibrahim Dabbashi, for whom Saif al-Islam's 20 February speech was a key factor in their decisions. Dabbashi on 21 February had written a *note verbale* to the Security Council requesting a discussion of the situation in Libya, initiating a dramatic five days in which Shalgham, asked by Qadhafi to fire mission staff, instead defected, announcing his position in a BBC interview on 24 February.[16] On 25 February Shalgham gave an impassioned speech to the Security Council comparing Qadhafi with Pol Pot and Hitler;[17] Dabbashi broke down in tears at the sight, and Shalgham embraced him. Dabbashi and Shalgham played no subsequent part in Security Council deliberations—as Tripoli had withdrawn confidence in them. But the spectacle was instrumental in shifting the positions of Russia and China to support UN Resolution 1970 which referred Libya to the ICC and imposed an arms embargo, travel ban, and asset freeze on the Qadhafi family and senior security officials.[18] Other Libyan diplomats and ambassadors also resigned and began making their way to Benghazi. These included Ali al-Isawi of the Libyan embassy in India, Abd al-Hafiz Qudur in Italy, and Salah al-Bishari in Indonesia.

Other politicians who had worked with Saif al-Islam on attempted political and economic reforms in the 2000s also joined the emerging political body. For example, Mahmud Jibril was a US-trained econo-mist who led the National Planning Council of Libya, as well as the National Economic Development Board, which had the status of a reg-ular ministry. As such, Jibril oversaw the production over three years of a 20,000-page blueprint charting Libya's economic future, includ-ing a 180-degree pivot from Africa to Europe and from a distribution economy to one containing market liberalisation reforms and a rejuve-nated private sector. Key to this was reconfiguring over US$200 billion in public sector construction and investment contracts that was politi-cally and economically controversial.[19] Jibril had also been a member of Saif al-Islam's constitutional committee, but joined the emergent revolution from Abu Dhabi.

Jibril and those around him brought with them Libyans with impor-tant international relationships that shaped early perceptions of the rebels[20]—Mahmud Shammam in Doha, Arif Ali Nayid in Abu Dhabi, Dabbashi in New York, and Qudur in Rome—and an ambition to orchestrate a managed transition of power away from the elder Qadhafi towards something that would realise the work they had begun under Saif al-Islam. From the beginning of the revolution the initial hope was that Saif al-Islam might support the February uprising and a political transition but this had been patently ruled out by his speech on 20 February 2011. Abd al-Jalil, for example, recalled that if Saif al-Islam's speech had been balanced, 'he would have been able to replace his father and things could have been resolved amicably and a constitution could have been drafted according to the people's needs.'[21]

Meanwhile in Benghazi, the nascent political movement created a headquarters at the al-Fadil hotel, fashioning an ad hoc communications system using Skype, a satellite dish, a magicJack from the Italians and an Inmarsat mobile satellite system provided early, by the UK.[22] This allowed the Benghazi movement to establish contact with Zintan and Misrata as well as some of the external defectors like Isawi and Jibril, who arrived in Benghazi on 28 February.

Immediately, Benghazi residents urged the council to regulate its functions, liberate the rest of the cities, create a 'vision' of the 'transitional phase', find a headquarters, create a media office, start receiving official delegations from humanitarian organisations, states, regional and international organisations, and work out diplomatic representation to the outside world.[23] Within twenty-four hours of coming into being, the NTC encountered a tsunami of expectations for which it was ill-prepared.

Structurally, the council, named the 'Interim Transitional National Council' in its founding statement of 5 March, to which both Mugharbi and Jalal contributed, comprised thirty members representing all of Libya's regions and all segments of Libyan society who presented themselves as the sole legitimate representative of the Libyan people. Its first act, based on the agreement of the municipal councils across the liberated areas, was to select Abd al-Jalil as president, and Ghugha as his deputy and official spokesperson for the council. Its immediate goals were to set protocols for its regular and emergency meetings and 'to make decisions in accordance with … the people's demands … the fall of the Qadhafi regime and the establishment of a civil, constitutional and democratic state.'[24]

In reality, little else had been defined concerning any aspect of the Interim Transitional National Council. A shared anxiety throughout the eclectic group of lawyers, academics, former Qadhafi ministers and ambassadors, youth, political prisoners, women, and regional representatives and Qadhafi oppositionists from the diaspora was to show that they had not seized nor assumed power. They felt they could only claim to speak and act on behalf of the Libyan people on issues where there was a broad consensus. Throughout the revolution and across constituencies this boiled down to only two points: the removal of Qadhafi and his family and the election of a legitimate body that could represent the Libyans in navigating their future. After forty-two years of Qadhafi, the Libyan opposition, obsessed about legitimate representation, trusted neither themselves nor the outside world, and both feared and embraced their new-found environment in the liberated areas, often leading to stasis and indecision over seemingly mundane issues.

This was reflected in the nomenclature of the NTC. They did not see themselves as a government, for to claim so was tantamount to equivalence with the unelected Qadhafi whom they sought to remove. While this was palatable to social sensibilities, in reality there were severe demands for administrative decision making on all aspects of daily life throughout the revolution. Some of the 17 February Coalition, led by Mismari, remained outside and at times critical of the new body with varying degrees of influence and success. Mugharbi left the NTC with a group of lawyers, writers, intellectuals, and political activists to join the think-tank styled Consultative Support Group, based at the Libyan International Medical University. On 28 February it published the pamphlet 'Urgent Steps to Activate the Work of the Libyan Transitional Council', urging the NTC to take on more responsibilities and to organise like a government.[25]

The NTC established a further body called the 'Crisis Management Committee' on 5 March. The 'Committee', led by Jibril, was delegated authority to 'run all foreign matters and to represent the foreign affairs of Libya' along with Isawi. The Council noted the need to appoint more members to this 'Executive Team' to run the vital sectors of the country. Both Jibril and Isawi were given a clearly defined goal: 'the right' to negotiate and communicate with the international community to accomplish international recognition of the Council, and nothing more. Finally, while noting the military imbalance between the regime and the revolutionaries, the Council implored the international community to 'protect the Libyan people from any further genocide and crimes against humanity' but without 'any direct military intervention on Libya soil'.[26]

Over time the Crisis Management Committee became an executive implementation body—the 'Executive Committee', with the NTC like a legislature responsible for devising policy. Perhaps a better division might have been external and internal affairs. However, the precise relationship between the NTC and the Executive Committee was never completely settled and was a source of tension throughout the revolution.[27] Early on, for example, the NTC in Benghazi only discovered after the fact that Jibril had announced outside the country in late March that he was the 'prime minister'. While many saw Jibril's ego at work here, Jibril's supporters interpreted this as his using the title mainly to ease recognition with the NTC's external patrons.[28] Certainly, external observers felt from the beginning of the revolution that Abd al-Jalil and Jibril were not close and did not always communicate with each other.[29]

The initial response among Libyans to these unintentionally opaque organisational manoeuvres was stoic acceptance and benefit of the doubt amid a wider spirit of volunteerism. But the NTC needed to respond to the crises at hand, the first of which was the mid-March convergence on Benghazi by Qadhafi's troops. This was turned around at the eleventh hour by United Nations Security Council resolution 1973 (UNSCR 1973) on 17 March 2011, and by the subsequent air campaign spearheaded by France. France was the first to recognise the NTC as the legitimate representative of the Libyan people on 10 March and had hosted an emergency summit in Paris with the Arab League, notably Qatar and the UAE, to conceptualise the military aspects of UNSCR 1973, which called for a ban on flights in Libyan airspace, or a 'no-fly zone'.[30]

On 19 March, as the fighting entered Benghazi's suburbs, encouraging Qadhafi's supporters to reemerge, mistakenly believing that the tide was turning, Yunis and the revolutionary military council quarrelled over the defence of the city.[31] After the crisis subsided at the end of March, some of the young fighters confronted the NTC in their offices, seeking better support, money and weapons. In turn, the NTC criticised the performance of the military and Yunis throughout its April sessions, as well as NATO, which the NTC explicitly blamed for its 'ambivalent posture', its 'delayed airstrikes', and its 'early reticence'—all of which it saw as having allowed Qadhafi to regroup.[32]

Democratic Libya: Whose vision?

At the first formal international conference on Libya in London on 29 March the NTC presented its 'Vision of a Democratic Libya', written by the 17 February Coalition member Fathi al-Ba'ja, who had joined the NTC and led its 'political affairs advisory committee'. Long on promise and short on detail, the vision committed the NTC to creating a modern, pluralistic, inclusive free state that would 'join the international community in rejecting and denouncing racism, discrimination and terrorism, while strongly supporting peace, democracy and freedom'.[33] Though clearly written for its external audience, like much of the earliest NTC pronouncements, it was nonetheless the first comprehensive vision that the NTC released and designed to project as favourable an image as possible to the outside world.[34]

The participants at the London meeting agreed on a more formal Libya Contact Group as a mechanism by which the Arab League, Organisation of the Islamic Conference (OIC), European Union (EU) and NATO would meet with the NTC monthly. Fittingly, in recognition of Qatar's burgeoning diplomatic, military and humanitarian support to the NTC, its first meeting was in Doha on 13 April, followed by Rome on 5 May. These and subsequent meetings were a huge distraction for the revolutionary leadership, albeit a necessary reality of cultivating external legitimacy and recognition.[35]

It took until the end of April for the NTC to further refine its internal organisation and complete a new transitional vision, a 'Roadmap for Libya', drafted by Ba'ja and heavily influenced by Jibril. The nine-page commentary and scenario analysis involved only one page of what could be called a roadmap. This outlined an ambitious timetable where after a ceasefire agreement—which presumed the abdication of the Qadhafi family as a precondition for a negotiated political transition—an 'interim government' would be drawn from the NTC but would also include three technocrats, plus two military officers and two security officers from the 'old regime' to 'avoid chaos during the transition phase'.[36] Consistent with the NTC's early debates on governance, only at this stage would this entity be called an 'interim government'. Thereafter, a representative National Congress would assemble with delegates from each city, town and village, which would replace the NTC as an interim government and appoint a committee to draft a constitution that, if approved by the Congress, would go to a national referendum. If approved nationally, parliamentary and presidential elections were to follow. The new government, once formed, would replace the interim government. The entire process was to be completed within nine months.

Objections swiftly arose. For the international community, the Road Map timeline was too short for a credible political transition involving a constitution-making process and fair elections. Benghazians criticised it for being originally written in English and without wide consultation. At any rate it catalysed a vibrant discussion throughout the country as to how to expand the initial NTC, how long the unelected body should endure, and whether it was to be replaced by election or appointment.

There were strong demands for immediate elections, however unrealistic, and a preoccupation as time went on with how the NTC members had been initially selected and therefore with the legitimacy of the NTC itself. Political Islamic currents who were not initially a part of the NTC, among them the cleric Ali Sallabi and the 'United Libyan Revolutionaries'—a bloc mainly comprising young fighters led by Faisal Muhammad al-Safi—were particularly adamant that the National Congress be elected as soon as possible. The original 17 February Coalition under Mismari also contributed vocally to the debate from outside the NTC concerning whether political parties should contest the elections, or whether only individuals could contest seats.

While these debates raged, some points of popular consensus emerged in Benghazi. The population tolerated the NTC for the initial transition period, but rejected any attempt to prolong its tenure. The popular mood was also against any negotiated transition as treasonous and an insult to those giving their lives on the frontline. Other popular demands were that NTC members reside in Libya, be qualified for their post, work to specific job descriptions, and publish their priorities.

Metamorphosis

In response to domestic demand and advice from the growing international diplomatic representation in Benghazi, the NTC underwent a management overhaul at the end of April to better cope with its expanding responsibilities. On 10 May the formation of the 'Free Libya Armed Forces' was declared, comprising an army and an air force, with Yunis as its commander.[37] The same day the Council summarised its progress in securing diplomatic recognition as the only legitimate body representing the Libyan people. France had recognised the body on 10 March, Qatar on 28 March (Qatar's recognition of the Council received 'oral support' from the Gulf Cooperation Council (GCC)), the Maldives on 3 April, and Italy on 4 April. On 22 April, Gambia became the first African state to recognise the NTC. By 13 May the Executive Office had expanded to fourteen separate portfolios, although the education position was unfilled.[38] Jibril was confirmed as head of the Office and in charge of international affairs, with Isawi as his deputy.[39]

The NTC also expanded from thirty-one to forty members. Representatives from Buntan, Gubba, and Benghazi had been named while those representing Ajdabiya, Zintan, Misrata, Nalut, Ghat, and Tripoli had not been disclosed due to security concerns.[40] During this expansion over April, the NTC incorporated representatives from twenty-three local councils from western, central, and southern Libya. These had been brought to meetings in Abu Dhabi on 9 May and Doha on 11 May, and delivered to Benghazi on a Qatari military plane on 12 May in time to attend a mass rally in Freedom Square, drawing the attention and ire of the Qadhafi government and allowing the NTC to credibly present itself as a national body. On 14 May those twenty-three regional representatives met with Abd al-Jalil at the al-Fadil Hotel and several representatives agreed to stay on in Benghazi and sit at the Council.[41]

Local councils were also organised ad hoc in each city to deal with utilities, emergency services, and security. Each council had ten to twelve members with at least one designated to sit on, and represent the community to, the NTC. Members were selected in public meetings on the basis of their experience, education and distance from the Qadhafi government, each council having a chairman, vice-chairman and, in theory, representatives against each of the Executive Office portfolios. Separately, the NTC decided to acknowledge the tribes of Libya, but not to formally incorporate them into any structures. Here there was a widespread consensus within the NTC that Libya's tribes were anachronistic and inconsistent with the NTC's vision of a modern state.

Through May the NTC also improved its media presence, rolling out a Facebook page, a new website, a live streaming site (NTC Libyan Media), an official print newsletter (*Council News*), and an FM radio station. It also posted YouTube videos of life proceeding apace in Benghazi, 'to counter the lies of Qadhafi', and footage of visiting foreign delegations. Libya Al Hurra TV, the first Benghazi-based television station to operate in Libya since the start of the revolution, began broadcasting on 30 May. There was also a rapid growth in the number of NGOs in the liberated areas.

This management overhaul and structural metamorphosis allowed for the impression that the NTC was better able to address the growing list of issues under its purview. This included efforts to help Misrata and communities displaced by fighting in the Nafusa Mountains; deal with the proliferation of security groups in Benghazi; tackle corruption on the Egyptian border, which was impeding imports; manage local councils; receive an increasing number of visiting delegations; and feed an insatiable and growing group of foreign patrons with the story that the NTC had a plan for everything, which it did not.

On 1 June a car bomb exploded outside the Tibesti hotel, driving several foreign delegations to seek more discreet premises in the suburbs. Additionally, the first concerns of a protracted stalemate on the battlefield had begun to sink in, and Qadhafi seemed more confident than ever.[42] More importantly, Qadhafi's armed forces and security brigades had forced the rebels back from two of the east's four main export terminals, Ra's Lanuf and Brega, and had line-of-sight coverage over a third at Zwaitina. That fighting had damaged a key oil pipeline, crippling the NTC's export of crude oil—which was essential to exchange for the import of refined products to enable electricity generation in eastern Libya.[43] There was a crucial side-campaign fought between both sides targeting control of the oil infrastructure which was underreported. But it was a key theatre in which the revolutionaries would ultimately prevail.[44]

Lawyers, money and recognition

The NTC knew early on that its legitimacy would in part be judged on its ability to pay salaries and otherwise run a wartime economy. One of its first acts on 19 March was to designate the Central Bank of Benghazi as a monetary authority and to establish the Arabian Gulf Oil Company (AGOCO) as a supervisory authority on oil production and policies in the country, based temporarily in Benghazi.[45] The primary lead on policy fell to the Executive Committee's 'minister for oil and finance', Ali Abd al-Salam Tarhuni, a career academic at the University of Washington in the US who had joined the NTC in Benghazi in early March. Effectively a one-man ministry, Tarhuni's challenges included ensuring liquidity of the Libyan dinar and foreign exchange, the flow of goods and services in the public and private sectors and securing financial support to pay salaries as well as for refined fuel products to generate electricity.[46] The sums required for salaries and refined fuel products were enormous and could only be realised through the release of Libyan sovereign assets held offshore and frozen by UNSCR 1970, since the NTC could not generate taxes or other revenues from income or businesses. However, releasing Libyan assets was fraught with legal, technical, and physical obstacles. Tarhuni's initial meetings with oil companies in Benghazi had failed largely because neither he nor the NTC could provide payment guarantees to the companies.

The Libya Contact Group was aware of the problem from the beginning. At the 29 March London conference, Qatar had volunteered to facilitate the sale of Libyan oil and to use the proceeds to meet Libya's 'humanitarian needs'.[47] The Qatari government, with encouragement from the UK and the US, asked the Geneva-based independent oil trader Vitol Group to supply the NTC with gasoline and fuel in exchange for crude oil from the eastern oilfields. On 30 March Vitol entered a formal barter contract with AGOCO to supply oil products to the liberated areas in exchange for crude oil and naptha. Given the Qataris' backing, Vitol was the only company prepared to deal with the NTC on credit terms as opposed to immediate payment.[48] It continued to supply them, even when payment was slow, eventually recouping the crude oil as well as the funds.[49]

The Vitol agreement literally kept the lights on in Benghazi, but because crude oil was being used as payment for refined products and not to generate revenue, Tarhuni and the NTC were fast entering a budget crisis. By June, of 180 million Libyan dinars (LYD) (US$146 million) in various banks in eastern Libya at the start of the revolution, there was only 40 million LYD (US$32 million) left for the population to withdraw. The NTC's financial situation was therefore critical; the 9 June Contact Group meeting in Abu Dhabi described it as a severe threat to the organisation. Interruption to electricity and water, lack of liquidity in banking and commerce, and limited security coverage for extraction from oil fields all 'affected the sustainability of the revolution'.[50] The NTC's forecasted revenues over the next six months from customs revenues and selling imported subsidised fuel still left an estimated deficit of 2.8 billion LYD, most of which was needed for salaries.[51]

Tarhuni had also made several unsuccessful approaches to the Sanctions Committee established under UNSCR 1970 and to the EU, via diplomatic envoys in Benghazi, to unfreeze Libyan assets abroad. However, until mid-July this route was not legally or politically possible. In legal terms, most states recognise other states, not governments nor political entities like the NTC. Politically, both China and Russia sat on the sanctions committee and were still grappling with the events unleashed by UNSCR 1970 and 1973. They were unsure if the NTC would prevail over Qadhafi and disinclined to agree an exemption. Many EU members were not persuaded to follow France's early recognition of the NTC as the legitimate government in Libya, due to both the legal question and questions of performance; recognition being generally accorded to entities like the NTC on the basis of administrative effectiveness, control of territory, and the degree to which they are representative of the population.

To ride out the budget crisis, the NTC relied, aside from the dwindling reserves held in Benghazi banks, on ad hoc pledges and donations from foreign countries, notably the combined pledge of $245 million for humanitarian assistance made at the 5 May Rome Contact Group. To receive these ad hoc pledges, the NTC agreed with the Contact Group to establish a Temporary Financial Mechanism (TFM), which would bypass the sanctions regime established by the UN Security Council. Specifically, the TFM would provide a vehicle that would allow the deposit of funds, bank transfers, and Letters of Credit, which the NTC could use to pay for salaries, public welfare, and food subsidies in the areas under its control. The TFM had to ensure the money was used transparently in accordance with international audit standards.

However the TFM took several crucial weeks to establish itself in Benghazi through June. At the Libya Contact Group meeting in Abu Dhabi on 9 June, Nayid and Jibril, on behalf of the NTC, therefore formally sought immediate financial aid to help pay for the oil imports to Benghazi and security and technical assistance to repair and secure damaged oil production facilities. They also asked the British to release 900 million LYD in recently made currency by the firm De La Rue frozen by UNSCR 1970. Finally they suggested urgent consideration be given to a cash injection and 'printing of money' in the event that the funds did not reach the NTC through the TFM or the unfreezing of assets.[52]

Still, the money pledged in the Rome, Doha and Abu Dhabi Contact Group meetings did not materialise, and it was Turkey that provided the first real injection of funds to the NTC at the end of June by way of $100 million in cash and $100 million of in-kind humanitarian assistance after intense lobbying by the NTC. It was a generous contribution from a country that had initially been seen by the NTC as siding with Qadhafi and hesitant to deal with the revolutionaries, recognising the NTC as the sole legitimate representative of the Libyan people only on 3 July.[53] The cash component was flown from Ankara to Benghazi in the NTC's BA146 Air Libya jet several days later.[54] Qatar also transferred $100 million as a loan guaranteed by Qasim Azuz, the governor of the Central Bank (Benghazi) of Libya, on 23 June 2011.[55]

However the Libyans remained profoundly frustrated by the slow materialisation of funds through the TFM. Three days prior to the 15 July Contact Group meeting in Istanbul, an exasperated Abd al-Jalil summoned the Contact Group's envoys and told them he would withdraw the NTC from the Contact Group until the funds promised to them had been paid. His gambit worked. The 15 July Contact Group meeting in Istanbul was to be a watershed for the NTC. With fighting entering its fifth month and Ramadan only two weeks away, the meeting was attended by thirty-two countries together with the UN, EU, NATO, the Arab League, the OIC, the GCC and, as invitees, the African Union, Brazil and India. Working assiduously behind the scenes Turkey had lobbied the participants intensely to stand more fully behind the NTC. The expanded Contact Group agreed to deal with the NTC as the 'legitimate governing authority in Libya ... welcomed its role in leading the transition process in Libya and expressed support for its efforts to broaden its popular base to embrace all Libyan people'.[56]

The same day Kuwait promptly transferred $50 million to the TFM. Bahrain transferred $5 million. Critically, the US finally recognised the NTC on 15 July, allowing the US to release $400 million against frozen funds in two tranches: $300 million on 31 August 2011 and $100 million on 1 Sept 2011. Germany, in a loan agreement against frozen funds provided $108,380,968 on 28 August allowing the TFM to pay $100 million to Vitol in three payments from July and to keep open the credit lines for further fuel supplies throughout the fall of Tripoli and afterwards. The largest tranche was $1 billion for public sector salaries released by Canada in October 2011.

Libyan exasperation with the Contact Group as seen in Abd al-Jalil's threat to withdraw from the group was real. In fact, neither side foresaw the practical challenge of shifting large sums of money through the international financial system to a nonsovereign entity like the NTC. Loopholes had to be found even after the NTC was recognised as the 'legitimate governing authority in Libya' by the Contact Group. For example, in Canada various firms claimed $700 million against

Libyan funds. However, the US Treasury was able to enforce an exemption against such claims and the funds were transferred from Canada via the US to the TFM.[57] For the duration of its existence—July through November 2011—the NTC would spend some $1.2 billion.[58]

Cash and liquidity

Distributing the cash to recipients on the ground presented its own challenges. Chief of these was the problem of liquidity, since Libyan dinars were held offshore or being hoarded within the country, which meant that nobody could withdraw sufficient cash from their bank accounts. In the Nafusa Mountains, salaries had not been paid since January due to the fighting. Some $15 million would be paid in two tranches in early August and September in the form of 'Family Assistance Handouts' in Zintan, Nalut, and Jadu. Dollars paid into the TFM would be exchanged for Libyan dinars through three currency traders in Benghazi, flown to the airstrip at Ruhaibat in the NTC's plane, then secured in local banks for onward transfer by local committees for distribution to families each of whom would receive on average 280 LYD (160 LYD per family and an additional 20 LYD for each family member).[59] The initial payments in the Nafusa Mountains helped the NTC gain the appearance of some control in this crucial theatre prior to the fall of Tripoli.

However, the overall liquidity problem in Libya would only be solved after the fall of the capital, and required releasing 900 million in Libyan dinars recently printed in the UK by the banknote firm De La Rue, but impounded by the British Navy under UNSCR 1970. A second batch of Libyans dinars had been held at an airport in London where an Africa Airways flight was to take it to the government in Tripoli. A lawyer from Jibril's office, Tariq al-Tumi, led negotiations with the British Foreign Office in June, but the UK attorney general ruled that legally, the dinars belonged to the Central Bank of Libya, which was subject to the asset freeze under UNSCR 1970, and as the British government did not yet recognise the NTC as the legitimate government, the NTC could not receive the currency. Even if the UK government were to recognise the NTC as the sole legitimate representative of the Libyan people, and the Central Bank in Benghazi as the 'legal Central Bank' in accordance with the NTC's 19 March decree, then the Central Bank in Benghazi would own the notes, but as it too was deemed subject to the asset freeze it would not be possible to transfer them. Little wonder Abd al-Jalil was frustrated.

As Ramadan and Eid approached—traditionally high-spending periods for the population—the NTC's credibility was threatened as the liquidity crisis worsened. The UK, despite being one of the NTC's strongest supporters and having the largest foreign mission in Benghazi since 5 March, only formally recognised the NTC as the legitimate governing authority in Libya on 27 July. A political decision rather than a legal view, it enabled Tumi's negotiations to proceed with the UK Foreign Office to allow the NTC *de jure* ownership of the 900 million LYD. Tumi then had to argue before the UN Sanctions Committee, controlled by the UN Security Council, that the dinars be released on humanitarian grounds. Initially, China rejected the application because derogatory comments about China made by an NTC member had been reported in a Hong Kong newspaper; after an apology, China cleared the second application.[60] On 30 August, the last day of Ramadan and ten days after the fall of Tripoli, Tumi and executives from De La Rue flew to Benghazi to negotiate the transfer of the dinars to the Benghazi branch of the National Bank with the UK Foreign Office's help, upon which an RAF plane brought the dinars from the UK a few hours later. Only at that point did the Libyans discover the total number of dinars not to be 900 million LYD, but two billion. The currency eased the liquidity crisis, and as such was a critical stabilisation measure after the fall of Tripoli.

The Yunis affair

In July, as the military campaign against Tripoli gained momentum in the Western Mountains, the NTC rapidly shifted its attention to the prospect of a post-Qadhafi political dispensation. Discussions concerning the transition framework intensified within the NTC, as did the arguments concerning military strategy for both Tripoli and the Brega front commanded by Yunis. Despite repeated attempts to take the latter town Yunis had been unable to shift the line of conflict west of Ajdabiya. Troops under his command in mid-July suffered some seventy dead and over 600 wounded in a three-pronged assault on Brega involving some of the heaviest NATO bombing of the war.

On 27 July an NTC delegation presented Yunis with a summons, signed by Isawi and stamped by the NTC's Ministry of Defence, to return from the Brega frontline to Benghazi to discuss military affairs.[61] After telephoned reassurances from Hasi at the rebel operations centre in Benghazi, Yunis set off with a small convoy of cars back to the city. Shortly Yunis took a call from a relative who asked why he had left the frontline and queried why the commander-in-chief was being recalled for investigation. Yunis told his relative that Hasi had reassured him everything was fine. After going through seven checkpoints Yunis made a final worried call to a cousin at 10am, saying they were being followed by a large number of heavily armed fighters. There was no further communication.[62]

On the Saturday after the killing, Abd al-Jalil gave a quixotic account of events, saying that Yunis had been taken into custody for investigation into complaints that he mismanaged forces and did not provide them with enough ammunition, supplies and food. Abd al-Jalil told reporters 'the recall of General Abd al-Fattah Yunis from Ajdabiya was based on a warrant issued with the knowledge of the Executive Committee'. But in an extraordinary disclosure he added that he didn't know 'why [it] was issued ... who was present at the meeting when the decision was made ... or on what basis the decision was made'.[63]

Every political transition, even in homogenous societies, is a daily referendum on identity, one's past, present, and future. While the complete circumstances around Yunis's killing have never been ascertained, his assassination may have been a revenge attack for his actions as interior minister under Qadhafi, dissatisfaction with his role in the inconclusive offensives against Brega, or allegations of continued contacts with Qadhafi and his officials. But the more candid explanations provided by those close to Yunis, Abd al-Jalil and Isawi, all point towards an internal crisis within the NTC leadership. One view sees Yunis as the unintended victim of a struggle for control of the Executive Office within the NTC and the defence and interior portfolios. In this view, Isawi signed the warrant to bring Yunis in for questioning as a way of discrediting the military commander and removing him as a potential foe. That he was assassinated was an unintended consequence. With Yunis discredited, and Jibril distrusted for his absence from Libya, the way was paved for Isawi, with the support of some of the revolutionary battalions, to take the helm of the Executive Office of the NTC, now an internationally recognised and, more importantly, solvent enterprise. The irony of it was that the incident politically finished Isawi.

Another view connects Yunis's death more explicitly with the two rival plans for the liberation of Tripoli. The NTC's 5 May Roadmap written by Ba'ja and Jibril had clearly spelled out roles for government police and military officers. Through Yunis and other intermediaries, Jibril and his Tripoli Taskforce had close contacts with a network of defected officers who might have provided the platform for a less chaotic transition, possibly with Jibril at the helm. This was not supported by many of the revolutionaries or, according to one well-placed observer, by Abd al-Jalil himself, as he feared a double-cross or coup. Discrediting Yunis (though not necessarily killing him) and replacing Jibril with Isawi, might enable the liberation of Tripoli and the broader political transition to occur on different terms.

If leadership is judged in terms of how one responds to adversity then Abd al-Jalil's moment had arrived. With Jibril silent and abroad, Abd al-Jalil had to convince a sceptical population that justice was being served. The revolution that had erupted against one of the most capricious and eccentric manifestations of political power in modern times, the Qadhafi regime, was at risk of being seen to abandon its principles.

Accordingly, Abd al-Jalil decided on 8 August to sack the entire Executive Office for its alleged implication in the Yunis affair. The differences between the NTC and the Executive Office, glaringly obvious through the Yunis affair, had not been settled, nor had either entity satisfactorily solved the conundrum in the eyes of the population of earning the right to govern, with dissatisfaction most evident against the Executive Office and its frequently absent chief, Jibril. While Jibril would remain as head of the Executive, he was asked to submit a new board for the NTC's approval and to spend less time outside the country. When Tripoli did fall at the end of August, like much of the military aspect of the revolution, it was not because of the NTC but in spite of it. Indeed, the revolution was officially without an executive body and would remain as such until October 2011.

The Constitutional Declaration

In the wake of Yunis's death the risk that the NTC would implode seemed real. Yet Abd al-Jalil had still to steer the framework for Libya's transition to representative government. This framework became known as the Constitutional Declaration, and its final provisions were negotiated against the backdrop of Yunis's death and while the military campaign in the Western Mountains proceeded apace.

Ever since the NTC's 5 May Roadmap had been published (and roundly criticised in Benghazi) the political and legal committees in the NTC had continued to develop a more detailed legal framework to guide its operations through the transition. Thus a new 'Constituent Covenant for the Transitional Period' was endorsed by the Executive Committee on 21 June and then circulated in Benghazi for comment. The 'Covenant' was to provide the 'basis for ruling in the transitional period until the approval of the permanent constitution in a general public referendum'.[64] But again, the Covenant was widely criticised by the population in Benghazi and by leading voices in both the 'secular' and 'Islamist' currents that were then emerging, specifically over Article 30 which allowed the NTC to endure until after a constitution-making process and subsequent legislative elections. In effect, the 'Covenant' was the same as the 5 May Roadmap and again proposed an unrealistic and rushed timeframe for the transition.

In the wake of the criticism at least four groups developed their own transitional plans, of varying quality, and a vibrant debate ensued across Benghazi. One was the 'Vision of the Political Process during the Transitional Phase', dated 27 June 2011, by the National Front for the Salvation of Libya, a diaspora opposition network who had returned to Benghazi to reanimate their political role. Another, the 'Draft of the Roadmap', was circulated by Zahi Magharbi's Consultative Support Group working from the Libyan International Medical University. A third proposal, the 'Draft of a Constitutional Declaration', came from a group of lawyers from the 17 February Coalition which included Gallal, Qadura, and Mismari.

Finally, Islamist groups also began to circulate their own versions of a transitional plan. One was the 'Roadmap and Political Future of Libya' plan, developed largely by two influential clerics, Ali and Muhammad Bu Sidra, in conjunction with revolutionary fighters under the name of the 'United Libyan Revolutionaries'.[65] The cleric Ali Sallabi also published a thirty-three-page, 206-article draft constitution, humbly presented 'for discussion', as an alternative vision for the transitional phase. Sallabi's proposed sequence drew on the plan developed by the United Libyan Revolutionaries, which became apparent when he asked Hana al-Gallal, his neighbour in Benghazi, to comment on it.[66]

Another widely discussed issue was whether Libya could manage a relatively early election without jeopardising the rest of the transition.

Here the debate was most heated. Supporters of the 5 May Road Map and its 21 June evolution, centred around Jibril and Ba'ja (who had largely written them), saw the Road Map as a binding document. Its key feature was the simplicity and speed with which the NTC could put a constitutionally elected government in place. Their thinking was that this was the most stable arrangement in the Libyan context, and that the process's speed would forestall challenges to its legitimacy and be the most expedient way of installing a new government to tackle the economic challenges facing Libya.[67] Jibril essentially believed that the Libyans did not have a sufficiently developed democratic culture to support an extended transition. Jibril also received international support for the simplicity of the process, which minimised the number of elections within the transition; the US, among others, vividly recalled how the transitional process in Iraq, with its multiple elections, had gone awry. But this thinking clashed head-on with a view held by the Muslim Brotherhood and other Islamist groups that the transition itself had to be overseen by an elected, legitimate body, and that legitimacy was worth risking the continuity and stability that a non-elected NTC, as presented in the 5 May Road Map and its 21 June evolution, would have provided.

In the final debates over drafting what would become the NTC's 'Constitutional Declaration', formally enacted on 3 August 2011, the latter view prevailed. While these debates ensued, the NTC completely rewrote Article 30 on 27 July by clearly spelling out the process for the NTC's dissolution and for National Congress elections within 240 days, or eight months, of the fall of Qadhafi. After this, the Article stipulated a formal 'end of war' announcement and that the NTC would move to Tripoli to form an interim government within thirty days. Within ninety days the interim government would call for elections for a National Congress of 200 members to be held within 240 days after the announcement of liberation. Once the new Congress convened the NTC would dissolve itself. The Congress would then choose a prime minister who would appoint a cabinet and form an interim government to be endorsed by the Congress. In parallel, the Congress would also choose a Constituent Committee that would have ninety days to draft a Constitution which would then be subject to a national referendum. Subsequent parliamentary elections would occur according to the Constitution followed by the formation of a constitutional government, thereby completing Libya's transition.

The Constitutional Declaration was a bittersweet achievement in various ways that fundamentally altered the relationships between the emerging factions within the NTC. Article 30 had been completed in emergency session on the evening of the day of Yunis's arrest, though it was never clear if the two events were connected. When final voting on all the provisions of the Declaration took place on 3 August, several key members of the NTC were absent—including Ba'ja, who had left for Washington, DC, for consultations. Jibril, Ba'ja and the Executive Office felt that the Muslim Brotherhood and others had taken advantage of the drama and tension of the moment to push through a fundamentally different sequence to what they envisaged. The NTC apparently had no internal bylaws for managing absentee voting at the time.[68]

On 10 August, when Ghugha and the chief of the NTC legal committee, Salwa al-Dghaili, introduced the Constitutional Declaration in a Benghazi press conference, they were almost mobbed by an angry audience that included original members of the 17 February Coalition such as Gallal, who felt the whole process had been conducted furtively and without genuine consultation. From their perspective, the Constitutional Declaration showed how the 'Islamist' (or Muslim Brotherhood) and 'secular' (or pro-Jibril) factions of the NTC had already started to position themselves for political power after the fall of Tripoli. In this respect, the 17 February Coalition saw both camps as being as bad as each other, with each supporting a transitional sequence which they thought would benefit them politically. The fact that key members of the NTC were away at this critical juncture, in this view, showed they did not understand their national responsibilities.[69] But irrespective of the result and the tense circumstances in which it was delivered, the NTC finally had a formal transition plan and the stage was now set for the internal uprising in Tripoli where the balance of forces remained as opaque as ever.

Conclusion

The 17 February Revolution was chaotic, with no one fully in charge of events. In these circumstances, the NTC and its Executive Office achieved a minimal threshold of political legitimacy to carry the revolutionary moment. It did this by expanding its national representation through the local councils, securing international recognition and financial support for the transition, and by deliberating a transparent path for a return to constitutional government. It set itself simple goals and did not pretend to be a government, and it was supported by a complex mix of mutually reinforcing internal and external constituencies, underpinned by popular support where Libyans of all stripes had a role to play. Ultimately it could not contain the emergence of political factions around the negotiations of the Constitutional Declaration and jockeying for influence for the imminent political transition. But it also included some extraordinary individual contributions, including from Yunis, whose early defection to the rebel side gave the NTC the initial space in which to organise, and whose death reflected the tensions emerging within the NTC over the transition. It also benefited from sheer luck: Qadhafi and Saif al-Islam's public responses to the uprising; the influence of neighbouring transitions in Tunisia and Egypt; and the unprecedented regional and international response in mid-March by the Arab League, the UN Security Council and NATO's no-fly zone, which perhaps saved it from annihilation.

3

THE FALL OF TRIPOLI

PART 1[1]

Peter Cole with *Umar Khan*

Tripoli—Libya's capital city, and home to almost one third of its population—was where the many strands of the Libyan revolution came together, and where they unravelled. The puzzle of engineering a revolution in Libya's capital stretched NATO's mandate and its members' political and military exposure, creating substantial divisions over the revolution's goals that shaped the contours of Libya's new politics.

Tripoli's history and geography defined its residents' affiliations for or against the revolution. The bedrock of revolutionary support came from poorer suburbs on the coastal outskirts—Suq al-Jum'a, Fashlum, Tajura—which, with their poor roads and groundwater, were never historically settled, but where under Mu'ammar al-Qadhafi many of Tripoli's old merchant and landed families relocated. These families were among those who suffered substantially from Qadhafi's 1970s *Green Book* redistributionism, losing property and business relationships to the government. Others could not afford the rising cost of living that the oil boom and urbanisation brought.

Around them, a new city sprang up, populated by the newly rich beneficiaries of Qadhafi's oil state. Over the 1970s and 1980s Tripoli saw an enormous influx of Libyans who staffed Libya's bureaucracy and oil services companies. Elites settled in grand villas in districts once populated by Tripoli's merchants, like Bin Ashur, Qirqarish, and Hayy al-Andalus, or in new suburban sprawl, such as Ain Zara to the southeast. Poorer migrants from central and southern Libya who staffed the security services and bureaucracy were housed in projects (*sha'biyat*) created in the entirely new suburbs of Abu Slim, Ghut al-Sha'al, Hadba, Qurji, and Gharghur on the 'airport road' between Qadhafi's main compound, Bab al-Aziziyya, and the international airport.

In 2011, there were pockets of revolutionary support across all these areas. But outside districts like Suq al-Jum'a, Tajura and Fashlum, these were isolated; few knew the background and loyalties of their neighbours. Qadhafi's security brigades were stronger in Tripoli than in Benghazi and the east, where the armed forces and *Sa'iqa* ('Thunderbolt') Special Forces in the Katibat Fadil, Benghazi's one large military base, largely stayed out of the conflict at Interior Minister Abd al-Fattah Yunis's discretion.[2] In Tripoli Qadhafi could rely particularly on two large 'rapid intervention' brigades: the Imhammad Imgharyif Brigade, commanded by al-Barrani Ishkal based within Qadhafi's compound at Bab al-Aziziyya, and the famous 32 Reinforced Brigade (*al-Liwa' 32 al-Mu'azzaza*) commanded by Khamis al-Qadhafi, which possessed three major bases covering approach roads to Tripoli from the west, east and south. Large well-equipped military bases also existed in Tarhuna and Gharyan near Tripoli. There existed other volunteer and paramilitary forces—the Revolutionary Guards, People's Guard, People's Resistance Forces, and even *kashshaf* (scouts), whom Musa Kusa, according to a US diplomat, instructed to prevent people gathering.[3] Similarly, criminals were released from prisons to threaten protestors.

While Benghazi, Misrata and Zintan's protests developed over 15–17 February, sympathisers in Tripoli discussed taking similar measures on Facebook, and on 17 February itself small protests occurred in Fashlum.[4] But major protests did not occur until 20 February, when Saif al-Islam al-Qadhafi made a fateful speech that led many defecting to the rebels to conclude that Qadhafi would not countenance political reform. The speech came after several weeks' efforts by Saif al-

Islam and his brothers to grapple with the protests spreading across Libya. Khamis had cut short a trip to the US in mid-January to apparently make military preparations.[5] Sa'adi al-Qadhafi flew personally to Benghazi's Katibat Fadil on 15 February to coordinate the Special Forces and address the town by public radio on 17 February, promising money, a new airport, and investment.[6] Saif al-Islam, on 16 February, approached the emergent 17 February Coalition in Benghazi, and some of the political opposition networks—Muslim Brotherhood, National Front for the Salvation of Libya (NFSL) and Libyan Islamic Fighting Group (LIFG), with whom he had fostered various reconciliations over the 2000s, to enquire how the protests could be peacefully defused.

With few exceptions, none of these groups fully expected events over 15–17 February 2011 to lead to revolution. Instead, they pressed Saif al-Islam to revive economic and constitutional reforms he had abandoned in the mid-2000s. The emergent 17 February Coalition in Benghazi issued such demands in the week preceding Saif al-Islam's speech, Fathi al-Ba'ja noting that on 16 February, their intention was 'not to create a revolution'.[7] On 17 February an emissary from Saif al-Islam approached the Coalition, asking 'What will it take for the protests to stop?'; they responded with similar limited demands, along with a ceasefire request.[8] Abdullah al-Sanusi flew at least two of the Coalition to Tripoli—Abd al-Salam al-Mismari and Abd al-Hafiz Ghugha—but released them both.[9]

The Muslim Brotherhood and NFSL had been politically neutralised by 2011,[10] their members in Tripoli quietly pursuing business or academic careers.[11] Over the 2000s a quasi-secret gathering called the 'Book Club' developed in Tripoli in the house of Nizar Kawan—a Muslim Brother with a shock of hair and winning smile that his colleagues joked could have fronted shampoo commercials—which presented its own reform 'initiative' (*mubadara*) to Saif al-Islam, in February 2011.[12] Meanwhile the LIFG and a younger generation of Libyan fighters, who had fought an insurgency against the regime during the 1990s, were undergoing a delicate programme of prisoner releases agreed between Saif al-Islam, the Doha-based scholar and cleric Ali Sallabi, and six leading commanders of the LIFG—Abd al-Hakim Bilhajj, Sami al-Sa'adi, Khalid Sharif, Miftah al-Dhuwadi, Abd al-Wahhab al-Qa'id and Mustafa Qanaifid. Saif al-Islam called Sallabi in Tripoli to ascertain the LIFG's position on 17 February 2011. Sallabi also asked that he revitalise his constitutional and political reforms. 'I am totally depressed by what you are saying,' Saif al-Islam al-Islam answered.[13]

By 20 February the Qadhafi family appeared no nearer to accommodating these requests for reform. Saif al-Islam's advisers appear to have been divided between advocating reform and defending the family rule.[14] Among the former were Muhammad al-Huni and NOC Chairman Shukri al-Ghanim, who claimed to have drafted a speech on 18 February promising reform, which compelled him to agree to a speech on 20 February.[15] That day, he is claimed by more than one eyewitness to have met his family at Bab al-Aziziyya to persuade his father to concede reform or retirement.[16] All current sources are silent on what happened thereafter,[17] but in his televised speech at 11pm, played on giant screens at Tripoli's Green Square, he sat dishevelled in front of a green map of Africa, and apparently without notes acknowledged his reach-out efforts, saying 'Many Libyans urged me to speak.' But his speech ended unambiguously: 'The army will play a big role—it is not the army of Tunisia or Egypt. It will support Qadhafi to the last minute. Now in Green Square people are shooting.'[18]

The 20–25 February protests

Following Saif al-Islam's speech, most eyewitnesses agree that probably thousands—'seas of people' as one put it[19]—poured into the streets. 'I thought the regime had fallen,' one observer who later played a substantial role in the underground opposition said.[20] Groups, mainly of youths, converged in Fashlum, Suq al-Jum'a and Tajura, where opposition to Qadhafi was strong, and Green Square.

They joined sporadic protests that had been running most of the day across the city. These met with unarmed police who swiftly pulled back—according to one interlocutor, Yunis, then still Interior Minister, had ordered police not to confront the demonstrators.[21] But after Saif al-Islam's speech police checkpoints were reinforced by the Imhammad Imgharyif and 32 Reinforced Brigades, and the People's Guard; as the crowds poured out following the speech, the first corroborated reports of security forces' shooting to kill outside some mosques occurred.[22] Still, some soldiers shot into the air; a fair number pulled back from the crowds, prompting protestors to occupy Green Square, whose abandonment gave protestors a surreal sense of liberation. In the chaos of the night, unknown groups set ablaze the internal security building overlooking Green Square, and, further west, the People's Hall, where Qadhafi's equivalent of a parliament met twice-yearly. Rumours flew through the crowds that Qadhafi had fled. In those strange moments, reality temporarily suspended, some went back and talked to the armed forces: 'They were nice, ordinary people,' one said, 'one of them said he was from this area and had friends here.'[23]

But the security brigades rallied swiftly, returning to Green Square at around 5am with six or seven unmarked vehicle-mounted anti-air-craft guns. With Green Square at risk of becoming a focal point for the emergent rebellion, the brigades shot to kill, scattering the last vestiges of protestors in the early dawn, killing several dozen and wounding scores more.[24]

Despite the shock of the killings, the 20 February protests raised giddy hopes at home and abroad, where rumours of Qadhafi's flight also circulated.[25] For some, the 'fear barrier' was broken. The security brigades withdrew almost entirely from Tajura and Suq al-Jum'a, but fortified themselves along Tripoli's central arterial roads. Small protests erupted outside state television on 21 February, then the justice ministry and local authorities headquarters on 22 February, and Mi'tiqa airbase on 25 February. Graffiti urging Qadhafi's downfall appeared in the streets. But the ruthlessness displayed at Green Square on the night of 20 February led thousands of others to stay home,[26] such that banks and shops stayed closed despite government text messages on 23 February requesting people to return to work.

Qadhafi's government rallied, and Qadhafi made three speeches over three days. The first on 21 February—a thirty-second appearance under a golf umbrella—reassured supporters that he had not fled the country.[27] Second, the next day, came the two-hour diatribe broadcast outside Bab al-Aziziyya whose climax generated two of the revolution's most enduring slogans—'Who are you?! [*Man antom!*]', and the ominous threat 'to cleanse Libya inch by inch, house by house, home by home, alley by alley, one by one until the country is cleansed from filth and impurity'.[28]

On Friday 25 February, Qadhafi's live midday appearance at Green Square promising to 'open the arsenals if necessary'[29] augured a second rerun of the 20 February protests. As Qadhafi spoke, the security brigades were stationed inside mosques during prayers, and at major public spaces. The shooting began after prayers. As on 20 February, some initially shot above the crowd—a prominent opposition activist said of a post-prayer confrontation: 'They were firing high—I could see the leaves on the trees being hit. They weren't serious about injuring people—they wanted to scatter us, and we did.'[30] But as the day wore on, more and more protests were met with shooting. Another protester, Hisham Bu Hajar, said: 'I came out of the mosque and went to the frontline of the demonstration asking the police not to fire. One was about ten metres away—I could see in his eyes he was listening. But then he reached for his shotgun and shot me in the right leg.'[31] A large march organised in Suq al-Jum'a and Tajura towards Green Square met a roadblock with gunmen stationed on the surrounding roofs which fired into the crowd.[32] A similar protest at the central Algeria Square also met trucks of security brigades. Some described the wounded being shot in the head, while reports that the security brigades targeted the wounded in hospitals appear to be accurate.[33] Though no figures exist, deaths were probably greater by far than occurred on 20 February, and ended hopes that Qadhafi could be persuaded into reform.

Tripoli's stifled opposition

Tripoli's opposition developed slowly and tentatively following the 25 February protests. The lack of armed or civil protest in Tripoli freed the Muhammad Imgharyif and 32 Reinforced Brigades to suppress nascent revolts in Zawiya over 4–9 March, and Misrata on 6 March. Internal security (*al-Amn al-Dakhili*) appeared unaffected, and its recruitment of family members as informants against their families kept fear of the agency alive: 'People within a household didn't know if one of them was working for security.'[34] Many family units divided along pro- and anti-Qadhafi lines, with different generations, and sometimes siblings and spouses, taking different views. These tensions sometimes destroyed families, particularly if informants confessed or were discovered. Uncounted divorces and family rifts occurred across the city.

Supporters of the emerging '17 February Revolution' were atomised by a warren of checkpoints run by the security brigades, through which movement was significantly risky.[35] Thus, youth groups' default option was to use media to broadcast their existence. In Fashlum, a small group of twenty named the Free Generation Movement cohered around the Mhani family, conducting civil disobedience acts. Their main outlets, YouTube and friendly media channels, lifted them from the shadows, but dictated the direction of their group towards ever more creative civil disobedience. These youth groups symbolised the atomised and fragmented nature of Tripoli's opposition—inexperienced but media-aware, with intense faith in world public opinion.[36]

Over time, approximately two hundred such clusters of supporters in Tripoli assembled, comprising almost three thousand persons[37] and slowly began to connect. Probably the most important early factor in their connection was bloodline. Within the security services, people passed information to trusted relatives, even those in Benghazi or the National Transitional Council (NTC), to protect family and clan. This dynamic was arguably more important than ideological support for the revolution. 'People working in the security services who may have hated their cousins ideologically would call them if they had orders to arrest them or burn their houses.'[38] Information security was so poor that, before long, rebel fighters had access to security brigades' radio frequencies, and vice versa. Though many had ideological or material interests to oppose Qadhafi, bloodlines usually determined whom they contacted to express such opinions.

The second factor connecting opposition cells in Tripoli was the possession of two-way satellites that allowed secure communications with the other side. A large black market for these devices emerged, with IT company heads and employees sourcing equipment and smuggling it in. A subset of those in these IT companies were informers for the government, leading to a small clandestine war. One IT head involved in smuggling, Abd al-Hamid Darrat, for example, was reported to the security services from within his own office.[39]

One such cell that coalesced around bloodline and communications technology grew from an apartment in Dhull Street. It centred around the Ra'is family; former Colonel Najm al-Din Ra'is, his brother Nasir, and Muhammad Ghazawi then serving in the army, whom Ra'is contacted on 21 February.[40] Najm al-Din's brother-in-law, Hussain al-Aib, was a senior military official privy to meetings taking place between Sanusi, Qadhafi's sons, and senior security officials such as Husni al-Inshi. Another, Nasir al-Amari, worked in internal security (*al-Amn al-Dakhili*). He was an IT company manager; using scanners and computer hardware he provided, the group transmitted documents and security updates to Ibrahim Dabbashi—the defected Libyan ambassador to the United Nations in the NTC and a family contact—and

Mahmud Jibril, head of the NTC's Executive—using satellite phones Dabbashi provided. Information provided included the passport numbers and names of foreign fighters being processed through the Prime Ministers' Office, and the security services' profiling of the military leaderships in Misrata, Zintan and Benghazi.[41]

Over time these clusters began learning of each other, and 'hubs' developed around those with access to weapons or communications. One example, important to subsequent events, was a network of forty-fifty security officials, largely from Suq al-Jum'a, 'hubbed' around army munitions officer Ali bin Zahra and Muhammad Shaikh, a general in the police's investigations department. Shaikh began working in March with a relative, Usama Shaikh, and later that month linked up with army officers General Jum'a Mishri and General Yunis al-Sahli.[42] Sahli then brought other officers into the networks like Fathi Ayyad, Abd al-Razzaq al-Igniyya, and then bin Zahra and his network of arms smugglers and officers. Another group of police and army officers—Mahmud Sharif, Hisham al-Litki, and Jamal Ghazawi—emerged in Slim Street, where they used a local mosque as their base of operations.[43] At this point, the network began consciously subdividing itself into mission-specific groups.

Meanwhile another network coalesced through political opposition circles, particularly the former NFSL and Muslim Brotherhood. These were equally isolated at first—since Brotherhood or NFSL members tended to know only a handful of others. One said 'we never even acknowledged each other in the street. Being a Muslim Brother in those days meant having a rope tied to your bed for a quick escape.'[44] Over March, former members rekindled relationships developed over decades in exile in Cairo, the US and Europe, meeting in each others' houses. From the Muslim Brotherhood, personalities such as Nizar Kawan, Sidiq al-Kabir, Mustafa Tir, Mustafa Nuh, Hisham Krikshi, Adnan Ghirwi and Salah Tunali became regular faces. From the NFSL there were Hisham Bu Hajar, Sadat al-Badri, Na'im Gharyani, Abd al-Majid Biuk, Muhammad Umaish and others. Again, satellite communications mattered; the house of Umaish, a burly poker-faced doctor from an old Dirna family, became the hub for day-long meetings, since he kept the satellite phone and internet connections with which the group contacted colleagues in Benghazi.

The group also met in the luxury carpet shops of Bu Hajar, a former army colonel and NFSL member who in the 1990s, as a young member of its military 'wing', was intended to be in the second 'wave' of a 1984 attack on Bab al-Aziziyya during an unsuccessful assassination attempt on Qadhafi.[45] It was Bu Hajar who had been shot in the leg by the hesitant police officer during the 25 February protests, which took him to Brussels, where from his hospital bed he watched the UN Security Council pass UNSCR 1970 on 17 March. He contacted his NFSL colleague Ali Zaidan, the Belgian government and Jibril, who by then was lobbying European ministers in Strasbourg to recognise the NTC. Once back, he mobilised former members of a youth club he ran into the 'Shabab al-Asima' or 'Youth of the Capital', and, due to his political connections, became an important fixture in the network.[46]

By the end of March, these three strands—the Brotherhood, NFSL and Bu Hajar's Shabab al-Asima—began focusing, through several endless meetings, on establishing a political alliance. They agreed to call themselves the 17 February Coalition (*I'tilaf Sab'at Ashr Fibrayir*, hereafter *I'tilaf*) and Nizar Kawan agreed to be a spokesman for the group, moving to Doha and using his political connections to announce *I'tilaf's* creation on Al Jazeera in early April.[47]

I'tilaf were perhaps the most vigorous in reaching out to the dozens of independent groups springing up across Tripoli, though they were never influential enough to control the uprising. Three personalities in particular were predominant in this reach-out. The first was Sadat al-Badri, a doctor and NFSL member until the early 2000s. Badri was one of the most energetic in seeking out cells such as Najm al-Din Ra'is's, with whom al-Badri had studied in the 1960s, and Muhammad Shaikh's, connecting them to each other.[48] At times, Badri spent days or weeks patiently enquiring in neighbourhoods after particular groups or cells. The second was Hisham Bu Hajar, whose background led him to be nominated as *I'tilaf's* first 'head'.[49]

The third was Mustafa Nuh, a former member of Qadhafi's intelligence apparatus and also a member of the Muslim Brotherhood. A sombre personality, Nuh had strong military and intelligence contacts, including with the security services networks. In April, Nuh emerged as head of a 'military council' for Tripoli at a meeting in Siyahiyya between the security service defectors Shaikh, Sahli, Nuh, Ghaddar, bin Zahra, Igniyya, Ayyad and others.[50] Shaikh said of the meeting, 'we agreed he outranked us; even those of higher rank deferred to him.'[51] The same month, *I'tilaf* also recognised Nuh as head of its 'military wing'. Nuh thus bridged the political networks of the Brotherhood and NFSL and sympathisers in the security services.

Nuh also worked with youth groups throughout Tripoli, via Bu Hajar and other contacts, including young Salafists and the younger generation of LIFG fighters in the capital, documenting the numbers, registrations, armouries and movements of security brigades within Tripoli over April. In time, Nuh worked with these youth groups to test response capacity, generating, for example, small shootings or *gelatina* (fishing explosive) attacks in suburbs, then simultaneously generating incidents elsewhere to map the response capacity of the brigades.[52] In this way, armed youth gangs began to develop, including among the Salafist youth subcultures of the city.[53]

By the end of March, the idea of generating mass protest in Tripoli was moribund. Bu Hajar organised *I'tilaf's* first and only public protest—a small gathering of thirty people in Bin Ashur on 7 April, which Bu Hajar taped and passed to Al Jazeera. The event passed unnoticed; twenty of the thirty who attended were from Bu Hajar's own family.[54] Hereon the various networks in Tripoli started working towards armed opposition. Hope had died that the 17 March establishment of a no-fly zone would lead to imminent liberation from Benghazi and a peaceful uprising in Tripoli. As Bu Hajar said: 'We thought the freedom fighters would come marching down from Benghazi—something we later realised was a fantasy.'[55]

The 'Plan to Liberate Tripoli' and the Tripoli Taskforce

The 'fantasy' of which Bu Hajar spoke was unravelling elsewhere in April. The frontline at Brega, east of Sirt, had stalled and the outcome of conflicts in Misrata and Nafusa Mountains was unclear. NATO's air support, begun on 31 March, was not immediately matching Libyans' high expectations, and Qadhafi's security brigades in Brega had shed uniforms and adapted tactics to compensate. Forces under Abd al-Fattah Yunis, now the rebels' chief of staff, had succumbed to squabbling with another general, Khalifa Hiftar, and an emerging mass of civilian volunteers.[56] A third effort to retake Brega, launched over the first week of April, was beaten back to Ajdabiya, with an accidental NATO air strike on rebel civilian fighters.[57] Yunis publically blamed NATO, flying to Brussels to press NATO leadership for stronger military support, such as the use of Apache helicopters.[58]

In the wake of military stalemate, a strand within the NTC emerged, backed by Abd al-Rahman Shalgham, Mahmud Jibril, and Fathi al-

Ba'ja, which supported a mediated solution based on negotiating Qadhafi's departure and creating a transitional council comprising members of Qadhafi's government and the NTC, which became the basis of the '5 May Roadmap'. The African Union was also promoting its own mediation efforts, and there was real consideration in NTC and diplomatic circles that the country might be split.

Simultaneously, however, covert efforts to bolster the rebels' military effectiveness were beginning. On 21 March, NTC Chairman Mustafa Abd al-Jalil authorised an approach to the Qatari government 'to negotiate the shipment of [weapons] supplies needed by the Council.'[59] Qatar had supported toppling Qadhafi from the outset, supporting, with the UAE, the Arab League's call for a no-fly zone over Libya. Qatar was also a likely sponsor since it used French weapons suppliers, and President Nicolas Sarkozy had politically 'recognised' the NTC on 10 March and had been a main sponsor of the no-fly zone at the UN. The Libya–Qatar meeting occurred in Doha on 22 March; the Qataris, according to a participant in the meeting, were specifically concerned about issues of legality, since French end-user certification on weapons sales forbade resupply to third parties. A shipment of twelve iridium (satellite) phones was made,[60] and once the Qataris obtained French permission over 24–25 March, one smuggled shipment of Milan anti-tank and foldable Zodiac weapons occurred.[61] At the 13 April Contact Group meeting in Doha, Qatar's prime minister made his country's willingness to supply weapons directly to rebels plain to the UN and NATO,[62] and the first Qatari plane shipment arrived the following week, at Tubruq airport,[63] with a second plane flying thereafter into Benghazi. Both shipments were directed to Yunis.

While supporting arms shipments through Tubruq and Benghazi, France also put significant pressure on the NTC's Executive Committee to find a solution to the military impasse. On 15 May, Sarkozy told Jibril that neither NATO nor France could 'support Libya's revolution forever'. 'It was a compelling argument, to be honest' Jibril said.[64] Jibril felt that he urgently needed to offer the international community a plan that looked credible. But at that point, he said, the NTC's information on Qadhafi's control centres was insufficient, supplemented discretionarily by Sudanese intelligence. 'We didn't know the mapping of Qadhafi's security, and thinking about a popular uprising in Tripoli while Qadhafi's operations rooms were still standing would have been a massacre.'[65]

On his return to Doha from the Paris meeting, Jibril was contacted, via the head of one of the rebels' newly emergent TV channels, by the head of a catering company serving Qadhafi's security services named Abd al-Majid Mliqta. Mliqta had crossed the Tunisian border in April with a flash drive containing coordinates for approximately twenty-seven operations rooms his catering company serviced. Jibril flew Mliqta to Doha, whereupon he used Mliqta's information to try and convince France and the international community to back a 'plan' hinging on a renewed assault on Brega by Yunis, concurrent with a largely peaceful uprising in Tripoli.[66] It hinged on the claim that NATO would destroy a selection of targets, including those twenty-seven operations rooms, using Mliqta's information. It also hinged on the prediction that the 'military council' of security service defectors in Tripoli could serve with Yunis as a transitional security entity.

Meanwhile a second, separate effort, first supported by the UK, to gather information to support toppling Tripoli occurred through a communications network with two-way satellites based in Dubai and Tripoli set up on 20 February 2011, and expanded to Qatar on 22 March. With other satellite nodes, including one set up in the NTC in the al-Fadil hotel on 20 February,[67] and two others later set up in Misrata by Muhammad bin Ra's Ali and in Zintan's 'English Teachers' Institute' (Ma'had al-Mu'allimin), these communications networks supported NATO targeting decision making and discreet special forces information-gathering operations in Tripoli.[68]

The coordinating figure in the Dubai and Tripoli hubs of that network was Arif Ali Nayid, a Sufi scholar and head of a telecommunications firm in Libya. Nayid had risen to prominence through his early lobbying on the NTC's behalf via the 'Free 'Ulama Network', which made early approaches to the Turkish government through contacts in the Nurçu Sufi movement and Nayid's preexisting contacts with the Turkish foreign minister, Ahmet Davutoglu, and prime minister, Recep Tayyip Erdogan. Nayid also made early representations to the British and US governments via Tony Blair's office and to the UAE's Abdullah al-Nahyan. This prominence led to Jibril's bringing Nayid on in a 'Support Office' within the Executive Office on 4 April.

On the sidelines of the 5 May Rome Contact Group meeting, the US team, under Secretary of State Hillary Clinton, expressed concern over the lack of any perceivable plan to stabilise Tripoli following Qadhafi's fall—an important barrier to its backing of the Libyan rebels.[69] These conversations led to Nayid's generating a two-page memo proposing a 'Tripoli Taskforce' within the Support Office to address both the military efforts to liberate Tripoli and its stabilisation. On 22 May Nayid flew to Benghazi to meet Abd al-Jalil, who authorised the Taskforce. The same day, Nayid briefed the memo to the NTC and to the EU's high representative, Baroness Ashton. He then met the 'International Stabilisation Response Team' (ISRT), set up after the Rome Contact Group Meeting between British, French, and Italian technocrats to pool experience from Afghanistan and Iraq.[70] The Taskforce interposed itself as its Libyan interlocutor and alternative, arguing that the ISRT alone would not receive sufficient buy-in from Libyans.[71] The Taskforce thus addressed the international community's queasiness, post-Iraq, over post-conflict stabilisation, while also placing itself at the centre of the growing web of foreign military and technical support arriving in Benghazi during May.

The 'Islamist' opposition

Jibril's plans and Nayid's sudden prominence in Benghazi attracted the attention of other political factions also arriving in May. As the NTC expanded to include other political and regional currents, Abd al-Jalil's concern over the growing influence Jibril possessed over the Tripoli portfolio, led to his balancing Jibril and the Tripoli Taskforce against other groups intending to play a role in the fall of Tripoli and post-Qadhafi Libya.[72]

Of these groups, a network in Benghazi and Tunis had emerged comprising mainly 'Islamist' groups—the Muslim Brotherhood and former LIFG, who objected particularly strenuously to Jibril's 5 May Roadmap and its vision of a mediated transition in partnership with defected security officers in Tripoli. Their worldview also clashed with those of the more internationalist Jibril—a political scientist trained in Egypt and the United States, who worked on privatisation and economic liberalisation reforms for the Libyan government from 2007–11[73]—and the Sufi scholar Nayid. These groups began the revolution spread across Libya, Europe and the Gulf; most of those who became influential in the fall of Tripoli did not arrive in Benghazi until May.

Just as Nayid and Jibril's networks coalesced around those able to access foreign influence-makers, so too did Islamist networks coalesce around similar brokers. Among the most important was the Doha-based cleric Ali Sallabi. Sallabi was influential for many reasons; his father was a founding Muslim Brotherhood member in Benghazi, and Sallabi was seen as an ideological guide for the movement though he himself remained above it. His close association with the head of the Association of Muslim Scholars, Yusuf al-Qaradawi, gave him access to Middle Eastern power circles, and he had worked with Saif al-Islam al-Qadhafi and the leading figures of the LIFG on their renunciation of armed *jihad* and prison releases. Through these networks Sallabi and others were able to convene a large gathering of Islamist and Islamic currents, called the 'National Gathering', in Istanbul in late April.

Discussions over how to influence the fall of Tripoli began in earnest at a meeting on the sidelines of the 'National Gathering' comprising around sixteen people from Tripoli, Kufra, Misrata and the eastern region. Those present, according to Sallabi, were 'primarily' from Islamist groups; their counterparts in Libya, including *I'tilaf* in Tripoli and Fawzi Bu Katif in Benghazi, were appraised by phone. 'In fact it was coordinating the various Islamist efforts across Libya. The prospect that the country might split was on the table, and this meeting was to look at our options should that occur.'[74]

One discussion was whether to support the NTC; 'we had been working for forty years to govern Libya as an Islamic country. When we heard the names of those on the NTC we were shocked… it wasn't just their [secular] ethical practices, but we didn't know their political inclinations.'[75] Participants agreed not to split from the NTC, but were divided over how to influence events. One current advocated opening dialogue channels with Qadhafi's government, prompting an effort by Sallabi to reach out, partly through tribal Maqarha networks, to senior security officials Abdullah Sanusi and Abu Zaid Dorda in May. Another pushed to escalate a military insurgency against Qadhafi and logistical support efforts from Tunisia, which they recognised required state support and allaying Western powers' concerns about their intentions, particularly of the former LIFG. 'The states most likely to offer us military support were Qatar and Sudan. But to convince NATO that we were safe, we had first to convince the Qatari and Turkish governments and allow them to convince NATO.'[76]

Following the meeting, several participants[77] converged on Benghazi over May. One was Abd al-Razzaq al-Aradi, a businessman and Brotherhood member. Part of *I'tilaf*'s founding in Tripoli, he escaped Tripoli in April (with the support of Muhammad Aqil, of the same Maqarha networks supporting Sallabi's outreach efforts to Sanusi and

Dorda)[78] and went to work with Sallabi in Doha, and thence to the Istanbul meeting, where he kept *I'tilaf* in Tripoli informed by phone. Aradi and Alamin Bilhajj, a senior Muslim Brotherhood member, decided after that meeting[79] to approach Abd al-Jalil in Tripoli and apply for NTC membership. *I'tilaf* nominated Bilhajj and Aradi as two of their six representatives to the NTC, which they read to Abd al-Jalil via Skype from Umaish's house.[80] The nominations created the first political tussle with Nayid, who had also been expanding the NTC's geographic representation by collecting 'local council representatives' from Libya's west and south[81] and flying them to Benghazi where, on 14 May, most joined the NTC.[82] The three Tripolitanians in the group, however, including Libya's subsequent interim prime minister, Abd al-Rahim al-Kib, were rejected by Abd al-Jalil in favour of *I'tilaf*'s list, although Kib later joined after the sudden death of one of *I'tilaf*'s nominees.[83]

Another participant at the Istanbul meeting was the former LIFG commander Miftah al-Dhuwadi, who had fled Tripoli in April to Tunisia via Zintan.[84] With another former LIFG commander, Abd al-Razzaq al-Usta, Dhuwadi set up a small training base in Nalut for a fighting unit called '17 February,'[85] then attended the Istanbul meeting, where participants agreed to facilitate logistical support for the nascent group from Tunis.[86] A third former LIFG commander, Abd al-Hakim Bilhajj, also fled Tripoli in April, travelling to Tunis by boat from Zuwara. Though he missed the Istanbul meeting, on Dhuwadi's return, the group transferred between one and two hundred former LIFG fighters from Europe and Tripoli into Nalut. They then flew to Benghazi in mid-May to connect with Sallabi and tour the eastern frontlines—since Bilhajj lacked a passport and had issues flying under his own name, Sallabi supplied him an alternately-named passport from Misrata's Interior Ministry branch. Sallabi also brokered the group's first meeting with Abd al-Jalil, who cautiously acknowledged them.[87]

Sallabi and Dhuwadi flew to Sudan at some point in the third week of May with one other former LIFG commander, utilising contacts gained from their time in exile in Sudan in the nineties to meet President Umar Bashir and lobby for military support for their fighters. Sudan was already well invested in assisting the rebels take Kufra, having sent ten armoured vehicles there in April. The Sudanese military at the meeting focused on the Nafusa front, with one saying: 'As soon as we have weapons in the Nafusa Mountains, you'll be in Tripoli in three months.'[88] At the time, there was no indication that the Tunisian government would support routing the weapons through its territory, so instead the meeting identified a route over the Libyan desert, using Tebu and Tuareg traffickers. From this meeting, and another subsequently in June, the Libyans secured $120 million in small arms paid for by Qatar, which was initially sent over the desert in eighteen shipments and met by Sallabi's brother, Isma'il, in Benghazi.[89]

Around the end of May,[90] Dhuwadi assembled the key elements of the network in Tunis to develop a plan for 'the approach of forces from Nafusa to Tripoli, and then securing Tripoli.'[91] The group at that point was still primarily former LIFG, including Abd al-Hakim Bilhajj, Usta, Sa'adi, Abd al-Basit Bu Hliqa, Ism ad-Din Smaita, and Abd al-Mun'im Matus. Aradi, newly the NTC representative to Tripoli, also attended and on returning to Benghazi, introduced the group to three more people: Umar Khadrawi, an Irish-Libyan friend from Ireland, an external security official named Ahmad Muqaddim and an army officer 'Abd al-Hakim', who both assisted with intelligence. The network stabilised into a planning committee of six—Abd al-Hakim Bilhajj; 'Abd al-Hakim'; Dhuwadi; Matus; Muqaddim; and Khadrawi—which met in Tunis over the first week of June before Bilhajj contacted Aradi asking to present their work to Abd al-Jalil.[92]

The plans collide

Abd al-Jalil's authorisation of Arif Ali Nayid's Tripoli Taskforce on 22 May sparked hostility from Aradi and Alamin Bilhajj towards the NTC, partly because they felt excluded, and partly because as Tripolitanians they bristled at other Libyans—Nayid and Jibril were both Warfalla—masterminding their liberation. They suspected Nayid of aggregating too large a role[93] and cast doubt on Jibril's claims that NATO would successfully hit Qadhafi's entire command structure at the rebels' convenience. Alamin Bilhajj said, 'we didn't know how many would be fighting inside Tripoli. What if NATO failed? What if the uprising failed? *That's* what we call a plan. Talk of 'twenty-eight targets'—that's not a plan.'[94]

Nayid's team spent the remainder of May developing the Taskforce with two UK officers, one French officer and two French special forces officers. But meanwhile conflict with Aradi and Sallabi was brewing over who should take charge: Nayid felt Aradi should be his deputy, while Sallabi insisted Aradi should take charge. Both parties appealed to Abd al-Jalil, who on 8 June convened an explosive meeting intended to iron out the differences between the two parties. Though both groups endeavoured to appear civil, the insults flew thick and fast. Nayid felt 'it was foolish to appoint the Muslim Brotherhood or LIFG; we needed someone who had an understanding with Western allies and whose motivations were clear.'[95] One of Nayid's supporters on the NTC, Mahmud Shammam, accused the Muslim Brotherhood of usurping the revolution. Aradi and the Tripoli NTC representatives threatened to resign *en masse*; one flew at Nayid, saying that as a member of the Warfalla tribe and non-Tripolitanian he had no right to determine Tripoli's fate.[96] Abd al-Hakim Bilhajj, who flew from Tunis to attend, refused to bring his group under Nayid, and Jibril, in Doha, refused to acknowledge Bilhajj. 'The whole problem was that it was "Jibril or Bilhajj", like Bilhajj is something else' said Bilhajj.[97] When it became clear that the two camps could not work together, Abd al-Jalil did not transfer responsibility for the Tripoli portfolio away from Nayid and Jibril. But it was also clear that the Taskforce could not continue. The next day, the Taskforce team packed up and relocated to Abu Dhabi, with Nayid hitching a ride on a plane with the Spanish foreign minister. 'Nayid was run out of town' recalled one western diplomat.[98] To protect himself and his team, Nayid wrote to Abd al-Jalil dissolving the Taskforce, placing it under Jibril's authority as a 'Stabilisation Committee.' 'I dissolved the Taskforce upwards,' Nayid said.[99]

The Qatari turn

The bitterness between the two camps intensified as it became clear that Sallabi and Bilhajj's networks succeeded in diverting Qatar's military sponsorship away from Jibril and Nayid's purview. While the first two French/Qatari shipments in March and April had been delivered to Abd al-Fattah Yunis with Jibril and Nayid's oversight, the first air shipment to Tubruq in mid-April caused an immediate scramble over the weapons between an army general, Khalifa Hiftar, and Sallabi's younger brother Isma'il.[100] Isma'il Sallabi, with Fawzi Bu Katif, a project manager for a Libyan oil company, was marshalling untrained young fighters on the eastern frontline into a coalition of fighters administered by Bu Katif, with funding and coordination from Aradi, Alamin Bilhajj and the 'Islamist' networks that convened in Istanbul in April.[101]

Afterwards, Ali Sallabi began approaching the Qatari Chief of Staff to influence the directing of further air shipments towards Isma'il.

Objections from Yunis and the international community were met by appointing an army officer, Muhammad Hadiyya, to audit the weapons routed to Isma'il Sallabi.[102] The weapons were stored in a farm belonging to a businessman contact of the Sallabis, Ashraf bin Isma'il, who transferred them to Isma'il and to others in the 'Islamist' network in western Libya, including a few small fishing boats with light arms and grenades hidden in nets to Tripoli. Over the end of May and early June, Ali Sallabi arranged for Dhuwadi to present their plan to the chief of staff of the Qatari Armed Forces in Benghazi, then subsequently in Doha, where their plan was put before the Emir.[103]

Partly in response, Misratan commanders began to complain in May that they were excluded from the Qatari aid, prompting Nayid to press Qatar in May to step up weapons deliveries to Misrata. Qatari funds had already allowed a Libyan Misratan network to procure three large vessels—a Croatian fishing boat, the *Sarha*, which held three shipping containers, a tug boat, the *Irada*, and a larger vessel, the *Sirt Star*, to transit humanitarian aid, arms sourced from Libyan weapons depots and fighters into Misrata. The Misrata Military Council sent Nayid one of their members, Muhammad bin Ra's Ali, to work in an operations room in Dubai's Kempinski Hotel. This enabled in May a further three to five[104] Qatari flights into Benghazi which were shipped across to Misrata aboard the *Sarha*, *Irada* and *Sirt Star*.[105] The Misratans also opened a small private channel with Dubai-based merchants and a Spain-registered company.[106]

By this point, the Qataris were concerned about the clear conflict between Nayid and Sallabi, and Yunis's diminishing authority. 'Their one big question,' a western diplomat recalled, 'was "Who is in charge?"'[107] The Qatari chief of staff went to Baida to press Abd al-Jalil on the issue; 'We needed a clear Libyan commander inside the plan, because we wanted to put the plan [presented by Sallabi] to NATO, which meant we needed a Libyan authority to follow.'[108] The Qatari account of that meeting was that Abd al-Jalil did not want Nayid to take sole responsibility for Tripoli. A Libyan security source close to Abd al-Jalil said, 'Abd al-Jalil was very worried about Mahmud Jibril's exerting influence over the Tripoli portfolio, and his contacts with military and security officials in Tripoli. He feared a coup of sorts.'[109]

Whatever the truth of these views, Abd al-Jalil created a separate institution over May to provide NTC authorisation for weapons transfers such as Qatar's—powers which were previously exercised personally by Abd al-Jalil, Yunis, Jibril, or Nayid. On 5 May he created a Ministry of Defence under Jalal Dghaili; both Abd al-Jalil[110] and Qatar[111] preferred working through this office, which gave the official Libyan sanction Qatar needed to formally route support to frontline fighters while coordinating with NATO and the international community. Aradi said that, 'the main supplier of weapons was Qatar, but as soon as it reached Libya they came under Ministry of Defence control. We never dealt directly with Qatar, just the minister.'[112]

Aside from the tensions between Abd al-Jalil, Yunis and Jibril, another element to Qatar's turn was their assessment of fighters' capabilities. Being such a small state, this was framed entirely by the chief of staff and the head of the Special Forces, which enabled them to act very quickly and decisively, with few internal bureaucratic obstacles to policymaking. Both were focused on delivering support to those they felt maximally capable, who for them were not the remnants of the armed forces, but civilian fighters in the field.[113] The latter felt, particularly, that groups such as the LIFG were more motivated and capable; their fighting background contrasted with the academic backgrounds of both Nayid and Jibril. Moreover, the Qataris were uncomfortable with both Jibril and Yunis's support for a ceasefire and mediated transition; Jibril, particularly, seemed to them resistant to expanding a military front in the west.

Qatari support was not, however, solely routed through Islamist networks, but also the aforementioned Misratan networks. Qatar directly flew in 20,000 tons of weapons over eighteen separate flights during the 2011 uprising, around thirteen of which were routed to frontline fighters.[114] Of these, seven were flown directly to Misrata airport beginning 12 June; the remaining six appear to have been delivered to bin Isma'il, and thence to Abd al-Hakim Bilhajj or Isma'il Sallabi.[115] The Misratan network, centred around Ramadan Zarmuh, Fathi Bashagha, Salim Jawha, Salah Badi and Salah al-Din,[116] was independent of Sallabi, and many of these individuals were flown to Doha to cement their own relationships with the Qataris.[117] Through business and family contacts, such as Ibrahim Dbaiba, Sallabi and Aradi later flew to Misrata to extend their own connections with the operations room there, but at least one member of that room insisted that they never controlled the network or distribution.[118]

Yet the spectacle of closeness between Bilhajj, Sallabi, Dghaili and Qatar, and its secrecy,[119] overshadowed the rest of Qatar's substantial military and nonmilitary aid across Libyan society. On returning to Benghazi from Baida, the Qatari delegation met Bilhajj for the first time.[120] Together, they flew to Tunis, where, around the time that Nayid's team was relocating to Abu Dhabi—they pulled together some commanders from the Jebel Nafusa and set out the basics of a plan in which the Nafusa Mountains fighters would push forward to the coast, to Zawiya and Sabratha, using coordination with the NATO air campaign that Qatar would provide. The Qataris presented the plan and their intentions to NATO liaisons, and also lobbied the Tunisian minister of defence and chief of staff to allow the transfer of heavy weapons to the Nafusa front through its territory. The Tunisian agreement on this obviated Sudan's earlier plans to transfer the aid up through Tebu and Tuareg networks.

Arming the Nafusa front

Both networks, working independently of each other, turned their intention in June and July to arming allied proxies in the Nafusa Mountains.

Qatar's growing support of the Sallabi network pushed Jibril and Nayid to seek more robust support from France, the UAE, and the US. This process began after Jibril's meeting with Sarkozy in May, whereupon he appointed a planning committee consisting of Mliqta, Ahmad al-Majbari and a scientist named Uthman Abd al-Jalil to be based in Djerba[121] and coordinate with France.[122] That same month, the French attempted several airdrops into Nafusa, but the Libyans perceived the operation as a failure; several drops exploded or were damaged.[123] A small Qatari weapons shipment, along with UAE-sourced non-lethal aid, was also smuggled into Zintan overland, via Tunis, in April in order to test the feasibility of that route.[124] With US and Emirati support, a small airstrip was therefore constructed on a straight piece of road at Haidat, a tiny village near the town of Rujban midway between Zintan and Nalut, chosen partly for that fact, so as to not provoke the then-tense relations between those two towns. The airstrip was only five metres wide, large enough to accommodate a small BA146 plane.[125]

On 15 June, after approximately five meetings with the French and NATO Chiefs of Staff,[126] Jibril and his planning committee again lobbied the French for weapons support in Paris, at a meeting attended by the French defence minister, intelligence chief and chief of staff, and a small British delegation. Having absorbed Nayid's Taskforce, Jibril was still pushing for a plan centred around an internal uprising in Tripoli supplemented by NATO strikes on command facilities using data such as that provided by Mliqta. Presenting Mliqta's data to Sarkozy, Jibril recalled that 'we wanted them to verify that those 27 operations rooms Mliqta identified were still in place. They came back to us with the finding that everything we had supplied them was accurate.'[127] According to Jibril, Sarkozy asked if the uprising could happen on 14 July, the anniversary of the French revolution. By now, however, Jibril and his planning committee were also incorporating the idea of arming groups from Nafusa Mountains,[128] and asked Sarkozy for arms shipments that could be routed to Tripoli and to Zintan in the Nafusa Mountains. 'I pulled a piece of paper from my pocket and said "This is what we need." He said "OK, our friends in Qatar will supply the arms at the right time."'[129]

Yet Jibril was caught unawares by the Qataris' new supply chain. Jibril had intended that the shipment of weapons designated for his group would be met at Benghazi's Banina airport by Majbari and Colonel Hadiyya, the army officer appointed to audit Qatari weapons supplies. But when the shipments arrived at the end of June it was Defence Minister Dghaili who received and routed them to bin Isma'il's stores. They were then collected by Abd al-Hakim Bilhajj during his time in Benghazi in early June. A civilian Airbus 320/310 from Libyan Airlines, Libya's national carrier, was borrowed after much wrangling, and the supplies flown in five to six flights from Benghazi to the Rujban airstrip, escorted and protected by NATO aircraft enforcing the no-fly zone.[130] Those weapons too heavy to be transported by air, including some of the priciest, were sent in three container shipments to Djerba in Tunisia, coordinated through the Tunisian chief of staff, Qatari officers and Dghaili, and driven overland to the Nafusa Mountains.[131] Another stormy meeting followed in which Abd al-Jalil tried to broker an agreement between Jibril's group, Sallabi, Dghaili, and bin Isma'il. The outspoken Mahmud Shammam exploded with rage towards bin Isma'il, furious that the NTC had given over weapons to those he called extremists.

Jibril and Nayid therefore looked increasingly to the UAE as a supplier. While the Qataris were able to reach an early understanding with the French on issues of end-user certification, the UAE was constrained by the US, which preferred that the Emiratis ship weapons of non-US origin.[132] But US objections were lifted by June, partly because of concerns over the Qatari supply chain. It also came coterminous with the Emiratis' diplomatic recognition of the NTC, which allowed Jibril, Nayid and his allies to use the embassy's legitimate authority as a representative of the Libyan state to request aid. The first Emirati shipment was flown by plane into the Nafusa Mountains on 9 June, with ten tonnes of weapons in around fifteen containers.[133] The UAE embassy in Tunis also opened a diplomatic track with the Tunisian government, enabling further shipments to be delivered overland.

A close relationship developed between Jibril, Zintani commanders and the UAE, whose supplies were exclusively delivered to Zintan's Usama Juwaili, along with around eight American-made sniper rifles,[134] and set up an operations room in Zintan with two Emirati officers. Timely as the UAE supplies were, Zintan by that point was already becoming strengthened with the capture of several key ammunition depots, and the use of tactics such as aiming captured guided missiles (whose targeting computers were decommissioned) at Qadhafi's military, which had important psychological effects. Juwaili therefore distributed some of the deliveries to Zintani allies in Zawiya.[135]

The group also turned to Sudan; a meeting with the Sudanese intelligence chief in Turkey paved the way for the two Misratans, bin Ra's Ali and Fawzi Abd al-Al, with Nayid and then Jibril, to visit Sudan for several meetings over late July.[136] There was some delay securing the agreement, since the Sudanese required Qatari funds to cover the cost of the supplies; to secure those funds, one Libyan participant said, 'we threatened to make a big fuss and distribute documentary photographs about the previous Qatari arms being smuggled to the mountains by Bilhajj.'[137] But once agreement was made, twelve[138] shipments were flown into Benghazi and Misrata airport on Sudanese Ilyushin aircraft in the first week of August.[139]

Jibril and Nayid also attempted to train a small group of Tripolitanian so-called 'special forces' as a 'Tripoli Guard' to secure and maintain key facilities. This was to have been led by Bu Hajar, who had fled Tripoli for Djerba, Tunisia in late April. In May, he smuggled 22 youths to Djerba, intending with Nayid to have them trained in Turkey and Qatar. When Qatar and Bilhajj opposed the plan, Bu Hajar instead, in June, travelled to Nafusa with Nizar Kawan and Salah al-Shirri to try and set up a fighting group there, which would eventually be called the 'Red Companies' (*Sarayat al-Hamra*), which by early August numbered around 430.[140] Funding came through for the group from Tripoli sources in late June. Sixteen of the original twenty-two youth, meanwhile, were sent to Benghazi for training by two French special forces agents.

Meanwhile, the Qatari chief of staff also travelled to the Nafusa Mountains around mid-June, arriving in Zintan by way of the Rujban airstrip by plane with Shammam of the NTC Executive Committee[141] a couple of weeks after the Emiratis' arrival. Qatar entered the west with little knowledge of the players on the ground, and the chief of staff's initial trip focused on trying to understand the main commanders, on ensuring that there were no issues between the Amazigh and Zintan that could spill into intra-rebel conflict. Limited offers of training were made to Juwaili,[142] and some Qatari officers remained behind in Zintan, at a school separate to the Emiratis' room,[143] and at Nalut to assess the rebels' needs and coordinate aid imported from Tatuine, where the Qataris had set up a further operations room and logistics hub.[144]

The Qatari operations rooms network not only helped coordinate the emerging mountain communities with each other, but also supported the rotating deployment of Qatari special forces into Nafusa to fight alongside and coordinate rebel advances with the NATO air campaign. Qatari weapons support in Nafusa, however, remained routed through Dghaili and Bilhajj. Bilhajj's network had developed friendly relations with Nalut, where their fighting groups were based, through an Amazigh LIFG member named Murad Zikri. But Bilhajj had been less successful in developing good working relations with Zintan. While some of Bilhajj's supplies went to Nalut and other friendly military councils, the majority went to two other Tripolitanian fighting groups, also receiving Qatari training.[145] One was the aforementioned '17 February Battalion' run by former LIFG commanders Miftah al-Dhuwadi and Abd al-Razzaq al-Usta in Nalut and Rujban, which numbered less than 200 fighters by mid-June. It contained volunteer youth and former LIFG fighters from Europe, Tripoli and a significant number of eastern Libyans, for whom Bilhajj arranged transit on boats and planes arriving from Benghazi.[146]

The second was the Tripoli Revolutionaries' Battalions (*Kata'ib Thuwwar Trablus*). Its head was Mahdi al-Harati, an Irish-Libyan activist who had been on the *Mavi Marmara* aid flotilla that defied Israel's blockade of Gaza in 2010.[147] Harati entered Benghazi in March, smuggled over the Sudanese border to Kufra, and with 25–30 close friends, most also Irish-Libyan, attempted to join the fighting in the east. The group was turned away by the NTC, but over April and May made contact with Bu Katif and began receiving Qatari training. In May, the group relocated to Nalut, and with Murad Zikri Harati negotiated the use of a school and funding from the same private Libyan and Gulf donor networks supporting Zikri, Usta, Bilhajj and others.[148] But unlike Bilhajj or even Bu Hajar, Harati lived daily with his group. Libyan expatriate volunteers coming to the Nafusa Mountains were attracted by Harati's genuine leadership skills, his access to higher-grade communications equipment and weaponry, and the 'elite' reputation granted by three weeks of physical and communications training from Qatari officers.[149] The group thus swelled to around 500 people by 1 August and reached around 1200 by Tripoli's fall.[150]

On 4–5 July, Jibril made a final attempt to bring the competing players together in a meeting in Abu Dhabi. Jibril hoped to bring Dghaili, Aradi, Nayid and Bu Hajar alongside his team into a committee of eight people. Bilhajj did not attend, being unable to travel to the UAE on his adopted passport; it is unclear if Jibril wished him to. Both Aradi and Nayid arrived at the meeting with their respective 'plans', though Nayid's version, a weighty Powerpoint presentation, was immediately leaked to a British broadsheet, rendering it worthless. Jibril divided the portfolio into 'Liberating and Securing' and 'Stabilisation' briefs. Nayid's team, rebranded the 'Stabilisation Committee,' was given the brief of securing essential supplies and services into the capital.

Aradi, Dghaili and Bu Hajar were brought into the 'Liberating and Securing' component, which continued with the plan drawn up by Jibril's team of identifying a list of targets in Tripoli, and coordinating with NATO to strike them at a point when the Tripoli underground were ready to rise up, and the Nafusa Mountains groups ready to descend towards the capital. The group would whittle down the list of targets, originally 120, to eighty-two, then sixty, then finally, in the days preceding the uprising, twenty-eight, and worked with NATO to target as many as possible during the Tripoli uprising. It expanded Jibril's team somewhat to include Bu Hajar from *I'tilaf* who was brought into the group at the Abu Dhabi meeting. But it did nothing to reconcile the larger tussle between Jibril and the Bilhajj network. The plan set out at Abu Dhabi pointedly had no role for Bilhajj, a fact lost on neither him nor Aradi, who returned from the meeting fuming at this perceived snub.[151] When Bu Hajar and Mliqta returned to Djerba in July to set up an 'operations room' with a third member of the group, Abd al-Majid Uthman, Dghaili, Bilhajj and the Qatari Chief of Staff visited them. Another spat erupted, Mliqta slammed his laptop closed, and insults flew over who was ultimately responsibile for the fall of Tripoli. The two groups continued to attempt to interact and patch things up over August, but the damage was done, and conflict between the 'Islamist' and 'secular' networks would plague the fall of Tripoli and beyond.

4

THE FALL OF TRIPOLI

PART 2

Peter Cole with *Umar Khan*

By July 2011, two rival 'plans' around the liberation and governance of Tripoli had emerged. One, centred around Mahmud Jibril of the National Transitional Council (NTC) and set out in Abu Dhabi on 4–5 July, envisaged a 'Liberating and Securing Committee' led by Hisham Bu Hajar, followed by a 'Stabilisation Committee' headed by Arif Ali Nayid. The second, centred around Qatari officials, Ali Sallabi, Abd al-Razzaq al-Aradi and increasingly Abd al-Hakim Bilhajj, involved arming and training fighters in Misrata and the Nafusa Mountains. Both relied heavily on the NATO air campaign and state allies within it.

This chapter discusses how parts of both plans succeeded, but much of both failed when confronted by a more chaotic reality. The Tripoli underground themselves armed and organised faster than anyone expected, through military networks and via Misrata, and pushed for an uprising before anyone was ready. Fighters from Misrata and the Nafusa Mountains entered the capital, which they had not planned to do; Bilhajj and Bu Hajar found their men outnumbered by the many Tripoli neighbourhood groups and thousands of Misratan and mountain fighters. The Stabilisation Committee found itself hampered by government ministries and at odds with Tripoli's 17 February Coalition (*I'tilaf Sab'at Ashr Fibrayir*, henceforth *I'tilaf*) and the Local Council they created. As Mu'ammar al-Qadhafi's rule receded, the problems of governing superseded the problems of fighting. Among the foremost political problems was dealing with the many armed groups that had emerged.

Arming the Tripoli underground

Despite the dual plans emerging in Benghazi, the Tripoli underground ultimately set the pace and manner of Tripoli's fall. However, influenced by the politicking around the plans, the *I'tilaf* network, supporting the efforts of Bu Hajar and Aradi, looked increasingly to Misrata and the Tripolitanian armed groups in the Nafusa Mountains. In contrast, the capital's network of security sector defectors and youth groups tried to foment an armed uprising from inside Tripoli in coordination with Jibril's 'Liberating and Securing' committee.

Most Tripoli cells sourced their weapons independently from Qadhafi's military, their sympathisers within playing an important role in procuring them. Mustafa Nuh and Muhammad Shaikh's Military Council started meeting discreetly in farmhouses and villas as their security service networks grew larger, and requisitioned or purchased small amounts of weapons directly from the military bases in Gharyan, Tarhuna and Bani Walid that were receiving large consignments of weaponry from Sirt.[1] Two officers, Farid Zintani, an aviation munitions officer, and Ali bin Zahra,[2] played particularly prominent roles in these efforts. Others, like Hussain al-Aib, the man passing out information from Abdullah al-Sanusi's meetings to the Executive Committee, wrote requisition letters for his family to sign out weapons from military stockpiles in Gharyan.[3] Hisham al-Litki, the former army officer in Slim Street, acquired €200,000 from private Libyan and Qatari sources, which he used to buy weapons from Bani Walid, smuggling them piecemeal back to Tripoli in a family car.[4] Similarly, others with family military connections drove to these depots at night, returning with two or three guns apiece hidden under the car bonnet, plastic bags, childrens' car seats and women's clothing. In this manner one Tarhuna resident smuggled up to a thousand guns, twenty per trip, to an NFSL contact, Nasir Zumid, since his Tarhuna registration plates and the green flags he displayed prevented his being searched at check-points.[5] In general these individuals circulated weapons to trusted families, and so cells developed that tended to hoard. Those who lacked military contacts ran huge risks; one group from Janzur, unable to gain weapons through established routes, tried to buy from what turned out to be a man working for the security brigades.[6]

Youth groups also acquired weapons by volunteering to fight for Qadhafi. In June and July Saif al-Islam announced the call-up of the People's Resistance Forces (PRF, *Quwwat al-Muqawama al-Sha'biyya*)— a volunteer reserve based on Qadhafi's concept of the 'armed people' (*al-sha'b al-musallah*) in which weapons were given to civilians who registered their ID. Tents sprang up across Tripoli; conferences and schools became registration centres and armouries. Eyewitnesses in military barracks recalled the 'tribalisation' of the PRF; weapons were allocated to groups of ten volunteers from the same tribe, each of whom vouched for their groups' tribe and political views. Hangars, armoured vehicles, guns and bullets were allocated to tribal groups such as the Maqarha and Warfalla.[7]

The PRF bolstered the opposition's confidence. Its untrained volunteers, unfamiliar with Tripoli's streets and social dynamics, manned Tripoli's checkpoints, where the opposition's interactions with them sometimes veered towards farce: I'tilaf's Hisham Krikshi, then working with his colleague Adnan Ghirwi on civic contingency preparations, recalled being stopped while transporting beds for a covert field hospital. He gave them the licence of a friend who happened to be registered as deaf; 'the men were distracted to arguing over whether a deaf guy could drive a car!'[8] The opposition relaxed. Precautions around meetings, such as faking documents or hiding data on flash drives, were forgotten. They began using Skype without apparent repercussions. 'We thought if they didn't come for you in twenty-four hours, they probably didn't know about you,' said Sadat al-Badri.[9] Muhammad Shaikh theorised that the scale of government monitoring was so overwhelming that anyone on a wanted list was only at serious risk for forty-eight hours, before new additions and priorities were added.[10]

The PRF also became excellent targets for *gelatina* (fishing explosive) attacks. Youth groups from Suq al-Jum'a, Siyahiyya and Tajura, aided by narrow alleyways and high concentrations of supporters attacked the tents, technicals and checkpoints. These attacks saw the emergence of Salafist fighters under leaders such as Abd al-Ra'uf Kara and Abd al-Latif Qudur in Suq al-Jum'a, which increased the pace of attacks on the rapid reaction force of the security brigades, headed by Muhammad Simarji, which policed the neighbourhood. By July, Sirmaji's Toyota vehicles withdrew—most were redeployed to Zlitan to shore up the frontline against Misratan forces[11]—their tents vanished from their streets, and they ceased registering new weapons to civilian volunteers. The armed groups they left behind in Suq al-Jum'a and Tajura grew aggressively confident, mounting a coordinated attack on the Four Points hotel, and a major crossroads checkpoint in central Suq al-Jum'a.

The Military Council also grew larger, as cells learned of each other, and more ambitious, meeting regularly to plan armed operations. The first major meeting of leaders and cells covering Tripoli occurred at the villa of an officer named Kamal Busir. After this, the network discussed specific operations; an early initiative, later abandoned, was the assassination of a prominent propagandist, Yusuf Shakir, who influenced young Libyans to fight for Qadhafi. A network of leading officers arose: Ali bin Zahra, Muhammad Shaikh, Farid al-Zintani, Abd al-Razzaq Ghaniyya, Yunis al-Sahli, Fituri al-Ghuraibi, Abd al-Ra'uf al-Sabiq and others. By the second meeting, planning officers—Kamal Busir, Fituri al-Ghuraibi, Abd al-Ra'uf Sabiq and Farid al-Zintani—were designated, and they began planning an audacious attempt to assassinate, on 23 July, security chiefs Sanusi and Mansur Daw' (heads of internal security and the People's Guard respectively), Prime Minister Umar al-Baghdadi, Saif al-Islam al-Qadhafi and other officials at their meeting in the upscale neighbourhood of Hayy al-Andalus.[12]

However the operation failed. The attacker, a young Salafi, firing an RPG at the hotel believed to contain the meeting, missed, and hit its roof. This provoked a dramatic crackdown by the security services. The chance detention at the Tunisian border of a Military Council member, Ali Abd al-Ra'uf, on suspicion of having a fake passport, provoked the unravelling of the council as the security services arrested anyone connected to him. Council members Abd al-Razzaq Ghaniya, Kamal Busir, Fituri al-Ghuraibi, Abd al-Ra'uf Sadiq, and Muhammad Ghaddur 'disappeared in one day, at the same moment.'[13] Nuh was arrested on 26 July. 'Nuh knew so many of our names and addresses that we were all endangered' said *I'tilaf*'s Muhammad Umaish.[14] 'We all knew we had to disappear' said Shaikh.[15] Umaish fled to Djerba; Shaikh and Sahli to a farm on the outskirts of Suq al-Jum'a. The arrests and scattering ceased after a few days, but disrupted opposition military coordination and communication at a crucial time; 'our structure was like grapes, connected only by one person. When everyone disappeared, the cells lost contact.'[16]

Tripoli's loss of a strongly-networked military council had significant consequences for how Tripoli fell, and the ensuing struggle for power. With the onset of Ramadan on 1 August, the armed cells of Suq al-Jum'a and Tajura agitated ever more aggressively for a coordinated uprising. UN sanctions were biting, with five-day-long fuel queues making life so intolerable that bicycles—a mythological rarity on Libyan streets—started to be used. Less quaintly, the increasingly agitated security forces were behaving egregiously, jumping fuel queues, barging into houses, stealing cars, and shooting those who objected. On 30 July, the armed group in Suq al-Jum'a led by Qudur threw down the gauntlet at an I'tilaf meeting, threatening to launch their own uprising before the start of Ramadan. They did so again on Friday 8 August.[17] Though many groups were still too ill-equipped by 8 August to launch an uprising,[18]—most shared guns between fighters and I'tilaf calculated that the network possessed three days of ammunition at best—several large shipments of weaponry from Misrata that week shifted the balance further in favour of groups like Qudur's in Suq al-Jum'a and Tajura.

The role of Misrata

Misrata's weapons support came late, though the arms trafficking network that supplied it had been developing for months. It had grown from a small group of Misratans who, in mid-March, sourced weapons from defected Libyan army units in Dirna, Tubruq and Benghazi, with letters signed off by Abd al-Fattah Yunis and Mustafa Abd al-Jalil of the NTC. The network sourced a Croatian fishing boat, the *Sarha*, which held three shipping containers per trip, soon supplemented by a tug boat, the *Irada*, and a larger vessel, the *Sirt Star*, and transited arms and fighters into Misrata.[19] A flotilla of small craft operated by Misratan battalion commanders also plied the waves, transiting black market weapons.[20]

Once Misrata's airport was secured on 15 May, Qatari C-17s and, later, Sudanese Ilyushin aircraft began flying weaponry into Misrata. The first Qatari shipment arrived on 12 June, with Ramadan Zarmuh among the logistical coordinators. Some of these shipments were explicitly designated for Tripoli, and were transferred to the Mirsa Battalion holding Misrata's port. Though according to that battalion and others in the network,[21] the amounts shipped by air were dwarfed by those Misratans had already stockpiled. The head of the Mirsa Battalion said; 'The 12 June shipment [for Tripoli] was 200 guns and 3,000 bullets—less than fifty bullets per gun! We added 50,000 bullets, seven RPG launchers, 170 RPGs and 250 grenades.'[22]

The Misratan deliveries were late because of the sheer difficulty they had in entering ports near Tripoli undetected. The first shipment made in early July was interdicted by the security services near Janzur—an event which seems to have contributed to Nuh's capture.[23] The next shipment of 500 guns, 160,000 bullets and 50 RPGs aboard a ship named the *Susa* left in mid-July, but the security services likewise attempted to interdict it by raiding the house of one of its Misratan crew. The *Susa* then rerouted to Girgis, southern Tunisia, where it sat two weeks in the harbour, and finally made its way to Qarabulli, a port just east of Tripoli, on 9 August. There, the weapons were sent to shore by dinghies, unloaded into three waiting vehicles by a police contact, and taken to Qudur's farm. On 14 and 19 August, two further shipments made their way to Qudur: a fishing trawler, the *Intisar*, via Tajura and a tugboat, the *Ganat*, via Tripoli Harbour. Each carried between them a further 900 guns, along with several dozen RPGs.[24]

Suq al-Jum'a and Tajura were hungry for action before Misrata's weapons even arrived, but their arrival bolstered their assertiveness towards those in *I'tilaf* who still felt unready for an uprising. On 14 August, at a coordination meeting in Siyahiyya, Qudur's cell again insisted on setting a date for an armed uprising on 17 August.

Preparing the 20 August uprising

After the Abu Dhabi conference, Jibril sent his 'Liberating and Securing' team—Abd al-Majid Mliqta, Ahmad al-Majbari and a scientist named Uthman Abd al-Jalil, later joined by Hisham Bu Hajar and three others[25]—to create an 'operations centre' in Djerba. There, for a few weeks, they collected and managed information on a list of fixed regime targets. But the room had little communication with NATO's air campaign; target data was passed to Jibril, thence to the Qataris and French, and the room would not be able to double-check whether targets were hit. Bu Hajar also built up his armed group, the Hamra Companies, in the Nafusa Mountains, and sent sixteen fighters to Majbari in Benghazi, where they were trained by two French special forces on securing certain infrastructure. Majbari trained a total of fifty-five people with the French special forces.[26]

The 'Liberating and Securing' team retained contact with security sector defectors including Shaikh, Ra'is, and Mabruk Imghirwi, to whom Majbari managed to deliver at least one shipment of weaponry via Qarabulli.[27] It reached out to community leaders of tribes supporting Qadhafi around the capital, hoping to gain support for a minimally violent entry into Tripoli. In July, a major development occurred with the defection of the head of the Imhammad Imgharyif Brigade in Bab al-Aziziyya, al-Barrani Ishkal, who reached out to Mustafa Abd al-Jalil and Jibril of the NTC via a Dubai-based businessman. Ishkal signalled that he would not oppose the toppling of Qadhafi when the time came.[28]

Within Tripoli, I'tilaf focused on organising the popular uprising,[29] establishing a coordinating committee in Siyahiyya, and media room in the nearby district of Qurji, to try and coordinate various neighbourhoods in a simultaneous uprising. Though tracking every group was impossible, eleven or twelve liaisons based at Siyahiyya each monitored four to five groups. They divided the city into thirty-one areas, each with small clusters of armed units, and tried to provide each with field hospitals and satellite phone communications, though the uprising happened too quickly for those supplies, brought from Tunisia, to be distributed, and most groups in fact used regular Libyan phone networks.[30] The committee encouraged a tactic they called 'lock and defend,' encouraging each neighbourhood to secure its street and avoid built-up downtown areas where loyalists could more easily defend themselves.[31]

But I'tilaf became substantially disillusioned with Jibril's committee in Djerba. After visiting Djerba in July, one member, Adil Bu Ghrain, felt that: 'There was nothing. I asked if they had military plans for liberating Tripoli beyond NATO strikes—they said no.'[32] After Nuh's arrest, I'tilaf's new leader was Imhammad Ghula—a mannered, articulate man who had been organising field hospitals in Suq al-Jum'a. Ghula disliked Jibril's group. 'They sent us this plan for attacking Qadhafi's command centres. They said they'd send people to carry out the attacks but they never came—they always said they were being trained in Benghazi, Tunisia, then somewhere else.'[33] When I'tilaf passed information to the Djerba room, the delay the latter had with NATO contrasted poorly with the Misratan operations room, which I'tilaf trusted more, and where there were British, French and Qatari officers in the room.[34] 'We were never really sure that they had direct contact... with Misrata we felt that [advisers] were sitting right there in the room, as we would straight away get information back, whereas with Djerba there was always a delay.'[35]

In early August, Jibril's team relocated to Zintan, setting up oppo- site the French and Emirati operations room. Coordination on target- ing was still an issue; despite being next door to NATO's room, Jibril's team still needed to communicate circuitously, first to Jibril, who then passed targeting information to Qatar, then to the French, then to NATO.[36] But gradually the two rooms developed trust and the team could verify whether the targets they were providing were being struck. The French and Emiratis gave valuable input on capabilities, asking the team to limit the list of potential targets to strike in Tripoli to twenty- eight, that being enough for a maximum sortie of seven planes to han- dle.[37] Jibril's team maintained regular liaisons with Bilhajj, Harati and Nafusa mountains fighters, though again the details of their plan they released outside the team was kept to a minimum.

But, simultaneously, Nafusa Mountains fighters advanced to effec- tively surround the capital by 17 August. This tipped momentum away from Jibril's planning committee, being instead coordinated on 27 July in Tatuine by the Qatari chief of staff, NATO liaisons, and the major commanders of the Nafusa Mountains, with Bilhajj and Mahdi al- Harati's network attending.[38] A significant deployment—perhaps around seventy[39]—of Qatari special forces fought alongside the Libyan rebels and relayed battle assessments to NATO so as to encourage the striking of targets at certain times. An adviser said; 'When NATO struck, [Qatari advisers] would send rebels to take over the target; if the rebels didn't, then the next day the regime would reinforce it, and NATO wouldn't be able to hit it a second time.' Advisers respected NATO's civilian protection mandate but adapted to it: 'NATO would never break its mandate, but they would follow moving targets if [given by advisers]. They were capable of seeing everything, but [advis- ers] would prioritise targeting for them.'[40] The late addition of two US Predator drones on 16 August,[41] significantly, cleared the coastal high- way between Zintan and Zawiya.

The astonishingly fast advance took many by surprise. When fighters took Gharyan and Zawiya on 16 and 17 August, morale peaked among the Tripoli opposition, who moved supplies to operations rooms openly and talked on domestic phone networks—a far cry from the fear that pervaded their early days. *I'tilaf's* plan itself was photocopied and distributed across the town.[42] To this extent, Qadhafi's rule had perhaps already collapsed. Some Tripoli opposition sources maintain that Qadhafi, who likely knew of the planned uprising, fled that day.[43]

The Tripoli Military Council

The seemingly imminent uprising refocused attention on 'the day after'. But the temporary scattering of the Tripoli opposition in July had disrupted internal efforts to set up a military council similar to those emerging across western Libya. Within *I'tilaf*, Nuh, now arrested, and Muhammad Umaish, who had fled to Djerba, had led efforts to cohere a council. The security service networks around bin Zahra, Shaikh, Zintani, Busir and so forth had continued to meet, but communication with each other and with the newly empowered armed groups in Suq al-Jum'a and Tajura had weakened. Contact with *I'tilaf* was at a low, routed through only one person, Mustafa Tir, and a split had occurred with Ghula, who preferred to coordinate *I'tilaf* with Misrata and Tripolitanian revolutionary battalions in the Nafusa Mountains, and delegated coordination with the security officers to Badri and Tir.[44]

The concept of a military council of defected officers was also heavily resisted by 'Islamists' within *I'tilaf* and by Tripoli's NTC representatives, who wished to see the Tripoli battalions groups in the Nafusa Mountains empowered. Yet these were profoundly disorganised. The main leaders—Harati of the Tripoli Revolutionaries' Battalions, Abd al-Hakim Bilhajj and Hisham Bu Hajar, spoke to and saw each other infrequently throughout the summer. Their main point of contact came through the Qatari operations rooms, and even then, Bilhajj often sent liaisons, Mahdi liaised through Nalut, and Bu Hajar through Zintan. The challenge was uniting them such that when Tripoli fell, they could provide some measure of security.[45]

On 17 August, the NTC's Tripoli representatives Alamin Bilhajj, Sidiq al-Kabir and Abd al-Rahim al-Kib convened the five fractious Tripoli battalions in Rijban to attempt to unite them under Hisham Bu Hajar's leadership—Bu Hajar having organised the 'official' military wing of *I'tilaf*, and perhaps too because he possessed good relations with Jibril's 'Liberating and Securing'Committee. Those present agreed he should head all five battalions under one 'Tripoli Brigade' (*Liwa' Trablus*).[46]

Abd al-Hakim Bilhajj, however, refused to accept Bu Hajar's appointment, proposing instead a former LIFG comrade, Abd al-Razzaq al-Usta. The Tripoli NTC representative Alamin Bilhajj—who had backed Bu Hajar—met Abd al-Hakim Bilhajj on the 18 August at 3am at his camp in Rujban to hammer out a compromise. A compromise was reached. Bu Hajar was to remain leader of the 'Tripoli Brigade' with general responsibility for 'liberating' Tripoli, while Bilhajj would head a Tripoli Military Council to 'secure' Tripoli after Qadhafi's fall. The NTC representatives in Rujban telephoned their allies in *I'tilaf*, Ghula and Salah Tunali, who assented. The Tripoli representatives formalised the request to the NTC over 18 August, but with time against them, little else was decided or agreed.[47]

Meanwhile the opposition cells in Tripoli were still pushing for an uprising on 17 August.[48] On 16 August, according to Jibril, Qatar's chief of staff called him to communicate to the Tripoli cells that NATO needed more time[49] because Qadhafi's military was drawing back to Tripoli.[50] Jibril suspected Qatar of stalling 'to buy time' for their military plan;[51] Qatari officials did not confirm Jibril's account of the call but said that 'our plan was that the Nafusa fighters would close the [western] coastal road, while Misrata would close the other so Qadhafi wouldn't escape. Then the Tripoli battalions would go inside.'[52] Bu Hajar and Mliqta passed the message on to Tripoli, in the process claiming that NATO would strike the twenty-eight targets they had identified. When only seven strikes occurred over 18–19 August, *I'tilaf* and the armed cells lost patience, insisting instead on moving on 20 August, before anyone—Jibril, Qatar, or NATO—was ready. The remainder of the strikes hit only on the twentieth, destroying twenty-four of the twenty-eight targets.[53]

Just before dusk on 20 August, Abd al-Jalil gave a televised speech, saying 'the noose is tightening.'[54] Though not, as subsequently misreported, a 'codeword', it was taken by Tripolitanians as a signal. After the dusk call to prayer had sounded, Tripoli's youth poured into the streets, and mosques across town repeatedly broadcast, hypnotically, the musical, undulating glorification of God, the *takbir*, which some activists had prerecorded. One was Krikshi, who had been doing civic contingency preparations for *I'tilaf*, who in his account did so at his daughter's request, while exhausted one evening: 'I did it right there on the sofa in my work clothes, staring at the ceiling.'[55] Krikshi's voice joined others echoing in the city: 'God is greatest; God is greatest; there is no God but God.' Gunfire erupted across the capital.

The coming of the revolutionaries

None were prepared for the speed with which the uprising advanced throughout the capital. Those watching from operations rooms and in Djerba, Doha, Dubai and Benghazi spoke of the strange disconnect between the reports coming from Tripoli and what they saw on their TV screens. A Libyan in NATO's operations centre in Misrata said that it seemed like their interlocutors weren't even in Tripoli.

Hundreds of small simultaneous battles had erupted. Generally, most streets faced one to two cars carrying at most five men apiece; major checkpoints faced four to five cars. Qadhafi's remaining security brigades almost instantly lost morale; those listening in at the NATO operations rooms in Misrata and Zintan heard an enemy overwhelmed with too many requirements from too many different sides, isolated from ammunition and each other. Those that could fled to one of Tripoli's many bases, bunkers or public buildings.

Excepting the well stocked armed groups in Suq al-Jum'a and Tajura, most of the youth fighters had fewer than forty-eight hours' ammunition, and were sharing guns. By the morning of 21 August, most youth in the Suq al-Jum'a, Tajura, Hayy al-Andalus, Fashlum, and southern Hadba had risen up, but were primarily securing their own streets. Southern half and central downtown Tripoli still flew green flags. The security brigades had retreated to Bab al-Aziziyya, and were fighting a rearguard action as a chain of state officials and civilians began evacuating down the unguarded southern roads to Tripoli Airport and to Bani Walid.[56]

At this point Misrata and Nafusa Mountain fighters swarmed into Tripoli. It is important to remember how unintended this was. The plan set out between the Qatari chief of staff and Misratan and Zintan-led mountain battalions, put together over several meetings in Doha and in Tatuine in late July, was that only the Tripoli battalions should enter Tripoli. Zintan agreed only to come down as far south as the area of Sahl al-Jafara, the plain skirting from Gharyan down to the coastal road at Zawiya. Likewise at Misrata, Salim Jawha felt that the urban terrain was too unknown to Misratan battalions.[57]

However, the Tripoli battalions were far from ready. Frantic calls from *I'tilaf's* communications hubs in Siyahiyya to Bu Hajar in Zintan on 20 August saw the latter telling them his battalion could not arrive until 22 August, prompting yelling and shouting down the line. Harati, fighting near Zawiya, also told the *I'tilaf* coordinators he could not get there in time.[58] This prompted Harati's men to drive from Zawiya straight to Tripoli in a twenty-four-hour slog, in close coordination with ground advisers, such that NATO could strike a key 32 Brigade base blocking his route at midday on 21 August, allowing Harati to arrive at Siyahiyya at sunset that day.[59]

The Tripoli battalions' disorganisation prompted Zintan's rushed entry into Tripoli that same day. While Harati was fighting east from Zawiya, Bilhajj and Bu Hajar drove up the southern route into Tripoli through Gharyan, where the bulk of Zintan's fighters were camped at an agricultural compound near a valley named Wadi al-Hayy. Bilhajj and Bu Hajar met the leading Zintani commander present, Faisal bin Sira, who commanded Nafusa Mountain fighters between Zintan, Tripoli and the coast, and one of his commanders, Mukhdar al-Akhdar. Bin Sira said that Zintan was not logistically ready to move,[60] but that since only Zintanis were covering the southern route running from Qadhafi's Bab al-Aziziyya compound past Tripoli International Airport, then Zintan should block off the airport road. In the chaos, Bilhajj left the meeting, ostensibly to support Harati's fighters in Zawiya. He may have taken with him the bulk of Bu Hajar's weapons and supplies.[61] Bu Hajar sat again with bin Sira and asked that the Zintanis help clear the airport road.[62] Zintan therefore abandoned whatever commitments it made to remain outside Tripoli. Akhdar not only led the Zintani force clearing the airport road, but subsequently occupied that airport for almost a year, leading Tripolitanians to darkly joke that the airport had become 'Zintan International'. The Zintani commanders Mukhtar al-Firnana and Usama Juwaili later acknowledged that once the descent began, Zintani commanders, who had consistently struggled with discipline, lost control of their fighters as the temptation to claim spoils became too much.[63]

Misrata had somewhat stronger coordination than Zintan with the larger Misratan battalions, its operations room, and the Tripolitanian operations rooms. Around 500 Misratans had travelled in by boat on 19 and 20 August to support the imminent uprisings, but not the battalions with their heavy weaponry.[64] But as the uprisings swept Suq al-

Jum'a and Tajura, effectively freeing both overnight, several battalions, apparently without informing their central command, sped west from Misrata. Since their primary means of communication were walkie-talkies—domestic phone coverage between Misrata and Tripoli was still cut—the Misratans briefly lost contact with each other. When they arrived at Tajura at 4am on 21 August, Qudur's cell in Suq al-Jum'a was surprised, and called Misrata's Military Council to ask if they were 'real Misratans'. But they were—and over the coming days, thousands of Misratan fighters poured in to the city.[65]

On 23 August the Misratan, Nafusa Mountain, and various Tripoli battalions converged on Qadhafi's compound at Bab al-Aziziyya. Many within the complex had fled, including Saif al-Islam and Daw', who left on 22 August. They had successfully mobilised enough civilian supporters to both thwart an alleged attempted NATO strike on the complex on 21 August[66] and to support a brief public appearance by Saif al-Islam on 22 August, designed to scotch rumours that he had been captured. A small encampment of unlucky soldiers and mercenaries remained along with snipers in high-rise blocks overlooking the complex, but with the astonishingly heavy gunfire levelled against them, the duration of fighting was brief.[67] As the fighters and world's media overran the complex, an Al Jazeera news cameraman embedded within Bilhajj's unit drove with him to Qadhafi's iconic statue of a clenched fist crushing a US fighter jet. Standing in front of the fist, Bilhajj, whom Al Jazeera presented as the head of the Tripoli Military Council and 'leader' of the forces overtaking Bab al-Aziziyya, said, 'The tyrant has fled, and we are chasing him.'[68]

News of the speech spread like wildfire across Libya. Few knew who Bilhajj or the Tripoli Military Council were; many commanders who did had only been introduced to him in July or August. To many the Al Jazeera speech felt like a coup. Misratans—who outnumbered all the western mountain, Tripolitanian and eastern fighters at Bab al-Aziziyya together, were apoplectic that a man commanding a couple of hundred fighters could claim to lead the forces toppling Tripoli. Zintanis were already uneasy about Bilhajj's spreading of weapons around Nafusa Mountain towns but felt that he had breached trust by not fighting with them from Wadi al-Hayy up the airport road, where they had incurred substantial losses. Some in the Tripoli underground also assumed that either Bu Hajar would head a post-revolutionary military body, or that the military or police would step in. Bilhajj's appearance, given the lack of strategy and communication between the fighters, inadvertently attracted a storm of criticism and speculation.

Governing the new order

Though aware of the date of the planned uprising, the NTC was critically unprepared for the speed of Tripoli's fall. Its three leading personalities—Abd al-Jalil, Jibril, and Ali Tarhuni—were in Baida, Doha and Benghazi respectively, and barely talking.[69] It was still reeling from the assassination of Abd al-Fattah Yunis, which had led to Abd al-Jalil's sacking the entire Executive Committee on 3 August. Though other army commanders converged on Tripoli, competing to replace Yunis, none had clear authority even within the armed forces. Sulaiman Mahmud al-Ubaidi, the army's interim chief of staff, moved across to assess and manage what was left of the armed forces; Khalifa Hiftar, who ultimately moved to Zawiya, appeared preoccupied with what remained of the army's armoured stockpiles in Tarhuna.[70]

A power vacuum therefore arose, into which stepped Tarhuni— 'shooting from the hip', in his words, without even a phone call to Abd al-Jalil or Jibril—who on 21 August negotiated a plane at Benghazi airport and flew to the Nafusa Mountains with $7m in cash. Meeting the NTC's justice and media ministers there, Tarhuni entered Tripoli with Zintan's assistance, travelling to a National Oil Corporation facility on 22 August, and thence to the Corinthia Hotel.[71]

Tarhuni identified several governance challenges—liquidity, healthcare and the disposal of dead bodies, fuel, food and water shortages. However from 22–25 August, security governance was an immediate political priority. Jibril, who remained in Doha until 25 August, had named a 'security committee', but most of these individuals were initially uncontactable in the chaos.[72] Likewise, Misratans were struggling with phone communications among their battalions, whilst Zintani-led mountain commanders had also lost control over their fighters, who had starting raiding in the capital. Communication issues abounded and the political and governance tensions that resulted over 23–30 August can be partly attributed to willful or circumstantial miscommunication.

These tensions manifested immediately in a behind-the-scenes dispute over who should announce Tripoli's liberation. Tarhuni's 25 August announcement of liberation at the Radisson Mahari hotel— during which he choked as the drama of the moment hit him—generated a flurry of behind-the-scenes manoeuvring from *I'tilaf*, Sallabi, Bilhajj and the Tripoli NTC representatives, who did not want the Executive Office to claim credit. Bu Hajar, upon whom the Executive Office was increasingly relying within Tripoli circles, stood beside Tarhuni during the conference, which deepened the enmity between him and Bilhajj: 'Bilhajj was calling me to not go and all this confused me. I thought maybe I'm doing something wrong.'[73]

Meanwhile efforts to address the governance challenges Tarhuni had noticed were underway from two competing groups; Nayid's Stabilisation Committee, and the 'Tripoli Local Council', set up by *I'tilaf* in Tunisia in August.

The Stabilisation Committee had spent July and August doing preparatory work with the UN and international community and local councils in the Nafusa Mountains. Its prominence in international circles enabled it to immediately meet the UN and Contact Group members in Dubai over 21–24 August and attend the fifth Contact Group meeting of 25 August. Yet the militia influx into Tripoli was outstripping the plans presented there, making some delegates uneasy, particularly during the 'Security Workshop' on 21 and 22 August. 'Dubai felt like the wrong place to be at the time,' one attendee said.[74]

But the value of the Committee's coordination would become apparent over subsequent days. On 26 August, the Committee met UN humanitarian divisions at Zarzis, Tunisia, to address the water, food and fuel shortages arising in Tripoli in the wake of the fighting. The Committee's move the next day to the Corinthia Hotel, where it met up with Tarhuni in the Prime Minister's Office, gave the UN and international relief efforts the necessary interlocutors to coordinate emergency water and fuel shipments via Malta and Tunisia. In Tripoli, it reopened the port—then taken by Harati's men[75]—and supervised the distribution of water from the ship to community and mosque leaders.[76] Likewise, a team of Libyans seconded from Libyan and international oil companies—Imad bin Rajab, Isam Qusbi and Faisal Qirqab—negotiated 500 million LYD of emergency cooking gas and diesel on credit from oil brokerages, which were brought in and unloaded at Zawiya.[77]

The Committee could also restore telecommunications and electricity services, due to its preparatory coordination with the US, UK and NATO. Telecommunications systems had been taken over as the rebels approached Tripoli, and the control servers hacked to broadcast pro-rebel SMS messaging.[78] The Committee had telecommunications network maps, and had previously contacted critical engineers at electrical and telecommunications companies through satellite phones to keep things running smoothly. It also met with the Central Bank to ensure the safety and availability of money,[79] while the UAE delivered police cars and internal organisational assistance through it to the Interior Ministry.

The Stabilisation Committee had little power to follow up on this initial emergency relief. Its ambitions were to function as an emergency government, but perhaps for this reason, the NTC and Jibril's Executive both distanced themselves,[80] opting instead to work through government ministries. On 30 August, the NTC called for all government employees to return to work, and NTC Executive Committee members were sent to oversee their respective ministries.[81] The UN and International Stabilisation Response Committee, invested in the Stabilisation Committee, found themselves disconnected from the ministries,[82] which were in turmoil following the flight of key decision makers and as bureaucrats hounded various IT managers, bureau chiefs, and real and alleged internal security employees out.[83] Ministries lacked emergency response capabilities. 'Every day I asked whoever was still at each ministry to tell us their capability,' Tarhuni later said, 'but the structure of government was not able to address the kind of problems we had.'[84] As governance problems mounted, the people of Tripoli themselves stepped into the gap:

From my first day in the Prime Ministers' office people would just come in with a plan. People I didn't even know, who I'd never met, would brief me without my telling them. I got two to three hours' sleep at most. So one was managing things, but with this tremendous power of the people basically solving problems on their own.[85]

The Tripoli Local Council, meanwhile, was convened by *I'tilaf*, the Tripoli NTC representatives Alamin Bilhajj, Abd al-Rahman al-Kib, and Sidiq al-Kabir, and a network of businessmen and professionals in a series of meetings at the Carthage Hotel in Tunisia in early August, with disruption and protest over the Muslim Brotherhood's perceived influence over the Council.[86] Its head was Abd al-Razzaq Bu Hajar, Hisham Bu Hajar's uncle and a wealthy cloth merchant who owned substantial parts of Tripoli's old medina. The Council aspired to motivate its network of Tripolitanian engineers, doctors, oil executives, and community and religious leaders to stabilise Tripoli, motivated greatly by Tripolitanian pride, and resistance to Nayid's Stabilisation Committee, seen as outsiders, governing their city. 'We do not want Benghazi or Bedu tribesmen to govern Tripoli' grumbled one donor and Tripoli grandee during the Council's formation.[87]

The Local Council's 'civil contingency committee' was led by Ghirwi and Krikshi, and had spent months inside Tripoli developing networks of professionals, businesses, field hospitals, and stockpiles of medicine, food and satellite communications. It arrived in Tripoli first over 21–23 August, and established early coordination with first-response international relief agencies like the ICRC. It pointedly did not meet the Stabilisation Committee and the two groups feuded constantly, sometimes duplicating effort and obstructing each other from finding the best solutions. Often they worked with the same local Tripolitanian networks; both, for example, had contacts with a network of volunteer doctors, who approached both sides when trying to secure emergency medical supplies, which in turn were sometimes simply taken from pharmacies and hospitals as well as aid channeled through the Stabilisation Committee or Local Council.

An example of such duplication was the Local Council's attempt to alleviate the gas shortages in Tripoli. Unaware or uninterested in the Stabilisation Committee's coordination with the UN, the Local Council learned of a liquefied natural gas tanker on a regular government delivery moored offshore through National Oil Corporation contacts. The contacts persuaded the captain to dock at Tripoli port, but unfortunately did so while downtown fighting was still raging. The captain panicked; the Council organised some Libyans to board the ship to stop it departing and unloaded the gas.

As with water supply, while the Stablisation Committee coordinated emergency relief shipments with the UN, the Council played a role mobilising neighbourhood youth militias to assist its distribution. The more substantial problem was that the aquifers that supplied Tripoli came from a source of Qadhafi's Great Manmade River at the village of Shwairif in al-Hasawna, near Sabha. The area was 600km to Tripoli's south, still under Qadhafi's control, and contained a Magarha community heavily loyal to Sanusi. The Tripoli Local Council located, equipped and sent nine volunteer engineers who were the first to reach the site. With friendly engineers from Shwairif, which was equally dependent on the aquifers, they ascertained that the reservoirs' power supply had been cut from Bani Walid, a loyalist area, and the back-up generators were in a nearby village held by Tuareg and Tebu members of Qadhafi's Faris and Maghawir Brigades. Competition emerged again: Nayid's Stabilisation Committee negotiated with the brigades through Uthnait al-Koni at the French/UAE operations room in Zintan, while the Tripoli Local Council mobilised nearby revolutionaries to fight them. When the brigades ultimately withdrew and the water flowed once more, Nayid announced it in a press conference while the revolutionaries were still fighting, and without mentioning the Local Council. A backstage spat again erupted, turning what might have been a unique example of complementarity between the two entities into more feuding, their competing claims of responsibility belying the number of independent Tripolitanians and Libyans working together on the same problems.[88]

Tripoli Military Council faces problems

Meanwhile, the lack of an accepted military council in Tripoli was obvious. Nuh and his arrested colleagues were not released from Abu Slim prison until 24 August. The security committee nominated by Jibril was initially sidelined[89] though subsequently appended to the police, intelligence and military—Mahmud Sharif and Muhammad Shaikh, for example, were appointed to the interior ministry, where they suffered from these institutions' incapacity, and had no political leverage over the several hundred revolutionary battalions and neighbourhood militias in the capital. Abd al-Hakim Bilhajj's Tripoli Military Council had generated prickly opposition from Zintan, I'tilaf and grassroots Tripoli militias. Battalions of all shades were occupying seized villas, police and military facilities, and armouries across the capital.

Competition between these groups and the armed forces over arms depots and security facilities was rife. The most valued commodities were the security service and intelligence documents held in various buildings across the capital, which all vanished within hours of the militias' entry.[90] Throughout September, armed groups came to blows over the right to guard—or simply take—arms caches. Zintanis hauled crates of naval torpedoes up to the mountains; Bilhajj's fighters and army soldiers angrily kicked landmines at each other while their superiors negotiated.[91]

Since Bilhajj still relied on his own men, Ali Sallabi arrived on 22 August to shore up support for the Tripoli Military Council, first building bridges with *I'tilaf*—most of whom still wished Hisham Bu Hajar to control it—and Bu Hajar's uncle, who headed the Local Council. He then convened various Tripolitanian commanders on 24 August at the Radisson Mahari hotel, and again at the Mi'tiqa airbase on 25 August. The Council was formally announced that same day, with Bilhajj as head, Harati and Hisham Bu Hajar as his deputies, and ten heads of local area military councils.[92]

Few Tripolitanian fighting groups in Suq al-Jum'a and Tajura accepted Bilhajj's leadership, nor that of any commander who had spent the conflict in the mountains. The Council was also unable to work with the security networks of Shaikh, Sharif and Nuh. Worse, Bilhajj tried on 25 August to bring former LIFG comrades—including those who had been in prison during the conflict—into leadership positions, raising enormous objections, and leading two LIFG commanders—Khalid Sharif and Abd al-Wahhab al-Qa'id—to depart the council immediately.[93]

To further improve Bilhajj's position Sallabi shuttled between Misrata and Zintan. Misratans were indignant about Al Jazeera's claim that Bilhajj liberated Tripoli, but at the same time Sallabi—himself Misratan—and the Misratan leadership shared a desire to limit the immediate resurgence of the armed forces, whom they had fought bitterly. Their being part of the same Qatari distribution networks meant that some prominent Misratans such as Ramadan Zarmuh and Ibrahim Dbaiba were already on warm terms with Sallabi.[94] By 23 September, when Misrata hosted the first nationwide conference of 'revolutionaries' (*thuwwar*), relations between Bilhajj and leading Misratan commanders had warmed.[95] The Misratans remained in Tripoli—no one had the political will or firepower to remove them—but acquiesced to the Tripoli Military Council.

Zintan, however, was not won over. Zintani commanders concerned with Tripoli—Juwaili, Mukhtar al-Firnana, Ibrahim al-Madani and Mukhdar al-Akhdar—were deeply sceptical over Bilhajj's routing of weaponry to Nafusa towns unfriendly to Zintan, and to his perceived abandonment of Zintan on the airport road. With their warmer relations with the Executive Committee and the UAE, they were more inclined to distrust Qatar and Bilhajj. Through a growing alliance with Jibril and their connections with the dormant army and security institutions, their commitment to remain in the capital to counter the influence of Misrata and the 'Islamist' militias deepened.[96]

Zintan also had many fighters that were born in Tripoli (*sukkan Trablus*). These fighters banded together under two previously unknown commanders; a former car mechanic called Abdullah Nakir, who established a rival military council called 'The Supreme Council of Tripoli Revolutionaries' and the brother of Jibril's ally Abd al-Majid Mliqta, who formed a battalion called Qa'qa'.[97]

Qa'qa' and Nakir's Council would be a sore headache for Bilhajj and Harati throughout September, coming to blows several times, with the latter blaming the former—with some justification—for car and house thefts in the city. Qa'qa' also, however, began providing personal security to Jibril, making them difficult to dislodge. Zintan's Mukhtar al-Akhdar used his position at the airport to prevent Bilhajj from travelling on the passport Sallabi had requisitioned for him five months earlier.[98] When the Tripoli Military Council tried to restrict the movement of heavy vehicles in the city, confiscating a Zintani technical, Nakir sent a convoy in response to arrest Bilhajj. The situation nearly came to war, with the Military Council gathering volunteers from Suq al-Jum'a, Tajura and Siyahiyya ready to attack.[99]

The Supreme Security Committee and the new Libyan politics

The political divisions surrounding the Tripoli Military Council and the Misratan and Zintani occupations in Tripoli made further coordination efforts impossible. A Libyan delegation comprising Abd al-Jalil, Jalal Dghaili, Bu Katif, Abd al-Hakim Bilhajj and Ramadan Zarmuh from Misrata travelled to Doha, then Abu Dhabi, on 29 and 30 August to meet the Qatari and Emirati leaderships and attend a NATO conference. Yet despite assurances of unity given there to the NATO leadership—who were expressly concerned with understanding the emergence of the Tripoli Military Council and 'Islamist' groups in the capital—Jibril's boycott of the delegation, and the absence of key Zintani commanders who were invited, underscored those divisions.[100] Furthermore, though the few leading commanders of the time were known to each other and the NTC, more and more new, unknown groups were springing up. This and the lack of a sufficiently legitimate political authority led attempts to unify armed groups to break down.

The first such attempt was a convention of over 200 commanders of armed groups in Tripoli on 26 August in Hadba. It intended to focus on coordination to avoid fighting in the city, and on immediately registering Tripolitanian fighters. However, no notable successes resulted from barring the act of meeting. Indeed Bilhajj, shortly after the meeting, made a speech requesting battalions from outside Tripoli to leave, which only raised suspicions that he was attempting to control the city.[101] A second attempt, convened by Ali Tarhuni between revolutionary battalion commanders and the defected security apparatus, dissolved in acrimony over who was even entitled to attend, the greatest division being between the battalions that had entered from outside, and the Tripolitanian groups who had risen from within.[102] One participant from the LIFG described feeling aghast as he watched a Tripolitanian police officer recount his experience in Qadhafi's security services protecting Qadhafi from assassination.[103]

Over a series of similar meetings in the Prime Minister's Office during the first week of September, Tarhuni thrashed out a four-point agenda that he, Jibril and the Stabilisation Committee wished to prioritise. The first point, which Jibril at one point threatened to unilaterally announce, was to dissolve all military councils inside Tripoli.[104] Though some rebels—the Zintani and Zawiyan constituencies—backed this, Bilhajj and the Misratans were strongly opposed. The second point was collecting all arms within the capital. Third and fourth was the transfer of prisoners and documents from the battalions to Executive Committee control.[105]

Though the four points were all, in practice, soundly rejected by the *thuwwar*, Tarhuni did by 7 September gain broad agreement to form a committee of thirteen people with nominal oversight and membership from all fighting groups in Tripoli to oversee these four points, headed by the defected police colonel Mahmud Sharif. It was with Zintan's Mukhtar al-Firnana, and Hisham Bu Hajar taking different subcommittees.[106] The committees were announced by Tarhuni in a joint press conference as the Supreme Security Committee (SSC).[107] Tarhuni and Jibril envisaged that the city's armed groups would register under it, to form a temporary and auxiliary security force until the police—whose stations and stores had been largely ransacked—could be reinstated.

The SSC, being initially a creation of the Executive Committee and containing several former police and military officers, saw itself as a direct competitor to the Tripoli Military Council for governance of the city. One original SSC member later noted that 'Internally you could see they were also trying to form a force to control the country, like the

Tripoli Military Council, and didn't want to participate in the others plan.'[108] Tensions between the two groups grew, the last straw being the SSC's insistence that all fighting groups in the capital provide men to the SSC. Bilhajj complained to Jibril over Tarhuni's adoption of the security portfolio, given his simultaneous handling of the oil and finance briefs and his work as de facto prime minister, and withdrew. The first iteration of the SSC survived for a mere two meetings—at the third only three people attended.[109]

To resolve the growing crisis between the two camps, Abd al-Jalil flew back to Tripoli on 11 September. Abd al-Jalil's absence from Tripoli reflected his concern that the NTC should not decamp Benghazi en masse for Tripoli.[110] He had hoped to keep Libya's leadership split between the two cities to appease eastern sensitivities. However, the growing political and security crisis in Tripoli compelled him to abandon this aim; when I'tilaf's Imhammad Ghula contacted him, for example, he almost threatened to split from the NTC entirely. 'I told him the Local Council was doing the government's job in Tripoli, that all diplomats were in contact with us. They should come at once otherwise we'll go to the media and start something new'.[111]

Abd al-Jalil then chaired a series of explosive meetings of the seventeen Military Council leaders in Tripoli over 11 and 12 September which culminated in his taking the SSC away from the Executive Committee.[112] By this point the two camps appeared almost in open war. At the first meeting on 11 September, Bilhajj had been 'accidentally' uninvited by SSC military chiefs, only to find out about the meeting, arrive and disrupt it.[113] At the second meeting at Mi'tiqa the Qatari chief of staff, igniting the already combustible mix, arrived with Bilhajj and Bu Katif. Jibril, who was planning that evening to announce the dissolution of military councils in Tripoli, was again furious, and the disagreements erupted; the chief of staff opposed dissolving the military councils and wished to postpone an upcoming visit of the French president, Nicolas Sarkozy, and British prime minister, David Cameron, on 16 September; Jibril insisted the visit proceed. However, pressure from Dghaili and Bu Katif on Jibril won through at the eleventh hour. At 7pm that evening, when Jibril appeared at the press conference with the seventeen council leaders, he had abandoned his threats.[114]

Abd al-Jalil removed the SSC from Executive Committee authority a few days later. Tarhuni recalled Abd al-Jalil phoning to break the news: 'As soon as I heard him say "Alaywi" [the diminutive form of

Ali, indicating affection.] I knew something was wrong.'[115] Control was transferred to three NTC members of varying political backgrounds—Aradi, the Misratan Fawzi Abd al-Aal, and the Sabhawi politician Abd al-Majid Saif al-Nasr.[116] The move ended the Executive Committee's hopes that a planned transition might be possible, and also spelt the end of the Executive's time in office. Jibril announced soon after that he would resign as soon as fighting in Sirt and Bani Walid ceased, and the 'Declaration of Liberation' formally declared. The country's emerging political blocs began to focus on who would control ministries in the next interim administration.

The new SSC management in Tripoli continued a process begun under Tarhuni of registering and paying fighters, spawning a new generation of politicised, state-funded armed groups within the SSC, which soon resembled a parallel, hybrid institution. When the Tripoli NTC representative Abd al-Rahim al-Kib took over the prime ministership from Jibril on 24 November 2011, agitation from armed groups in Tripoli for payment was spiralling out of control, as were public sector pay strikes. Though Kib's administration resisted, the simultaneous pressure of a 20% government budget deficit due to the 2011 conflict compelled Kib, Abd al-Jalil, Sidiq Kabir—by then the governor of the Central Bank—and the finance minister to petition the UN Security Council to unfreeze government assets. On 5 December, over $100 billion was released under UNSCR 2016, and the government, and Local Council and municipal buildings across Tripoli, immediately came under enormous pressure from armed groups. 'They nearly took the doors off their hinges,' Krikshi at the Local Council said.[117] On 18 December, Kib, after being surrounded by armed fighters at his offices in Tripoli, stated he would personally ensure that anyone registered at a military or local council, and registered with the government, would be paid. Thus began Libya's incorporation of militias into a bloated, hybrid security sector, all but outside state control.

Zintani and Misratan occupation in Tripoli would continue, but Bilhajj arguably never recovered from his association with Qatar and the Tripoli Military Council. As the SSC began paying state salaries, the Council quietly faded from view. One of Bilhajj's former LIFG colleagues in the council later reflected: 'The chief achievement of the Tripoli Military Council was as a transition point for us. We successfully prevented the old regime from regaining power, but ultimately, our friends and allies in the council went on to positions in the SSC and the ministries.'[118] Bilhajj would not be among them; having moved into politics, he would go on to contest and lose a seat in the 7 July elections. As for Qatar, the exposure it felt as diplomats and media increasingly became aware of its role led to its feeling 'burnt'. Its role in the fall of Tripoli would haunt it for some time.[119]

Tripoli's haphazard fall created the contours and dividing lines that would shape politics in the upcoming transitional era. It created competing visions over the type of transition Libya should experience, and who should and shouldn't be empowered. Accordingly, it created political blocs who aligned themselves with those visions which would survive over the lifetime of the NTC and its successor, the General National Congress. As the rebels moved from the relatively simple politics of being united against Qadhafi, to the more complex questions of what should come after, they found themselves challenged, and often divided. The struggle to topple and then govern Tripoli was but the first chapter in a larger story—the struggle to build a new state upon the remnants of the old.

5

NATO'S INTERVENTION

Frederic Wehrey

Introduction

Without NATO, the ability of the Libyan uprisings to successfully topple Mu'ammar al-Qadhafi was in serious doubt. Most scholarship on
the NATO campaign has accordingly centred on its successes and its
implications for Western interests and policy. Airpower advocates
parsed the campaign for evidence of a new 'Libyan model' for aerial
intervention that integrates the effects of intelligence, surveillance,
reconnaissance (ISR), precision munitions, and domestic opposition
forces, aided by allied ground advisers—a variation of the 'Northern
Alliance' model employed in Afghanistan.[1] Foreign policy mavens
applauded the intervention as a seismic break from the costly nationbuilding exercises of Iraq and Afghanistan—although criticism of this
'light footprint' approach followed in the wake of the attack on the US
mission in Benghazi on 11 September 2012. Others see the campaign
as NATO's finest hour: a 'genuine, if moderate success' for the North
Atlantic alliance that demonstrated its continued relevance in an age of
unilateralism and mounting scepticism.[2]

Airpower helped to shift the tide of battle at crucial stages of the revolution—most notably during the initial defence of Benghazi, the break-out from the epic siege of Misrata, and the entry of opposition forces into Tripoli from the Western Mountains. An oft-overlooked enabler of these successes was the arrival of foreign ground advisers which, besides coordinating the delivery of arms and training to anti-Qadhafi forces,[3] helped improve the precision and responsiveness of coalition airstrikes. Finally, NATO airpower appeared to have a disproportionately psychological effect on the battlefield that is difficult to measure, but nonetheless emerges repeatedly in the accounts of both loyalists and revolutionaries.

But beyond noting these successes, the conduct of NATO's air campaign raises important debates about the intervention and its legacy. These include how effective airpower was, how cohesive the coalition was, and what coordination existed between NATO, its member forces, and Libyan revolutionaries on the ground. Few asked Libyans themselves what they thought of the campaign's effectiveness. This chapter aims to do this, examining the implicit, tacit partnership between NATO—or more accurately, NATO's individual member forces—and Libyan revolutionaries. It draws from interviews conducted in March and September 2012 and May 2013 among Libyan revolutionary leaders, field commanders, rank-and-file fighters, and ordinary citizens in the war's four crucial fronts: Benghazi and Brega; Misrata; the western Nafusa Mountains; and finally Tripoli itself.

In many ways, the partnership was marked by strains, frustrations, and exasperation due to differences over the scope and mandate of the intervention, its execution, and the military inexperience of the Libyan rebels. But there was also remarkable cohesion and cooperation, often in creative ways, which overcame the limitations of strategy, organisation and experience that affected NATO operations, the Libyans, and NATO member states.

NATO's interlocutors in Libya: The role of military defectors

NATO's entry into the conflict began on 19 March as a US- and French-led coalition, with NATO itself taking over on 31 March. Though rebel fighters were still organising themselves, an early network of military defectors had sprung up, aiming to play coordinating and intermediary roles. The various operations rooms these defectors were setting up in Zintan, Misrata, and Benghazi during this time later became important communication nodes for NATO.

Initially, most of those fighting against Qadhafi were enthusiastic volunteers with little or no military experience—students, day labourers, mechanics, professionals, volunteers from the Libyan diaspora, and the unemployed. Many were little more than neighbourhood guard forces, organised into loose 'battalions' (*kata'ib*; singular, *katiba*), composed of anywhere from twenty to 200 men. But by the end of March, in the key urban centres of the war—Benghazi, Misrata, and Zintan—greater coherence, organisation, and discipline had emerged, although in a model quite different from Western military thinking. This included the establishment of makeshift 'command centres' or 'operations rooms' (*ghuraf al-amaliyat*). As time progressed, these grew more sophisticated, playing a greater role in the operations of the frontline forces. In all cases they were staffed, at least in part, by former military officers. While they had limited influence over fighters' actions, their coordination efforts helped NATO filter the flood of information that resulted.

In Benghazi, defected officers from the Libyan Special Forces (colloquially known as the *Quwwat Sa'iqa* or 'Lightning Force') were among the most crucial interlocutors with NATO. The *Sa'iqa* was an elite force under the direct command of the then-interior minister, Abd al-Fattah Yunis, and whose officers, like Yunis, were drawn from notable eastern families.[4] The *Sa'iqa* was at the forefront of suppressing the insurgency by the Libyan Islamic Fighting Group (LIFG) in the 1990s, yet in the early stages of the Libyan uprising, it defected with Yunis. The unit's second-in-command, Colonel Abd al-Salam al-Hasi, was instrumental in setting up a central intelligence and communications cell in Benghazi that liaised with NATO member states.

Elsewhere, many coordinators came from the Air Force, which had defected in large numbers in both the east and west. On 21 February, shortly after the uprising began, Libyan Air Force officers at Benghazi's Banina Air Base declared their allegiance to the revolt. Gamal Abdel Nasser Air Base in nearby Tubruq quickly followed suit. The officers at these bases initially formed the 'Free Libya Air Force', adding an aging fleet of MiG-23s, MiG-21s, and Mi-24/35s to the anti-Qadhafi struggle. These pilots flew a variety of missions, beginning 5 March, against Libyan armed forces near Ajdabiya and Ra's Lanuf: close air support, maritime interdiction, reconnaissance, and at least one attempted air-to-air intercept of a loyalist fighter plane. By several accounts, they flew roughly forty sorties from the start of the revolt until 19 March.[5]

The 19 March imposition of a no-fly zone, which applied to both rebels and the government, ended these efforts; NATO aircraft escorted the Free Libya Air Force jets back to Banina, where they were grounded. On 20 March, multilateral forces destroyed the remaining air defence radar at Banina—a strike that left the base commander perplexed and angry.[6] Despite this misunderstanding, Benghazian Air Force officers played a critical role in staffing the operations rooms that liaised with NATO and also offered the base as a storage and assembly point for subsequent rebel assistance to Misrata.[7]

Similarly in Misrata, officers at the Misrata Air Force Academy defected en masse, sabotaging the Galeb trainer aircraft and Hind helicopters at the base. They participated in the Misrata Military Council in early March, and became instrumental in creating its operations rooms and communications infrastructures. Salah Badi, who helped form the first military committee inside Misrata in the early days of the war—and later formed a prominent revolutionary *katiba*—was a former pilot.[8] The head of Misrata opposition's radio rooms, Colonel Muhammad Abd al-Jawad, was a former operations room chief at the Misrata Air Base. Fathi Ali Bashagha, who became the main interlocutor between NATO and the Misratan opposition, was also a pilot, serving as a former instructor pilot at the Misrata Air Force Academy.[9] These officers were augmented by other ex-military officers and soldiers, including Salim Jawha, a former artillery colonel, who would emerge from the war as the leader of the Misratan forces, playing a critical role in coordinating the western sector of Misrata. This network of individuals influenced the creation of a system for managing and coordinating information that over time grew robust—by June, it was able to coordinate the efforts of hundreds of individual *kata'ib* on the city's three main fronts. Their efforts were enabled by the widespread use of the Global Positioning System, satellite phones, and a central operations room where the positions of friendly and hostile forces, civilian sites, and potential targets were plotted on Google Earth with remarkable precision.

In the Nafusa Mountains, Air Force officers had a similar influence on NATO relationships after western advisers began to arrive in May. Many officers at Tripoli's Mitiga Air Base fled into to the Nafusa

Mountains and created a network, reinforced initially by Muhammad al-Madani, a defected officer from Zintan, which sustained communication between the various Nafusa Mountain communities.[10] One network became the 'Western Region Military Council', led by Colonel Mukhtar al-Firnana, a former army logistics officer. Its operations centres in Zintan and Nalut were staffed by roughly a dozen former Air Force officers who acted as the rebels' liaison with foreign ground advisers. As in Misrata and Benghazi, they had an at times tenuous relationship with fighters on the ground. Nonetheless, among the most important for NATO was former Colonel Jum'a Imdakhum, previously also an Air Force pilot, who coordinated all airstrikes with the advisers.[11]

The fact that Western allies had longstanding relationships with several of these defecting officers—from both the Air Force and army—through attaché and security cooperation activities helped established these networks. Men such as Colonel Bashagha in Misrata and Colonel Imdakhum in Zintan emerged as the principal interlocutors with NATO because of a combination of their English language facility, military experience, and stature in local communities. In the US case, for example, the Department of Defense had established an Office of Security Cooperation at the Defense Attaché Office (DAO) in the US Embassy in Tripoli starting in 2008. Personal relationships established between DAO personnel and several of these officers who defected to the opposition ranks would prove crucial to coordinating NATO operations with opposition ground forces, managing the opposition's battle-space, and reconnoitring targets. As the war progressed, they were to work closely with foreign advisers on the ground to call in airstrikes and conduct battle damage assessment. Nonetheless the depth of such relationships should not be overstated—much was focused on exchange visits, English-language instruction, spare parts, and some very rudimentary professional military education. In several cases, this outreach was conducted with individuals who would later fight to the very end for Qadhafi.

'We were not their air force': NATO's rules of engagement

On 17 March, the United Nations Security Council passed Resolution 1973 (UNSCR 1973), authorising 'all necessary means' to protect Libyan civilians. Two days later, on 19 March, French aircraft struck armoured columns approaching the outskirts of Benghazi at approximately 4.45pm in an eleventh-hour intervention that Benghazi residents recount with breathless admiration. A US-led coalition codenamed Operation Odyssey Dawn then carried out the suppression of much of Libya's air defence systems—a crucial prerequisite for establishing the no-fly zone.[12]

The civilian protect mission was subsequently brought under NATO authority after arduous four-way talks between the United States, Britain, France, and NATO. Twelve days after the first strikes, the US ceded leadership of the campaign to NATO under the new name of Operation Unified Protector. France and Britain conducted the majority of strikes, with Belgium, Denmark, Norway, Italy, Sweden, and Canada playing a supportive role. In tandem, NATO warships and aircraft began patrolling the approaches to Libyan territorial waters to enforce an arms embargo on the conflict as required by the UN resolution.

More than any other facet of the intervention, NATO's civilian protection mandate was the subject of ambiguity, haziness, and frustration among anti-Qadhafi forces. Prior to UNSCR 1973, President Obama and his British and French counterparts had given speeches clearly indicating that Qadhafi's continued rule was unacceptable. Yet early in the actual military campaign, both NATO and the US sent strong signals about the limitations on its role: in its so-called 'warning order' to deployed forces, the Pentagon reemphasised the civilian protection mission. Echoing this, President Obama stated emphatically in a 23 March speech that the US was not pursuing regime change. Yet at a ministerial meeting in April in Berlin, the definition of 'threat to civilians'—originally understood to arise from any side, including the National Transitional Council (NTC)—was revised to apply only to the armed forces serving Qadhafi, anywhere in the country. Even thereafter, as will be discussed below, in the actual execution of air operations NATO commanders came close to applying the mandate against the rebel forces in their attack on Sirt.

The United Nations never defined Unified Protector's end-state—the point by which all threats to civilians were deemed neutralised. In many respects, this haziness about the actual relationship between the NATO coalition and the anti-Qadhafi forces was essential to cement the diverse views and concerns of the coalition and retain 'top cover' from the United Nations. Anything more specific calling for Qadhafi's ouster would not have passed the UN Security Council, given China and Russia's opposition to such a move.

Despite its haziness, the parameters of the civilian protection mandate had several consequences for the relationship between NATO and anti-Qadhafi forces. Here it is critical to distinguish between the forces and capabilities that belonged to NATO, the organisation enforcing the no-fly zone—which did not set foot on Libyan soil throughout the engagement—and those of its member states—who did.

Firstly, NATO, unlike its member states, had no liaison office or direct line of communication with anti-Qadhafi forces. As one senior NATO officer emphasised: 'There was no coordination or communication between NATO military forces—as a coalition—and the anti-Qadhafi fighters. Full stop. Our mandate was to protect civilians. We were not their air force.'[13] But while ostensibly noble, in fact this absence of liaison between NATO and the rebels was to increase dramatically the influence played by the individual NATO states, who did in fact establish lines of communication, liaison units embedded in the rebels' operations rooms, and, in the second half of the campaign, ground advisers who moved with the rebels' advancing frontlines.

Secondly, the mandate meant that NATO, again unlike its member states, was scrupulous in not taking sides during tactical engagements. It did not see itself as providing the 'close air support' that some of its member states wished of it. 'If our pilots saw a fight between technicals, they would treat them both as legal combatants and did not intervene,' noted a senior NATO commander.[14] Indeed, in executing the UN mandate, the coalition's air forces came close to striking rebel forces who were believed to be threatening civilians. 'We were prepared to strike anti-Qadhafi forces if they had targeted civilians. Toward the end of the war, in Sirt, we came very, very close,' noted a senior NATO planner.[15]

Thirdly, the civilian protection mandate compelled NATO to select fixed, strategic targets—known in military parlance as 'deliberate targets'. Only those facilities—whether ammunition depots, storage bunkers, or command posts—that could be proved to be supporting an attack on civilians were struck. This focus frequently at times slowed down the targeting process; some targets required ministerial approval.[16] Unlike the aerial campaign in Iraq, there was no effort to cripple Qadhafi's government through a massive attack on infrastructure such as roads, bridges, and electrical grids. 'We left the country's infrastructure intact,' noted the NATO commander. 'We hit only one road in seven months and this was in Brega.'[17] The consequences of this for the post-Qadhafi transition were profound.

Dynamic targets: NATO's limits

While NATO focused initially on its lists of 'deliberate' (fixed) targets, the more time-intensive process of identifying 'dynamic' targets (mobile, time-sensitive targets, usually identified by pilots or reconnaissance assets during battle) proved much more challenging. Though NATO's early disruption of Libyan command and control facilities meant that Qadhafi was unable to coordinate concentrated firepower at key junctures, the 'dynamic targets'—the army and security brigades, in other words—still had to be dealt with, since NATO judged these targets to pose the greatest threat to civilians. Here, however NATO faced significant limits over and above its mandate to avoid civilian casualties without explicitly supporting the rebels.

NATO faced a significant shortfall of both aircraft and, crucially, the intelligence, surveillance, and reconnaissance (ISR) assets needed to vet and corroborate targets. Of the former, only 130 combat aircraft, supplied by eighteen NATO members, were available, only fifty-five of which could carry out air-to-ground ops. This gave NATO an average capacity of forty-five strikes per day, and a further seventy sorties. By 9 September, NATO would have flown a total of 8,390 strikes and 22,342 sorties—a number which stretched the capacity of some member states, including the UK and Norway, almost to their limits.[18]

Regarding the latter, the line-of-sight requirements needed for NATO to hit 'dynamic targets' were significant. Before a dynamic target could be struck, it had to be vetted by a lengthy process: positive visual identification by the pilot, geographic position (was the target east or west of frontlines established with rebel forces?), and corroboration through ISR assets, such as Predator drones. The US provided a sizeable proportion of the ISR assets used, including thirteen S&R aircraft, two Predator drones, a Global Hawk (high-altitude unmanned), and various jamming equipment; later on, it would share previously restricted satellite imagery and signals intercepts, further improving NATO's capabilities during the Western Mountains campaign and assault on Tripoli.

Faced with limited resources, NATO needed to prioritise. 'The anti-Qadhafi forces had unrealistic expectations about our coverage,' argued one NATO commander. 'We were stretched thin. They thought the sky would be black with NATO aircraft.'[19] NATO therefore had to prioritise its aircraft and intelligence assets to only those fronts where it believed civilians were most endangered. As noted by the NATO commander:

First above all was Brega. Qadhafi's forces were swarming all over the city; we knew we had to stop them or they would take Benghazi. Next was Misrata, which was hanging by its fingertips. We had to keep the port open to save the population. Eventually we moved forces over to the West.[20]

Managing the information flow: Challenges of corroboration and competition among operations rooms

The Libyan rebels supplemented NATO's own sources of information—and it was on this that the tacit partnership between NATO and Libyan opposition fluctuated. The Libyan opposition forces did not merely try to adapt their strategies and movements to NATO's air campaign, but tried directly to influence its targeting process. Anti-Qadhafi activists and fighters across the country formed a complex network of spotters, informants, forward observers and battle damage assessors. Anyone with a cell phone, Google Earth, Skype, Twitter, or e-mail was in a position to report, and all of these conduits were used to pass coordinates, pictures, and other data. As the war progressed the quality of the reporting improved. The problem that mission planners faced, therefore, was not a shortage of targeting information, but rather a flood of it. The challenge of vetting the sources alone was extraordinary. Furthermore, the data needed corroborating with other collection platforms, transforming it into intelligence, and then determining what was actionable and what wasn't. The information overload was exacerbated by the proliferation of 'operations centres' allied with specific rebel factions who established their own separate channels with individual outside forces. These included Djerba, Zintan, Misrata, two in Benghazi and one in Dubai.

At first, the only conduit to NATO for opposition commanders across Libya was a makeshift operations room set up near the Great Manmade River project in Benghazi. It was run by Colonel Abd al-Salam al-Hasi, a Libyan army defector from the Libyan Special Forces (*Quwwat al-Sa'iqa*) commanded by Yunis whom he appointed to coordinate with NATO. Hasi's role primarily involved running daily coordination meetings at the operation room, where members of the NATO coalition had sent representatives. He also became the focal point for intelligence reporting from fronts across Libya and passed it on to these NATO representatives.

That said, there were limits to Hasi's span of influence. The volume of information he received, in his words, was overwhelming: 'my phone grew too hot to touch'.[21] More significantly, distrust grew in April between the defected armed forces, of whom Hasi was a senior member, and civilian fighters in the east. By May, the three largest groupings of civilian fighters—the '17 February Battalion', the 'Umar al-Mukhtar Battalion', and the '17 February Coalition' banded together as the 'Gathering of Revolutionary Companies' reporting directly to the NTC's newly created 'Ministry of Defence' and possessing its own reporting channels to NATO members' representatives.[22] Under the surface, a campaign of killings of former military intelligence and internal security officers was beginning. This political situation limited Hasi's purview still further, along with that of Yunis. According to a Western military officer who interfaced extensively with Hasi: 'It was unclear what his span of control was. He was certainly tight with Yunis. But it was not clear about the 17 February Battalion.'[23]

Through March and April, NATO members began building their own relationships with fighting forces across Libya, deploying special forces, and subsequently liaison officers, dedicated to training and improving coordination between rebel forces. However, rivalry between Qatar and the United Arab Emirates contributed to a fragmented information flow and undermined Hasi. Although Emirati advisers supported Hasi's operations room, Qatari forces backed another operations room in Zuwaitina that had been set up by the 17 February Revolutionary Battalion and the Rafallah al-Sahati Companies—two prominent fighting units manned and led by Islamists who, in some cases, had been on the receiving end of the Special Forces' counterinsurgency campaign in the late 1990s.

The widening political fissures in the eastern-based opposition and Qatar's ascendancy were reflected in Hasi's gradual sidelining in information coordination.[24] Referring to Qatar, a senior NATO officer said: 'Qatar had representatives in Hasi's meetings, but Hasi didn't know about Qatar moving equipment in. It was really grey where Hasi's influence started and stopped.'[25] As the lack of trust and communication between the intervening countries and the opposition grew, Hasi himself acknowledged his own gradual marginalisation, telling a news reporter in June 2011: 'Sometimes support comes too late. We contact [NATO] through an intermediary. There is no hot line between us and them. I feel like I am dealing with the hotel's room service.'[26] Echoing this, Yunis at one pointed quipped that the Libyan *thuwwar* were 'at the mercy of Qadhafi and NATO at the same time'.[27]

A third room with Emirati sponsorship was in rivalry to both Hasi and the Qatari-backed faction. This room was set up in March by Mahmud Jibril's affiliates on the Executive Council of the NTC in Dubai, with British MI6 oversight, and liaised via satellite phones, which the British provided and Jibril's affiliates distributed, with a network of contacts in Benghazi, Nafusa and Misrata. It was later staffed by US personnel from the Department of Defense's United States Africa Command (AFRICOM). This room provided targeting coordinates to AFRICOM and, to a lesser extent, the British. 'The British gave no dialogue or feedback about the information we provided. It was all one way. Once AFRICOM came it was more of a dialogue; they would give us more feedback and let us know their priorities.' AFRICOM wanted the room to be 'exclusive to AFRICOM; they were fine if we shared with the British but they wanted to know about this'.[28]

Importantly, this room had no contact with either of the operations rooms in Benghazi (Hasi's room) or Zwaitina. This room also appeared to have minimal contact with the Qataris—at times they would let the Qataris know if information was passed up to AFRICOM. But in general this room had an antagonistic relationship with the Qatari-backed faction. 'The Qataris undercut us; they were always one step ahead of us,' noted one member of the Dubai room.[29]

The information NATO received from all of these different sources flowed to the 'Ground Effects Cell' at NATO Headquarters, where member nations also had liaison officers. Any intelligence that individual member nations collected from opposition forces was passed to NATO's commanders via the liaison officers in this cell. The process for vetting and processing intelligence was thorough and time consuming. 'It was a very roundabout way,'[30] the NATO officer noted. NATO never acted based on a single report from a 'human source', i.e. a Libyan providing coordinates, without corroborating it through its own intelligence assets. Some interlocutors noted that it would typically take four to five days for information passed via a Libyan informant to be acted upon.[31]

In the early weeks of NATO's intervention, its lack of a liaison office with rebel forces, combined with the seemingly ponderous intelligence corroboration cycle led to a consequent slow tempo of attacks which frustrated opposition commanders and fighters on the ground. Libyan commanders developed a nuanced understanding of the reasons behind NATO's initially slow intelligence cycle—as a Misratan commander said:

We knew NATO was slow for several reasons. It didn't trust us, because early on it didn't have people on the ground. NATO was under tremendous pressure not to make a mistake. It had too much data and information, from across the country. And it had to balance strategic and tactical targets. Finally, we knew that NATO is a committee. We had to explain to our youth the nature of (UNSCR) 1973 ... that it was meant to protect civilians. And if you have a gun in your hand you are not a civilian.[32]

The consequences of NATO's lack of direct liaison and consequently circuitous target verification were greatest and deadliest in the west— Tripoli, Misrata, and the Western Mountains. In Tripoli, an initial surge in bombings under the US-led operation Odyssey Dawn (19– 25 March) slowed once NATO's Unified Protector took over, due to the cumbersome target nomination process that ensued—each member nation had an effective veto over any target, known in NATO vernacular as a 'red card'. In other cases, the lack of ISR assets and logistic support such as aerial refueling slowed operations and slowed the campaign. The net impact of these delays was acutely felt on the ground. Opposition supporters were confused and angry. 'Everyone thought the regime would be finished if you had just kept going,' noted one defector in Tripoli.[33]

From February to late May, NATO deployed few reconnaissance assets to Tripoli and the Nafusa Mountains, seeing the situation in first Brega, and then Misrata as the more urgent priority. This limited the number of strikes that could be carried out, since NATO's rules of engagement required that the target be verified via sight. When the operations room in Benghazi was the only conduit to NATO, the chain of communication was simply too long and unwieldy for NATO to react. Therefore, though Qadhafi had few military units in the region prior to the revolution[34] he was able to reinforce these units with impunity, ferrying troops and armour from Tripoli and accessing ammunition depots in the area that were untouched by NATO strikes. Rebel commanders, meanwhile, found themselves wrong-footed by the unwieldy communication chain. One commander and military defector, Mukhtar Firnana, said:

Early in the war, I had planned an attack on Zintan's storage depot ... the NTC in Benghazi said go ahead. Then, when I was a few kilometres away, they said turn back. NATO will strike this. NATO struck it only three months later. The fighters came back to me angry, saying I had failed them.[35]

The scarcity of NATO airpower effectively stalled the Nafusa offensive once the mountain towns of Zintan, Yefren, Wazin, Nalut, and Kikla had risen up.[36] Without airpower, these towns were unable to move out of their foothills and into the plains north of the Nafusa. Instead, it began fortifying its positions, with Zintan digging an elaborate 40km trench network around itself.[37] Of course, there were other reasons as well for the stalemate, including the opposition's own logistical problems, lack of organisation, and shortage of ammunition. One commander noted that the pause was necessary to regroup and train volunteers.

Among the Tripoli cells, there was no direct contact with NATO until 20 August—all contact went through Misrata and an operations room set up in Djerba, Tunisia, by Jibril and run by Abd al-Majid Mliqta. The Tripoli cells coordinated with NATO via Hisham Bu Hajar who was in the operations room—all through the internet and occasionally Skype. On 20 August, that changed, when NATO began striking targets. The Tripoli cells received calls from NATO about the locations of strikes. In one instance, a Tripoli rebel commander received a call from 'a NATO guy' letting him know that one side of Bab al-Aziziyya was undefended—clear evidence that NATO member forces were not simply engaged in a protection role but actively supporting rebel movements on the ground with strikes and overhead intelligence from sensors and satellites.

Elsewhere across the country, the Tripoli cells had limited coordination. 'We had zero coordination with the Benghazi operations room, except through the NTC—we had nothing to plan with them,' noted a key commander of the Tripoli cells. 'We coordinated with Misrata and Zawiya. After the fall of Tripoli we were in contact with all of the operations rooms, we gave them the frequency of loyalist forces' radios.'[38]

The role of ground advisers

By April, the limitations of NATO's slow intelligence cycle, compounded by the limited assets it was able to deploy, had become clear. To adapt, NATO member states began deploying their own ground advisers[39] directly into the operations theatres of Brega, Misrata, and the Western Mountains. By every account, the presence of advisers working with Libyan anti-Qadhafi forces had a transformative effect on airpower. Libyan interlocutors described how, in the operations rooms of Misrata, Zintan, and Benghazi, these advisers built trust between NATO and the fighters on the ground, sped up the flow of information, and, therefore, most importantly, improved the pace and precision of airstrikes.

Nowhere was this more apparent than in Misrata. Before the arrival of foreign ground advisers, NATO struggled. 'Misrata was tough,' acknowledged one NATO commander. 'We couldn't get in the middle of urban fighting. We wrestled with questions like, "is this infrastructure? Is it within our mandate?".'[40] Many interviewees in Misrata expressed frequent exasperation over this aversion to striking targets in densely crowded urban areas. This was nowhere more apparent than in the Misratans' repeated but unsuccessful pleas, via Benghazi and its own communications room led by Bashagha, for NATO to strike the tall Insurance Building—a notorious sniper's nest and the most contested structure in the city. NATO judged destroying the building to risk too much collateral damage.

The arrival of foreign ground advisers did not change these considerations for NATO, but their ability to coordinate rebels' movements with NATO airstrikes helped break the siege and launch the westward assault toward Tripoli. Although many of the details remain unknown, there was reportedly a period of intense collaboration between NATO members and the opposition that preceded the actual arrival of Western advisers to Libya. This included a team of three French advisers visiting the city for a short period in April and the Misratan opposition leadership meeting a senior NATO commander on board the French aircraft carrier Charles de Gaulle sometime in May. 'The first thing he told us,' recalled one Misratan participant, 'is that we are not attacking the Libyan people.'[41]

By mid-May, three or four additional French advisers set up a constant presence.[42] According to one planner, the French reportedly travelled around the frontlines incessantly, exposing themselves on numerous occasions to fire. Yet despite this, there was still a lengthy process of trust building. 'They were always double-checking our data against their maps,' noted one Misratan. 'We started taking our informants directly to [them] or letting them talk to them via Skype.'[43] According to a Misratan commander, these advisers were focused initially on securing the port in the northeast quadrant of the city and, subsequently in late June, supporting the Misratan assault on Tawergha to the south. Their role was described as three-fold: 'to coordinate NATO attacks on fixed targets before a Misratan assault; to prevent reinforcements from flowing in to the area; and to provide air cover'.[44]

By early June, four British advisers arrived, focusing on the western front. Misratans had a more favourable impression of the British. 'We became friends in two or three days; they were eating our food with us and always travelling with us to the front,' noted one commander. The British were also the most proactive in assisting the Misratans in planning for a breakout of the city in late June. 'When the British came, we started to act,' noted the Misratan commander. 'We had a meeting with them in June and they told us, "You must start your offensive [out of the city] before Ramadan [July]."'[45]

In breaking the siege, the British and French advisers called in coordinates to NATO command centres via radio or satellite phone—Misratan witnesses stated the advisers did not have direct links to aircraft. Both countries developed reputations for being more responsive, asking fewer questions about the information being passed, and, most importantly, acting on it. 'The French were everywhere and the easiest to work with,' noted one Misratan planner. 'They never asked questions like, "where did you get this?" They just took the data and said thank you. The British were the best. The people who worked with the British had 50 to 60 per cent of their targets hit. The worst were the Americans.'[46] In many cases, though, the response time between a particular target being fixed by the ground observers and a strike was described as 'minutes'. 'NATO was covering our advance,' noted one commander. In describing ground-to-air coordination in the Misratan breakout toward Dafniyya, a village on the western front of the city, he showed on a map how airstrikes—guided by ground advisers—enabled the right flank of the Misratan assault to envelop Qadhafi's forces.

Ground advisers and the Nafusa Mountains/Tripoli

In the western Nafusa campaign, ground advisers played a similarly significant role. Initially, Qatari and Emirati advisers arriving in June proved crucial to improving the targeting process and, most critically, coordinating weapons shipment, communications, and training. This relationship was fraught with friction and competition, resulting in the Qataris eclipsing the Emirati role by working more closely with Naluti Amazigh and the small Tripolitanian groups gathered in Nalut and Rijban under Abd al-Hakim Bilhajj and Mahdi al-Harati, who did not coordinate well with the Zintanis during the push toward Tripoli. The Zintani fighters under Usama Juwaili and Mukhtar Firnana, meanwhile, developed a closer relationship with Emiratis. In June, French and British advisers arrived, setting up their own operations room in Zintan. However, as was the case in Misrata and in the east, their presence was not without friction or misunderstanding.

In the early stages of the campaign, some Nafusa field commanders seemed to resent the limits imposed by these advisers, particularly the French, who appeared to be focused initially on target reconnoitring, training, and advising.[46] Again, much of this stemmed from inflated expectations by Nafusa commanders about NATO's responsiveness and ability to cover vast swathes of the battlefield with limited assets. The Nafusa front faced the additional challenge of uncertainty and caution from NATO about the composition of rebel forces—rumours abounded about jihadist and al-Qa'ida elements fighting in the area. Initial Western ground personnel were therefore intended to discern who exactly the rebels were before close collaboration ensued. 'Once the CIA figured out we weren't al-Qa'ida, everything started falling into place,' quipped one rebel on the Nafusa front.[48]

As the campaign progressed, Zintan-based commanders and liaison officers spoke fondly of the French role in the west, particularly during the latter stages of the campaign. The French reportedly provided forty ground advisers in total who coordinated weapons delivery, training, and target coordination.[49] They also played a role in smoothing out differences between various rebel factions in the Nafusa. 'The French were moving with us everywhere, by foot and car. They returned fire on several occasions,' noted one defector from the Libyan Air Force who worked in the Zintan operations room and subsequently participated in the final assault on Tripoli.[50]

Tactical adaptation on both sides

NATO's unique mandate and restrictions, and the increasingly important role played by ground advisers, forced both loyalist forces and anti-Qadhafi forces to adapt their tactics. The first adaptation was made by loyalist forces. As early as 25 March, by the time Operation Unified Protector took over from Odyssey Dawn, Qadhafi's troops had transitioned from armour and conventional military vehicles, to civilian vehicles mounted with anti-aircraft guns—the same vehicles employed by the rebels.

In response, opposition forces began marking their vehicles with a large 'Z' or 'N' on the hood or roof; very soon, however, loyalist forces began imitating this. The opposition then switched to painting their hoods with a yellow or orange fluorescent paint. When Qadhafi's military started copying these colours, the opposition used flags fastened to the hoods of their vehicles—the colours of these flags would be announced hours before an assault. Later, revolutionary battalion commanders, usually the lead vehicle in a group of ten or so, were given a laser beacon by foreign ground advisers.

In addition, Qadhafi's forces began placing artillery batteries and parking tanks inside schools, mosques, civilian dwellings, or under covered markets. As the battles for Misrata and Brega wore on, NATO focused increasingly on degrading artillery and GRAD capabilities and interdicting reinforcements. Consequently, loyalist forces did not adjust their barrages for accuracy because, fearing airstrikes, they would 'shoot and scoot'.

Rebel commanders understood the limitations of airpower in densely populated areas and tried to adapt. A Benghazi-based commander recalled how, in the early stages of the uprising, Yunis exhorted the *thuwwar* to stop Qadhafi's forces before they entered the city; once inside the city, he stated, airpower would be useless. Similarly, the Misrata military planner exhorted his colleagues to push the enemy outside the city's environs, 'otherwise we will be just like Zawiya'—a reference to a coastal city west of Tripoli that Qaddafi forces had occupied en masse, thus negating the application of airpower. In late April, opposition commanders in Misrata realised NATO was powerless to stop the shelling of the harbour from nearby Tawergha because Qadhafi's forces, camouflaged in civilian vehicles, had ensconced artillery teams near a mosque and inside schools. In the Nafusa, a commander involved in the initial assault on Aziziyya, a town just south of Tripoli, noted that the presence of loyalist forces disguised as civilians meant that 'NATO couldn't help; it was our problem and we had to do it on our own'.[51]

The rebels prized attack helicopters, particularly the Apache, deployed by British and US forces.[52] Armed with heavy-calibre machine guns, sensors, and Hellfire missiles, the slow-moving aircraft were ideal for supporting rebels in close engagements and interdicting reinforcements. Though not deployed to the battlefield until the final week of May, Apaches played a particularly significant role in striking loyalist 'technicals', accounting for nearly half of these vehicles destroyed in the conflict. Both sides appeared to hold this aircraft in awe, and it quickly became a sought after asset by rebel commanders, particularly early in the Nafusa campaign. Apaches also proved pivotal in supporting the final assault on Tripoli. 'Our main help during the Tripoli battle was from the Apaches,' noted one senior Libyan commander in the Tripoli battle. 'They cleared the west Janzur area for us. When tanks were moving the Apaches were responsive within an hour.'[53]

For their part, loyalist forces reportedly offered rewards for downing an Apache. That said, the Apaches' deployment was circumscribed by stringent requirements for ISR support, restrictive rules of engagement (ROE), and technical limits on sortie generation (most Apaches were launched from British and US ships). Much of its reputation, therefore, appears to have been fed by its performance in Afghanistan and bolstered by the use of psychological operations (PSYOP) leaflets dropped by NATO forces onto loyalist forces in Misrata and in the east that bore a picture of an Apache.

Collateral damage and civilian deaths

The NATO campaign caused limited civilian casualties. That said, there were mistakes and errors—Many were only confirmed later by independent on-the-ground observers. A Human Rights Watch report noted seventy-two deaths; the *New York Times* found forty and possibly seventy; a UN commission found sixty. But the availability of improved ISR and precision munitions, combined with tightly defined rules of engagement, limited casualties—particularly when compared to past interventions. NATO's air intervention in Kosovo's civil war, for example, saw an estimated 500 civilians killed by air strikes.

Opposition interlocutors admitted mistakes on several occasions. The indiscipline and overzealousness of young volunteers, combined with poor communication or ineffective lines of command, frequently resulted in anti-Qadhafi forces straying into NATO's line of fire. On the eastern front of Misrata, after the loyalist Hamza Brigade started using technicals to harass the city's defenders, French warplanes began striking near the Qasr al-Ahmad harbour. Misrata's operations room warned the *kata'ib* about the no-go zone, but several crossed this line and eight rebels were killed by French strikes.[54] Interviews with fighters from this group after the attack were striking in that fighters acknowledge their comrades' error and did not resent NATO for their actions. Similarly in the Nafusa Mountains, in the battle for Ghazaya, a strategic town near Gharyan, anti-Qadhafi forces breached the opposition front and were killed by a NATO strike. According to one planner, this was a blatant violation of orders.[55]

In several cases, young fighters believed a rumour that was circulating that NATO was deliberately allowing Qadhafi forces to flee with their vehicles and tanks. Full of exuberance, they crossed the frontlines into the no-go zones to capture the equipment and try to cut off the loyalists' escape.[56] In the western mountain region, one interlocutor attributed a cultural component to this dynamic: 'In our culture, you have to capture your enemy's weapons or he will use them again against you.'[57] In one case, an opposition fighter captured a tank and drove it back toward the opposition lines with the gun turret still facing forward toward his comrades. The tank was quickly struck by NATO.[58] In other cases, command and control was a problem. There were simply not enough radios or phones to control the scattershot movements of dispersed *kata'ib*.[59]

Revolutionary fighters were often reluctant to publicise errant strikes and casualties for fear that NATO would stand down operations for the next three or four days.[60] In other cases, there was fear that Qadhafi's government would exploit the mistake for propaganda purposes. In Tripoli, for example, a *katiba* commander described an instance when a NATO strike had demolished an apartment block in Tripoli's Suq al-Jum'a neighbourhood. The residents, guided by an underground *katiba*, quickly hid the bomb fragments.[61]

Toward the end of the war, in the Qadhafi strongholds of Bani Walid and Sirt, civilian casualties were more widespread. NATO commanders acknowledged the difficulty of discerning civilians from pro-Qadhafi holdouts. 'It was pickup truck against pickup truck,' noted the NATO air commander. 'It was difficult for us.'[62] Echoing this, a Misratan fighter involved in the assault related how errant NATO air strikes that killed civilians compelled many in the city to switch sides to Qadhafi.[63]

Conclusion: A new model for intervention?

Libyan accounts of the NATO campaign paint a picture of partnership in which Libyans were more active collaborators than is commonly assumed. At the same time, this cooperation was marked by significant strains, divisions, and frustrations born of the opposition's military inexperience as well as restrictions on NATO's resources. Nonetheless, both sides exhibited significant creativity and adaptation as the conflict dragged on.

The Libyans that worked with NATO were nearly unanimous in their appreciation of the campaign's strategic impact. Most obviously, intervention from the air proved crucial to stopping Qaddafi's advance into Benghazi, enabling the opposition to establish a base of operations. In the war's pivotal battle—the siege of Misrata—airpower had a limited direct effect on the street fighting that raged when Qadhafi's forces occupied nearly three-quarters of the city from March to mid-May. But airpower proved essential to limiting the effectiveness of loyalist artillery barrages, slowing loyalist reinforcements, and keeping the port open, which enabled humanitarian supplies and weapons to be shipped in to the opposition. Once Qaddafi's forces were pushed beyond the city's environs, NATO airpower—guided by foreign advisers—proved crucial in aiding the opposition break-out toward Tawergha in the south and Dafniyya/Zlitan in the west. This dynamic continued in the final assault on Sirt.

The campaign profoundly fortified the opposition's resolve in ways difficult to measure. Many Libyan interviewees evinced confidence that, man-for-man, the opposition could outfight Qadhafi's forces using superior morale and resolve, but NATO levelled the playing field. 'The air embargo from NATO was a big help to the 17 February Revolution', noted one commander in the Tripoli assault. 'It allowed us to fight the Qadhafi forces face-to-face, on even ground even though they had better equipment.'[64] Opposition commanders and planners were also acutely aware of the tension between dynamic and strategic targeting, and especially how NATO's mandate under UNSCR 1973 limited its ability to provide responsive close air support. Regarding collateral damage, many were quick to acknowledge their own inexperience, disorganisation, and poor command and control, as well as NATO's mistakes and, most commonly, the fog of war. This nuanced understanding, however, did not lessen their frustration at the lack of strategic support during critical stages of the campaign. This was especially evident in the Nafusa Mountains, where early interdiction against loyalist reinforcements from Tripoli and strikes against the area's ammunition depots might have hastened the opposition's advance and saved lives. In Misrata, there was similar exasperation with the lack of air support early in the war, but there was also an appreciation for the difficulties NATO faced in conducting close air support in the city's densely populated, urban battlespace.

In both the Nafusa and Misrata fronts, however, much of the consternation was eased with the arrival of Western, Qatari and Emirati advisers. By every account, the presence of foreign ground personnel in the command posts of Misrata, Zintan, and Benghazi had a transformative effect—building trust between NATO members and the opposition, improving the targeting cycle, and bolstering the general coordination ground with air operations. As noted, this was aided by the presence of former Libyan military officers inside the opposition ranks and the presence of a liberated zone—Benghazi—from which the opposition could coordinate support to Misrata and the west in the early stages of the war.

With these factors in mind, the Libya campaign represented a variation of the so-called 'Afghan model' where the combination of precision airpower, ground advisers, supplies, and training helped local allies overcome their stark deficiencies in initial fighting capability. But how applicable is this model elsewhere? How much of it rested on factors that were unique to the Libyan context? Most crucially, there were two key prerequisites for the synergistic effect of ground advisers, domestic forces, and precision airstrikes. Chief among these was time. NATO's extended attrition campaign against Qadhafi's fielded forces allowed for the revolutionaries to close the skill gap with their adversaries. But second was political and operational unity among local combatants working with Western ground advisers.

6

THE UNITED NATIONS' ROLE
IN THE FIRST YEAR OF THE TRANSITION

Ian Martin[1]

The mood at the Tripoli polling centre where I watched voting begin at 8am on 7 July 2012 was jubilant. The polling centre staff completed their preparations with the utmost care, faithful to the training they had received. Separate queues of women and men waited patiently but eagerly, and the first who had cast their votes emerged to hold aloft their fingers, now tipped with indelible ink, crying 'Allahu Akbar'. But my colleagues in Benghazi, 650km away to the east, began the day with apprehension. The previous evening, a helicopter transporting electoral materials had been shot at, and a young worker for the election commission, Abdullah Hasan al-Bara'si, had died. This came after the commission's offices in Benghazi and Tubruq were stormed, and a key warehouse in a third eastern city, Ajdabiya, set on fire; in the latter case, only two days before the poll, ballot papers for 46 polling centres had to be reprinted in Dubai and flown in, to enable the affected polling stations to open on 7 July, or soon thereafter. We knew to expect further violent attempts to disrupt the poll in eastern Libya on election day itself.

For the United Nations (UN), this represented the key moment in the first year of our support to Libya's transition. Ten months previously, on 7 September 2011, within days of the defeat of Mu'ammar al-Qadhafi's forces in Tripoli, UN Secretary-General Ban Ki-moon wrote to the Security Council proposing the establishment of an integrated UN Support Mission in Libya (UNSMIL) as requested by the chairman of the Executive Office of the National Transitional Council (NTC), Mahmud Jibril. On 16 September, the Security Council, which had become bitterly divided over the implementation of the NATO-led military operation that it had mandated to protect civilians, nonetheless voted unanimously to establish UNSMIL.

The UN system was more than usually prepared for the task. At the London Conference on Libya held on 29 March 2011, Secretary-General Ban Ki-moon had agreed that the UN would coordinate international assistance after the conflict. On 10 March, he had appointed Abd al-Ilah al-Khatib, a former foreign minister of Jordan, as his special envoy to seek to mediate a peaceful transition; in late April, he appointed me as special adviser to coordinate the UN's post-conflict planning, and to engage as appropriate with multilateral and bilateral actors.

This chapter describes the planning of the UN's role in post-conflict Libya, the launching of UNSMIL, and the UN contribution to the first year of Libya's transition, until a new government took office in late 2012. It addresses three main areas of UN engagement: the General National Congress (GNC) election; the security sector; and human rights, transitional justice and rule of law. It discusses difficult issues confronting the UN: How far to engage Libyans in planning ahead while the outcome of the conflict was unknown and the legitimacy of transitional leadership uncertain? Where to draw the line between technical advice on international good practice and national ownership of highly contested decisions regarding the electoral system? How far and how fast to engage in sensitive areas of the security sector, amid confusion and fragmentation of official responsibilities? How to uphold and advance UN norms and values regarding human rights and empowerment of women in a context combining revolutionary zeal and traditional culture? It describes a UN mission that endeavoured, in a difficult security context, to maintain a light footprint and deliver targeted assistance corresponding to Libyan wishes, respectful of national ownership while advocating UN principles.

Planning and launching UNSMIL

From spring 2011, all relevant parts of the UN system, including the World Bank, together analysed the key challenges for post-conflict support to Libya in what I termed a 'preassessment' process. Planning required learning the views of Libyans themselves, but which Libyans? With the conflict's outcome uncertain, UN engagement with Libyan actors was a sensitive issue. France was the first government to recognise the NTC as 'the sole legitimate representative of the Libyan people',[2] and others accorded different degrees of recognition, but critics, including some Security Council members, regarded this as premature. The UN participated in the Contact Group on Libya, which extended support to the NTC, but the Security Council's formal position, and the efforts of the African Union, were to seek a ceasefire and political solution that would meet 'the legitimate aspirations of the Libyan people',[3] and Special Envoy Khatib was seeking to mediate a peaceful transition, with possible interim power-sharing, between the NTC and what remained of Qadhafi's government in Tripoli.

Through my own visits to Benghazi, soundings by political officers deployed there, and discussions with NTC representatives, the UN learnt how the emerging leadership and civil society envisaged our future role. We discovered that the role played by the UN Commission, headed by Adrian Pelt, in the emergence of independent Libya in 1949–51, and in the negotiation of its first constitution, was well-remembered (although long-forgotten by the UN), and left positive expectations of UN support in 2011. But the Libyans making their revolution were determined to control that transition, and were wary, with the Iraq experience in mind, of post-conflict situations dominated by external actors. The Qadhafi years had fostered mistrust of the international community, even though the NTC wanted to open up Libya's access to international good practice.

While the conflict raged, I set out five principles to the Security Council and Contact Group for international engagement in post-conflict Libya. The first was national ownership—Libya's future must be determined by its people, with the UN helping them realise their aspirations. The second was to respond speedily, with proposals ready for early UN engagement beyond ongoing humanitarian efforts, whenever political developments required. Thirdly, international assistance should be effectively coordinated, and the transitional authorities in Tripoli not be overburdened by multiple, uncoordinated assessments or missions offering support, however well intentioned.

A fourth principle was that international assistance should understand the unique nature of Qadhafi's rule and Libya's combination of national wealth and institutional poverty, which made Libya very different from recent post-conflict situations in Afghanistan, Iraq, Kosovo or Timor-Leste. The fifth principle was humility—not the most obvious characteristic of external agencies, but it is hard to dispute that the international community's record in post-conflict transitions displays at least as many mistakes as successes.

Our NTC interlocutors consistently identified three areas where they expected UN assistance. Foremost was support for democratic elections—Libya's first in over four decades. Only a small minority of Libyans could recall the last election, held under King Idris in 1965. Moreover, political parties had been banned after the first post-independence election in 1952, as well as under Qadhafi. Following the election of a National Congress, the UN would be expected to continue supporting the democratic transition during the drafting of a new constitution, a constitutional referendum, and then the first elections under new constitutional provisions.

Secondly, the NTC expected UN advice in establishing public security, through reforming and developing the police and security forces, integrating within them some of the revolutionary fighters, and asserting control over the vast array of weapons, many taken from military stockpiles. Third came assistance in transitional justice, human rights protection and building rule of law. Addressing legacies of the past would require bringing to justice the worst violators of human rights; establishing the fate of thousands of missing persons; compensating victims; and promoting reconciliation. Along with these specifics went a more general recognition of the need for international support to develop aspects of governance that Qadhafi had inhibited.

The NTC—indeed all Libyan interlocutors—firmly wished to avoid foreign 'boots on the ground', despite the military advice from some Arab and western countries received during the conflict, largely unacknowledged at the time. There was sensitivity even to UN contingency planning for the possible deployment of up to 200 unarmed military observers to monitor any potential ceasefire, and possible temporary armed protection for them. This ceased to be relevant after Qadhafi's defeat.

The planning and deployment of UN peace operations have often been slow and cumbersome, insufficiently responsive to urgent needs and hard to modify once launched. To combine the objectives of speed of response and national ownership, the secretary-general proposed a phased approach, deploying a team for three months for immediate support, while exploring the UN's role with the new Libyan authorities and emerging civil society. The first UNSMIL team was quickly deployed in Tripoli—I myself had arrived even before the mission was mandated on 16 September and my appointment to head it—joining UN humanitarian agencies already on the ground. We offered support to the NTC's Executive Committee and Stabilisation Team, but despite their efforts encountered an initial vacuum of governance. It gradually became clear that Jibril and other key members of the NTC Executive Committee would not be part of the interim government, which the NTC's Constitutional Declaration said would be formed within thirty days of the announcement of liberation. This came after Sirt's fall and Qadhafi's death, on 23 October 2011. Abd al-Rahim al-Kib was elected prime minister of the interim government on 1 November, and it was 24 November before he and his ministerial team took office.

Accordingly, the deployment of UN staff was deliberately gradual. The key consideration was Libyan counterparts' readiness to engage in different fields, which developed slowly. As there was no government for the UN to consult with in undertaking full mission planning during the initial three-month mandate, the Security Council on 2 December agreed to a three-month extension. Meanwhile, growing international concern regarding the flow of arms and ammunition out of Libya led the Council to explicitly mandate UNSMIL to assist Libyan efforts to address the threats of proliferation.

The General National Congress election

The 23 October Declaration of Liberation started the clock running towards the election deadline, set by the NTC's Constitutional Declaration, adopted after much debate in Benghazi in August 2011. It required the NTC to adopt electoral legislation and establish an election commission within ninety days of the Declaration of Liberation, which would manage elections to a 200-member GNC within 240 days of the Declaration. The UN's Electoral Assistance Division had already detailed the decisions required for this process. Electoral experts made early visits—the first to Benghazi before the fall of Tripoli—and were among the first UNSMIL staff to be deployed. They engaged with NTC lawyers who were beginning to draft electoral legislation. However, it was not until November 2011 that the NTC appointed an Electoral Committee (EC) from among its members, to study what was needed for the process, carry out consultations, draft legislation, and prepare for the NTC's appointment of the commission's chairman and members. Only then was it clear with whom UNSMIL was to work in setting the framework which the election commission would later implement.

UNSMIL advisers soon established an excellent relationship with the EC, as it drafted two laws: a relatively straightforward one establishing the election commission, and a more complex one to define the electoral process. The initial draft law on the electoral process, which—as the UN advised—the EC made public for consultation, had major flaws, but its members were open to UN advice in amending it; in addition to many technical improvements, they accepted greater inclusiveness regarding the eligibility of voters and candidates. However, the political choices regarding the electoral system—proportional or majoritarian—and the allocation of constituencies, which would prove highly controversial among Libya's regions and cities, had to be made by the NTC, advised by the EC, with the UN offering technical advice and comparative analysis from other countries. The EC engaged the public as they confronted difficult and inevitably contentious choices, but consultation was limited by a tight timetable, inexperience in all quarters regarding electoral issues, poor communication through a nascent media, and no established mechanisms for engaging civil society.

The most difficult issue was balancing a politically acceptable representation of Libya's historic regions—the former Tripolitania, Cyrenaica and Fezzan—with the distribution of its population. Of the 200 GNC seats, the EC allocated one hundred to the west, including Tripoli; sixty to the east, including Benghazi; and forty to the south and centre. This was unacceptable to many in the east, who sought parity among the regions, regardless of Tripolitania's greater population. Further disputes about relative representation extended down to the level of individual cities and towns, with each jealously comparing the number of seats it had been allocated with its neighbours and rivals.

The NTC's second contentious choice was the role of political parties. As parties were outlawed from Libyan political life since 1952, some felt that premature recognition of parties would favour those already most organised underground. Others felt that localised elections without parties would leave tribal loyalties dominant, privileging old power structures. The debate resulted in a 'mixed parallel' electoral system, with 80 members to be elected from proportional representation lists of political 'entities' and 120 as individuals on a majoritarian basis. The NTC concluded that the timescale did not permit legislating for the proper long-term registration of political parties, so the acceptance of candidate lists from emerging political or other groupings—referred to as 'entities' as they were not yet registered parties—was left to the election commission.

The EC had still to negotiate the constituencies among the claims of different cities and communities. It did so through horse-trading over seat allocations and boundaries among NTC members and other community representatives, and by modifying the parallel system to accommodate their concerns. The outcome was thirteen electoral districts divided into seventy-three constituencies. In the effort to squeeze out extra seats to meet local demands, nineteen constituencies would elect only individual candidates in the majoritarian race, four would participate only in the proportional representation race, while 50 would take part in both. Of the 120 individual members, 40 would be elected by first past the post in single member constituencies, and 80 by single nontransferable vote in 29 multi-member constituencies. This was not an outcome any electoral expert would have recommended, and it was criticised for its complexity, and for not fully respecting the principle of equality of suffrage.[4] But the understandable priority for the EC and the NTC was the accommodation of as many community concerns as possible. Grumbling at perceived under-representation continued, but the EC must be credited with finding compromises which were sometimes messy, but which saw communities make the best of the participation that this first election offered them.

The debate over special measures to promote representation of women in the GNC was of particular interest to the UN. The NTC rejected the EC's initial proposal of a 10 per cent quota. For a while it seemed that there might be no special measures, which would have meant very little representation of women. Secretary-General Ban Ki-moon wrote to the NTC advocating special measures, and UNSMIL worked with women's and other civil society groups in support of this goal. Eventually the NTC decided to require that women candidates should alternate with men on the lists put forward in the proportional race by political entities, and that an entity entering lists in multiple constituencies should alternate men and women at the head of its lists.

Having begun late, the NTC could not complete its electoral discussions before the ninety-day deadline. On 18 January 2012, on the basis of the EC's revised recommendations, it established a High National Election Commission (HNEC), and named its members, sworn in on 12 February. Though the main electoral law defining the electoral process was passed by the NTC on 28 January, further negotiation over constituencies and seat allocation handicapped the HNEC.

The HNEC faced formidable challenges: members from different regions and cities who had never worked together; no electoral experience or useful precedents; and no offices, staff, or internal regulations. Moreover, Libya's new civil society, emerging political parties, media and population at large were unfamiliar with electoral issues and suspicious of the intentions of the new leaders. The HNEC would have to undertake a completely new registration of electors, since what records existed were unreliable, and organise an election in under five months— and much less than that by the time the NTC decided on the final constituency allocation; all in a highly uncertain security environment.

UN electoral advisers were co-located with the HNEC as it addressed these tasks, along with colleagues from other international organisations working in a UN-coordinated framework. They offered expertise in operational and security planning, procurement of electoral materials, data management, voter registration, logistics and field operations, training of registration and polling staff, candidate/entity nomination, complaints mechanisms, public outreach and external relations. The team contributed policy and technical advice on issues such as enhancing access and participation in electoral processes.

Despite early internal tensions, the HNEC addressed these issues with determination, as well as some trepidation, opening voter registration on 1 May at over 1,500 registration centres. Voter education had hardly begun, and early registration was slow, especially of women. Soon, however, public enthusiasm overtook scepticism, and the registration period was extended for a third week. In the end, 2.87 million of an estimated 3.2 to 3.5 million eligible voters registered, 45 per cent of whom were women. Meanwhile, candidates came forward with equal enthusiasm: 2,501 independent candidates and 142 political entities with 1,207 candidates on their lists registered in the allotted timeframe.

Public confidence grew in the NTC's intention to proceed with the election, while the HNEC showed itself capable of doing so. Successful locally organised elections for city councils in Misrata and Benghazi significantly increased positive expectations. The NTC's target date of 19 June, however, proved unrealistic, as candidates had to be vetted by a High Commission on Integrity and Patriotism established by the NTC before ballot papers could be printed, and political entities and candidates needed at least a minimum period to advertise themselves to voters and to campaign. In the face of great reluctance from NTC Chairman Mustafa Abd al-Jalil to envisage any postponement, the HNEC's recommendation of an election date of 7 July was accepted.

Abd al-Jalil's reluctance came not just from the desire to maintain the timetable of the NTC's Constitutional Declaration; a delay of less than three weeks was an extraordinary achievement, and considerably more time than this had been consumed by the NTC's delayed decision making. Rather, it came from his growing concern at threats to disrupt the election in eastern Libya by a political movement which, throughout the spring and early summer of 2012, had advanced demands for federalism outside the framework of constitution-making set out by the NTC, and on 3 May threatened an election boycott. This had little noticeable effect on voter registration in eastern Libya, although their denunciation of the east's seat allocation commanded wider sympathy. But their leaders, having excluded themselves from the election and political process, threatened violence if it went ahead. The NTC had already responded to eastern disaffection regarding seat allocation by deciding in March 2012 that the new constitution should be drafted not by the GNC itself, but by a sixty-person body it would appoint on the basis of equal representation from the three regions. Just days before the poll, Abd al-Jalil persuaded the NTC to further concede that this body should be directly elected, twenty members by each region, and take decisions only by a majority of two-thirds plus one.

This concession, and the efforts of many, including the UN, to dissuade those threatening violence, did not fully avert the threatened disruption. HNEC staff defied the threats as they replaced sabotaged election materials, and public revulsion at the eve-of-poll death of HNEC worker Bara'si strengthened the determination of voters and staff when further attacks on polling stations in the east were attempted on election day. The few deaths that occurred in clashes that day were of persons attempting sabotage.

Security fears were not, however, limited to eastern Libya. Recent fighting in Kufra in the south, and between the Zintan and Mashashiya tribes in the Nafusa Mountains, had displaced would-be voters. But all situations were sufficiently stabilised for polling to take place on 7 July, except for two polling centres in Kufra. There, concerted efforts by the HNEC and the UN led the Tebu leadership to agree to enable voting on 10 and 11 July. This further indicated the HNEC's commitment to an inclusive election, which included special voting arrangements for internally displaced Tawerghans, Tuaregs and Mashashiya.

In all, over 1.7 million Libyans cast their votes—62 per cent of registered voters. The well-ordered process was a credit to the HNEC's training of its nearly 40,000 staff. All observers were impressed by the spirit of the elections as men and women, young and old, amassed in queues at polling stations with the pride and emotion of people long denied democratic freedoms, many of them from families which had suffered or lost family for the right they were exercising. Over 25,000 domestic observers and agents were accredited, as well as 190 international observers from ten organisations: their assessments were overwhelmingly positive, notwithstanding recommendations for future improvements.

The HNEC's transparency continued during the count, which was inevitably lengthy due to the complex mixed electoral system. The campaign period saw no conflicts between candidates or their supporters, very few allegations of misconduct, and general observance of the voluntary code of conduct that the UN had helped to facilitate; there were no significant disputes regarding the results. But expectations that the Justice and Construction Party, established by the Muslim Brotherhood, would benefit from years of covert organisation and emulate the successes of similar parties in Tunisia and Egypt were confounded when it received only just over 10 per cent of the vote and seventeen of the eighty proportional representation seats, while the National Forces Alliance headed by Mahmud Jibril garnered 48 per cent of the vote and thirty-nine seats. The allegiances or alliances of the 120 individuals elected in local constituencies would only gradually emerge when the GNC began to vote.

Thirty-three women were elected among the 200 members, thirty-two on the lists of political entities and just one as an individual candidate, making clear that the special measures were essential for achieving women's representation. On 8 August 2012, the NTC dissolved, as Chairman Abd al-Jalil symbolically transferred power to the oldest member of the GNC. The interim government remained as caretaker until the GNC elected a new prime minister.

The election's success meant that UNSMIL, working with the UN Development Programme and the UN Office for Project Services, and coordinating other international actors, delivered on what most Libyans regarded as the highest priority for UN support. It did so with a lighter electoral operation than in many other post-conflict contexts, with (at its peak) only fifty-five international electoral advisers, based in three locations: Tripoli, Benghazi and Sabha. Early elections met the imperative to create a new legislature and government with demonstrable legitimacy, which had become urgent as public confidence in the NTC and the interim government declined. The performance of the HNEC demonstrated Libyans' capabilities in a new institutional setting. Whatever the NTC's failings, it fulfilled the key responsibility of a transitional authority—the peaceful and democratic transfer of power.

The security sector

The UN's assessment left no doubt that the combined legacy of Qadhafi's rule and the revolution would be immense challenges in the security sector. However, discussions with the NTC—in a context of inevitable sensitivity regarding external military involvement—left the roles that might be requested of the UN unclear. The NTC requested support for police development and programmes for revolutionary fighters and weapons control, but not advice on reshaping the military.

The end of fighting left Libya with hundreds of armed groups—*kata'ib* (battalions, singular *katiba*)—giving varying degrees of allegiance to the NTC but with no single chain of command even within individual cities or towns. All described themselves as *thuwwar* (revolutionaries). Some warranted the term, having fought to wrest control of their localities from government forces; of these, some remained in place, becoming the local protectors of their communities, while others—notably from Misrata, the Nafusa Mountains and the east—joined the battles in Tripoli, Bani Walid and Sirt. Others saw little or no fighting, but emerged to fill the security vacuum in their localities. Such groups included many that emerged in Tripoli during its fall, remnants of the army which defected in the east and largely sat out the fighting, and others in western towns that had stayed neutral or loyal to Qadhafi, transferring their allegiance only once the success of the revolution was assured. Lastly, groups that were little more than armed gangs formed opportunistically, especially in Tripoli, to take advantage of immediate and later rewards to 'revolutionaries', or in the worst cases to engage in personal vengeance, kidnap for ransom or other crimes.[5] The complexity, and internal tensions, within this diverse spectrum were enhanced by an ideological divide that emerged between some who preferred a managed transition with the participation of elements of the former government's security forces, and those revolutionaries—particularly Misratans, civilian fighters from the east and former members of the Libyan Islamic Fighting Group—who wanted to exclude these elements. Local military councils brought together the more responsible leadership of the armed groups and linked them to local civilian authorities.

The security situation did not allow early demobilisation: major fighting continued until Qadhafi's remaining forces were defeated in Sirt in mid-October, and concern at potential destabilisation by Qadhafi loyalists, planned or encouraged by those taking refuge in neighbouring countries, continued long after his death. Vital installations throughout the country were guarded by revolutionary battalions, who distrusted the remnants of the army, weakened as their weapons stocks had mostly been destroyed by NATO strikes or ransacked by armed groups. In January 2012, the NTC appointed an officer who fought with the revolutionaries, Yusuf al-Manqush, as chief of staff of the Libyan Armed Forces, to begin building a trusted and effective army. The Libyan Police had not attracted the hatred reserved for Qadhafi's parallel internal security apparatus, and there was soon a desire to see them back on the streets. But their development into a well-trained, robust force, able to tackle crime in cities awash with weapons, and into which some 15,000 criminals had been released from prisons by the Qadhafi government, would also be a lengthy process. As a series of local conflicts erupted, it was clear that the army alone did not have the forces required to intervene effectively.

The new authorities began by pressing local military councils to reduce the checkpoints and visible armed presence, especially of heavy weapons, in the cities; equipping and deploying what police were available; and negotiating—with difficulty—the handover at key state facilities to security elements under a greater degree of authority of the interim government, which initially often meant the more disciplined revolutionary battalions. The government announced that it would develop plans for the future of 75,000 revolutionaries through the Ministries of Interior, Defence and Labour, each integrating 25,000 into the police, armed forces or civilian life. In practice, the government failed to coordinate overlapping exercises to register the revolutionaries, and grossly mismanaged payments to them. The most comprehensive registration, by the Warriors Affairs Commission—a body established by the NTC itself, which had unclear relations with the relevant ministries—at one point exceeded 200,000, before it was reduced by screening.

Meanwhile, the need to complement the severely limited capacities of the police and army and to establish some state authority over the battalions led to the establishment of the Supreme Security Committee (SSC) and the Libya Shield Forces (LSF). The NTC initially established a three-member SSC in October 2011 to assert a degree of control over the armed groups operating in Tripoli. When one of the three members, NTC Misrata representative Fawzi Abd al-Al, became interior minister, he established a reconfigured SSC within the Ministry, bringing thousands of battalion members onto its payroll through local SSC branches. The minister's decision of 28 December 2011 gave the SSC not only immediate law and order responsibilities, but also authority to investigate elements of the former government and other intelligence functions.

In practice, the ministry—even the SSC's central headquarters—had only limited authority over local SSC branches, and while some SSC members were disciplined in carrying out security functions, including during the election, others abused their status or simply did not present themselves for work. Relations between the Libyan Police and the SSC were tense, exacerbated by the higher salaries paid to SSC members, and local-level coordination was mostly very poor. Soon the interim government became strongly concerned about the implications of this parallel security force, but addressing its future was left to the successor government.

In late March and April 2012, heavy fighting erupted in the two main southern cities, Sabha and Kufra, and in the west, between the towns of Zuwara, on one side, and Jumail and Riqdalin on the other. Armed Forces Chief Manqush deployed what regular troops he could, but they were clearly inadequate to impose and maintain ceasefires, and indeed revolutionary battalions feeling some responsibility—or community loyalty—towards each situation did not await orders before intervening themselves. The country's major coalitions of revolutionary battalions formalised their preexisting ad hoc deployments into conflict zones into the LSF, presenting this to the prime minister and armed forces chief at a conference in Misrata in April 2012. The interim government agreed to contract the LSF as auxiliaries, nominally under the command of the armed forces chief. However, while the neutrality of the army in local conflicts was generally accepted, the LSF was sometimes accused of taking sides, notably in Kufra, where it was replaced after Tebu accusations of partiality. Besides the LSF, Defence Minister Usama al-Juwaili and the deputy defence minister given responsibility for border security, Sidiq Mabruk al-Ghaithi, separately accorded legitimacy—and funding—to battalions not under the command of the armed forces chief. The problem of how to deal with the remaining armed groups resisting state authority—especially those occupying public property in Tripoli—remained unresolved.

While Libyans struggled with the legacy of the conflict for its security sector, Libya's neighbours and the wider international community were alarmed by the threats from unsecured arms and ammunition, and their actual and potential travel across unsecured borders.

The destruction of Qadhafi's declared chemical weapons and materials, supervised by the Organisation for the Prohibition of Chemical Weapons (OPCW) had been suspended in February 2011. After Qadhafi's defeat, revolutionary battalions allied to the NTC had controlled the relevant sites, as well as previously undeclared additional sites which came to light: the interim government cooperated fully with the OPCW in making further declarations, ensuring the security of stocks, and resuming inspections and destruction. The International Atomic Energy Authority (IAEA) was similarly satisfied as to the security of nuclear material—6,400 barrels of 'yellowcake' stored for peaceful uses—and the interim government's intention to sell it to a foreign bidder.

The fate of Libya's stockpile of shoulder-fired anti-aircraft missiles, known as MANPADS (Man-Portable Air Defence Systems) was less clear. It was uncertain how many had survived NATO operations and were serviceable, and whether they had already been looted and transferred out of Libya, or remained to be brought under proper control inside the country. Other heavy and light weapons, munitions and mines, initially unsecured or in the hands of revolutionary battalions or other armed groups, carried the threat of regional proliferation. Meanwhile, newly laid mines—mostly by Qadhafi's forces along shifting frontlines—and large quantities of unexploded ordnance, much of it in residential areas, posed great hazards to the local population.

Under Qadhafi, controls over trafficking of goods and persons across Libya's land borders of some 4,348km had been limited, capricious and often corrupt, but not entirely ineffective. The conflict saw the wholesale replacement of state authority by local armed groups and ad hoc authorities, especially in the south. This eliminated what controls had existed and created new competition and conflict over trafficking opportunities.[6] Readily available arms and ammunition brought new possibilities for lucrative smuggling. The NTC's plans for border security, drawn up with foreign military advisers as the conflict was ending, were never harmonised into a single plan and remained on paper pending the formation of the interim government and beyond. Meanwhile the government became increasingly concerned by an influx of irregular migrants detained in conditions they recognised as wholly unsatisfactory.

The UN's involvement with the threat of mines and unexploded ordnance, and weapons proliferation, began very soon after the beginning of the uprising, when the UN Mine Action Service commenced efforts behind the frontlines in eastern Libya. With increased access across the country after the conflict's end, UNSMIL facilitated information exchange and coordination regarding chemical weapons and nuclear material stockpiles among Libyan actors, bilateral partners offering assistance and the international agencies OPCW and IAEA, and supported the latter's early country visits. Similar coordination was begun regarding the larger problem of MANPADS, arms and munitions, and regarding border security, pending an assessment of border management to be led by the European Union. In November and December 2011, the Security Council expressed international concern via two resolutions which mandated UNSMIL's to support Libyan efforts to address all proliferation threats. In addition to bilateral discussions and agreements with neighbouring countries, the interim government convened a Regional Ministerial Meeting on Border Security in March 2012, with all Libya's neighbours plus Mali, Mauritania and Morocco, but there was little follow-up beyond its contribution to bilateral discussions. The European Union border management assessment reported in May 2012, but implementation awaited the new government.

The UN quickly deployed police advisers in its initial team in September 2011. They encountered much confusion on the Libyan side caused by poor control and coordination within the Interior Ministry and uncertainty regarding the postings and empowerment of senior officers. The UN team assisted the ministry in coordinating some nations' offers to establish a police advisory or training presence in Libya, or to offer training in their own facilities. Results were mixed, at best. The largest out-of-country training of 'revolutionaries' as police, in Jordan, revealed Libyans' poor preparation and unrealistic expectations, and some were repatriated after unruly behaviour. Meanwhile, the overwhelming priority became election security preparations; here the role of UN police advisers was appreciated, but in reality the Libyan police made only a limited contribution to election security, with a greater role being played by the SSC and revolutionary battalions. Over time, the deficiencies of decision making within the Interior Ministry, its lack of coordination with other ministries and the dangers emerging from the creation of the SSC became increasingly apparent. But only a new government, with a stronger mandate and longer timeframe, could address these issues, which required a coordinated approach to the security sector, including a vision, structure and long-term strategy for the Libyan Police. The international community too would need to offer a strategic and coordinated approach, and not merely isolated training packages.

UNSMIL attempted to promote such coordination and strategic policymaking among Libyan security sector actors by persuading and then assisting the Prime Minister's Office to organise an inter-ministerial retreat in February, but governmental follow-up was extremely weak. Relations among the key Libyan actors were poor, sometimes with public criticism of each other. Qadhafi had wanted no Ministry of Defence, which therefore had to be created anew with no constitutional basis and no experience of civilian oversight of the military. Relations between Defence Minister Juwaili and Armed Forces Chief Manqush were poor, and both were critical of Deputy Defence Minister Ghaithi's responsibility for border security and funding of forces with a separate chain of command. The relationship between the Ministries of Defence and Interior over border security was also ill-defined and tense. Neither the security ministries, nor the Ministry of

Labour, worked happily with the Warriors Affairs Commission, which answered directly to the prime minister and had no defined relationship with relevant ministries to fulfil its intended functions. In the field of mine action, weapons and ammunition control, too, the government failed to settle competing claims among Libyan actors, including a newly-established Libyan Mine Action Centre which had donor support but poor relations with the army.

Such institutional confusion and tensions meant that despite individual initiatives there was no comprehensive government strategy for addressing the future of revolutionary fighters, whether by integration into the security forces or return to civilian life, and this severely restricted the ability of the international community to assist. Any progress was limited and piecemeal. After a period of dealing with bilateral actors, who were offering their own advice and assistance to parts of the problem, Armed Forces Chief Manqush, with the agreement of the minister of defence, asked the UN to coordinate advice from countries he selected to develop a Defence White Paper as a framework for reconstituting the armed forces. UNSMIL's engagement across the security sector enabled the UN to discuss its fragmentation with the Office of the Prime Minister, and to propose a national security coordination committee, as well as further mechanisms for coordination in relation both to mine action, arms and ammunition, and to demobilisation, disarmament and reintegration. But by that point, the government was approaching the July elections and therefore its own end. The UN therefore prepared advice for the incoming government, which would have a stronger mandate to address the security sector and its multiple, fragmented actors, with the legitimacy flowing from an election in which security was voters' foremost concern.

Human rights, transitional justice and rule of law

Libya faced a heavy legacy of human rights violations—arbitrary detention, torture, summary and extrajudicial executions, and unresolved disappearances, already of concern to the UN and documented over the years by nongovernmental organisations. At issue was how quickly human rights would become protected by a reformed justice system, new national institutions and a vigorous civil society, and what UN and other international role should assist and operate alongside that.

Libya's uprising was ignited in February 2011 by a planned demonstration by the relatives of the victims of the worst single massacre by the Qadhafi government, when over 1,200 inmates were killed in Abu Slim prison in June 1996, and by the arrest of their lawyer in Benghazi; it became a revolution in the name of human rights and justice. The 2011 conflict added new war crimes, crimes against humanity and other violations of human rights and international humanitarian law. The UN Human Rights Council had promptly mandated an International Commission of Inquiry to document the latter; its access to Libya was limited while fighting continued, although it issued an interim report in June 2011. UNSMIL facilitated the Commission's post-conflict investigative visits for its final March 2012 report, and an assessment of the scope and scale of conflict-related sexual violence by the Office of the Special Representative of the Secretary-General on Sexual Violence in Conflict.

Further terrible evidence soon emerged of the crimes of the Qadhafi government over the decades and during the fighting in Tripoli in late August 2011, when some of its remaining political prisoners were massacred and relatives tried to discover the fate of their loved ones. Several mass graves were discovered, while survivors emerged to testify to years of detention, torture and mistreatment. Although many of the worst crimes during the conflict were committed by Qadhafi's loyalists, it became clear that the revolutionaries too had committed serious abuses, especially during the final fighting in Sirt, culminating in the deaths after capture of Qadhafi and his son Mu'tasim.

The most urgent demand was determining the fate of the missing, as relatives sought the exhumation of remains long before proper arrangements for identification were possible. The NTC established a National Commission for the Search for and Identification of Missing Persons, and the interim government later subsumed its work into a new Ministry for the Affairs of Families of Martyrs and Missing Persons. UNSMIL sought to mobilise international expertise to advise on what would inevitably be the task of many years.

There was strong public demand for bringing to justice the worst perpetrators of past abuses, and insistence that this occur in Libya, reflected in almost universal opposition to conceding to possible decisions of the International Criminal Court (ICC) that Saif al-Islam al-Qadhafi or Abdullah al-Sanusi, once captured, should be handed over to it. A strong basis for these objections was that the ICC's jurisdiction extended only to international crimes during the conflict, and not to the many charges which might emerge from Libyan investigations into the entire period of Qadhafi's rule, which in the case of Sanusi would likely include the Abu Slim massacre itself and other human rights crimes.

The NTC had adopted the language of 'transitional justice' and was in a hurry to enact a transitional justice law, but had little appetite for debate about how to best combine national reconciliation with the need for truth and justice. Despite the NTC drafters' willingness to receive UN advice on international best practice, the advice given was little reflected in the law made public by the NTC in February 2012. This law established a Fact-finding and Reconciliation Commission to investigate human rights violations since Qadhafi's 1969 coup and compensate victims; the NTC appointed senior Libyan judges to the body, but its further composition and method of work were still being considered when the NTC and the interim government left office. The long time period and the scope and scale of human rights violations committed would make the task of truth-seeking extremely daunting. The UN promoted civil society discussions and access to international experience, and sought to reopen debate among members of the GNC, when an improved draft reflecting UN comments would be considered.

Meanwhile, the present as well as the past required attention to human rights and justice. Qadhafi had released most criminal prisoners, and those political prisoners who survived were liberated with his defeat. The victorious revolutionary battalions took into custody the last of his fighters and other alleged loyalists, making little distinction between merely having fought for the government and direct participation in violations of human rights or humanitarian law. Among those detained, amid exaggerated accusations of being 'mercenaries', were many sub-Saharan Africans, some of them legal or illegal migrant workers rounded up after fighting ceased. Some of the prisoners were brutalised when first detained, and UNSMIL's visits and reports of nongovernmental organisations made it increasingly clear that torture and ill-treatment, sometimes resulting in deaths in custody, were continuing, particularly where detainees were interrogated to extract confessions or information about other alleged perpetrators.

The interim government committed itself to transferring detainees out of the hands of revolutionary battalions into state custody. It faced acute shortages, of physical facilities—many prisons had been destroyed—and of judicial police, who managed prisons. Some battalions did their best to provide decent conditions and treatment, seeing themselves as fulfilling a responsibility which they wanted the state to assume as soon as possible. Some suspected that those they regarded as guilty would if handed over be released, or were continuing efforts to track down more of those they held responsible for atrocities. Some Misratan revolutionaries, in particular, persisted in interrogating under torture detainees from Tawergha, a dark-skinned community south of Misrata from where Qadhafi's 32 Brigade had launched its offensive against that city, whom the Misratans accused of committing rape and other atrocities. In August 2011, Tawergha was emptied and razed by Misratan battalions, but suspects continued to be hunted across Libya and abducted outside the law. In Tripoli, too, alleged fighters and government loyalists were sometimes newly seized and held in secret detention centres, and reports of torture came also from battalion-run centres in Zawiya and Zintan.

The UN's efforts to mitigate this situation were threefold. First, it tried to mobilise international support to overcome bottlenecks the state faced in transferring prisoners to its own custody, by accelerating the training of additional judicial police. Second, it contributed international expertise to develop state prosecutors' capacity to screen detainees. Third, with the evidence of UNSMIL's visits to places of detention, it pressed the authorities to carry out their own inspections and investigate custodial deaths and torture, even while the state lacked the immediate capacity to take all prisoners into its own custody. Our strong direct representations to the highest levels of the interim government were supported by public statements, including briefings to the Security Council, by myself and the high commissioner for human rights. The lack of action by the government was highly disappointing. It was international and local pressure, as members of local councils became concerned for their communities' reputation, and some emerging human rights nongovernmental organisations began monitoring detention and speaking out, which led to some mitigation of treatment and a handful of releases.

All these challenges required a functioning judicial system, not just as a matter of principle, but as a very practical necessity for resolving conflicts, which persisted or flared up in different parts of the country, creating conditions for new human rights violations. Thus, in Bani Walid, communities refused to surrender accused persons to their perceived enemies rather than to state detention and impartial justice. However, the judicial system under the former government was politicised, corrupt, inefficient, and poorly trained. It lacked independence, and parallel institutions and contradictory legislative and regulatory frameworks prevailed. But many judges and lawyers had played leading roles in the NTC and the revolution, and their commitment to judicial reform was strong. The NTC proclaimed the independence of the judiciary in its Constitutional Declaration, and legislated early to distance the judiciary from the executive. But the courts only slowly became functional again as staff returned to work, and insecurity remained a constraint; prosecutors and judges faced threats and intimidation from revolutionaries.

In May 2012, the President of the Supreme Judicial Council established a national committee to report on judicial reform, which the UN began advising, together with the Ministry of Justice's review of the Penal Code. UNSMIL also advised the Office of the Prosecutor-General, through several workshops and expert missions, on formulating and communicating a strategy for investigating and prosecuting past crimes focused on the most senior former government members and on serious crimes. This would promote releasing persons against whom there was no evidence or who were not accused of serious crimes, and fair trials for those who ought to be prosecuted.

There was little immediate prospect that justice would extend to human rights violations by revolutionaries themselves. The NTC passed laws containing provisions for amnesty, but their language was open to different interpretations, as it depended on whether acts were deemed 'to promote or protect the revolution'. In any event, prosecution or even effective investigation remained highly unlikely.

But there were prospects elsewhere of translating the revulsion against Qadhafi's crimes into a culture of human rights protection. Training in human rights monitoring was among UN's best work with new civil society organisations. The NTC established a National Council for Civil Liberties and Human Rights, which joined with Libyan lawyers and others in condemning the NTC's April 2012 law 'Criminalising the Glorification of the Dictator' as violating freedom of expression. The Supreme Court struck down the law, finding it incompatible with the human rights guarantees of the Constitutional Declaration—as the UN had said it was with international standards. Ministers in the interim government no longer denied or justified ongoing violations, and generally authorised access to places of detention, although their personal human rights orientation did not result in effective government action. Some of the successful GNC candidates had strong records as human rights defenders.

Lustration is a significant aspect of transitional justice, where officials of a government with a record of human rights violations may not be individually criminally liable, but may be excluded from public office. In Libya, controversy raged around what acts or association with the previous government should justify exclusion. The NTC established a High Commission on Integrity and Patriotism to apply criteria that it specified, with decisions subject to judicial appeal, which disqualified some election candidates, and later some of those elected. However, both the appropriate criteria and due process in their application remained matters for much future debate, to which the UN offered international human rights standards and experience of vetting or lustration in transitional contexts elsewhere.

Libya had become a country where many had a strong sense of human rights values, accountability and transparency, precisely because its citizens had for so long been denied them, but where these remained in tension with instincts for revenge. The UN was publicly and privately critical of ongoing violations while supporting the development of capacities to end them. The protection of human rights in Libya would depend on the commitment of Libyans themselves to fulfil the promise of their revolution to build a new state in which the rule of law was respected, and this remained a priority task for the newly elected GNC and its government.

The transition

A special representative of the secretary-general and a political mission, whatever the specifics of its mandate, represent the UN in trying to help to keep an overall post-conflict transition, with all its inevitable difficulties, on track. Undoubtedly, the UN's greatest contribution in the first year was to the credibility of the election, which was not only a matter of confidence in the technical assistance of the UN's electoral support team, but also of UNSMIL's constant interaction with key Libyan political actors and civil society. This required a fine balance between supporting the overall acceptability of the electoral process, without intervening and making the UN responsible for highly contested decisions about the electoral system and constituency allocation. In a context where there was widespread, but unjustified, public scepticism about the NTC's commitment to holding the election and transferring power, and about the integrity of the process, the UN could offer significant reassurance through the media and a myriad of inter-actions with civil society and political actors. Libyans often referred to the UN involvement in the election as a guarantee of its integrity—sometimes citing the UN's role in the emergence of independent Libya in 1949–51.

The UN did not attempt to intervene at key moments of internal dis-array, most notably an attempt within the NTC in April 2012 to replace Prime Minister Kib, believing that these decisions were best left to Libyans to work through. However, the UN did urge eastern feder-alist elements not to pursue plans for parallel governance and military structures, and to make their case within the constitutional and politi-cal process without presenting unrealistic ultimatums to the NTC, and to desist from violence to obstruct the elections.

Although UNSMIL's political officers were based in Tripoli and Benghazi, with only periodic visits to the south and elsewhere, the UN's political and humanitarian teams made some contribution to assuaging local conflicts. Intense communication, often by telephone, between UNSMIL and all conflict parties, for example in Kufra, did something to cool passions and discourage further violence, and the prompt dispatch of humanitarian teams was consistently welcomed, even when there was little need for relief beyond the capacity of Libyan entities. It was, however, difficult to contribute to resolving the under-lying roots of local conflicts. Libya showed considerable capacity for mobilising short-term mediation teams, through local notables and tribal leaderships, and there was also state engagement through NTC members and designees of the interim government. However, once the immediate crisis was calmed, there was rarely sustained attention to underlying causes, which required government action. UNSMIL engaged heavily in the most threatening local contexts, particularly in Bani Walid, and in the consequences of past local conflict and displacement, particularly the need for mediation between Tawergha and Misrata, but formal third party mediation was never invited by the relevant authorities, even when conflict parties would have welcomed it.

Reconciliation, despite NTC and government commitment, faced major hurdles from communities opposed during the revolution, and regarding individuals associated with the Qadhafi government. The UN emphasised that public discussion, well-communicated policies, and action on transitional justice were essential, but as noted, the authorities made little progress. The UN engaged with communities that saw themselves as discriminated against by the new authorities, such as Sirt and Bani Walid, although lack of delivery by central government and inadequate resources available to local government were nationwide deficiencies. At the time of transition to the GNC and new government, the main challenges of reconciliation still lay ahead.

While making clear its respect for national ownership, UNSMIL publicly expressed its responsibility to promote UN norms and values. As well as the overall commitment to human rights standards, this included actively promoting the political and other participation of women. The UN engaged with civil society organisations, including womens' associations, who along with young people of both genders felt that their post-conflict opportunities did not reflect their contribution to the revolution. The Amazigh, Tebu and Tuareg minorities were assured of the UN's commitment to minority and indigenous peoples' rights, and were promised that these would be reflected in the UN position in the forthcoming constitutional debate.

Could the UN have done more to assist the NTC and the interim government during the first year of Libya's transition? If the greatest achievement of the period was the success of the GNC election, the greatest failure was the lack of progress in the security sector. But even if the UN had better anticipated the extent of its role and had more assertively offered advice and assistance, it is doubtful that it could have overcome the limitations to what could be achieved before a stronger government with a basis of democratic legitimacy was in place, and without real dialogue between government and leaders of revolutionary battalions. Nor is it likely that pressing for a more direct UN mediation role would have enabled it to contribute better to assuaging local conflicts and promoting reconciliation.

The most serious regional consequence of the collapse of the Qadhafi government was the added impetus that the return of hardened Tuareg fighters and the availability of Libyan weaponry gave to the collapse of the Malian state. Analyses which attribute the crisis of northern Mali to the Libyan revolution too often ignore the decades of Tuareg disaffection and rebellion, as well as the penetration of Islamic extremism, drug-trafficking and government inaction or complicity, which preceded events in Libya. But undeniably, the failure to secure Qadhafi's extraordinary stockpiles of arms and ammunition, or to more urgently address Libya's border security, severely exacerbated the crisis in Mali, and posed wider regional threats. These were far beyond UNSMIL's limited mandate and capacity, and should have received a higher and earlier level of attention and commitment by the intervening member states.

The new Libya faces many challenges beyond the three central areas of UNSMIL's work. Among them are the overall development of the national and local institutions of a modern state and decentralisation of its services, while changing the outlook of an old and bloated bureaucracy; the diversification of the economy and the creation of employment opportunities, especially for the youth, while fighting corruption in the management of the nation's wealth; and the proper regulation of migrant labour in a manner advantageous to Libya and its neighbours, while respecting migrants' human rights. The UN began to contribute, through its agencies, to developing capacity in central public administration, including government coordination of international assistance, and in key sectors, such as health and education—tasks that will extend far beyond the term of the new government. It also offered advice on the decentralisation of services that did not need to await the constitutional debate and could be speedily implemented to mitigate the sense of overcentralisation, which was strongest in the east and south but shared by western towns.

Positive Libyan perceptions of the UN's roles in 1949–51 and in 2011 presented probably the most welcoming context for UN support in the Arab world, notwithstanding security threats faced by the UN and others faced. UNSMIL sought to maintain that welcome by displaying genuine respect for national ownership and a relatively light footprint and low profile compared to post-conflict missions elsewhere. Although the most fundamental lesson of the UN's approach to its post-conflict role in Libya is that the uniqueness of each situation should be reflected in the planning of international missions, this experience may be worth taking into account in other post-conflict contexts. Peace operations are too often discussed as if large peacekeeping missions are the only option in the UN's toolbox. UNSMIL showed again the potential of special political missions deployed by the UN's Department of Political Affairs.[7]

The attack on the US's Benghazi consulate on 11 September 2012, in which US Ambassador Chris Stevens and three colleagues died, intensified pessimism about Libya's future. Libyans themselves were the harshest critics of their public servants, and had years of divisions and mistrust to overcome. Realistic assessments needed to reflect the terrible legacy of the Qadhafi decades, and the ways in which many Libyans remained true to the spirit of the revolution. Libyans stepped up to work for their communities through local councils, often with funding from their own pockets and those of local businessmen. Expatriates had returned to contribute to building a new state as well as to the private sector. A vibrant civil society was looking for new ways to focus the energies applied to humanitarian efforts during the conflict. Women and young people were showing determination to be part of the future as they had been of the revolution itself. Minorities were liberated from the fear that had repressed even the expression of their demands to end discrimination against them.

Inexperience and unrealistic expectations regarding the speed of change meant that this energy sometimes quickly turned to anger, frustration, and threatened violence. Our hope at the end of the transition's first year was that a democratically elected legislature would truly represent long-separated communities and provide the basis for a government with the legitimacy and authority to tackle, in particular, the issue of security and integration of the revolutionaries. The election was a necessary precondition for this hardest of challenges, but it would also require unity of purpose within a new government, support from the GNC, and further mobilisation of civil society acting on behalf of the peaceful majority of Libya's people. Would these be achievable in the period ahead?

7

CONFRONTING QADHAFI'S LEGACY

TRANSITIONAL JUSTICE IN LIBYA

Marieke Wierda[1]

Introduction

Immediately following the 17 February Revolution, the political climate for transitional justice was promising. Libyans had a historic opportunity to create a new society. The struggle for freedom from oppression lay at the heart of Libya's 17 February Revolution.[2] The rebels' decisive victory permitted the National Transitional Council (NTC) to make decisions unencumbered by compromises with the previous government, as is often the case in other transitions, and offered an opportunity to embrace its values in a new constitution. Reconciliation and legacy issues were among the NTC's priorities and the first minister of justice, Muhammad al-Alaqi, drafted a transitional justice law before Libya's liberation day on 23 October 2011.[3] However, some two years later, its prospects remained largely unrealised, and matters of transitional justice became trapped in acts of score-settling and revenge.

The term 'transitional justice' 'comprises the full range of processes and mechanisms associated with a society's attempts to come to terms with a legacy of large-scale past abuses'.[4] These processes enable societies to repudiate those abuses and achieve reconciliation by ending impunity and ensuring accountability. In the last two decades, transitional justice measures—criminal justice, truth seeking mechanisms, reparations, and institutional reforms—have become essential to peace-building after conflict, figuring prominently in democratic transitions in Latin America and post-apartheid South Africa.[5]

This chapter explores the trajectory of transitional justice in Libya. It begins by examining its impediments, including the length and scope of abuses it would cover, and the justice paradox inherent in liberation movements, which in Libya's case led to a far-reaching law on 'political isolation'. The chapter then lays out the transitional justice approaches being implemented in Libya at time of writing, concluding that transitional justice remains critical as an alternative to vigilante justice or revenge acts against perceived perpetrators, privileging instead support to victims and strengthening Libya's new institutions and culture of human rights. Where appropriate, the chapter discusses the role of the international community, particularly the United Nations Support Mission in Libya (UNSMIL) and the International Criminal Court (ICC), in promoting transitional justice in Libya.[6]

Crimes, past and present

a. Qadhafi's legacy

By most definitions of international law as well as under Libya's criminal code,[7] Mu'ammar al-Qadhafi's crimes against his own people were systematic and severe. Over four decades, the internal state security infrastructure (*al-Amn al-Dakhili*) menaced the population, creating a climate of fear, and acted with impunity.[8] The state machinery itself perpetrated alleged crimes and human rights violations such as summary executions, widespread disappearances and torture,[9] through the use of political courts and 'black hole' prisons for political opponents including Abu Slim and Ain Zara; suppression of cultural rights; and discriminatory policies against minorities. In addition, Qadhafi also divested people from their private property and chronically underinvested in social services such as health and education. This legacy fuelled revenge acts at the individual and communal levels following Qadhafi's fall.

The most significant atrocity of the Qadhafi era was the 1996 mass killing at Abu Slim prison. Abu Slim housed political prisoners, usually arrested without warrants and held incommunicado and in deplorable conditions for years. Torture was endemic. Detainees were allowed limited access to their families, denied medical treatment and deprived of any recreational activities or outdoor space for long periods of time. On 28 June 1996, prisoners rioted, calling for better conditions or for their cases to be processed. After negotiations with senior government officials—allegedly including intelligence chief and Qadhafi's brother-in-law Abdullah al-Sanusi—soldiers arrived, herding the prisoners into courtyards. They then threw grenades at the prisoners, shooting those attempting to flee. Within two days, over 1,200 prisoners were dead.

Family members were not informed of the deaths until 2008, when a Benghazi court ruled that authorities must reveal the whereabouts of thirty-three individuals believed to have died in Abu Slim.[10] Some families chose to receive compensation for the deaths, but others refused and subsequently regularly protested in Benghazi. The protest sparking the revolution was led by Abu Slim victims' families after two prominent members of the Organising Committee of Families of Victims of Abu Slim were arrested.

Qadhafi altered the country's laws to prosecute political opponents. Law No. 71/1972 systematically prohibited political organisation and dissent, and any parties, associations or activities based on ideology contrary to the principles of the Revolution of 1 September 1969, with regular and visible enforcement of the death penalty.[11] Many Libyans remember publicly broadcasted hangings at the Tripoli campus of al-Fath University and the main square in Benghazi on 7 April 1977 of students who had demonstrated against the government one year earlier.

The revolution itself occasioned a new wave of legal violations by Qadhafi's forces. Qadhafi's response to the demonstrations in February 2011 was characteristically harsh, vowing on 23 February 'to cleanse Libya inch by inch, house by house, home by home, alley by alley, one by one until the country is cleansed from filth and impurity.'[12] Although there was no mass killing of civilians nor use of aircraft or anti-aircraft guns, as was reported by some news agencies at the time, government forces did fire live ammunition at protestors without warning.[13] Security brigades used weapons prohibited by certain international treaties such as landmines and cluster munitions,[14] and indiscriminately attacked civilians in Zawiya, Nalut, Zintan and Yefren using unguided Grad rockets and artillery. The government also arrested hundreds in Tripoli, Misrata and the Nafusa Mountains.[15]

Detainees were held in overcrowded shipping containers and warehouses, with poor ventilation, inadequate hygiene facilities and with insufficient food and water provision. Torture was widespread at detention facilities in Khums, Qal'a and Yarmuk.[16]

Several extrajudicial executions also occurred. At the Yarmuk detention centre at Qal'at al-Furjan in Tripoli, over 100 detainees were allegedly executed in their cell by guards from the 32 Brigade[17] on 23 August 2011. The Commission of Inquiry and other human rights groups documented several additional incidents of extrajudicial executions by security brigades during the conflict, including instances of captured revolutionary fighters being shot with their hands bound behind their backs.[18]

Some allegations remain shrouded in mystery for lack of evidence, such as activists' allegations that Tawerghan fighters raped thousands of Misratan women during their occupation of Misrata in March and April 2011.[19] The ICC prosecutor seized on this allegation, publicly declaring in June 2011 that he believed Qadhafi was using rape as a weapon of war and suggesting there were 'hundreds of victims',[20] though at the time of writing no evidence of such a campaign had emerged. The Commission of Inquiry likewise said that it received 'no substantiated information indicating that individual Tawergha or organised groups of Tawergha men raped women in Misrata or elsewhere'.[21] A report on conflict-related sexual violence presented to the Security Council in January 2012 was similarly inconclusive, but found some cases of rape against both men and women during the conflict.[22]

b. The challenges of liberation

Libyan revolutionaries (*thuwwar*), despite accruing international political recognition, did not emerge blameless from the fighting. During the revolution, revolutionary battalions on occasion meted out retributive justice, including most famously killing Qadhafi, his son Mu'tasim and Defence Minister, Abu Bakr Yunis Jabir. A Human Rights Watch report attributed Qadhafi's death to an unclear combination of shrapnel wounds, beatings, and gunshots.[23] International organisations condemned his killing as a human rights violation, but in Libya it satisfied a vague sense of popular 'justice'. Few argued that he should have been kept alive to face trial.

Arbitrary arrests by revolutionary battalions occurred in large numbers after Tripoli came under their control. Hundreds of perceived loyalists, including former security sector and government employees, were rounded up. Battalions arrested over 8,000 persons throughout Libya and detained them in prisons and informal detention centres throughout the country, releasing only a small number. Many were kept in poor conditions, mistreated, and denied access to medical facilities and to judicial authorities.

More substantial vengeance was meted out against the Tawerghans and other communities, particularly in the Nafusa Mountains,[24] who allegedly fought for Qadhafi. Misratan battalions attacked Tawergha on 14 August 2011 after Grad rockets were shot towards Misrata from there. At that time most residents had fled,[25] and months after their departure looting and systematic demolition of housing continued. Graffiti on the remaining walls read 'Tawergha was'. Tawerghans relocated to internally displaced persons (IDP) camps and host families in Benghazi, Tripoli, Sirt, Zlitan, Jufra and Khums, but were still subject to arrests by Misratans at camps, private residences and checkpoints.[26] While Tawerghan community leaders admitted there were persons in their community who committed atrocities and ought to be tried, and publicly apologised to Misrata's local council, they also maintained that they were subjected to collective punishment, and continued advocating a return to their city.

Pro-revolutionary fighters also committed revenge killings of Qadhafi's Revolutionary Committees, Revolutionary Guards and the Internal Security Agency,[27] and used unguided rockets, artillery and rocket-propelled grenades in their onslaught on Sirt, Qadhafi's final hiding place. Many civilian casualties were reported in this battle.[28] At the Mahari Hotel in Sirt, on 20 or 21 October 2011, an estimated sixty-five to seventy-eight bodies were discovered, some with their hands bound, with civilian residents mixed in among members of Qadhafi's close protection unit.[29]

Finally, migrant workers were mistreated by both sides in the conflict, including having their houses searched arbitrarily, and being beaten and subjected to cruel treatment.[30] This behaviour, fuelled by discriminatory attitudes towards sub-Saharan Africans, continued after the revolution.[31]

The post-revolution political climate in Libya

Post-revolutionary Libya faced a transitional justice dilemma familiar to many post-conflict countries: it faced considerable public pressure to immediately deliver justice in a potentially large number of past and current cases, while inheriting a justice system weakened by decades of neglect and political interference and unable to deal with such cases in large numbers. Under these pressures Libyan policymakers had little opportunity to reflect on the merits or mechanics of transitional justice.

Libyan justice officials, with UN support, examined comparative experiences, including those of South Africa or former Yugoslavia. However, these experiences were perceived as having limited relevance, since the Libyan conflict was not ethnically, racially or religiously motivated. Regional examples did not carry much weight for different reasons. Iraq's transitional justice processes were judged less salient because of the occupation of Iraq by the US-led coalition, combined with Iraq's intense sectarian violence.[32] Similarly, the Moroccan Commission on Equity and Reconciliation, which took place under the auspices of King Muhammad VI, was not part of a transition and failed to promote criminal accountability. Consequently, some Libyans associated it with impunity.

But while no single case study can be applied universally, the Libyan situation presented certain dilemmas common to transitions. One was the overwhelming number of perpetrators implicated in the crimes committed under Qadhafi's government and on his orders, which were many more than could possibly be tried. Membership of Qadhafi's intricate security web was vast; for instance, Qadhafi's Revolutionary Committees, used to identify and persecute political opponents, numbered between 60,000 and 100,000.[33] The Internal Security Agency monitored political opposition groups and had jurisdiction over political prisons.[34] The Revolutionary Guard, part of the armed forces, was tasked with ensuring loyalty to the government and suppressing any opposition.[35] Security brigades such as the 32 Reinforced Brigade, led by Qadhafi's son Khamis, also played an important role in matters of internal security.[36]

A related problem was that many Libyans who may not have participated directly in acts of oppression benefited financially from the former government. A large number, of over half a million, were exiled to Tunisia, Egypt and other countries following the revolution. Furthermore, several former opposition figures returned to Libya under the reconciliation efforts of Saif al-Islam al-Qadhafi, including many who are prominent in Libyan politics today. The question of who should be punished for which actions (or affiliations) was therefore highly contentious, while mere affiliation often implicated entire families, tribes or regions.

The question of pursuing evenhanded justice for Libya's troubled past was complicated by the decisive victory of rebel forces over Qadhafi—unique in transitional contexts—which spawned a heroic narrative of civilians overthrowing an oppressive regime, which to some extent precluded full accountability of crimes committed by revolutionaries (*thuwwar*) in that process. Consequently revolutionaries resisted questioning their narrative of martyrdom and sacrifice for freedom, and consequently argued that pressure to hold them accountable came from external actors: international NGOs; the United Nations (UN); or the ICC. They accordingly criticised the international community for not sufficiently condemning Qadhafi's crimes while he was in power, notwithstanding human rights organisations' reports from that era, particularly on the Abu Slim massacre.

While this sentiment is understandable after an uprising against a repressive government, other post-conflict transitions demonstrate that a one-sided approach to accountability leads over time to impunity and a deterioration in fundamental human rights, which creates new grievances. In post-revolutionary Libya, this potential was illustrated in the passage of the Political and Administrative Isolation Law.

a. Political isolation instead of transitional justice?

In the climate described above, some Libyan political actors gave high political priority to excluding or 'isolating' those associated with the former government from power.

Excluding persons from public office is characteristic of post-dictatorship transitions and can help encourage institutional reform. Accordingly, the United Nations defined a vetting process as 'assessing integrity to determine suitability for public employment',[37] 'usually entail[ing] a formal process for the identification and removal of individuals responsible for abuses, especially from police, prison service, the army and the judiciary'.[38] The concept of 'integrity' used here is predicated on an individual's past conduct, such as involvement in crimes or corruption, in contrast to political purges, which are generally based on a person's affiliation. By this definition, the 'Debaathification' policy in Iraq was a purge, based on an individual's membership of

Saddam Hussain's Ba'th Party. Debaathification is blamed for under-mining stability and rule of law in post-war Iraq and fomenting an insurgency.

Libya's version of this process, domestically called 'political isola-tion' (*al-azl al-siyasi*), evolved over 2012 and 2013. With the lessons of Debaathification in mind, during the 2011 revolution the NTC pro-posed a relatively modest process that would exclude only those with, in Chairman Mustafa Abd al-Jalil's formulation, 'blood on their hands.' But in summer 2012, the NTC set up a High Commission on Integrity and Patriotism (Integrity Commission). Its purview included the upcoming directly-elected transitional legislature, the General National Congress (GNC), as well as government officials, diplomats and members of other national institutions, including the security sec-tor but not the judiciary. The Commission excluded all the Tuareg members elected to the GNC as well as the two representatives from Bani Walid. Increasingly, the process became more about current polit-ical power struggles than addressing the past.

Political pressure to pass a wider law remained. In December 2012, the GNC formed a committee to discuss proposals to enshrine the Integrity Commission's mandate in a 'political isolation' law that would mandate a still wider exclusion. The revolutionaries (*thuwwar*) exerted considerable pressure on GNC members in the lead-up to the vote, including an occupation of the Ministries of Foreign Affairs and Justice in May 2013.

It became increasingly difficult to publicly oppose the bill, which was fuelled by strongly voiced public sentiment that Qadhafi-era offi-cials ought to be ousted, backed by armed actors clearly willing to use force to ensure its passage. Accordingly key political blocs in the GNC all officially supported the bill, including the Salafist-oriented 'Loyalty to the Martyrs' bloc, parts of the Muslim Brotherhood-affiliated Justice and Construction Party, the National Front party of President Muhammad Mugharyif and the National Forces Coalition of Mahmud Jibril, even though the latter had a lot to lose through the bill. Privately, the bill was opposed by leading figures but few dared to voice their opposition publicly. Compromises to the bill were attempted, but rejected right up until the last minute. These included exceptions for those who joined the revolution early, which affected the National Forces Coalition. Conversely, a clause excluding those who had 'rec-onciled' with the former regime, which would have affected the

Muslim Brotherhood and former Libyan Islamic Fighting Group, was dropped from the final version.

On 5 May 2013, the GNC adopted the law by an overwhelming majority, with extensive implications for Libya's future political landscape. Article 1 contained substantial criteria specifying positions held or behaviour occurring from 1 September 1969 to 23 October 2011 that were considered grounds for exclusion. Reflecting the 'bottom-up' rule of the Qadhafi regime, the positions affected include not only national, ministerial, military, and security ambassadorial positions, but local level mayors, college deans and their deputies, student union leaders, and those who held leading positions in institutions related to the Qadhafi family or its businesses. Behaviours constituting grounds for exclusion were 'opposing the revolution'; theft of property or money; cooperation with security apparatuses in acts such as killing, imprisonment or torture; or glorifying the former regime leader or his regime. Though the full remit of the law would depend on its implementation, in principle those meeting its criteria would be barred for ten years from holding legislative, judicial or executive posts; directorships of ministerial departments; oversight of constituent bodies; security, military or diplomatic posts; and leadership positions in political bodies, higher education and media institutions. The law was criticised by the United Nations as disproportionate and vague, and the UN warned it could violate the civil and political rights of many citizens.

The Integrity Commission—renamed the High Commission for the Application of the Criteria for Public Positions—was mandated to implement this law starting in June 2013. Under advice from the United Nations, it amended its procedures to allow those under scrutiny to present evidence before the committee to defend themselves, and to retain the right to appeal the Commission's decision to local administrative courts and the Supreme Court.

Some government institutions, however, resisted the law. The judiciary, for example, went on strike in early June 2013 to protest being vetted against Article 1 by the Supreme Judicial Council, which it feared would lead to large numbers being removed. The Supreme Judicial Council then proposed an amendment to the law to limit its potential application to the judiciary. Similarly, the law was resisted by the armed forces, which established its own Integrity Commission.

In many respects the law was highly flawed. Some provisions unduly infringed international human rights, such as the right to nondiscrimination and to participation in public affairs. While purporting to deal with the past, it risked constituting a comprehensive political purge used mostly to exclude current political rivals. It risked negatively impacting national reconciliation efforts and creating a new class of disaffected people. It also risked depleting Libya's institutions of valuable human resources precisely at a time when institution-building presented significant challenges. In some respects, the law presented the symbolic break with the past that many Libyans said they wanted. But public awareness of the law's long-term implications was often weak and drowned in details very much shaped by power struggles between political factions rather than transitional justice considerations. It remains to be seen whether a more balanced view towards excluding those associated with the former regime will prevail.

b. Reconciliation in the Libyan context

During the political isolation debates, many Libyans argued that reconciliation—and the trust in government justice institutions it necessitated—required those they held responsible for past crimes to be brought to justice first. However, practical constraints on the capacity of the judiciary limited criminal prosecution to only egregious offenders.

Fortuitously, Libya possessed cultural and religious traditions for intercommunal or tribal reconciliation, incorporating principles of Islamic *shari'a* law such as compensation (*diyya*), whereby the family of the victim of a serious crime such as murder agrees to accept compensation instead of insisting on the death penalty against the perpetrator. Broader community conflict resolution (*musalaha*) mechanisms also existed. The prime minister and NTC, as well as GNC, often dispatched 'reconciliation committees' to mediate local conflicts that erupted during the transition across Libya: between Tebu and Zway in Kufra; Tabu, Tuareg and Arabs in Sabha, Murzuq and Ghadames; Zawiya and the Warshafana tribe on the western coast; Mashashiya and Zintan in the Nafusa Mountains; and in Bani Walid.[39] On occasion, these delegations of *hukama'* (wise men or persons of social standing) negotiated ceasefires between warring factions. In other situations, such as in Bani Walid, they were less successful. However, reconciliation committees were usually restricted to mediation and negotiating ceasefires rather than addressing root causes of conflict.

The reconciliation committees promoted 'national reconciliation' and national unity (*al-wahda al-wataniyya*), topics on which several large conferences were held, convening hundreds of delegates from across Libya. The discussions employed an Islamic discourse, particularly a December 2011 conference attended by the influential cleric Shaikh Yusuf al-Qaradawi, Libyan Grand Mufti Sadiq al-Gharyani, and Rashid Al-Ghannushi, the head of Tunisia's Ennahda Party. Unfortunately, many of these events became rallies in favour of the revolution. They did not present a roadmap for national reconciliation that involved concrete steps to discuss, confront or resolve outstanding grievances between communities.

Without such a roadmap, many revolutionaries (*thuwwar*) felt that 'reconciliation' was a code word for compromise towards the former regime. They and others were concerned about continuing corruption and nepotism within the bureaucracy, and wanted to 'cleanse' its ranks from the 'remnants' of the old regime (*azlam al-nizam al-sabiq*). Dissatisfaction with the NTC's and GNC's record on tackling corruption fed that demand for more reform. While some clerics, judges and politicians promoted reconciliation with Qadhafi's supporters in exile, the majority did not favour reconciliation without accountability, and did not see transitional justice mechanisms as being the pathway to reconciliation.

c. Illegal detentions

With the collapse of the police and armed forces after the revolution, revolutionary battalions undertook law enforcement roles themselves, and this was legitimised under NTC Law 38. Many battalions were also registered under the structures of the Supreme Security Committee, a temporary law enforcement body under the Interior Ministry in the absence of an effectively functioning police, and to some extent the judicial police (Libya's correction service). From the start, revolutionary battalions arrested and interrogated detainees related to the 2011 conflict.

As of writing, around 8,000 conflict-related detainees remain in custody in Libya.[40] Some battalions continued operating their own detention facilities, which reflected their inherent lack of faith in the justice system and central government, but also compounded its weakness. Others moved nominally under the judicial police, military police or Interior Ministry. Torture prevailed in a number of battalion-controlled and Supreme Security Committee facilities, particularly in Misrata, Zawiya, Zlitan, and Tripoli. By October 2013, UNSMIL had uncovered twenty-seven cases of deaths in custody under torture in total, most of which had occurred in the preceding twelve months.[41]

Redressing those arbitrary detentions and any accompanying abuses, including torture and deaths in custody, became the main human rights priority for Libya's Ministry of Justice and international and local human rights organisations. Justice Minister Salah Marghani, a former human rights activist who assumed his position in October 2012, launched a plan to bring all facilities currently controlled by revolutionaries under the control of the Ministry of Justice, starting with Misrata; and training sufficient numbers of judicial police to guard the prisons, as numbers were previously insufficient. Conditions of detention generally improved when facilities were taken over by the regular judicial police, which by mid-2013 controlled about 50 per cent, or 4,000, of the conflict-related detainees. The remaining 4,000 stayed in the custody of the Military Police, Supreme Security Committee or outside state custody. However, progress was slow. Resolving the issue of detentions required a more fundamental acceptance of the authority of the state over criminal justice issues by the *thuwwar* and a commitment to disarm accordingly. These steps still remain illusive, while some detainees remained valuable political bargaining chips for regional interests, particularly high-level detainees such as Saif al-Islam al-Qadhafi.

Setting the stage for transitional justice

The influence of the *thuwwar* meant that Libyan authorities struggled to implement transitional justice alongside other priorities, such as conducting elections and dealing with security challenges. Nevertheless, the NTC and GNC were able to partially implement some mechanisms, commencing trials for senior former regime figures, engaging the ICC, introducing an amnesty law for revolutionaries, revising the transitional justice law; introducing haphazard reparations (though with no property restitution), and establishing a ministry dealing with missing persons.

a. Trials of former senior regime members

Libya had a unique opportunity to try former regime members, despite its weak justice system. The Qadhafi regime operated two parallel legal systems: Revolutionary Courts for political opponents[42] and an ordinary criminal justice system for nonpolitical crimes. This division to some extent insulated the criminal justice system from political interference. Nevertheless, the government's arbitrary laws and decrees interfered with the legal order. Additionally, judges, prosecutors, public defenders and members of both legal systems were considered a single corps, resulting in the regular reassignment or moving around of judges as a means of controlling dissent.

After Qadhafi's fall, the 3 August Constitutional Declaration provided that only Libyan laws that were consistent with itself should be applied.[43] It prioritised the establishment of a new Supreme Judicial Council, composed of judges, and chaired by the president of the Supreme Court, to regulate administrative matters related to the judiciary and to bolster its independence. This Council later formed a committee to make recommendations on crucial judicial reforms, including restructuring the judiciary and courts, and to revise Libya's Criminal Code to align it with international norms.

Though judges and public prosecutors returned to work after the revolution, poor security impeded their work. They faced consistent threats and intimidation: even the first general prosecutor was assassinated after he left office. Consequently judges were reluctant to hold regular court sessions in most parts of the country and particularly the east, except in family and civil law cases.

Libya's main challenge, as in most transitional contexts, was the impossibility of trying everyone detained or allegedly involved in past crimes, as this would involve thousands of trials for which the Ministry of Justice had neither the personnel nor the capacity. It could not manage expectations: revolutionary battalions reacted negatively when prosecutors tried to release detainees, while the public expected, unrealistically, that all 'criminals' would be tried. But bringing trials to international standards required significant time and resources. To put the dilemma in perspective, the Bosnian War Crimes Chamber—a domestic court with international assistance considered quite successful—had, since its creation in 2004, convicted only around 110 individuals, in around eighty trials, by 2012.[44]

Libya's legal code also posed challenges. Its criminal code did not include international crimes, nor certain complex forms of criminal responsibility that would help to prove responsibility of senior leaders. While torture was defined as a crime in the Libyan penal code and in a

165

post-revolution law criminalising torture, there had been few investigations into its incidences.[45] There was also little public support in Libya for the establishment of a special court or tribunal to this end, which Libyans associated with the revolutionary courts of the Qadhafi era.

Trials of leading former regime figures were therefore brought before the ordinary courts but progressed slowly. Several senior leaders were charged in 2012, and in September 2013, the general prosecutor opened joint proceedings against over thirty senior regime figures for crimes committed during the revolution in 2011. Those charged included Saif al-Islam; his recently extradited brother, Sa'adi al-Qadhafi; former head of internal security, Sanusi; former secretary of the General People's Committee (prime minister-equivalent), Umar Baghdadi al-Mahmudi; former chief of external intelligence and Libyan permanent representative to the United Nations, Abu Zaid Dorda; Mansur Daw', Ahmad Ibrahim, Khalid Tantush and others. In these processes Libya did not, as of writing, access the experience or special investigative techniques of prosecutors in other post-conflict environments who faced similar challenges: for example, in selecting which of the many cases to pursue or how to link the architects of crimes to actual abuses.[46] The reason for this may be linked to Libya's reluctance to grant access to international advisers such as the UN due to ICC litigation (see below), or the fact that these investigations are usually confidential in the Libyan legal system.

Looking forward, criminal trials are likely to play an important part in Libya's transition. If victims, as well as revolutionaries, see that the general prosecutor is investigating and prosecuting the most important cases from the Qadhafi era, putting together strong cases to be presented in fair trials, this in itself will create confidence that the legal system is playing its role in the delivery of justice.

b. On a collision course with the ICC?

Libya's own trial efforts were spurred along as a result of the ICC's efforts to exert jurisdiction. The UN Security Council referred the Libyan situation to the ICC on 25 February 2011. Immediately, civil society groups in Benghazi and Misrata worked with the NTC to collect evidence for it. Consequently, on 16 May 2011, the ICC prosecutor requested the issuance of arrest warrants against Qadhafi, Sanusi and Saif al-Islam, for 'crimes against humanity' including persecution and murder allegedly committed from 15 February 2011 until at least 28 February 2011. The ICC's Pre-Trial Chamber issued the arrest warrants on 27 June 2011. Though it is difficult to know whether they affected the ultimate outcome of the conflict, they had an immediate effect on revolutionaries' morale by further legitimising their cause.

After the death of Qadhafi on 20 October 2011, Saif al-Islam and Sanusi remained at large until their capture on 19 November 2011 near Sabha, Libya and 17 March 2012 at Nouakchott airport in Mauritania respectively. The ICC Prosecutor paid visits to Libya in November 2011, a month after Qadhafi's death, to persuade the Libyans to surrender Saif al-Islam to the ICC, but from the inception of the NTC, the Libyan authorities remained adamant that they wished to hold his trial in Libya. On 30 April 2012, Libya filed an admissibility challenge before the ICC, arguing that it had opened an investigation against Saif al-Islam and should be allowed to proceed.

Matters were complicated further when a battalion in Zintan detained four ICC staff members in early June 2012. The Libyan government upheld the Zintanis' accusation that Australian lawyer Melinda Taylor of the ICC's Office of Public Defence Counsel was carrying a recording device and documents that were said to contravene state security, in particular a communication by one of Saif al-Islam's associates, Muhammad Isma'il. It took over a month to secure the release of the four, necessitating a ceremony where the president of the ICC came to Zintan and expressed regret for the events, promising an ICC inquiry into what had happened. But in an environment where international organisations are often presumed to have agendas, the entire episode increased ordinary Libyans' suspicions of the ICC. On 17 January 2013, Saif al-Islam appeared in court in Zintan, for charges against him regarding breaches of national security related to Melinda Taylor's visit. Similar charges were brought against Melinda Taylor and her colleague *in absentia*.

On 5 September 2012, Sanusi was extradited to Libya from Mauritania, following months of speculation as to whether Mauritania was going to hand him to France, the US or the ICC. For Libyans, his extradition was highly significant because Sanusi was widely viewed as one of the most powerful enforcers of Qadhafi's rule, and was thus implicated in many crimes outside the ICC's jurisdiction, including the Abu Slim massacre. On arriving in Libya, Sanusi did not appear in public but was interrogated on a wide range of issues, most predating the revolution.

On 31 May 2012 the ICC's Pre-Trial Chamber ruled on the admissibility challenge filed by Libya in the case of Saif al-Islam.[47] It concluded that it had been unable 'to discern the actual contours of the national case against Saif al-Islam'; in other words that Libya had not demonstrated that the domestic investigation covered the same case as was before the Court, which was a legal requirement necessary for the challenge to succeed. It also noted that while Libya, assisted by national governments and regional and international organisations, had deployed significant efforts to rebuild institutions, restore the rule of law and enhance capacity, the ICC considered Libyan authorities unable to carry out the proceedings against Saif al-Islam for three reasons. First, it considered that the Libyan government could not secure his transfer from Zintan into state custody. Second, it judged the judicial system unable to obtain witness testimonies, exercise full control over detention facilities and provide adequate witness protection. Third, it saw significant impediments to securing legal representation for Saif al-Islam, given the security situation in Libya and the risks faced by lawyers representing former government figures. The Court stipulated that Libya could bring a new challenge of admissibility in the future, and Libya appealed the decision, only to be dismissed.

In contrast, the ICC's subsequent decision over Sanusi on 11 October 2013 was that the case against him was inadmissible in The Hague. The Pre-Trial Chamber found that the Libyan investigations against Sanusi included the same conduct as was being investigated by the ICC and concluded that Libya was willing to try him despite his being unrepresented, in addition to the absence of witness protection and the government's inability to control certain detention facilities. The decisive factor that differed from the Saif al-Islam case was that the Libyan authorities already had Sanusi in custody, and had gathered far more evidence against him than Saif al-Islam.[48]

There remained no appetite among the Libyan authorities to surrender Saif al-Islam or Sanusi to the ICC. Many Libyans considered it essential to transitional justice that Saif al-Islam and Sanusi be tried in Libya for the full scope of crimes for which they stood accused, not simply the events of 17–25 February 2011, which is the temporal jurisdiction of the ICC.

c. Amnesty for revolutionary fighters

Amnesties, as transitional tools, grant legal certainty to specific categories of offenders, thereby promoting reconciliation.[49] However, the United Nations does not recognise amnesties for genocide, crimes against humanity, war crimes or serious violations of human rights. In Libya amnesties were primarily used to erase questions of liability on behalf of the *thuwwar*. Law 38, on 'special measures for the transitional period' passed in May 2012, stated in article 4 that that 'there shall be no penalty for military, security, or civil actions dictated by the February 17 Revolution performed by revolutionaries with the goal of promoting or protecting the revolution'. This language seemingly granted a broad amnesty to *thuwwar*, but left open the question of whether offences such as torture could be said to 'promote the revolution'.

Law 38 was subsequently revised in April 2013, when the justice minister introduced a law entitled 'Criminalisation of Torture, Enforced Disappearances, and Discrimination' which explicitly applied to revolutionary fighters and sought to deter those crimes. The law created controversy in the GNC—opponents eliminated a provision specifying that crimes committed in the name of the revolution should incur increased penalties—but was, nevertheless, passed in April 2013. But it effectively diminished the scope of the amnesty granted in Law 38 and sent a clear message from the government that such acts by *thuwwar* would no longer be tolerated. The *thuwwar* resisted the law, arguing that it was wrong to 'criminalise' them when they had liberated the nation. It led to heightened tensions between *thuwwar* and the Ministry of Justice, which was then occupied in the context of the discussions on the Political Isolation Law.

d. Fact-finding and its potential in Libya

'Truth-seeking' or 'fact-finding' processes are cornerstones of transitional justice. Truth and Reconciliation Commissions, as implemented in Peru or South Africa, can diagnose a society's ills and make recommendations for the future. Their broad and socially dynamic approach engages the public and can encourage society to consider why certain crimes happened and to evaluate and thus reform institutions that sanctioned those crimes. For example, South Africa's Truth and Reconciliation Commission held hearings that dealt with the role of the business community or church in upholding the apartheid system.

The value of truth commissions thus lies in exploring the root causes of violations. In Libya, these include the operations of state institutions themselves, as well as legacies of oppression and discrimination against certain political tribal and ethnic groups.

In February 2012, the NTC passed its first transitional justice law, known as Law 17, 'Laying a Foundation for National Reconciliation and Transitional Justice'. Unlike in Tunisia, there was no broad public consultation on the law, despite the importance of the social issues at stake. Law 17 did not clearly define the overall goals of the transitional justice process, wavering between addressing the massive human rights violations of Qadhafi's era and providing a dispute settlement mechanism for individual cases; the only reference to victims was in relation to compensation.

In 2012 the justice minister tabled a new draft law to remedy some flaws of the old and bolster its ability to address broader transitional justice questions. The new version of the law, passed through the General National Congress in September 2013, significantly strengthened the proposal for a Fact-Finding and Reconciliation Commission, aligning it further with truth commissions instituted in other countries. For instance, truth commissions usually produce a final report of their findings, with recommendations for reforms; Law 17 did not require this but the 2013 law did. The law also eliminated the statute of limitations for serious political crimes committed prior to 1997.

A crucial matter that remained undecided was whether fact-finding processes should address the crimes of the Qadhafi era or focus initially on events during the revolution. While Qadhafi-era crimes (such as the Abu Slim massacre) are relatively well known—their public nature was intentional, with executions of political opponents often carried out where they could be witnessed or televised, as with the hangings of student activists at Tripoli University—details such as the whereabouts of human remains are often unknown. In contrast, some events of the 17 February Revolution were much disputed, and could have benefited from immediate investigation. Yet some Libyans expressed anxiety at placing those events before a fact-finding commission, citing national unity or reconciliation, that the 'wounds are still fresh' and the 'fever needs to go down in order to heal the body'.[50]

Initial fact-finding efforts consequently remained passive, lacking in social dynamism and concentrating on historical events while avoiding more contentious contemporary topics. For instance, under Law 17 the

GNC established a Fact-Finding and Reconciliation Commission composed exclusively of senior male judges. It was intended as to focus on individual cases rather than compiling an overall, integrated historical record or even looking at particular incidents. The Commission opened branch offices at courts of appeal in various cities, strengthening the perception that the process was quasi-judicial—neither a court nor a truth commission. It issued calls for information but few members of the public engaged with it. The GNC passed a decree mandating a separate fact-finding commission for the Abu Slim massacre[51], but it has not been established yet.

e. Reparations in the Libyan context

Qadhafi's governments used 'handouts' to appease particular constituencies or garner their loyalty. This culture remains in Libya today, creating a haphazard approach to reparations for victims. For instance, the NTC passed a decree granting monthly payments only to former political prisoners. War-wounded then occupied the GNC until they got assurances of financial support. The Council of Ministers passed a separate decree compensating victims of sexual violence. Regular promises of payments and other benefits were also made to *thuwwar*. As of writing, these laws are yet to result in actual reparations. But without a comprehensive truth-seeking process—which the 2013 transitional justice law may yet develop—there was no coherent approach to reparations, simply because the potential categories of victims and kinds of violations were not explored.

Property restitution too was a significant unresolved challenge. Qadhafi's laws on property, particularly Law 4, which declared 'the house is the property of the one who lives in it', divested thousands of their properties. The laws were so arbitrary that after the revolution, almost 50 per cent of real estate in Benghazi and Tripoli was disputed between their original owners and those who acquired properties in good faith under Qadhafi. As of writing, Libya has been unable to establish a mechanism to deal with these inequities in property distribution.[52]

f. Missing persons: A victim-centred approach?

The plight of persons missing during Qadhafi's rule—such as many of those suspected killed in Abu Slim—became politicised by the revolution. The issue's scope spanned forty-two years of Qadhafi's rule, including Libya's several wars abroad, such as in Uganda and Chad, and the 17 February Revolution itself. The exact number of missing persons in Libya is currently unknown, but is reliably presumed to run in the thousands. Families of the missing demand that the government search for and identify their remains.

In other societies, notably Argentina and Chile, families of the disappeared drove the transitional justice process. In Libya, the plight of the missing still has great potential to do so. Focusing on missing persons can increase awareness of the plight of all victims, since the impact is the same for all families regardless of their political or social affiliations. Information on missing persons can be used to build a national historical record, which can allow a coherent approach to setting reparation entitlements for families. Those with knowledge of missing persons can be encouraged to share information, even if they are currently in detention or are perpetrators.

During the revolution, the NTC mandated a Commission on the Search and Identification for Missing Persons, composed of prominent scientists, which started preliminary work including on the aforementioned Yarmuk massacre. However, the post-revolution interim government dissolved the Commission by cabinet decision, creating instead a Ministry for the Affairs of Families of Martyrs and Missing Persons. This politicised missing persons issues by combining the issues of 'martyrs' with 'missing', resulting in discriminatory treatment for families of missing persons who were not 'martyrs', particularly in terms of payments. It alienated the scientific community, including a prominent geneticist who subsequently set up Libya's only DNA lab.

The ministry also lacked experience and technical skills. It made public statements that the search for and identification of missing persons would be resolved within months, even though such a process takes years or even decades. It embarked on exhuming and collecting DNA samples in Bin Jawad without applying proper protocols, sending those samples to a lab in Bosnia. Bodies were wrongly identified and given to the wrong relatives. Libya's lack of forensic anthropologists and archaeologists, as well as a legal framework to deal with missing persons, left many issues such as the management of genetic material and date protection unregulated. While international actors rushed to give assistance, including those as varied as the International Committee for Missing Persons, the South Korean government, and

Repsol, the oil company, the overall strategy remained haphazard and opportunistic, leading to further mistakes.

Illustrating the twin issues of politicisation and skills deficits, in May 2013, Misratan prosecutorial authorities announced that a mass grave was discovered near Tawergha. The announcement was politically provocative, as they claimed that it contained Misratan revolutionaries, and it was timed shortly before the Tawerghans planned a unilateral return to their town, which was later postponed. The Tawergha Council denied Misrata's claims, stating that the bodies were a Tawergha family killed in a NATO airstrike, and demanded an international investigation, saying they did not trust the Ministry of Martyrs and Missing Persons. The Ministry exhumed eleven bodies but was unable to identify them. Even if it could, the issue's political sensitivity risked sparking further acts of vengeance.

The plight of missing persons is thus highly illustrative of the challenges facing transitional justice in Libya generally. Public expectations were high, and policymakers found themselves making impossible promises to appease public demand. It was easier to rally around politically popular causes such as assistance to martyrs, than promoting egalitarianism in issues such as determining the fate of those who died fighting for Qadhafi, or who disappeared after the revolution. Much work remained to foster understanding that victims hail from across the political spectrum and that their rights matter regardless, in addition to developing legal frameworks and technical capabilities.

None of these challenges are surprising considering the repression and length of Qadhafi's rule, and the tumultuous nature of Libya's transition. However, if victims can be dealt with evenhandedly, through an independent and competent search and an identification process which treats all victims with dignity, this will contribute greatly towards post-Qadhafi reconciliation.

Conclusion

Revolutionary zeal manifested itself in widespread detentions of perceived Qadhafi supporters, a strong desire for punishment and a desire to further protect the revolution by purging former government officials through 'political isolation'. In this context, it was difficult for Libya to forge a path to reconciliation. Grievances and score-settling festered between local communities.

Transitional justice in Libya emphasised political isolation, and trial and punishment of former regime figures. More victim-oriented measures, such as reparations or the search for and identification of missing persons, were often implemented in ways that further sought to privilege revolutionaries and martyrs. These approaches risked exacerbating Libya's divisions and will make it more difficult to forge national unity.

What could be a better way forward? Fact-finding can help Libyans come to a more nuanced understanding of their history, and resolve specific disputed incidents such as the antagonism between the cities of Misrata and Tawergha, or the Abu Slim massacre. Demobilising militias and strengthening institutions can help address the complex issues fuelling conflicts in different parts of the country. As of writing, strengthening the security sector and rule of law, and ending conflict-related detentions, are urgent priorities. Victim-oriented measures, which do not discriminate between those who supported the revolution and those who did not, will contribute to reconciliation.

Building legitimate state institutions to prevent future violations may be the most important long-term transitional justice goal for Libya. Only with more security and an established rule of law can political oppression, arbitrary detentions, torture and disappearances belong to the past. This requires strengthening Libya's justice and security institutions and drafting a constitution that enshrines fundamental rights. Only then will Libyans succeed in fully turning the page on Qadhafi's legacy.

PART 2

SUB-NATIONAL IDENTITIES
AND NARRATIVES

8

FINDING THEIR PLACE

LIBYA'S ISLAMISTS DURING AND AFTER THE REVOLUTION

Mary Fitzgerald

Introduction[1]

The grey walls of Abu Slim prison rise high and forbidding over the hardscrabble central Tripoli neighbourhood that gives the now abandoned prison its name. Its history, along with that of its thousands of former prisoners, is key to understanding the diverse range of groups and individuals collectively described as Islamist in Libya.

Islamism can be defined as support for the introduction of Islamic tenets into political life through the implementation of *sharia*, the moral and legal code derived from the Qur'an and examples of the prophet Muhammad's life by religious scholars. This admittedly loose definition allows the classification of both movements and individuals who strive for that goal as Islamist.[2] Those referred to as such in this chapter self-describe as 'Islamists' (*Islamiyun*) to distinguish themselves from Muslims (*Muslimun*). Alamin Bilhajj, a wiry academic who headed the *shura* (advisory) council of Libya's Muslim Brotherhood in early 2011, offers this definition: 'To be Islamist is to believe that every-thing, including politics and economics, should be according to Islam.'[3]

The constellation of rebel groups that sprang up during the 2011 revolution—particularly in eastern Libya, long a hotbed of religiously-tinged opposition to the regime—was a microcosm of the broad spectrum of Islamist ideologies, ranging from members of the Muslim Brotherhood, to Salafists, to a *takfiri* minority who sanctioned killing Muslims deemed insufficiently pious. They included those whose political vision was rooted in the framework of the modern nation-state and others who reject the statist approach in favour of the *umma*, the universal community of Muslims, based on *sharia* law.[4]

As they and other nonaligned Islamists variously participated in the uprising and planned for its aftermath, they had to seriously examine what, beyond opposition to Qadhafi, they stood for and how they could work together.

Libya's two main Islamist opposition groups—the Libyan branch of the Muslim Brotherhood and the more militant Libyan Islamic Fighting Group (LIFG)—were almost neutralised on the eve of the revolution due to decades of repression followed by tentative reconciliation with Qadhafi in 2005–11. Libya's Muslim Brotherhood, the country's oldest and largest Islamist group, originated largely as a student movement influenced by Egyptian Brothers who taught at Libyan universities after fleeing Egyptian President Gamal Abdel Nasser's crackdown in the mid-1950s. Unlike in its birthplace, Egypt, the Brotherhood in Libya never had a proper opportunity to practise the blend of political activism and charitable work that founder Hasan al-Banna hoped would 'Islamicise' society from the bottom up.

When Mu'ammar al-Qadhafi, who was greatly influenced by Nasser, came to power in 1969, he outlawed the organisation, driving it outside Libya, where many of the current leadership were initially exposed to it, typically as students in Europe, the US and Canada. Much of the Libyan Brotherhood's organisational structure today is rooted in the overseas networks that subsequently developed. In the early 1980s, the Brotherhood embarked on a disastrous attempt to build on its meagre presence in Libya; scores were imprisoned in Abu Slim and several executed, their public hangings televised. Qadhafi targeted the movement again in 1998, rounding up and imprisoning over 150 senior members.[5]

The second largest group in Abu Slim after the Brotherhood was the LIFG, formed by Libyans who, after fighting the Soviets in Afghanistan, returned home to battle Qadhafi, whom they considered apostate. For much of its lifespan the LIFG was opposed to democracy; one of its leaders, Sami al-Sa'adi, denounced it as a Western concept in a book he wrote in his mid-twenties setting out the group's ideology. In the mid-1990s the LIFG was routed after directly confronting the regime, which inflicted huge losses on the group during clashes in eastern Libya's 'Green Mountains'. Hundreds of survivors were jailed. Those who escaped abroad included leaders like Sa'adi and Abd al-Hakim Bilhajj (no relation to the Brotherhood's Alamin Bilhajj), both rendered to Libya in 2004 with US and British assistance. By 2005, Abu Slim was home to over half of the LIFG's *shura* council, several of whom had begun rethinking the group's strategy. In 2005, Saif al-Islam Qadhafi and the Benghazi-born, Qatar-based scholar Ali Sallabi, him-self a former Abu Slim inmate, began a dialogue with its imprisoned leadership which resulted in a 400-page recantation of violent struggle, authored by six members of its *shura* council: Bilhajj, Sa'adi, Miftah al-Dhuwadi, Khalid al-Sharif, Abd al-Wahhab al-Qa'id and Mustafa Qanaifid. The LIFG's often bitter experience of armed conflict, not just in Libya but also Afghanistan and Algeria, where it supported and later fell out with the Armed Islamic Group, or GIA, was instrumental in the change. The renunciation in 2009 led to a mass release of LIFG prisoners, including Bilhajj, Sharif and Sa'adi, the following year. Over 100 others, Dhuwadi and Qa'id among them, remained in Abu Slim.[6]

If anything united Libya's disparate Islamists, it was not so much ideology—beyond a shared and often vaguely formulated wish for governance rooted in *sharia* law—as the bonds formed during incarceration in Abu Slim. Many imprisoned there speak of it as a formative experience, during which ideologies, strategies and tactics were debated. It personally affected the Brotherhood, the LIFG, and scores of youth who were not members of such groups but were nonetheless imprisoned for their perceived religious inclinations. The June 1996 massacre of some 1,200 inmates, most of them Islamists, after negotiations broke down following a prisoner protest for better conditions, particularly fed into the notion of sacrifice that frames the Islamist narrative in Libya.

'Ironically, you could say one year in Abu Slim was worth several on the outside in that we could talk with less fear,' recalled Abdullah Shamia, a professor of economics at Benghazi University and senior Brotherhood figure who spent eight years in Abu Slim, and later held the economics portfolio in the National Transitional Council (NTC).[7] Similarly, Sallabi, who was to become a pivotal networker and organiser during the revolution, observed: 'There were former prisoners in every Libyan city, with relationships of great trust which created a strong, secure network which grew quickly during the revolution because it was difficult to disrupt.'[8]

Protests over several years by women demanding justice for relatives who had died in the Abu Slim massacre prepared the ground for wider demonstrations against Qadhafi in February 2011, as did the 15 February arrest of Fathi Tirbil, a young Benghazi lawyer who represented the Abu Slim families (and who lost three relatives himself) which sparked rallies by lawyers and judges who joined the families in demanding his release. Thus, two days ahead of a planned 'Day of Rage' inspired by events in Egypt and Tunisia, Benghazi erupted in demonstrations that later tipped into armed uprising.

Once underway, revenge for what was considered Qadhafi's worst atrocity was central to the revolution's narrative. As one Benghazi protester put it in late February 2011: 'The Abu Slim massacre is the deepest wound in our country and we want vengeance.'[9] Several armed groups were named after those killed in 1996. The walls of Benghazi's seafront courthouse, where the NTC was originally headquartered, were covered with faded photographs of the victims. When rebel fighters poured into Tripoli in August 2011, they used rocks and metal bars to smash the locks off cell doors at Abu Slim, freeing thousands of inmates, most of whom immediately joined the revolution.

The Muslim Brotherhood and the LIFG on the eve of revolution

As Libya stood on the cusp of revolution, the Muslim Brotherhood was suffering a crisis of credibility. Opposition circles saw it as having compromised with Qadhafi after it began a cautious engagement in 1999 to secure the release of its members in Abu Slim. When Saif al-Islam attempted to dialogue with dissident groups in the early 2000s the Brotherhood responded positively, boycotting the first Libyan pan-opposition conference in London in 2005 that called for Qadhafi's overthrow. Brotherhood detainees were consequently freed in 2006, but other opposition factions spoke bitterly of what they considered a betrayal.[10]

By February 2011, the Libyan Muslim Brotherhood was fragmented. 'There was the leadership outside the country and there were those inside Libya, of whom around 153 of us who had been imprisoned remained under surveillance,' explained Abd al-Latif Karmus, a professor of law at Tripoli University and former prisoner who became head of the Brotherhood's *shura* council after the revolution.[11]

The overseas leadership, scattered across Europe and north America, closely followed events unfolding in Tunisia and Egypt. On 30 and 31 January, some sixty senior figures met in an Islamic cultural centre outside Zurich. Discussing the upcoming 17 February 'Day of Rage', 'the big question,' recalled Alamin Bilhajj, was whether Libya would follow Tunisia's and Egypt's example. 'We concluded that Libyans would demand things like a constitution and abolishing Qadhafi's Revolutionary Committees but not regime change. We were sure Qadhafi would try to suppress it.'[12]

The exiled leadership established offices in Tunisia and Egypt to channel humanitarian aid and smuggled satellite phones into Libya to contact members inside. On 19 February, they met again in Switzerland to discuss what seemed like unstoppable momentum in Benghazi and other eastern towns. 'We wrote a question on a white board: should we stick with [Saif al-Islam's] reform programme or dismiss it and go with the revolution?' Bilhajj said. 'The consensus was, "we are with the revolution".'

Alamin was sent by the Brotherhood's exiled leader, Sulaiman Abd al-Qadir, to organise on the ground in Libya. Before crossing the Egyptian border on 1 March, Alamin stopped in Qatar to meet other Libyan Brotherhood figures, including Isma'il Gritly, who worked at Al Jazeera. He also met Sallabi, who had left the Muslim Brotherhood some years before but retained similar views and personal ties to leading Brothers. Alamin was concerned that his name was on Egyptian blacklists, then still enforced: Sallabi's connections with the Qatari establishment facilitated Alamin's travel with an Al Jazeera news team on a military plane taking humanitarian aid from Qatar to Egypt.

Inside Libya, what remained of the Brotherhood's network—estimated in 2009 to number only a few thousand[13]—sprang to life. In Benghazi, preachers aligned with the Brotherhood delivered sermons urging people to join the growing protests. Shamia communicated with other Brotherhood members across eastern Libya, coordinating humanitarian aid coming from Egypt. In a country where civil society organisations were banned, the Brotherhood's trusted decades-old clandestine networks could swiftly dispense this aid. 'We worked as individuals not as a movement,' said Shamia. 'But I knew and trusted these people—they form my network—so it was natural to work that way.'[14] Similar networks emerged in Tripoli, partly from regular meetings held at the home of Nizar Kawan, a foreign ministry official and secret Brotherhood member. 'It was difficult to organise as a group at that time, particularly in Tripoli because of the tight security,' said Abd al-Latif Karmus, also one of the Tripoli-based Brothers.[15]

By early 2011, the men who once formed the backbone of the LIFG were also scattered across Europe and the Middle East. While never officially disbanded, the LIFG had become inactive. Several individual members remained subject to UN sanctions. The angry young men who founded the group were now middle-aged and mellowed, having disavowed armed struggle in Abu Slim. Many had sunk into near resignation to the status quo.

While LIFG members in Libya remained under surveillance or in jail, those in Europe, particularly the UK, tried to find the group's place in the revolution. In fraught discussions, some believed events in Tunisia and Egypt would inevitably affect Libya, but others were pessimistic given the previous failures of the National Front for the Salvation of Libya's attack on Bab al-Aziziyya in 1984 and the LIFG's own routing in the late 1990s. Senior figures in London, chiefly Abd al-Basit Bu Hliqa, a London-based businessman and LIFG *shura* council member, and Anis al-Sharif, who once drafted LIFG communiqués, argued that the LIFG needed to publicly relaunch as the Libyan Islamic Movement for Change (LIMC) to match the calls for peaceful protest sweeping Libya. Other members opposed this, arguing that it would jeopardise a scheduled release of LIFG prisoners from Abu Slim on 14 February. When the release did not happen, Sharif and Bu Hliqa announced the LIMC. Fears it would affect the prisoners proved unfounded. Early on 16 February over 200 inmates walked out of Abu Slim and into the beginning of a revolution. Among them were senior LIFG figures who would play prominent roles in the uprising, chiefly Dhuwadi and Qa'id. 'At the time, officials were hesitant about releasing us,' said Dhuwadi. 'Some were very opposed, and argued about whether our release would calm things down or worsen the situation if we joined the revolution.'[16]

While Dhuwadi left for Tunisia after briefly visiting his hometown of Sabratha, connecting with the influential Zintan leader Muhammad al-Madani on the way, Qa'id, Sa'adi, Abd al-Hakim Bilhajj and Khalid al-Sharif were summoned by Saif al-Islam and Qadhafi's security chief Abdullah al-Sanusi, who pressed them to denounce the protests in eastern Libya. Sa'di and Sharif were later detained in Abu Slim until rebel forces entered Tripoli in August. Bilhajj eluded arrest, and escaped to Tunis via Zuwara, where he connected with Dhuwadi and other revolutionaries. Qa'id fled southwards over the border, disguising himself as a migrant worker and travelling to Sudan, from where he flew to Benghazi in June. Linking with LIFG associates and former Abu Slim inmates there, Qa'id later commanded an armed group during the advance on Sabha after the fall of Tripoli.

Early organisation

On 27 February, as the Muslim Brotherhood was rekindling its networks, and with the LIFG still under pressure in Tripoli, Mustafa Abd al-Jalil, Qadhafi's former justice minister, announced the establishment of the National Transitional Council. Alamin Bilhajj had reached Benghazi when the first meeting of the body occurred in the city's Tibesti Hotel. Bilhajj and other Brotherhood figures were dismayed by the names of its members, mostly academics or lawyers, whom the Brotherhood viewed as too liberal. 'This was not an NTC that represented all of Libya, the real Libya,' Bilhajj recalled. 'One problem concerned geographical representation, the other was the type of people. Libya is a conservative country; how come there were no conservative people in the NTC?'[17] Such misgivings were not limited to the Brotherhood. Devout youths in Benghazi joining the rag-tag armed groups streaming to the eastern front accused some NTC members of drinking alcohol or having extra-marital affairs, and fuelled early rumours of a possible 'counter-revolution'.[18]

A more serious effort to challenge the NTC's composition began with a meeting initiated by Sallabi in Istanbul in April attended by members of the Brotherhood and the former LIFG, along with other nonaligned figures. From the Brotherhood came Sulaiman Abd al-Qadir, Alamin Bilhajj, Nizar Kawan, Isma'il Gritly and Abd al-Razzaq al-Aradi—a businessman from Tripoli who had distanced himself from the Brotherhood after returning to Libya some years previously. The LIMC was represented by Dhuwadi, Bu Hliqa and Anis al-Sharif—its remaining leaders had been either imprisoned or were fleeing Libya. All agreed on the need to counter more 'secular' elements within the

NTC and the wider uprising. 'There was a fear that the secularists wanted to be the political frame of the revolution and deny the Islamists any role,' Sharif recalled. 'The question was how we would cooperate and organise during and after the revolution. We decided to set up a national umbrella movement including Islamists from all sides and nationalists who accepted Islam as a [political and legal] frame of reference.'[19] The movement, named the National Gathering (*al-Tajummu' al-Watani*) was envisaged as a civil society initiative that could later be transformed into a political party. 'We did not want to create an Islamic party or push an Islamic revolution because while the majority of the Libyan people are Muslims, they are not Islamists,' said Alamin Bilhajj. 'The idea was to create something bigger, more nationalist in tone, but conservative.'[20]

The National Gathering planned a caravan across eastern Libya in early May to canvass support among community leaders and tribal elders. Before that, however, they had to decide how to engage—or not—with the NTC. The first option—attempting to bring the NTC down—was swiftly rejected as dangerous; the second—establishing a rival entity—was dismissed to preserve a united front to the world. The result was a qualified endorsement and a pledge to demand a more diverse NTC.

The delegation chosen for the May trip, originally to include Sallabi, Alamin Bilhajj, Aradi, Bu Hliqa and Anis al-Sharif, was thus also tasked with lobbying Abd al-Jalil for representation on the NTC. Yet almost immediately tensions arose within the National Gathering as members prioritised their own plans based on personal and other commitments. Only the Brotherhood members Alamin Bilhajj and Abd al-Razzaq al-Aradi made it to Benghazi that month to press for inclusion on the NTC.

Their attempt was fraught with suspicion and misunderstanding. During a private meeting with Abd al-Jalil, Alamin Bilhajj and Aradi built their case on securing a Tripoli seat, which the Brotherhood had asked Alamin to do. According to Alamin, Abd al-Jalil, aware of criticisms that the NTC was unrepresentative, welcomed the fact the two men were Tripolitanians, and that Alamin was a senior Brotherhood figure. After travelling to the UK to resign as president of the Muslim Association of Britain, Bilhajj became one of six new Tripoli representatives on the NTC, openly declaring his Brotherhood affiliation by introducing himself at his first NTC meeting as head of its *shura* council.

The Muslim Brotherhood's entry into the NTC triggered deep unease within the council. In opposition, a more secular-leaning camp formed around Fathi al-Ba'ja, a political science professor from Benghazi who headed the NTC's political committee, along with executive committee members Abd al-Hafiz Ghugha, Mahmud Shammam, Ahmad Gebreel and Mahmud Jibril. Tensions between the camps became impossible to bridge. Ba'ja's acerbic wit—at one point he scotched a Brotherhood effort to legislate for a National Guard by comparing it to the Iranian Revolutionary Guard—clashed with Alamin's sensitive personality. Alamin Bilhajj threatened resignation several times during the lifetime of the NTC, often over perceived slights, as when Abd al-Jalil remarked on the need to avoid 'ideological conflict' within the council, or during one explosive meeting after the NTC declared liberation in late October 2011, when Ghugha loosed a stream of invective, claiming the Brotherhood was controlling the council and Abd al-Jalil was too close to them. Alamin became tearful. 'I said, "If the problem is the Brotherhood, I will not be here" and I walked out of the meeting.'[21]

Despite these fears, the total official Brotherhood members in the NTC and its executive board numbered less than ten out of some 100, far lower than its opponents claimed. In May, Bilhajj and Aradi were joined by Brotherhood members Ramadan Khalid, who represented the northwestern town of Msallata, and Ahmad Dayikh from the eastern town of Baida. Salim al-Tabib, from Tajura near Tripoli, was appointed in the council's final months. Two Brotherhood members served on the executive committee: Shamia and Salam Shaikhi, an imam who returned from Manchester in the UK to adopt the religious affairs portfolio.

Yet these Brotherhood members made common cause with other NTC members who shared similar views on Libya's future. Three in particular were considered close to the Brotherhood: Ali al-Isawi, vice-chair of the executive committee until its dissolution in August, Jalal al-Dghaili, the NTC's defence minister, and Anwar Fituri, responsible for transport and communication. 'These people believed that Libya is an Islamic country and our laws should reflect that. We called them the middle group between Islamists and secularists because, though they had not joined our groups, they thought similarly,' explained Bilhajj.[22] Shamia estimated that this bloc, which he described as 'the Islamic current' comprised around half of the NTC. Ghugha and others in the opposing camp saw Abd al-Jalil himself as sharing this current's conservative views. Some were particularly hardline: at least two—Muhammad Rimash from Sirt and Mubarak al-Futmani from Bani Walid—protested the appointment of two women as ministers in the November 2011 interim government.

The NTC's more secular-leaning members were also unsettled by the Brotherhood's efficiency. In their eyes, the Brotherhood formed a small but tightly knit group within. 'When they arrived with their laptops and suits, they seemed more organised than us, as if they arrived with a plan,' said Ba'ja.[23] Alamin Bilhajj regularly briefed senior Brotherhood figures on the internal workings of the NTC, who in turn created a special committee to, as Bilhajj put it, 'help me gather information so my role in the NTC would be better'.[24]

Two principal issues generated the most tension between the self-described 'Islamic current' within the NTC and their opponents. Indeed, many NTC members primarily identified each other as 'Islamist' or 'secularist' according to their stance on these matters. One, during the drafting of the electoral law in early 2012, was the question of allocating General National Congress (GNC) seats to political party candidates versus individuals. 'Secularists' argued that since political parties had been previously banned, a party-based system would benefit groups like the Brotherhood that had existing networks to build on. 'Islamists' countered that an individual-based system would deepen regional and tribal fault lines by empowering local elites. The fact that Alamin Bilhajj was deputy chairman of the NTC committee, tasked with supervising the drafting of the electoral law, exacerbated the concerns of Fathi al-Ba'ja who pushed unsuccessfully to prohibit political parties based on religious, ethnic or tribal affiliations. In the end, a hybrid system allowing for both individual and party lists was agreed, with 120 of the GNC's 200 seats allocated to individual candidates.

The second contentious issue was the place of *sharia* law in the NTC's roadmap for the transition. One prototype, completed by an NTC team including Benghazi law professor Salwa al-Daghili and distributed to members in June 2011, referred to Islam as 'the religion of the state', with *sharia* 'a' main source of legislation. A handful of NTC members—including but not limited to those from the Brotherhood—insisted on describing *sharia* as 'the' principal source. Abd al-Jalil supported the original text. 'I was so shocked,' recalled Bilhajj. 'I met the Brotherhood that day and told them Libyans may be Muslims but I believe they don't understand Islam.'[25] The wording prompted demonstrations against the proposed text—some involving armed Salafists—in Benghazi and other towns, while Sallabi and other prominent religious figures lobbied Abd al-Jalil and the NTC. Though Libya's diverse range of Islamists differed in their interpretations of *sharia*—the Brotherhood, for example, cleaved to less literal readings than the Salafists—and how such laws might be implemented, they united to oppose the draft. 'They raised petitions and then came to us saying this is what civil society wants,' said Fathi al-Ba'ja. 'There was a lot of pressure to change it.'[26]

The protests prompted Abd al-Jalil to call another vote, which, to Ba'ja's dismay, took place with several NTC members absent. That vote resulted in the wording being changed. Abd al-Jalil used his first speech in Tripoli's Martyrs Square on 13 September after Qadhafi's ouster to announce that *sharia* would be 'the' main source of legislation, and later repeated this at Libya's official liberation ceremony on 23 October 2011, promising to annul laws contradicting *sharia*. His specific—and, according to an aide, improvised[27]—endorsement of polygamy raised eyebrows inside and outside Libya. Some close to Abd al-Jalil interpreted his remarks as an effort to placate more militant elements who had begun flexing their muscles in eastern Libya.

The rise of militancy in the east

The former LIFG represented Libya's older generation of militant Islamists, who, by the late 1990s, were either exiled, jailed or being monitored. But the younger generation, which included sons and nephews of those rounded up or killed in the 1990s, were exposed to more radical ideological currents emerging in the 2000s.

Many of those younger hardliners emerged from Libya's sizeable and diverse Salafist firmament. Salafism has deep roots in Libya, particularly in the east, but its contemporary expression takes three broad strands. The first and largest derives from Saudi scholar Rabi' al-Madkhali, who preaches obedience to the *wali al-amr* or ruler and discourages political dissent. Libya's *madkhali shaikhs* were therefore initially opposed to the 2011 revolution, with some utilised by the government for propaganda. After Qadhafi's death, *madkhali* Salafists largely reverted back to their quietist, apolitical ways, though some were involved in attacking Sufi shrines and mosques across the country. The second strand comprises an older generation of Salafists, including members or associates of the former LIFG, who took part in the revolution and later embraced political participation, whether by voting or running as candidates.

The third is a small but significant current which rejects democracy in favour of more *salafi-jihadist* or *takfiri* ideologies promoting armed action as the best way to spur sociopolitical change. This strand emerged mainly in Benghazi and Dirna, two eastern cities with long histories of Islamist opposition, including young men who went to fight in Afghanistan and Iraq and returned steeped in more radical ideas.

Their views towards the NTC, before and after Qadhafi's ousting, were often ambivalent, and sometimes hostile. 'Some didn't go to the frontline much because they had a problem with the NTC's legitimacy,' said one former LIFG member who spent much of the revolution in Benghazi. 'We thought we could talk to them, convince them, contain them … but despite assurances that Islam would be the main source of legislation in the future, they still questioned what we were fighting for.'[28] At times that questioning transformed into something more sinister. 'Some played on the Arabic name of the NTC, calling it the *majlis al-wadani* [pagan council]', recounted Ba'ja, whose self-declared secularist and liberal views made him particularly hated. 'They sent us death threats.'[29]

Dirna was particularly reputed, in the words of the late American diplomat Christopher Stevens, killed in an attack on the US consulate in Benghazi in September 2012, as 'a wellspring of Libyan foreign fighters'.[30] Scores of Dirnawis fought the Soviets in Afghanistan, and several of its youth died in the Abu Slim prison massacre. Repression, high unemployment, and the influence of local veteran *jihadists* all contributed to radicalising a new generation. After 2003, over fifty Dirnawis went to Iraq aiming to become suicide bombers—the largest number from any city outside Iraq.[31]

Three individuals from this more militant Dirnawi seam became prominent during the revolution. One was Abd al-Hakim al-Hisadi, who was briefly involved with the LIFG in the late 1990s before drifting into more radical circles in Afghanistan and Pakistan. Another was Sufyan bin Qumu, who likewise spent much of the 1990s in Afghanistan, but never joined the LIFG. Bin Qumu was captured in Pakistan in late 2001, sent to Guantanamo Bay and transferred to Libya in 2007. The third was Abd al-Basit Azuz, said by his peers to be a long-standing associate of al-Qa'ida leader Ayman al-Zawahiri. Azuz left Afghanistan in the early 1990s and moved to the United Kingdom where he lived for almost two decades before leaving for the tribal borderlands between Afghanistan and Pakistan. He arrived in eastern Libya in summer 2011, reportedly at al-Zawahiri's behest.[32]

Initially Hisadi and bin Qumu's presence risked discouraging international support: several regime officials, including Saif al-Islam al-Qadhafi, drew attention to both in February 2011, claiming that Hisadi planned to establish an 'emirate' in Dirna—which Hisadi denied. As the NTC took shape in early March, the newly-announced Libyan Islamic Movement for Change (LIMC) decided to approach it 'to send a clear message that we would support them with no separate plan',[33] according to Bu Hliqa, who made the trip with two LIFG veterans of the 1980s war in Afghanistan: Abd al-Razzaq al-Usta, who had later gained asylum in the UK, and Abd al-Mun'im al-Madhuni, a burly member of the LIFG *shura* council known by his *nom de guerre* 'Urwa' who was legendary as the commander who organised the 1996 assassination attempt on Qadhafi that prompted the regime's fierce backlash. After fleeing to Syria then Turkey, Urwa returned to Afghanistan. He was one of around a dozen LIFG members who fled to Iran after 9/11, most of whom made their way back to Libya after the 2011 uprising began.[34]

The LIMC wanted to limit Hisadi and Qumu's impact on the NTC's chances of gaining UN Security Council support for a no-fly zone. 'We wanted to pass a message that we were not extremists, that what we did in the past was because there was no other way to change the regime unless by force,' said Bu Hliqa. After he and Urwa entered Libya overland from Egypt—Usta fell victim to the travel ban Egyptian authorities were still enforcing against the LIFG—they met with LIFG members and former *jihadists* in Tubruq and Dirna. 'We told them we must be under the NTC; whoever can fight must go to the frontline and whoever cannot must help in other ways.'[35]

In Dirna, Hisadi promised to cooperate but bin Qumu declined to meet Bu Hliqa and Urwa—the former Guantanamo inmate had already started organising his own small group. When Azuz arrived in eastern Libya later that summer, he too was met by senior former LIFG figures who knew him from the UK. 'We made it very clear to him that al-Qa'ida is not part of our strategy in this revolution and we decided not to allow him any active role,' said one of those who met him. 'He said he had made a mistake going to Afghanistan and he had no agenda of his own. Later we were told he was still in contact with these people outside.'[36]

In March, Bu Hliqa and Urwa met Abd al-Jalil to introduce the LIMC and its position on the revolution. Abd al-Jalil and other NTC officials questioned them over possible affiliations with al-Qa'ida. While some former LIFG members like Abu Laith al-Libi and Abu Yahya al-Libi had joined al-Qa'ida, the LIFG leadership had, in 2007, refuted a claim made by Abu Laith al-Libi and al-Qa'ida leader Ayman al-Zawahiri that the LIFG had merged with al-Qa'ida. They insisted the LIFG never agreed with or assisted al-Qa'ida's war against the West and that Sa'adi and Abd al-Hakim Bilhajj had made this clear in meetings with Osama bin Laden in Afghanistan. 'We had no other goal but to get rid of Qadhafi,' said Bilhajj.[37] The NTC demanded assurances the LIMC was not linked with external groups. 'They wanted to ensure that no people were coming from outside Libya—they said this was a red line.'[38]

The two men moved on to Benghazi and then further west to view the frontline. 'There were groups fighting with no coordination,' recalled Bu Hliqa. 'We thought it cannot work like this, we need to be one army. We decided to start organising ourselves and then see how we can work with others.'[39] Thus Bu Hliqa and Urwa joined with Hasan al-Hamr—an oil engineer from Benghazi whose brother had died in Abu Slim—to form an armed group. Bu Hliqa suggested they name it after Umar al-Mukhtar, the Libyan resistance fighter whose image and slogan 'We win or we die' had become part of the revolution's iconography. They bought weaponry in the mountain town of al-Marj with 100,000 Libyan dinars borrowed from a contact in Ajdabiya and formed the group with 300 men—100 from the defected military and the remainder, including former LIFG members, in eastern Libya. 'There was no attempt to classify people as LIFG or non-LIFG,' as Bu Hliqa put it. Despite Urwa's death on the frontline near Ajdabiya in mid-April—described by many in the LIMC as their biggest loss of the revolution—the Umar al-Mukhtar Battalion became one of the largest in the east, eventually comprising around 1,000 members.

The Umar al-Mukhtar Battalion joined two similarly-sized groups formed from the youth flocking to the frontline. One was the 17 February Battalion helmed by Fawzi Bu Katif, an oil project manager and Brotherhood member from Benghazi imprisoned in Abu Slim for over a decade. Bu Katif had been active within a group of military defectors in Benghazi in the week following 15 February. By 27 February the proto-NTC nominated him to head a 'military committee' of defectors from the city's police force such as Ashur Shwail, and several military commanders, enabling Bu Katif to set up a small base in Benghazi, where officers instructed youth in basic weapons training.

These youth were unaligned with any specific political grouping, though again, former Abu Slim prisoners were highly prominent. Those in the 17 February Battalion coalesced around two former Abu Slim inmates; Isma'il Sallabi, the younger—and more radical—brother of Ali Sallabi and Rafallah al-Sahati, an oil engineer, whose group adopted his name when he was killed on 17 March. Another five or six groups coalesced around the bin Hamid brothers, Wisam and Hussain, and called themselves the 17 February Coalition. From Dirna came the Abu Slim Martyrs Battalion, founded by former LIFG member Salim Dirby, which had many former inmates of the jail within its ranks. Dirby's brother had perished in the 1996 massacre.

It is tempting to characterise these fighting groups, which consolidated in Brega and Ajdabiya in April 2011, as 'Islamist' given the preponderance of self-described Islamists in their ranks. But this label was adopted retrospectively. At the time, the groups were a muddle of youth from across the sociopolitical and social spectrum holding the Brega frontline. 'There was no sense of Islamists organising separately to the others,' said Abd al-Basit Bu Hliqa.[40] 'Umar al-Mukhtar was mixed, as was the 17 February Coalition. At the frontline we had people getting drunk at night and others complaining about them.' The 17 February Battalion was equally diverse. 'I had LIFG people, I had *jihadi* people, I had *takfiri* people, I had all types,' recalled Bu Katif. 'But nobody was taking a separate stand or waving their own flag at that time.'[41]

By late May, the groups need to coordinate with each other, and with NATO, across a frontline spanning 40km, led to the creation of an umbrella organisation—the Gathering of Revolutionary Companies (GRC) (*Tajummu' Sarayat al-Thuwwar*) comprising the 17 February Battalion, the Umar al-Mukhtar Battalion, and the 17 February Coalition. Three people from each formed the GRC leadership, with Bu Katif the overall leader. While rank and file fighters were mixed, the GRC's leadership was drawn from what Bu Hliqa described as the Islamist spectrum. The 17 February Battalion was represented by Bu

Katif, Isma'il Sallabi and Mustafa Sagizli, a businessman considered close to the Brotherhood. The Umar al-Mukhtar Battalion was represented by Bu Hliqa, Hamr and Abd al-Jawad al-Badin, one of the imprisoned LIFG cadres released on 16 February.[42] From the 17 February Coalition were Wisam Bin Hamid[43] and Mustafa Ruba', an oil engineer and former prisoner. 'It was not a plan, these were simply the people most active on the frontline,' said Bu Hliqa.

The GRC threatened the relevance and leadership of General Abd al-Fattah Yunis, the former interior minister who became chief of staff of the rebel forces. Yunis was important to the NTC—his defection on 20 February was one of the events that precipitated the fall of Benghazi, since he commanded the Sa'iqa ("Thunderbolt') Special Forces in the area that might have resisted the protests. But Islamists distrusted him because he had been one of Qadhafi's closest aides, having joined his coup against King Idris in 1969. In several roles within Libya's security apparatus, Yunis had overseen the detention of political dissidents. As rebel chief of staff, he made infrequent visits to the frontline, instead jockeying for position with Khalifa Hiftar, an army defector who returned from long-term exile in the US in March to declare himself field commander. Fathi al-Ba'ja recalled protests against Yunis at the NTC's headquarters by clerics demanding he be punished for his role snuffing out Islamist groups in eastern Libya. Whispering campaigns accused him of secretly maintaining ties to Qadhafi. State media hinted at such contacts to sow discord among the rebel forces.

In June, the newly-formed GRC met with Mustafa Abd al-Jalil, who asked Yunis and Hiftar to attend, along with several NTC members including Alamin Bilhajj and Fathi Tirbil, the lawyer for the Abu Slim families. After giving a frank assessment of the Brega frontline and upbraiding the NTC for its perceived lack of support, the GRC leaders requested that they come under the NTC's Defence Ministry and that Fawzi Bu Katif become deputy defence minister. The GRC insisted that any new armed group should get permission from the Defence Ministry before joining the front. All present agreed, and the NTC allocated the GRC 500,000 dinars to buy weapons and vehicles. 'Yunis expressed regret for the situation up to then and said we would work together,' recalled Abd al-Basit Bu Hliqa. An operations room was established in Zwaitina, some 150km west of Benghazi, and planning to retake Brega began.

But on 28 July, Yunis was killed in Benghazi by an obscure rebel unit, threatening the cohesion of both the NTC and the frontline.

Yunis's death, which occurred after the NTC issued a summons for his questioning, exposed fissures and intrigue within the opposition. The summons were carried out by some within the GRC: Ruba' was among those who brought Yunis to Benghazi, though Bu Katif later insisted that Ruba' did not do so under GRC orders. What happened between Yunis's arrival in Benghazi and the discovery of his mutilated body and those of two aides on the city outskirts hours later remains unclear. The group believed to have killed him was named after Abu Ubaida bin Jarrah, one of the Prophet Muhammad's companions. It contained several former inmates of Abu Slim prison, some of whom adhered to *takfiri* ideology. A witness claimed the two men who shot Yunis dead shouted that he was a traitor who had killed their father in Dirna. 'The nature of the killing suggests it was an act of personal revenge,' NTC head Abd al-Jalil said at the time. The assassination deepened divisions between the defected armed forces Yunis commanded and civilian armed groups such as the GRC. Though the NTC had been afforded political recognition by the US, Britain and thirty-one other countries and was close to passing its constitutional declaration, Abd al-Jalil was compelled to dismiss the entire Executive Committee on 8 August after elders from Yunis's Ubaida tribe accused Isawi, Dghaila, and Shaikhi of conspiring with extremists to kill the general.

By August 2011, Libya's Islamists had tried tentatively and not entirely successfully to achieve closer unity from their fragmented starting point in February 2011. They also attempted to exert greater influence on the direction of the revolution, working in the process with senior figures in the NTC, Yunis, and other Libyans, but could not reconcile themselves with their different vision for the country's future. 'We shared a common goal to get rid of Qadhafi but that was it,' said one prominent nonaligned Islamist from Benghazi.[44] They also had to confront more hardline elements within their own movements and the wider Islamist milieu. In killing Yunis, such elements not only imperilled the entire revolution, they also deepened the suspicions of more secular-leaning Libyans over the Islamists' motives.

Tension with 'secularists'

Tensions wrought by Yunis's killing, coupled with those that arose over the planning for the fall of Tripoli, divided Libya's revolutionaries further into two broad camps that pitted the Islamist spectrum against

193

its opponents in the NTC and what remained of the army and police. Their struggle burst into the open shortly after Qadhafi's routing from Tripoli in late August when Ali Sallabi appeared on Al Jazeera to denounce Jibril and his associates in the NTC as 'extremist secularists' who would guide Libya into 'a new era of tyranny and dictatorship' that could be 'worse than Qadhafi'. Abd al-Hakim Bilhajj, by then head of the Tripoli Military Council, echoed similar, though more nuanced, sentiments in a *Guardian* opinion article later that month, arguing that 'Libya's Islamists have announced their commitment to democracy; despite this, some reject their participation and call for them to be marginalised,' he wrote. 'It is as though they want to push Islamists towards a nondemocratic option by alienating them.'[45]

Bilhajj's article was designed for an international audience, but Sallabi's explosive denunciation of Jibril and his allies on Al Jazeera had the greater impact across Libya. In several respects it backfired. Many who otherwise shared Sallabi's wariness of Jibril felt the highly personalised broadside went too far given that Qadhafi and much of his inner circle were still at large. Ordinary Libyans who knew Sallabi only through his frequent TV appearances during the revolution bristled at how he purported to speak for all Libyans. Protests decrying Sallabi took place in Tripoli and Benghazi. Several within Sallabi's circle, including some who had agreed to cooperate on the National Gathering initiative of April 2011, baulked at how divisive his remarks proved and fretted that it would cost him valuable political currency. One of Sallabi's close associates was told by his tribe to distance himself from the cleric.[46]

At the first National Gathering meeting after Tripoli's fall, heated exchanges occurred over the incident and Sallabi ultimately agreed to take a backseat advisory role. 'Ali Sallabi was seen as somewhat toxic after the Al Jazeera controversy,' said one attendee.[47] The episode revealed the limits of Sallabi's influence, which was often overstated by both his supporters and opponents. He utilised longstanding contacts, particularly within the Islamist firmament, to bring together disparate rebel groupings, proving to be a useful interlocutor between the opposition and Qatar. He also tried to negotiate the Qadhafi family's departure from Libya with Abd al-Jalil's blessing. However, subsequent media reports hailing him as the country's most influential political figure were wide of the mark. So too were more secular-leaning revolutionaries who portrayed him as the mastermind of an Islamist conspiracy to take over Libya. Contrary to what people like Ba'ja (who described Sallabi as 'the godfather of the Islamic trend' in Libya)[48] believed, Sallabi was not universally admired among Libya's Islamists. Indeed, several considered him well-meaning but impulsive and lacking in political *nous*.

The Muslim Brotherhood goes it alone

Sallabi's National Gathering represented the ideal of bringing Libya's Islamists together politically under an inclusive nationalist umbrella. Sallabi had long believed that an explicitly Islamist political party would not fare well in Libya. He understood that Libyan society was different to that in neighbouring Egypt and Tunisia, where the divide between liberalism and conservatism was more pronounced. He felt most Libyans took for granted that Islam would play a role in guiding public life, but that did not necessarily translate into support for political Islam, which had not had the opportunity to spread in Libya as it had in Egypt and other countries. Instead, Sallabi argued, parties with a nationalist agenda that also respected faith and tradition would have the broadest appeal.[49]

Yet within months of the fall of Tripoli the National Gathering fell apart. The Muslim Brotherhood pulled out following several acrimonious meetings in which members failed to agree on its structure. Some accused the Brotherhood of trying to wrest control. 'The others came to the meetings with the predisposed idea that the Muslim Brotherhood was only there to dominate and that they needed to be wary of us,' said Abdullah Shamia, the NTC's economics minister. 'We in the Brotherhood felt that if they could not trust us to be open, honest and without a hidden agenda, then it could not work. So we left.'[50]

The Brotherhood's decision to abandon the National Gathering came after a period of self-assessment that began soon after the rebels claimed the capital. Abd al-Latif Karmus, the senior Brotherhood official, recalled the first meeting of its key figures at a luxury Tripoli hotel. Several of the former exiles, prisoners and hitherto clandestine members were meeting each other for the first time, prompting no little wariness at first. 'It was a little strange, like being in a dark cave for a long time before emerging blinking into the sun,' said Karmus.[51] They agreed to hold a General Congress in Benghazi that November. It would be the Libyan Brotherhood's ninth congress, and the third held inside Libya (its first and second General Congresses were held secretly in 1992 and 1996). 'The Benghazi Congress was the Brotherhood's official declaration that we were back,' said Shamia. 'It sent the message that we wanted to spread and revive our group and our ideas.'[52]

Some 700 people attended the Benghazi Congress. Proceedings were tinged with emotion. 'It was the first time we had all come together,' recalled Alamin Bilhajj; 'It was overwhelming.' NTC officials who were members of or close to the Brotherhood attended, including Shamia, Shaikhi and Dghaili, then the outgoing defence minister. The mood was jubilant but focused on restructuring and strategising. By the Congress's close, the Brotherhood had increased its consultative council membership from eleven to thirty people, and elected a new leader; Bashir al-Kubti, an accountant who had lived in Los Angeles for several decades before returning to Libya that March.

The organisation also decided to formally enter politics. After debating the different party political models adopted by the Brotherhood and other Islamist movements in Egypt, Tunisia, Turkey, Morocco and Jordan, the Libyan Brothers decided not to create their own party but to join with others 'of a similar mindset' in founding one. Like the Freedom and Justice Party established by the Muslim Brotherhood in Egypt in 2011—which included a number of Coptic Christians—the party's membership would not be restricted to the Brotherhood and its structure and decision-making process would be separate. The decision to establish a party independent of, but affiliated to, the Brotherhood showed that the Brothers were unsure of their standing in Libya after years of Qadhafi's propaganda against the movement, and felt they needed to present a more diverse—and therefore more palatable— front to potential voters. As one mid-ranking Brother put it: 'We could not do it alone.'[53]

The November Congress also featured international speakers including members of Tunisia's Islamist Ennahda party, which had triumphed in national elections the month before, and the Syrian Muslim Brotherhood. Such international connections were also evident the following month when senior Brotherhood leaders convened a conference on 'national reconciliation' which Abd al-Jalil, interim prime minister Abd al-Rahim al-Kib and Libya's Grand Mufti Sheikh Sadiq al-Gharyani attended. The Brotherhood invited the leader of Tunisia's Ennahda, Rachid Ghannouchi, and Shaikh Yusuf al-Qaradawi, a highly influential Doha-based Egyptian cleric close to the Brotherhood who headed the International Union of Muslim Scholars, of which Shaikhi and Ali Sallabi were members.

However, the presence of such figures prompted some NTC members to withdraw from the conference because 'they saw it as propaganda for the Brotherhood'.[54] The Libyan Brothers were criticised for their connections with the global Brotherhood movement particularly during the 2012 election campaign when rivals accused them of following diktats from their Egyptian equivalent. Brotherhood figures running for election either as individual candidates or with its affiliated Justice and Construction Party (JCP), launched in March 2012, became highly sensitive about its perceived internationalism, and were at pains to stress their independence from Brotherhood movements elsewhere.

The LIFG's existential crisis

With Qadhafi gone, the LIFG (recently rebranded the LIMC) faced an existential crisis. Its founding goal of dislodging Qadhafi by force, abandoned during the Abu Slim reconciliation process in 2009, was revived and achieved during the revolution. Now, members asked themselves what, if anything, the group stood for.

The LIFG's purpose was not only unclear to its own members; some Libyans still suspected the group was affiliated to al-Qa'ida, despite its firm denials. In February 2011, Sa'adi al-Qadhafi had offered Khalid al-Sharif and Abd al-Wahhab al-Qa'id 'millions of dinars' to bring al-Qa'ida to fight on Qadhafi's side in Libya.[55] That autumn, Sa'adi called Abd al-Hakim Bilhajj from exile in Niger to attempt the same stratagem, hinting that Sa'adi himself was contacting al-Qa'ida. 'How can you put your hand in that of the West?' Sa'adi purportedly asked; '[Sa'adi] argued that cooperating with NATO violated Islamic principles, adding, "the Crusaders will now set up their military bases in Libya".'[56]

Furthermore, LIFG members were moving on, taking prominent security and ministerial positions in the interim government. Shortly after his release from Abu Slim during Tripoli's fall, Khalid al-Sharif established a 'National Guard', which aimed to prevent former regime elements escaping across the Tunisian border, and ran its own prisons; when it came under the Ministry of Defence in February 2013, Sharif became the minister's deputy in charge of borders and protection of key facilities. Sadiq al-Ghaithi al-Ubaidi, a former LIFG prisoner from

Tubruq in eastern Libya, became another deputy defence minister, while Dhuwadi became deputy minister for the martyrs and the missing. Under Kib's successor, Ali Zaidan, Bu Hliqa was appointed deputy interior minister and Sami al-Sa'adi was offered, but declined, the post of minister for the martyrs and missing. Their rise had less to do with their LIFG past than with political factors relating to their individual experiences during the revolution, as well as personal tribal and regional connections. This further raised the question of what relevance, if any, the LIFG/LIMC had.

To address these issues the former LIFG/LIMC called a three-day Congress in November 2011. 'It was difficult because this group had not been working openly and therefore had no chance to really think about its political side,' said Bu Hliqa. 'There were so many questions: shall we join the political game or do we move towards preaching (da'wa) instead? Do we dissolve the group now that our original mission is done?'[57]

The Congress reflected how diverse the group had become: the 400-or-so attendees who streamed into a hall in Tripoli's Tobacts Hotel included men in pinstriped suits and men in traditional Libyan dress, men with bushy beards and men with none, men who had been lucky to avoid incarceration and men whose faces betrayed years of imprisonment, torture or life on the run. 'It was the first time so many sat together in the same room,' said one of the organisers, Isma'il Kamuka, a London-based LIFG member who had been jailed in Britain in 2007 for providing funding and false documentation for the group. 'Before that we had been scattered everywhere. People shared their stories and experiences. It was very emotional.'[58] Most were meeting each other for the first time. 'Because we were a secret group, we never really knew each other,' said Bu Hliqa. 'You knew someone through the phone or through other people. Even if you met someone on a mission, you only knew the other's nickname. This was the first time to get to know each other, to talk about our past and our future.'[59]

As Kamuka saw it, the movement could take one of two paths: 'We could sit at home, write our history and honour our sacrifice but leaving it there. Or we could fight in another way—not armed struggle, but building a new Libya.'

But the conference ended with no clear strategy for the future. Delegates voted to change the name of the LIMC to the Islamic Movement for Reform (Harakat al-Islah al-Islamiyya). They elected a new consultative committee, comprising most previous LIFG *shura* council members including Abd al-Hakim Bilhajj, Dhuwadi, Khalid al-Sharif, Qa'id and Bu Hliqa, and headed by Sami al-Sa'adi, the LIFG's former religious guide. No one objected to Libya's democratic path. 'I expected that some people might think democracy is unIslamic, but even those who had been in prison were okay with it,' said Bu Hliqa.[60] In an emotional speech at a June 2012 ceremony marking the anniversary of the Abu Slim massacre, Qa'id urged those present to honour their sacrifice by voting in the forthcoming elections—which was significant, given Qa'id's relation to Abu Yahya al-Libi and his consequent reputation among Abu Slim inmates.[61]

The shift in the LIFG's attitudes to democracy reflected broader trends in Muslim-majority countries in the first decade of the twenty-first century that were hastened by the wave of uprisings across the Middle East and North Africa in 2011. 'In the past we said that participation in any democratic or political activity is prohibited,' said Sa'adi. 'We were not mature, politically speaking, and focused more on the practical reality of armed struggle more than researching the political landscape. We have experienced many things since then and have seen what happened in other Muslim countries. Many had followed what had happened in Turkey [where the ruling AK party had Islamist roots], and they liked it.'[62] For Bilhajj, both Turkey and Malaysia, where he had spent time before his rendition to Libya, offered lessons. 'They succeeded in developing their countries and their economies, and in establishing effective institutions that provide justice and welfare for their people ... This experience is worth aspiring towards.'[63] The electoral success of Ennahda in Tunisia and the Muslim Brotherhood in Egypt in late 2011 banished any lingering doubts about democracy. 'From an Islamic point of view, one must reform or change one's thinking when one realises there is a better way,' Sa'adi said. 'Libya was changing and we wanted to be involved.'[64]

Those within Libya's Islamist firmament who had embraced political participation split into three main parties prior to the country's elections in July 2012.

The first was the party discussed at the Muslim Brotherhood's November Congress, launched the following March as the Justice and Construction Party (JCP). While the Brotherhood stressed that JCP membership was independent and open to everyone, they could not dispel the widespread assumption that the party was the Brotherhood's political arm. This perception was not helped by the fact that several of its founders were well-known Brotherhood members, and by the JCP's election of a former head of the Brotherhood's *shura* council, Muhammad Sawan, as its leader. A former Abu Slim prisoner, Sawan lacked charisma, but had a strong base due to his Misratan origins.

From the ashes of the failed National Gathering attempt to unite Libya's Islamists under a broad nationalist umbrella came the Homeland Party (*al-Watan*). Its slogan, 'All Partners for the Homeland', reflected its diverse membership. The Homeland Party's most recognisable face was Abd al-Hakim Bilhajj, who stepped down as head of the Tripoli Military Council to join the party. Its ranks included affluent business people with no Islamist background, Muslim Brotherhood members, including former Al Jazeera journalist Isma'il Gritly, and more liberal Libyans who were involved in civil society efforts during the revolution, including Lamia Bu Sidra, a British-educated engineer whose glossy billboard pictures in Benghazi, where she was top of the party list, featured her without hijab.

The third party to emerge was the Moderate Nation (*al-Umma al-Wasat*),[65] founded by Sami al-Sa'adi. Several of its members had started with the Homeland Party but bridled over its inclusive approach. Members of the Moderate Nation, which included a far larger cohort of the former LIFG, including Khalid al-Sharif, Dhuwadi and Qa'id, described it as a more explicitly 'Islamic' party. '*Umma al-Wasat* is more religious with clear Islamic targets,' said Khalid al-Sharif, meaning it was less ambiguous than others on how strictly future legislation would be *sharia*-compliant.[66]

These parties faced two challenges in preparing for the July elections. The first was distinguishing themselves from rival entities, including the National Forces Alliance (NFA) led by former interim prime minister Jibril. Many Islamist politicians detested Jibril for his political background heading a national planning board under Qadhafi, his perceived liberalism, and his barely concealed antipathy for Islamists. Almost all parties running in the election—including those, like the NFA, considered more liberal—adopted variations on the same vision of Libya as a democratic civil state with an 'Islamic frame of reference' that the JCP articulated at its launch.[67] This allowed the NFA's election campaign, which featured religious rhetoric and imagery such as a blind *shaikh* running as a candidate in Tripoli, to 'steal our clothes and our language' in the words of one independent Islamist candidate in Benghazi.[68]

The second, more difficult, challenge was countering negative public opinion of Islamists more generally, and the Brotherhood in particular, due to Qadhafi's propaganda and because the Brothers never had the opportunity to correct those perceptions in Libya—for example by providing social services as the Egyptian Brotherhood had over decades. 'Some people here think the Muslim Brotherhood is something to be frightened of. They confuse us with extreme factions,' JCP leader Muhammad Sawan said shortly before the poll. He and other Brotherhood figures expressed vague confidence in correcting these perceptions over time.[69]

The three parties also courted the more politically engaged of Libya's Salafists. No Libyan equivalent to Egypt's Salafist al-Nur party, which had surprised analysts with its strong parliamentary election performance in late 2011, emerged. A few small political Salafist groupings formed, the largest of which was named Asala, whose campaign posters featured its female candidates wearing the *niqab* or full-face veil. A senior Asala figure stressed that the group only contested the elections to ensure the Salafist perspective was heard in any constitutional deliberations, and it did not have faith in, nor wish to enter, a party political system.[70]

At the other end of the Salafist spectrum were those who considered elections inherently unIslamic. Some of these had previously joined revolutionary battalions but from late 2011 began forming their own groups committed to implementing *sharia* in Libya. One, Muhammad al-Zahawi, a former Abu Slim inmate from Benghazi who had fought in the myriad units under the GRC in Brega, gave an interview to a local TV station voicing his opposition to the poll. Zahawi's circle in Benghazi included another former Abu Slim prisoner, Ahmad Abu Khattala, commander of the Abu Ubaida bin al-Jarrah Battalion accused of killing Abd al-Fattah Yunis in July 2011. According to Abu Khattala, the battalion was disbanded after the revolution and several of its members joined Zahawi in a new group named Ansar al-Sharia. It attracted around 250 members from different units across Benghazi, including Fawzi Barawi, a former army officer who had fought with the 17 February Battalion and later sat on Ansar al-Sharia's leadership council.[71]

The first that many in Benghazi heard of Ansar al-Sharia was when it led a parade of pickup trucks loaded with heavy weaponry along the city's seafront in June 2012, calling for the immediate imposition of *sharia* law. Several vehicles were emblazoned with the group's distinctive insignia; two raised Kalashnikovs surrounding a clenched fist with raised forefinger above an open Quran. The rally, which included fighters from towns such as Dirna, was met with a counter-demonstration by locals, some of whom blasted rap music and threw stones. More mainstream Islamists looked on dismayed. 'We all want *sharia* but they are sending out a message that this will be *sharia* through the barrel of a gun,' said one. 'This is hardly a way to persuade people.'[72]

Similar movements sprang up in Dirna. The town's largest armed group, the Abu Slim Martyrs Battalion, split over supporting the democratic transition. Its leader, former LIFG member Salim Dirby, was in favour of democracy, but others believed it to be contrary to Islam. Several of the latter joined the Dirna version of Ansar al-Sharia, established and led by Sufian bin Qumu in early 2012 and apparently unaffiliated with the Benghazi faction.[73] Other Salafist groups emerged. Azuz and a former LIFG member named Abdullah Sabir established the Nur Battalion, which opposed the 7 July elections. While Nur maintained that it contributed to local security and later came under the nominal control of the Interior Ministry, its uncompromising social mores rankled with many Dirna residents who accused it and others of intimidating women who did not observe hijab and threatening radio stations that played music.[74] Assassinations in the town targeted critics of these and other armed Salafists who swaggered around Dirna with black flags featuring Quranic inscriptions.

Libyans fighting with *salafi-jihadist* or *takfiri* groups abroad also returned during the post-revolutionary period, including a dozen or so Dirnawis who fought with *jihadist* groups in Mali. 'Many of these *takfiris*, some of whom had been with al-Qa'ida in Mali, said they didn't trust the NTC,' said one senior member of the former LIFG. 'We asked them what they were doing here and they said they just wanted to return home.'[75]

Conclusion

Despite the JCP, Homeland and Moderate Nation parties' relative confidence following Islamist successes in Tunisia and Egypt, the three parties fared poorly. The JCP fielded seventy-three candidates but garnered seventeen out of the eighty seats allocated for parties, against the NFA's thirty-nine. Two candidates won from the Moderate Nation; the

Homeland Party failed to secure any seats. But media reports portraying the result as a triumph for the 'liberal' NFA over Islamists were misleading, since they did not account for individual candidates holding 120 out of the assembly's 200 seats. More individual candidates identified with the self-described 'Islamic current' than the NFA: these included some twenty Salafists, many associated with Asala, and JCP and Moderate Nation members or affiliates who ran as individual candidates.

Accusations of Qatari support, rooted in the belief that Doha had favoured Islamist-leaning fighters during the revolution, dogged the Homeland Party and JCP throughout the campaign. The Homeland Party's purple-and-white livery prompted jokes comparing it to Qatar's maroon-and-white flag. Jibril's NFA exploited these rumours, culminating in a blunt televised warning by Libya's UN envoy Abd al-Rahman Shalgham days before the ballot that Libya faced a stark choice between 'one of the world's finest planning minds' (Jibril) and Qatar. JCP and Homeland Party officials later felt that their failure to properly challenge Shalgham's remarks played a significant role in their parties' lacklustre performance in the election.[76]

The increasingly assertive, though ostensibly independent, pronouncements of the Grand Mufti, Sadiq al-Ghariani, also proved a hindrance. Ghariani was considered part of Libya's mainstream Salafist-oriented current, and his early declaration of the revolution as religiously legitimate in February 2011 ensured his promotion to head of the reestablished Dar al-Ifta', the body responsible for interpreting Islamic law, a year later. On 6 July, Ghariani declared voting for parties that would limit *sharia* to be 'unIslamic' which outraged more liberal Libyans who saw it as a direct attack on Jibril's NFA. Some within the Islamist spectrum feared it would prove counterproductive. 'Shaikh al-Ghariani shouldn't tell people how to vote,' said the Brotherhood's leader Bashir al-Kubti some days after the election. 'It is best if he stays out of politics.'[77]

The poor showing for the JCP, Homeland Party and Moderate Nation on party lists left Libya's politically engaged Islamists feeling bruised. Subsequent soul-searching triggered fresh acrimony and resignations within the parties. Several were content to blame the results on fear-mongering by the NFA, buttressed by the effects on public opinion of Qadhafi's demonising of Islamists. But others admitted that their inability first to unite, and second to produce from their ranks a figure with as wide appeal as Jibril, then seemed to have contributed to their defeat.[78] Days before the election, former LIFG member Anis al-Sharif, a founding member of the Homeland Party who quit early on due to internal party squabbling, said he feared Libya would witness the reverse of what had happened in Tunisia and Egypt, where more liberal elements who failed to join forces lost to the more organised Islamists of Ennahda and the Muslim Brotherhood.[79] 'The lesson is that we should not split into smaller parties,' said Imhammad Ghula, a Tripoli real estate dealer who was one of the Homeland Party's founders. 'The Islamists' split was less about goals or missions than it was about rivalries and jealousies.'[80]

The failure of Libya's self-described 'Islamic current' to unite during and after the revolution and the failure of their political parties to achieve an electoral majority did not mean they were a spent force. Their subsequent rallying in the General National Congress, assisted by savvy alliances made by the JCP, resulted in Islamists retaining significant influence in Libya's new politics. Outside the GNC, these political factions were bolstered by nonaligned Islamists within the quasi-official security structures that grew out of battalions formed during the 2011 revolution. The Brotherhood also registered itself as a nongovernmental organisation in August 2012 in efforts to put down roots in Libyan society, just as its Egyptian counterpart had. But as the Muslim Brotherhood and much of the former LIFG contended with more radical elements, both critical of their engagement in politics and determined to disrupt the country's democratic trajectory, the latter's behaviour risked further damaging the image of the entire 'Islamic current'. This struggle within will continue to define Libya's Islamist landscape for some time to come.

9

BARQA REBORN?

EASTERN REGIONALISM
AND LIBYA'S POLITICAL TRANSITION

Sean Kane[1]

In the spring of 2011 Benghazi was a place of promise. A spirit of volunteerism permeated the city, which overflowed with international flags and the red, black and green tricolour of Libya's pre-Qadhafi monarchy. At the time of Mu'ammar al-Qadhafi's death in October 2011, twelve-year old boys were still acting as traffic police in Libya's congested second city and eastern Libya was considered the most stable part of the country.

Since that date, however, the region's prospects have become bleaker. Rising Islamic militancy across the east led to increased attacks on foreign targets, most significantly the killing of US Ambassador Christopher Stevens on 11 September 2012. Separately, a 'federalist' movement that rejected the National Transitional Council (NTC) and its transition plan emerged, announcing itself in March 2012 in an assemblage of eastern tribal dignitaries and academics in Benghazi. The movement proclaimed autonomy under a federal system and adopted eastern Libya's historical name: Barqa. Alleging that the NTC had not addressed Qadhafi's political and economic marginalisation of their region, the Barqa movement called on easterners to boycott the country's 7 July 2012 elections—the tangible expression of the core political right for which many eastern Libyans had sacrificied so much. What does such a dramatic turnaround signify for the 'new Libya'?

To answer these complex questions it is necessary to understand Libya's prior experiment with federalism and the traditional power structures in its east that sought to reassert themselves via the 2011 revolution. The east's federalist movement, at least as expressed by those who provocatively declared a federal region of Barqa in early 2012, has struggled with a lack of focus to its proposals, internal divisions and criticism that it is a non-representative vehicle for the interests of the region's historical tribal elite. Nonetheless, the movement was tapping into a broadly held eastern interest in autonomy and growing disaffection with Libya's post-Qadhafi political transition in what was rapidly becoming the most troubled part of the country. This broader alienation of the east is a challenge for the viability of the new Libyan state order and explains why the NTC quickly made substantial political concessions to the nascent 'federalist' movement.

An accidental and reluctant state

Following the first protests against Qadhafi's rule, the 17 February Coalition—a group of lawyers and academics in Benghazi—together with regional local councils and a network of defected diplomats and former government officials established the NTC as the political representation of the Libyan revolution. They presented themselves as the vanguard of a national movement and sole representative of 'all Libya'. Their founding statement emphasised that Benghazi was only their temporary headquarters until the capital, Tripoli, was liberated, and was careful to cite 'representation' from cities and towns outside the east.[2] Throughout the conflict, its leadership repeatedly proclaimed that victory required liberating of the entire country, publicly spurning rumours that Qadhafi's government might accept an eastern regional enclave.[3] The then-head of the education portfolio for the NTC, Hana al-Jalal, underscored this in March 2011, posting to Facebook that 'he [Qadhafi] tried to break us and reduce our nationalism' and reaffirmed easterners' belief in Libya's unity saying that the east was waiting for 'dear Tripoli' to rise up.

While all Libyan towns and regions ultimately recognised the NTC at some stage during the conflict of February to October 2011—and sent representatives to it—its legitimacy was limited by the over-representation of Libyans from the east among its founders. During the conflict, the necessity to present a united front to garner international support curbed potential disaffection with this state of affairs. The Council's frequent proclamations of national unity were meant to signal domestically and internationally that the NTC was not only an eastern movement or the reincarnation of the autonomous emirate that briefly existed in eastern Libya twice during the twentieth century.

This nationalist narrative was important because of Libya's historical characterisation as an accidental and reluctant state, defined by a discontinuous geography punctuated by regional socio-political rivalries. In December 1951, the United Kingdom of Libya emerged from UN stewardship as a union of regions. Previously, during Ottoman rule, Libya consisted of three states or provinces (*wilayat*, sing: *wilaya*): Tripolitania, Cyrenaica (Barqa in Arabic) and Fezzan, roughly corresponding to the country's current west, east, and south. Geographically separated by the Gulf of Sirt and the country's vast central desert, the three regions developed distinct social and political structures. After World War II, they experienced separate colonial administrations, with two separate British military authorities administering Barqa and Tripolitania and the French administering Fezzan.

Then, as now, the vast majority of the population lived along the Mediterranean Coast, where the Italians had forcibly conjoined the administration of Tripolitania and Barqa. Western Tripolitania was relatively urbanised, represented about two-thirds of the population, and was politically heterogeneous, comprising divergent local municipal and economic interests. Its attempt at founding the Arab world's first republic in 1918 foundered amidst internal infighting.

In contrast, the eastern region of Barqa was more traditional and cohesive, with social and political solidarity structured around the Sanusiyya (an Islamic religious order) and Bedouin tribal systems.[4] The Sanusiyya were a religious Sufi order in North Africa and parts of the Arabian peninsula founded in Mecca in the mid-nineteenth century by the Grand Sanusi, Sayyid Muhammad bin Ali al-Sanusi. Concerned with the decline of Islamic thought and spirituality among the Bedouin tribes, the Sanusi order created a vast network of lodges that spanned Barqa, parts of Egypt, the Arabian peninsula and the Sudan. In Barqa, the Sanusi order established an institutional authority that transcended but did not usurp existing Bedouin tribal governance traditions.[5]

'Tribe' in Libya may be understood as a social organisation based on some form of shared solidarity based on common descent, long and close contact, common geography, or some combination of these and other factors.[6] In Barqa specifically, shared lineage associations are the determining factor in tribal identity. The nine leading Sa'adi tribes of Barqa originally migrated to Libya from Arabia almost 1,000 years ago and claim descent from a common maternal ancestor named Sa'ada. Known as the freeborn or noble tribes (al-hurr), they own their home-lands through conquest and historically collected in-kind tribute from client tribes (murabatin) on their lands. One branch, the Jibarna, settled the western coast stretching from Benghazi to Sirt, including modern-day Ajdabiya and Brega; the second, the Harabi, settled the interior Green Mountains, covering modern-day Marj, Baida, and Tubruq.[7]

Sanusi leadership and common ancestry provided the east with a strong regional identity and unity that one historian described as Barqa's 'greatest asset',[8] which to some extent persists until today. The tribe remains a major source of personal identity and social organisation in eastern Libyan society, and perhaps acted as an invisible political unit under Qadhafi.[9] Historically, it allowed Barqa to more effectively resist outsiders, such as the Italian colonisers in 1911, and left it better placed to gain political recognition from European colonial powers. In this respect, Italy briefly gave Barqa dispensation to govern itself as the Autonomous Emirate of Cyrenaica from 1920 to 1929 under the head of the Sanusi Order, as did the post-World War II British civil and military administration until the creation of the new Libyan state in 1951. Historical antecedents for eastern autonomy therefore remained in the living memory of the NTC in early 2011 and, subsequently, those leading the federalist movement in 2012.

Similar to post-2011 Libya, the newly independent Libya of 1947 struggled with divergent views among its notables over the political, administrative and economic structure of the new state. Notwithstanding these centrifugal tendencies, in order to assure their independence, Tripolitania and Fezzan accepted the Allied powers' selection of Idris al-Sanusi, heir to the Sanusiyya movement and grandson of the original Grand Sanusi, as king of Libya.[10] Yet they negotiated a loose federation where the regional administrations had greater authority and resources than the national government. This period only ended in

1963, when the incredible influx of revenues created by the commercial exploitation of oil led to the 'first deliberate attempt'[11] to centrally
administer Libya as ten states rather than three federal regions. In
today's Libya, the term 'federalism' (*fidraliyya*) is almost exclusively
associated with this federal era of 1951–1963; indeed, the post-2011
Barqa movement aimed to straightforwardly restore the 1951 constitution and system of government.

In its third chapter, the 1951 constitution accorded executive and
legislative power on subjects of national concern to the federal government—King Idris and his executive. But in critical areas such as taxa-
tion, economic development and mineral wealth, the federal government depended on regional governments to enforce the rule of law and
collect tax revenues. Moreover, the federal system created an elaborate
administration that rotated the capital between Tripoli and Benghazi
(with Idris's court transiting between the two cities), an upper house of
parliament directly selected by regional administrations, regional leg-
islatures and courts, and even regional border crossings and customs.
Reflecting the relative balance of power, regional administrations
employed almost ten times more civil servants than the federal government and the Cyrenaica Defence Force outnumbered the army.[12]

Even beyond this formal constitutional arrangement, leading Sa'adi
tribal notables of eastern Libya enjoyed substantial influence. Libyan
historian Amal Obeidi described the symbiosis between the Sanusis
and the Bedouin tribes of Barqa as 'almost complete', arguing the kingdom was dominated in its first decade and part of its second by tribal,
family and religious networks.[13] The king's unofficial Royal *diwan* (an
advisory group), populated by Sa'adi tribal notables, held substantial
power. Many of these same individuals held official positions in the
cabinet, diplomatic corps, national bureaucracies and the Cyrenaica
Defence Force. Local government boundaries also aligned with the
frontiers of the Sa'adi tribes' homelands, whose leaders dominated
local administrative positions.[14]

These constitutional and cultural governing arrangements were
upended by the large-scale commercial exploitation of oil during the
1960s. Oil made modern Libya but also laid bare the problems with
the country's brand of federalism, and led to the creation of its first
central administration, and the reformation of the kingdom, in 1963.
As Libya went within eight years from being one of the world's poor-
est countries, with a subsistence economy, to its fourth largest oil

exporter, the federal system proved ill-equipped to meet the consequent demand for unified economic policies and development plans, uniform contracting regimes for exploration and production and clear, national legislation.[15]

Complicating matters further, the country's largest underground oil structures straddled the historical boundary between Barqa and Tripolitania in the Sirt Basin.[16] This was particularly sensitive, given the Sanusis' failed attempt in 1917 to extend their power westwards into Tripolitania, which had been forcibly repulsed in a battle near the town of Bani Walid. A system leaving autonomous regions responsible for hydrocarbon management invited new disputes in petroleum reservoir management and practical problems in constructing refining facilities and pipelines. Historian John Wright argues that the centralisation of the state in 1963 was partly a political response to many early oil finds being located in Barqa and the need to ensure that the oil was seen as 'Libyan' rather than 'eastern'.[17] Qadhafi likewise sought to suppress any resource regionalism by symbolically moving the headquarters of the National Oil Corporation from Benghazi to Tripoli in 1970.

With oil exports representing over 90 per cent of Libya's public revenues and 75 per cent of its national budget, an essential question raised by the revived eastern federalist sentiment today is whether feelings of regional ownership of oil will now find political purchase. Saif al-Islam al-Qadhafi played on this possibility in a televised speech in the first days of the 2011 revolution, asking 'how will we divide the oil among us', and forecasting 'chaos' over revenue sharing.[18]

The uneasy eastern revolutionary coalition

After Qadhafi's 1969 coup, he swiftly consolidated his authority by attempting to dismantle the elite and tribal structures that had underpinned the monarchy. During the first phase of his rule, great efforts were made to eliminate tribal loyalties and attachments. In the east particularly, his government purged Sanusi officers from the armed forces, dismantled Sufi orders and expropriated land from Sa'adi tribal leaders.[19] Qadhafi understood that the tribal society in the east could seriously threaten his new rule; indeed Barqa remained a locus of opposition against Qadhafi's rule.

Unsurprisingly then, scions of the traditional eastern elite returned to play prominent leadership roles in both the NTC and then, afterwards, the Barqa federalist movement. The decision early on in the revolution to defect by the Ubaida, Bara'sa and Awaghir, the largest Sa'adi tribal groupings in and around Benghazi and in the Green Mountains (al-Jabal al-Akhdar), damaged the Qadhafi government's hold on the eastern region.[20] Members of the Sa'adi tribes also came to hold senior leadership positions in the NTC and its military structures, such as NTC Chairman Mustafa Abd al-Jalil of the Bara'sa tribe and the revolutionaries' chief of staff, General Abd al-Fattah Yunis of the Ubaida tribe. Speaking to the presumed enduring significance of the Sanusi name, Ahmad Zubair al-Sanusi, the great-nephew of the deposed King Idris, was a founding member of the NTC before agreeing to become the head of the newly formed Transitional Council of Barqa in 2012.

Nevertheless the February 2011 uprising in the east was not merely a tribal movement. While research by historian Amal Obeidi indicates that the tribe remains one of Libya's strongest sociopolitical units, eastern society is not the same as that of the current generation's parents and grandparents. Obeidi for example found that during the 1990s nearly half of Libyan university students favoured dropping tribal identity in Libyan society.[21]

Thus in 2011, in parallel to the reassertion of traditional power structures, Benghazi also saw a flowering of political activism, free speech and independent civil society. Over 200 political and civic networks and independent media organisations were quickly mobilised by women, exiles, youth and religious conservatives.[22] These groups formed the backbone of a volunteer movement that performed virtually all state functions: garbage collection, telecommunication services, neighbourhood watches, medical treatment and humanitarian assistance.[23]

Libyan urban and middle-class youth were particularly prominent in this political activism and volunteering, as well as frontline fighting, winning acknowledgement from the NTC as playing 'the most important role' and representing the 'foundation of the revolution'.[24] The key youth group was the 17 February Movement, which claimed 100 affiliated organisations. Present from the first protests of the revolution, it was largely composed of young, urban, middle-class citizens, most possessing higher educations. Beyond the 17 February Movement, women's groups and returning diaspora also supported the NTC through volunteerism, technical advice, fundraising and media outreach. These youth and civil society activists tended to be wary of traditional tribal elites and their past dealings with the Qadhafi government. They also charged that the NTC leadership and traditional tribal aristocracy sought to 'hijack' their revolution.[25]

The resurgence of the eastern Sa'adi tribes was also attenuated by eastern Islamist groups, including the Muslim Brotherhood, the former Libyan Islamic Fighting Group (LIFG) and other nonaligned political and militant Salafists and Islamists who had gained credibility through frontline fighting.[26] These groups were also traditionally wary and sometimes hostile towards the region's tribal elite, with veterans of the LIFG from Dirna and the Green Mountains bearing particular animosity towards Yunis and his Ubaida tribe. The Ubaida had traditionally formed the backbone of the Libyan army in the east, which had undertaken major air and ground assaults against a LIFG-led insurgency against Qadhafi in 1996 and 1998.

Eastern Islamists presented themselves as a moral alternative not just to secular institutions of government but also to the nepotism and clientelism of tribes, as well as the sometimes destructive competition among powerful tribal associations.[27] They appeared most established in parts of the east where the Sa'adi tribes were not present, notably certain neighbourhoods of Benghazi and, especially, the city of Dirna. Major parts of these populaces migrated from Misrata and other western Libyan cities during the mid-twentieth century and thus shared few genealogical ties with the nine Sa'adi tribes.[28] Religion—and political Islam specifically—may have therefore become an alternative form of social solidarity and political identity for these migrant families. In the coming months, the Islamists often took opposing positions to secular and tribal figures in the NTC. For example, during NTC negotiations over the electoral law, Muslim Brotherhood members opposed an electoral system of individual representatives (as opposed to party representatives) out of concern it could lead to 'tribalism and regionalism.'[29]

During the revolution itself, these fissures did not fatally undermine the NTC or the civil society that supported it because of their common opposition towards Qadhafi. Even after his death, the opposition in the east still shared the perception that the region was sidelined during Qadhafi's rule and that revolution required tearing down this legacy of centralised rule. Abd al-Qadir Qadura, a prominent Benghazi professor of constitutional law who wrote an influential paper on the need for equal regional representation in Libya's first elections, evocatively compared the engrained effects of centralisation on Libya's psyche to nicotine stains on longtime smokers' fingers.[30] In Qadura's, and other easterners' minds, completing the revolution went beyond Qadhafi's overthrow to dismantling his perceived legacy of centralisation.

However, while easterners might have agreed on the perniciousness of centralism, they were divided on how to address it, with the Barqa movement's tribally infused federalism proving controversial among civil society, youth and Islamists. As early as 20 July 2011, the east's leading tribes initiated discussions on a new Libyan federation during a conference in Benghazi entitled 'First Federal Conference for Libyan Victory', which promoted the advantages of federalism for Libya and pointedly did not invite NTC leaders. In October 2011, an even more suggestively titled meeting of the 'Inhabitants of Barqa' was held in Baida—symbolic to federalists as the site of the very first Sanusi lodge and summer capital of King Idris. Foreshadowing things to come, both conferences were heavily criticised within the broader revolutionary coalition as promoting tribal divisions.[31]

From triumph to discontent

When Libya's 'liberation' was formally declared on 23 October 2011, the ceremony marking the declaration was held in Benghazi rather than Tripoli. The speakers were predominately from the east with political and military leaders from other regions playing less prominent roles.[32] While public opinion research during the uprising should be treated cautiously, one survey of eastern Libya conducted in October 2011 found that 84 per cent of the eastern population felt that the country was moving in the right direction (only 6 per cent felt it was not).[33] Given how quickly eastern disaffection reappeared as the NTC relocated to Tripoli, the liberation celebrations may have represented the high-water mark for the victorious east's status in Libya's political transition.

Citizens across Libya shared in the economic dislocation of Qadhafi's rule, especially during the international sanctions of the 1980s and 1990s. But the east probably suffered the greatest political and economic reversal of fortunes under Qadhafi. The rent-seeking behaviour of eastern elites and the Sa'adi tribes under the monarchy and their outsized political influence undoubtedly fed the popular disillusionment that fuelled Qadhafi's Revolutionary Officers' 1969 coup. Under Qadhafi, the east's favoured status was replaced by what regional inhabitants saw as systematic discrimination and centralised control from Tripoli aimed at forestalling rebellion. Islamists shared this feeling of deliberate neglect, claiming that Dirna and other traditional Islamist areas in the eastern Green Mountains became 'the most marginalised cities in the east' as punishment for their role in the mid-1990s Islamist insurgency.[34]

Following the triumphant transfer of the NTC to Tripoli in October 2011, these shared eastern feelings of inequality quickly flourished and provided space for federalist calls for autonomy, especially as the Council's relocation was accompanied by much of the international diplomatic community. According to Ali Tarhuni, Abd al-Jalil had therefore resisted the relocation as long as possible and wished initially only to relocate the Executive, relenting only when the security disputes in Tripoli between Abd al-Hakim Bilhajj and Mahmud Jibril compelled his presence. It did not help that the Council's westward move unintentionally echoed Qadhafi's aforementioned relocation of government and symbolic institutions (such as the national airline carrier and National Oil Company) from Benghazi to Tripoli.[35] These sensitivities were exacerbated by the Council's necessary effort to improve its regional balance by selecting western Libyans for the majority of cabinet positions in the interim government.

Once the NTC and interim government reverted to Tripoli, Benghazi activists and the lawyers and university professors involved in launching the NTC began to allege that there was a stealthy return to the *status quo ante*. Some months later, a senior member of the Barqa movement pointed to the NTC's relocation of Libya's equivalent of the social security administration to Tripoli and the alleged marginalisation of easterners in lists for graduate scholarships abroad and ambassadorial appointments as key complaints behind their drive for autonomy.[36]

The resentment was compounded by proprietary eastern feelings over the revolution and a perception that western towns were late to support it. Parallels were drawn to the spotty resistance of Tripolitania to the Italian colonial occupation and a popular refrain emerged claiming that 'Tripoli continued erecting statues to the tyrant [Qadhafi] until the week before he fell'.[37]

These views soon manifested themselves in the streets. Within six weeks of Qadhafi's death, the first significant post-revolution protests against the NTC were held in Benghazi. On 12 December 2011, approximately 200 people protested in Tree Square, the site of the first rallies that launched the revolution. They criticised the NTC for considering a draft transitional justice law to pursue reconciliation with Qadhafi supporters (seen as influential and more numerous in the west) and a lack of transparency in its decision making. Protestors charged that 'the regime has not changed ... it is the same which oppresses and marginalises cities'.[38]

Keenly sensitive to the ramifications of eastern discontent, the NTC that same day released a statement recognising that 'Benghazi hosted the revolution ... and was one of the factors that enabled its success' and acknowledging that 'since the revolution the people of Benghazi feel marginalised and forgotten'.[39] The Council named Benghazi Libya's economic capital, promising that administrative decentralisation would follow, and committed to monthly meetings there—but made little progress on these promises during its remaining months in power.

The representation dilemma

Rising eastern disaffection quickly tinged Libya's political transition. On 3 August 2011 the NTC had released a Constitutional Declaration that included a roadmap towards permanent democratic institutions. It began with the 'liberation' of Libya from the Qadhafi family, followed in eight months by elections to replace the self-appointed NTC with a 200-member directly elected General National Congress (GNC) which would act as a transitional parliament and oversee the drafting of Libya's new constitution.

From the start, this Declaration was buffeted by regional contention. Early drafts foresaw the NTC, with its outsized representation from Benghazi and the east, supervising the entirety of Libya's transition and constitutional drafting process. The NTC's Tripoli representatives and their contacts in the still regime-held capital pushed instead to replace the NTC with the directly elected GNC, partly to ensure a stronger role for western Libya in the transition.[40]

By November 2011, debates over apportioning regional representation in the GNC were well underway. With an estimated two-thirds of Libya's 6.5 million people living in its west, eastern figures from across the political spectrum argued against an electoral formula for the GNC based on population-based proportional representation. They feared such an approach could result in Tripoli dominating the body and hence constitution-making, potentially leading to a reestablishment of centralised control. Consequently, these diverse eastern trends called for a geographically defined system of electoral districts, where each of Libya's regions would have equal representation in the GNC regardless of population size.

Tripoli and the west understandably disagreed. They also recalled the historical precedent of the provisional National Constitutional Assembly that drafted Libya's independence constitution in 1951. Selected by UN Commissioner Adrian Pelt on the basis that the three regions should each have twenty representatives despite their population differences,[41] its equal geographic balance effectively allowed Barqa and Fezzan representatives to outvote Tripolitania on key questions despite the latter having twice their combined population. This was in fact the outcome in 1951 on the question of federalism in the independence constitution. Western Libyan political leaders were therefore wary of resurrecting this formula in 2012 for the election of the GNC.

The first draft of the electoral law was released on 3 January 2012. Frustrated by the murky process surrounding its drafting and a minute ten-day period for public comment, eastern tribal leaders, political parties and civil society all seized upon the provision stipulating the apportionment of seats between electoral constituencies and regions. The relevant article read as follows: 'The country shall be divided into electoral districts (constituencies) for the organisation of elections, provided observation of the ratio of population and geographical area.'[42]

At three major public discussions in Benghazi hosted by different eastern political currents, audiences repeatedly focused on this article. One was organised by the NTC at the Benghazi International University on 5 January 2012 with the head of the committee who drafted the law; a second by the Muslim Brotherhood at the Da'wa Islamiyya Conference Centre on 8 January 2012 and a third by the Benghazi University Faculty of Law on 9 January 2012.[43] The common sentiment running through the meetings was 'equality between regions' as the basis for drafting a constitution and that 'Tripoli' needed to know that the law in its current form was unacceptable.[44] Some participants emotionally described the offending article as a 'black mark' on the whole law that could spark a new revolution.[45] During the meetings, participants implicitly admonished western Libyans, suggesting 'that those who sided with Qadhafi should not be given seats or allowed to vote on par with supporters of the revolution'.[46]

Despite lack of consensus on this key point, the NTC tried to stick closely to the Constitutional Declaration's timetable, which required adopting the law by 20 January 2011. This resulted in violent protest on 21 January: as the Council met in a special session in Benghazi to finalise the elections law, hundreds of angry armed protestors, some of whom had camped outside for three weeks, ransacked the NTC's Benghazi headquarters claiming that the law was being drafted without public consultation.[47] Several Council members fled, in some cases jumping out of back windows.[48]

The sacking of the NTC headquarters shook up the NTC leadership, leading to the resignation of Deputy Chairman Abd al-Hafiz Ghugha and, in a concession to protestors' concerns, the NTC delayed the law's passage to allow independent Libyan legal experts to review the bill. The law was finally adopted on 12 February 2012, but deferred the explosive regional representation issue, stating merely 'electoral districts based on population and geography will be determined and announced by The [High National Electoral] Commission within two weeks'.[49] This announcement did not occur, however, until 14 March 2012. The final compromise announced was 102 seats for western Libya, sixty for the east and thirty-eight for the centre and south. Throughout the ensuing months, easterners protested what they saw as their underrepresentation in the General National Conference. As late as 1 July, protestors against the representation formula occupied the city's election commission building.[50]

Though there were other controversial election issues, such as participation of political parties, election quotas for women and lustration of Qadhafi-era officials, it spoke to the political significance of the question of regional balance in representation that it took the longest to resolve. The end result contributed to a probably unrealistic but nonetheless strongly held sense of political disenfranchisement in the east. Against a backdrop of continuing economic stagnation and halting reconstruction efforts, it allowed initially marginal discussions of federalism to find purchase.

Back to the future

On 6 March 2012, almost a year to the day from the NTC's Founding Statement, an estimated 3,000 tribal leaders, military commanders and political figures gathered in Benghazi to unilaterally declare the creation of a new Barqa federal region. Its leadership comprised over 350 tribal representatives, professionals and ex-revolutionaries, and claimed representation from across Barqa.[51] One analyst's typology of the movement articulated three main constituencies: intellectuals and former members of the exiled opposition from the cities of Benghazi and Dirna; the region's Sa'adi tribal establishment; and parts of the region's old army officer class, often closely related to tribal leaders, who had defected early in the revolution.[52]

The tribal establishment participating in the Barqa Conference included the most important tribes from both the Harabi and Jibarna branches of the Sa'adi, from the eastern and western halves of Barqa, respectively. The two largest Jibarna tribes were represented, namely the Awaghir (possibly the second most numerous tribe in the east and the major tribe around Benghazi) and the Marghaba (the largest tribe in the oil-rich Sirt Basin). Meanwhile, the Ubaida, the dominant tribe within the Harabi branch and the second largest tribal confederation in Libya, played a key role organising the conference. Smaller Harabi tribes such as the Hasa and the Dursa were also present. Also participating were commanders from the Barqa Military Council, a loose coordinating entity of sixty-one eastern revolutionary battalions commanded by Hamid al-Hasi, a former army colonel with extensive frontline experience during the revolution and a member of the Sa'adi Hasa tribe.[53]

The Bara'sa tribe, which after the Ubaida was the most powerful Harabi tribe in eastern Libya's Green Mountains, was, however, conspicuously absent. Despite their homeland, in and around Baida, being the site of the first Sanusi lodge, this tribe maintained a distance from the federalism initiative out of respect for Abd al-Jalil, one of its prominent sons.

The Declaration issued by the Barqa Conference unanimously rejected the proposed distribution of seats for the GNC elections then being negotiated. Looking to the past for solutions, they argued that the 1951 Constitution promulgated at independence still had legal standing. The Conference dismissed the 1963 amendments made to the 1951 Charter to centralise administration of the kingdom after the discovery of oil as a 'violation' and also refused to recognise the NTC's 3 August 2011 Constitutional Declaration.[54] Completing the historic symbolism, the gathering named Ahmad Zubair al-Sanusi, an NTC member, political prisoner under the Qadhafi regime and great-nephew of the deposed King Idris, as head of the newly formed Transitional Council of Barqa.

218

While the Barqa Declaration was vague on what powers an autonomous Barqa region would claim, conference participants were less circumspect. Some indicated that Barqa, with Benghazi as its capital, would have its own parliament, police force and courts while running basic services like housing and education. While foreign policy and the armed forces would remain with the central authorities, different ideas appeared to be circulating regarding what would happen with regional finances and the management of oil resources.[55]

The conference's closing statement emphasised that its calls for federalism were not tantamount to separatism, but rather the best means to address eastern feelings of marginalisation and keep Libya as 'a unified and sovereign state'. While the declaration carried no official standing it highlighted the increased prominence of a movement that only a few months ago existed at the fringes of politics in eastern Libyan politics.

The NTC swiftly characterised the Barqa Declaration, given its entire rejection of the Constitutional Declaration and transitional process, as 'sedition' sponsored by counterrevolutionary forces and a threat to national unity. Abd al-Jalil, despite his own eastern roots, vaguely threatened to forcefully block the self-styled region's creation.[56] Protests extolling national unity were held across Libya on 9 March 2012, with thousands gathering in central Tripoli's Martyrs Square to chant 'No to federalism' and 'Libya is one'. Most major political movements also condemned the Barqa Declaration, including both Islamist and liberal groups.[57] Libya's leading mufti, Sadiq al-Gharyani, declared that rejecting federalism was a religious duty for all Libyans. Even Egypt, Tunisia, and the Organisation of the Islamic Conference expressed support for a unified Libya.

Yet the NTC's subsequent actions revealed the depth of its disquiet with the eastern protests and Barqa movement. The interim authorities quickly announced that, at Prime Minister Abd al-Rahim al-Kib's initiative, they would prepare a law on administrative decentralisation while immediately opening offices in Benghazi and Sabha (the largest city in southern Libya) to 'avert the policy of federalism to run the state's affairs'.[58]

Most dramatically however, on 13 March 2012, the NTC announced its first amendment to the Constitutional Declaration. While the General National Congress was originally free to select the constitutional drafting committee, it was now charged to emulate 'the Sixty

Committee established to develop the Libya Independence Constitution in 1951' in picking drafters. Moreover, all drafting decisions would require a two-thirds plus one majority.[59] The intent was clear: to dispel anxieties about the regional distribution in the GNC, the east was conceded equal geographic representation in the body that would draft the new constitutional text and an effective veto in its decision making. Despite this concession, however, discontent only heightened in the east. Federalists rejected the amendment, claiming that the appointed constitutional body would still be beholden to a GNC numerically dominated by western Libyans.

Meanwhile, the NTC's promised law on administrative decentralisation did not materialise and the Barqa Council held a follow-up meeting in Baida on 10 April 2012 in King Idris's summer capital. The Council rejected the new electoral law, announced a 200-member governing council and, echoing the monarchy's tribally recruited Cyrenaica Defence Force, announced a regional guard to protect the Barqa region.[60,61] Most worryingly to the NTC, the Barqa Council also, as the GNC elections approached, called for eastern residents to boycott the polls in favour of a referendum on establishing a federal region.

Fearing a boycott would undermine the legitimacy of the elections, Abd al-Jalil made a surprise announcement on 5 July 2012—the eve of the historic vote. Amending the Constitutional Declaration once again, the NTC acceded to a core federalist demand, entirely removing responsibility for supervising the drafting of the constitution from the GNC. Instead, they proposed that the sixty members of the constitutional commission would be directly elected and that the commission would have equal representation at twenty members each, from Tripolitania, Barqa and Fezzan respectively.[62]

This second amendment, one of the NTC's final acts, was a contrasting bookend to its founding statement of February 2011, which carefully presented the NTC as representing a unified, national movement. The Barqa federalists meanwhile had substantially succeeded in shaping the political debate and the transitional process of statebuilding around their own regionalist vision.

Barqa reborn?

Barqa's federalist movement should not be conflated with more general eastern estrangement concerning Libya's transition, which appeared to be almost universally felt by eastern Libya's political class. At the start of the Libyan transition in October 2011, public opinion polling found that only 7 per cent of eastern respondents favoured a federal system.[63] This suggested a weak base of public receptivity for federalists to build upon and that eastern autonomy had not been a major popular motivator for the 17 February Revolution. Even at the time of the Barqa Council's founding conference in early March 2012, eastern support for the movement's proffered brand of federalism still appeared mixed.

Some of the strongest resistance to the Barqa movement in fact came from the east, where preemptive protests criticising it were held in Benghazi prior to the 6 March 2012 conference. Protests continued after the conference, where major eastern cities saw rallies as part of nationwide demonstrations against federalism. Local governing councils in Benghazi, Dirna, Baida and Tubruq—including not only the east's largest cities but also Barqa's putative capital—also denied recognition to the Interim Barqa Council, as did the most powerful eastern-based militia coalition, the Gathering of Revolutionary Companies (*Tajammu' Sarayat al-Thuwwar*). Similarly, a joint statement from 120 of Benghazi's youth and civil society organisations rejected federalism despite characterising a centrally administered state as 'an abomination'. In all, these reactions to the Barqa initiative illustrate that eastern estrangement from Tripoli did not automatically translate into support for the federalists.[64]

More fundamentally, the Barqa Council was a controversial standard bearer for a federal system. In both composition and principal proposition, the Barqa Council represented a return to the east's historic power structures. As one eastern political figure commented, 'This step [declaring autonomy] has been taken by families who in the past had prestige and think that if they do this they can return to the past.'[65] These remarks referred to the underpinning role of the Ubaida, Marghaba and Awaghir tribes in forming the Barqa Council and their elite status under the Sanusi monarchy (especially the Ubaida, probably the most influential tribe at that time).

The Sa'adi tribes certainly played a key role in the 17 February Revolution, but their mobilising power spoke perhaps to the lack of other avenues for political organisation under Qadhafi, who banned civil society, parties and trade unions.[66] The aforementioned eruption of civil society, youth groups, political parties, revolutionary battalions

THE LIBYAN REVOLUTION AND ITS AFTERMATH

and Islamist networks in the east had given eastern Libyans options to politically organise outside of or across tribalism, and indeed in some cases to resist tribalism. For example, it is unlikely that Ahmad Zubair al-Sanusi's forefathers received anything like the caustic treatment he did on Facebook following the Barqa founding conference in March 2012, where he was depicted as a senile and crying infant.

Indeed, with some 57 per cent of the Libyan population under the age of thirty, a state consciously modelled on how Libya looked in the 1950s and 1960s seems anachronistic. This was borne out at workshops conducted by the author on elections and constitution making in several eastern cities from December 2011 to May 2012. In these sessions, young Libyans proved mostly unaware of their country's federal past and emotionally described national unity as having been the chief rallying cry in their rush to the frontlines.[67]

The tribal politics of the Barqa Council also undermined its own goal of attaining an inclusive regional movement. The Bara'sa distanced themselves from the initiative largely on tribal grounds, namely respect for Abd al-Jalil, as well as due to their strained relations with the Ubaida.[68] Tribes from smaller eastern towns, particularly the oil-rich Sirt Basin, saw the movement as Benghazi-centric: while some of the Marghaba tribe dominant in this area did participate, other Marghaba, and representatives of the Majabar and Zway tribes[69] from the oil towns of Ajdabiya, Ra's Lanuf, Brega and Jalu did not want to trade centralism in Tripoli for centralism in Benghazi. Rather than see an autonomous eastern federal region that might diminish their local influence, they envisaged ten or more national provinces that would allow their area to manage its own affairs and oil production independently of Benghazi.[70] Some tribal and local council leaders from this oil crescent were more militant, threatening to cut supply to eastern oil terminals if 'Benghazi' unilaterally declared autonomy.[71]

The Barqa initiative also suffered because its eastern and tribal orientation lost it support from significant parts of Benghazi and Dirna, who, as mentioned, were descended from migrants from Misrata and other western Libyan towns. These descendants were especially wary about a 'tribal project' masquerading as a federal region of Barqa in which they feared becoming second-class citizens. Dirna political activists were 'completely against federalism' because 'up to 80 per cent of the city' was originally from western Libya and they were worried that the original Sa'adi Bedouin would ask them to return if federalism was implemented.[72] Dirnawis therefore favoured municipal and economic decentralisation over federalism. This stance also had historical echoes. Adrian Pelt, the UN commissioner who oversaw Libyan independence, wrote that during the mid-1940s that the Dirna branch of the main political organisation advocating Libyan independence favoured 'complete unity between the [Libyan] provinces' while the traditional elite that populated the Benghazi branch favoured federalism.[73]

Libya's traditional tribal leaders also encountered opposition among Islamist groups, who hailed not just from Dirna and Benghazi, but also some of the same areas of the Green Mountains as the Sa'adi Harabi tribes. The Barqa initiative failed to span this faultline; instead, attendees at the March 2012 Barqa founding conference blamed Islamists for anti-federalist protests.[74] Similarly, Tubruq, an Ubaida and federalist stronghold, resisted the Muslim Brotherhood's Freedom and Justice Party's efforts to open a local representation office.[75] Islamists returned the favour: one kidnapped Libyan journalist said that the first thing his allegedly Islamist abductors told him was, 'You are a dirty Bedouin. You want federalism.'[76] Indeed the rivalry between political Islamists and tribally oriented federalists in the east had some undertones of an identity conflict between the 'original' Sa'adi tribal inhabitants of the region and more recent migrants to the area from western Libya.

But perhaps the Barqa initiative's key limitation related to its tactical decisions. Even the growing group in the east interested in exploring federalism felt discomfort with the self-appointed and tribally associated Barqa Council unilaterally adopting a historically loaded model of federalism while professing to speak for the entire region. Of equal frustration was the issuance of that controversial declaration prior to dialogue with Libya's other regions, rendering the concept of federalism toxic in the rest of the country. There was even grudging acknowledgement of Abd al-Jalil's remark that the Barqa movement represented 'a group of people imposing their views on the Libyan people … before they vote on it and express their ideas'.[77]

The Council's call for a boycott of the elections and perceived links to efforts to sabotage the vote were even more deleterious to its standing. Prior to the polls, the Barqa Regional Guard and Barqa Military Council set up roadblocks in Wadi al-Ahmar near Sirt (the traditional boundary between Barqa and Tripolitania) to stop ballot boxes entering the east, shut down five oil export terminals in the Gulf of Sirt and occupied the elections commission building in Benghazi, where the

Barqa fighters quickly came into conflict with opposing local Benghazi groups. Armed groups that many easterners assumed were linked to federalists also fired at a helicopter ferrying election materials to Benghazi (killing one Libyan poll worker) and burned down a warehouse storing elections supplies in Ajdabiya.[78]

This sabotage backfired, and as on election day Benghazi and the east generally ignored the Barqa Council's boycott call. The High National Election Commission estimated turnout across Libya at 62 per cent, whereas turnout in eastern Libya was an almost identical 60 per cent. In Benghazi, the political centre of gravity of the federalism movement, turnout was 66 per cent.[79] Online, social media network posts praised Benghazi residents for delivering federalists a 'slap to the face' by voting in large numbers.[80] Post-election focus groups found that participants in eastern cities took great pride in the 7 July elections, comparing them to townwide Eid feasts or wedding celebrations. Most interviewees indicated that they had voted due to a combination of civic responsibility, honouring the principles of the 17 February Revolution and the sheer novelty and excitement of participating in the country's first elections in over four decades.[81]

A clearer debate on the autonomy sought by federalists, and a political compromise on the eastern region's status, thus did not emerge under the NTC's watch. This was partly because the Barqa Council's March 2012 founding declaration never specified the administrative arrangements and distribution of powers the movement sought. The movement thus became caricatured by its opponents, including local and national Islamist figures, as a cover to control Barqa's abundant natural wealth and resurrect a neo-patrimonial system where the leading Sa'adi tribes controlled the distribution of oil-funded public sector and parastatal jobs, investment projects, social allowances and subsidies. One example of this sentiment expressed within the east's complex identity politics was given by Ahmad al-Zlitny (whose last name suggests his family's origins from the western town of Zlitan), spokesman for a Benghazi-based Islamist group lobbying for the imposition Islamic law, who stated: 'We don't have a problem with federalism, but this is just about tribal power.'[82]

Nevertheless, this dismissal also ignores the east's much more fundamental feelings of alienation from the new order it ironically helped to force into being in February 2011. As some leading national political figures later acknowledged, it was poor governance from the centre and lawlessness that led many easterners to consider federalism as a solution.[83]

Whither the east and the new Libya?

To develop a functioning and financially sustainable polity, Libya will need to separate legitimate eastern anxieties from more extreme self-rule demands. The Sa'da tribes cannot realistically expect to regain the status they held under the Sanusi monarchy, nor Benghazi its status as the NTC's seat of power in 2011. While poor service delivery, halting reconstruction and continued security instability are interpreted in the east as evidence of continuing marginalisation by Tripoli, these complex problems are endemic throughout Libya. But Barqa and other parts of Libya's periphery clearly should be more integrated into national political decision making, government administration and economic planning than they were under Qadhafi.

In fact, caught up in the emotion of the term 'federalism' and its connotations of separatism in the Arab world, commonalities between the east and the rest of the country on local autonomy have been overlooked. Major power centres in western Libya, such as the port city of Misrata (and for that matter some in eastern cities like Dirna and Ajdabiya), have consistently favoured strong municipal or provincial authorities with their own decentralised authorities and independent budgets. Public opinion polling suggests that a 'decentralised state' is the preferred allocation of powers between central and local governments by 57 per cent of Libyans and 62 per cent of easterners.[84]

As Libya begins the multi-year task of institution building, advocates of federalism, decentralisation and even the status quo of relative centralisation will ultimately have to agree on the apportionment of state powers. While it is difficult to confidently predict the shape of this *modus vivendi*, what is clear is that maintaining a stable Libya will be difficult if its politically hyperactive eastern region does not buy into the new order.

The choices made by Libya's new rulers suggest that they understand that even popular electoral mandates do not exempt them from this axiom. Given that this chapter has argued that the Barqa movement only had marginal popularity in the east, one might logically ask why the NTC made such broad concessions to it. The first answer is that unlike most of the localist demands being directed towards the NTC, the Council perceived renewed alienation from eastern Libya as a clear strategic threat to the transition.

A quick glance at two key issues, oil and water, reveals how the viability of the new Libya could be undermined if eastern alienation becomes a permanent feature of the political landscape. In any scenario, Libya's oil will need to finance government and an equal standard of services and development across the country. However, approximately two-thirds of production comes from the eastern region (and a further 25 per cent from the south).[85] Similarly, regarding, water resources, the largest of the country's four major underground water reservoirs is located near the southeastern town of Kufra within the historical boundaries of Barqa.[86] As King Idris and his advisers foresaw when they changed the state system in the 1960s, should these resources be seen as 'eastern' rather than 'Libyan,' the consequences for Libya's political and financial stability would be grave. A collapsed debate on federalism and decentralisation could lead to just such a situation. So while the NTC was clearly responding to federalist pressure when it twice altered its transition plan during 2012, it should not be overlooked that its concessions on regional representation in the constitution drafting process reflected demands being raised by the broader eastern population *before* the federalist movement burst onto the scene.

The second likely motivation of the NTC was the extent to which the region has set trends in Libyan politics. Resistance to Italian occupation, the shaping of the 1951 independence constitution, and most recently with the 2011 revolution, all emanated from Benghazi. The NTC likely concluded that even the unpopular Barqa movement risked inspiring other autonomy advocates. Despite, or perhaps because of the NTC's concessions to the Barqa movement's militancy and pressure tactics, copycats did emerge in 2013. While according to opinion polls federalism continued to remain unpopular in the east,[87] July 2013 saw a new group of eastern federalists seize control of the major oil export facilities in the oil crescent of the Sirt Basin.

Demanding more autonomy and revenue for the eastern region, this second-generation federalism movement tended to be conflated with Ahmad Zubair al-Sanusi's Interim Barqa Council.[88] They were in fact a separate group and an illuminating contrast to the older Sa'adi elite. Initially calling themselves the Barqa Youth Movement, the blockade action was led by a thirty-three-year old named Ibrahim Jadran who had risen to prominence fighting on the frontlines in 2011. Jadran and his battle-tested supporters hailed not from Benghazi and the Green Mountains but from the oil crescent in the eastern Sirt Basin that this chapter has noted is wary of trading Tripolitanian centralism for administration by Benghazi. Within three months, Jadran's closure of oil terminals had sparked a more than 90 per cent reduction in Libyan oil exports and cost the central government as much as $5 billion.[89]

Even more worryingly for the NTC's successors, Jadran's action inspired imitation in other parts of the country, including a symbolic declaration of a federal region of Fezzan; oil and water pipelines from southwest Libya being cut by local groups seeking to have their grievances redressed by Tripoli; and Amazigh (Berber) activists in the western Nafusa Mountains cutting gas export lines to press demands for recognition of their indigenous language in the new constitution. In taking such pains to respond to a tribally based Barqa movement that seemed to have endogenous limits to its political appeal, the NTC may first and foremost have been trying to forestall the eastern Sa'adi tribal elite from letting the federalism and resource regionalism genie out of the bottle.

10

HISTORY'S WARRIORS

THE EMERGENCE OF REVOLUTIONARY BATTALIONS
IN MISRATA

Brian McQuinn

Introduction

On 17 September 2011, seven months into the war, hundreds of
Misratan revolutionary battalions[1] parked their vehicles armed with
anti-aircraft guns in long rows along the four-lane highway to Sirt,
anticipating the final battle of the uprising. Despite the tension, men
slept under their trucks shaded from the 44°C temperatures, prayed
in small groups along the desert highway or debated the whereabouts
of Mu'ammar al-Qadhafi and his sons. NATO airstrikes on the
Libyan army's frontlines signaled their advance. As plumes of smoke
rose up, Muhammad, a thirty-two-year-old oil company executive
turned fighter, pointed at a man carrying a large orange and blue
painting. It depicted a landscape of palm trees and desert with two
lines of men running at each other firing World War I bolt-action
rifles. The Italian soldiers, dressed in their characteristic green uniforms and tall white helmets, are falling to men dressed in long white

robes and orange capes. At the centre of the painting is a bearded man on a white horse leading the charge. The painting's caption reads, 'The battle of Qardabiyya ... the battle for national unity.'

'History is today. It has all come full circle,' Muhammad asserted. He handed me his smartphone, which displayed a black-and-white image of the same bearded man in the painting: Ramadan al-Suwaihli—the most prominent Misratan leader of the insurgency against Italian colonial rule. His image was ubiquitous in Misrata. Suwaihli's image was often accompanied by a grainy black-and-white photograph of the fighter's own grandfather who fought 'with Suwaihli'.

Muhammad continued:

Ramadan al-Suwaihli created the Tripolitania Republic in 1918, the first republic in the Middle East. He fought the Italian occupation right here [pointing to the desert in front of us]. That is why the man wanted you to see that picture. But Suwaihli failed and then Qadhafi erased him from history along with the republic. But it is our destiny as Misratans to fulfil Suwaihli's dream. When Sirt falls, we will finally have our republic. It took 100 years, but we can feel our grandfathers with us today.[2]

Moments later, the Misratan fighters sped down the highway in a coordinated cacophony, jamming through the narrow opening in the government fortifications created by the airstrikes, and pushed into Sirt's outskirts. Finding little resistance in Tripoli, or other towns recently overrun by Misratan forces, no one foresaw what awaited them: two months of bloody fighting and Qadhafi.

Misrata emerged from the 17 February Revolution more emboldened than at any time, perhaps, since the Tripolitania Republic, controlling the majority of experienced fighters and weaponry in Libya.[3] Their confidence derived from working together as a garrison town to repel Qadhafi's armed forces and security brigades through ingenuity, good fortune and the city's tight-knit social networks. The shared trauma and triumph became central tenets of Misratans' individual and collective narratives.[4]

This chapter argues that Misratans' self-reliance and vision of Libya are rooted in its history and reinforced by insurgency: first against Italian colonial authority from 1911–1933 and then the 2011 revolution. Particular attention is paid to the inception of the revolutionary battalions and neighbourhood executive committees that oversaw them. Initially composed of three-to-five-person street-fighting cells, the groups coalesced into 236 organisations, some capable of operating tank divisions and coordinating using Global Positioning System devices and Google Earth mapping technology. Their tactics, often portrayed as chaotic and disorganised, were learned during the urban guerrilla campaign and are more accurately characterised as decentralised and adaptive.

The chapter first examines the historical events and personalities that underpin Misratans' sense of manifest destiny. It then reviews the three stages of the fighting in Misrata, detailing the inception of the armed resistance and civilian authority. It concludes by examining how these two narratives, one historic and the other contemporary, shaped each other and, in turn, Misratans' visions for its role in Libya's future.

The Tripolitania Republic (1918–1922)

The sense of historical destiny adopted by Muhammad and his peers was mythologised. The Tripolitania Republic was a brief four-year experiment in republican government during the Italian occupation (1911–1933) of Libya in which Misratans, and Suwaihli in particular, played a leading role.[5] During Qadhafi's era, the history of this republic and its founders was erased. Instead, Qadhafi lionised the eastern insurgency leader Umar al-Mukhtar, whom the Italians publicly hanged in 1931.[6]

The Tripolitania Republic emerged from the power struggles between Italy and the Ottoman Empire. Motivated by colonial conquest, Italy invaded Libya in October 1911, at the time a province of the Ottoman Empire. Distracted by unrest in the Balkans, the Ottoman Empire quickly sued for peace, leaving Libya's status ambiguous—claimed by Italy but not fully ceded by the Ottomans. Libya's elite split their loyalties between the Italians and the Ottoman Empire. With the outbreak of World War I in 1914, Italy and the Ottoman Empire were again engaged in open conflict.[7]

The Ottomans supported Libyan resistance to Italian occupation by supplying weapons and advisers. They initially allied with the Sanusi Order in the east to encourage attacks on British positions in Egypt. After being defeated by the British, however, the Ottomans, led by General Nuri Bay, retreated west to Misrata. Once there, the Ottoman officers found ready friends among local commanders who had been harassing Italian forces outside Tripoli and Khums for months. Ramadan al-Suwaihli played a prominent role in Misrata, his reputation built on his military success against the Italians at Qardabiyya (the battle depicted in the painting). The Ottomans and Germans subsequently used Misrata's deep-water port as a main supply route for reinforcements and supplies into Libya, allowing Suwaihli to strengthen his political influence and arm Misratan forces. By the end of 1917, Suwaihli was appointed governor of an autonomous territory, which included most of eastern Tripolitania.

The Republic only lasted four years, however. Internal strife between its leaders—Suwaihli, Sulaiman al-Baruni, Ahmad al-Murayyid, and Abd al-Nibi Bilkhair—and the coming to power of the Fascists in Rome spelled the end of the Arab world's first republican government. In October 1922, Mussolini's regime abdicated all previous agreements, triggering a renewed insurgency in Libya. Unlike previous Italian governments, which preferred diplomacy, the Fascists resorted to brute force. Over the next decade, almost half of Libya's population perished as a result of mass executions and the interment of a majority of Cyrenaica's population in camps with poor sanitation and water.[8] The insurgency did not die until its leader Umar al-Mukhtar was publically hanged in September 1931 in front of thousands of onlookers.[9]

Despite the short-lived nature of the Republic and Misrata's autonomy, the experience was, as the vignette above illustrated, formative to the city's collective narrative. While the values of self-reliance and autonomy are legacies of Bedouin culture in Libya,[10] Suwaihli came to embody these virtues for Misratans. The insurgency against Qadhafi in 2011 was subsequently framed by, and reinforced, these same values and narratives. Nevertheless, while this provides insight into Misratans' framing of the war, the cohesion and group morphology of the fighting units, and their symbiotic links to the community's neighbourhoods, were also a product of how the war unfolded in Misrata.

Armed resistance in Misrata

The armed conflict in Misrata lasted almost the entire revolution, beginning on 19 February 2011 and continuing until the fall of Tripoli on 20 August 2011. Yet even after the city was no longer encircled by the armed forces and security brigades, its forces continued to fight, first in Tripoli and then later in Sirt, 250km to the southeast of the city. This chapter argues that understanding Misrata's revolutionary battalions it is necessary to study their inception, which is presented in three stages: the initial success of the Misratan protestors; the occupation of Tripoli Street; and finally, the emergence of revolutionary battalions. While each stage describes a distinct phase in the fighting, this tripartite depiction is a simplification of a complex and fluid situation. Nevertheless, it serves as a productive framework for describing the interaction between the conflict environment and the nascent military and civilian organisations bourgeoning from it.

The research presented here is based on interviews conducted between July 2011 and March 2012 with more than three hundred fighters, commanders and civilians. The interviews prioritised political and military events, as my fieldwork focused on the cohesion and the accumulative organisation of fighting units. The majority of interviews were with individuals born and raised in Misrata. Their views, when taken together, portray a distinctly Misratan perspective on the war and its inception. This reliance on individual accounts is unavoidable in the study of civil wars at the micro-level as there is no archival data.[11] The chronology is subjective and incomplete as my interlocutors were only a fraction of the 280,000 residents who witnessed or shaped events in the city.[12]

Stage 1: Initial success of Misratan forces

Misratans' collective narrative of the revolution begins with the protests on 19 February 2011. This history obscures, however, smaller protests for and against the government in the preceding weeks. During this time, clandestine opposition groups attempted coordinated action. Al-Tuhami Bu Zian, a forty-eight-year-old imam and father of two, was involved in one of the early clandestine political cells that later organised one of the largest early protests. Bu Zian explained that only two members of their original group of six survived the uprising. He would preside over the funeral of the first protestor killed during the 19 February demonstrations—a turning point for protest in Misrata. He later became a commander of a revolutionary battalion and a prominent leader among the battalion commanders on the western frontlines.

In late January, the National Conference for the Libyan Opposition (NCLO), an organisation established in May 2005 by exiled opposition figures in London, called for a 'Day of Rage' on 17 February 2011. This proclamation galvanised the nascent opposition domestically and internationally, becoming a rallying call and coordination mechanism for political action. The date was significant because six years earlier, security forces killed as many as twelve protesters during a demonstration that began as a protest against the Danish cartoons of the Prophet Muhammad but quickly morphed into calls for political change in Libya.[13]

During this time, Qadhafi organised pro-government rallies across the country to strengthen his public image. In Misrata, these began on 13 February. They included the widespread distribution of pamphlets and posters trumpeting Qadhafi's successes and revered status. As 17 February approached, Misratan residents began receiving threatening text messages, warning that anyone joining anti-government protests would be killed. Misratan residents often emphasised that those participating in these pro-government events were not originally from Misrata—either bussed in from outside the city or from families linked to Qadhafi. This claim underscored a recurrent theme in the city's collective narrative: 'true' Misratans opposed Qadhafi from the onset of the revolution and anyone in the city supporting Qadhafi did not have his or her family roots in Misrata (and were therefore not 'true' Misratans). While this assertion is almost certainly incorrect, it purges Misratans' collective conscience of two uncomfortable realities: first, many Misratan residents did initially participate in pro-Qadhafi demonstrations and, secondly, it was events in Benghazi that incited Misratans to action.

Late on 15 February 2011, a small peaceful protest began outside the police station in Benghazi after Fathi Tirbil—a well-known human rights lawyer who represented the families of the victims of the 1996 massacre at Abu Slim prison—was arrested.[14] This spontaneous gathering quickly expanded into a crowd of thousands and devolved into violence, leaving thirty-eight protestors injured.[15] The violence continued into the next day, inspiring anti-government demonstrations in Baida and Zintan.[16] Asked why protests did not take place in Misrata, Bu Zian explained, 'In Misrata, the majority of the people were wealthy, they did not care whether Qadhafi stayed or went, but when this happened, everything changed. We all have family in Benghazi. By killing people there, Qadhafi made a mistake: he forced us to choose sides.'[17] These familial networks would figure prominently in the organisation and funding of weapon and humanitarian shipments from Benghazi—especially in the early days of fighting before civilian and military authorities were established.

Misratan activists debated fiercely over how and when to respond to the killing of protesters in Benghazi. Sporadic protests erupted in Misrata the next day but were quickly put down by government forces. This changed on 19 February when it was rumoured that a protest would begin at the main mosque downtown following afternoon prayers. Learning of the protest, local police in riot gear cordoned off the streets surrounding the mosque. This left only 30 to 40 protesters in the mosque. Bu Zian described the moment, 'When we came out of the mosque and saw no one else waiting for us, we were sure we would not survive the hour.'[18] Unbeknownst to them, individuals blocked from meeting at the mosque began smaller protests throughout the city. As in Benghazi, the protests began peacefully. In response, the security personnel did not use deadly force to break up the protests, choosing instead to intimidate and beat protesters. This led to running skirmishes throughout the city as groups of protesters congregated, only to be scattered by security forces.

During the night, Khalid Bu Shahma, one of the approximately thirty-five protestors injured in the melee, died in the Misratan Central Hospital.[19] His death became the turning point for the protests. While hundreds of people were involved in the protests on 19 February, thousands of residents attended Bu Shahma's funeral the next day.

After the funeral, Mustafa, Bu Shahma's father, emerged from the crowd and addressed the mourners. The nine people interviewed about the funeral provided remarkably similar accounts of his speech, including Bu Zian who was standing beside Mustafa having just presided over the funeral of his son. Osama Karami, a twenty-five-year-old electrical engineer, recalled his words: 'Thank you for coming to my son's funeral. He is a martyr. But I do not want you to say that you are sorry for my loss. I do not want you to come to my house and give me condolences. I want you to go to the main square and shout it.'[20] Each individual who witnessed the speech remarked how struck they were that Mustafa depicted his son as a martyr (*shahid*). This declaration, which was inaccurate because Islamic authorities in Libya had not yet declared the uprising a *jihad* (holy struggle),[21] was a provocative political statement.

After the funeral, the crowd walked towards Misrata's main square, near the courthouse—seen by Misratans and Qadhafi officials alike as the primary symbol of administrative control. About ten blocks from the square, they confronted the army and the Imhammad Imgharyif

Brigade along with the 32 Reinforced Brigade (32 Brigade), Qadhafi's rapid intervention (often called his 'personal protection') forces. Only days before, they had put down resistance in Zawiya, killing nine.[22] This was a dramatic escalation in the government's response to the protests, signalling a crackdown. The security brigades began firing heavy machine guns over the heads of protestors to disperse the crowds.

Protesters described the terror of the deafening sound of heavy weapons fire and the sensation of bullets flying just overhead. The clashes quickly turned deadly; while accounts differ, thirty to forty protesters died and hundreds were injured.[23] Hundreds were taken into custody, many of whom remain missing. Dozens were found six months later in detention centres after the fall of Tripoli on 20 August 2011. Interviews with two of the prisoners captured that day recounted stories of unremitting torture while in custody.

At approximately 8pm a rumour circulated that Qadhafi had fled to Venezuela. Shortly afterwards the army and Imhammad Imgharyif Brigade withdrew to bases at the airport and Military College, both on the western outskirts of the city. Protestors ransacked and burned security-related facilities including the Internal Police building. Scenes of violence turned into nightlong celebrations. This dramatic turn of events is often attributed to a statement made by the Italian ambassador, Francesco Trupiani, in Tripoli suggesting that Qadhafi had flown to South America. An alternative (and more likely) explanation, recounted by various civilian leaders in Misrata, is a negotiation between al-Barrani Ishkal, the head of the Imhammad Imgharyif Brigade, and senior Misratan notables. The truce, as explained by one Misratan notable, stipulated that neither the Misratan protestors nor the Imhammad Imgharyif Brigade would instigate violence. Qadhafi military forces would not enter Misrata until 6 March 2011, giving the city two crucial weeks to organise and prepare.

The protestors gained an important ally during the first day of protests when the commentators from the radio station in Misrata came out in support of the revolution. Misrata FM was one of the only sources of information, inspiration and coordination in the early days of the fighting. This was especially so after the mobile phone network was shut down by Qadhafi forces in early March 2011. As one Misratan described, 'We always had Misrata FM on, it reminded us that we were united.'[24] More vexing for the Qadhafi government was the station's broadcasting range—extending to Homs in the west, including Bani Walid, and Tawergha to the east—as its continued dissent contradicted government claims that it controlled Misrata.

Emergence of civilian authority:

Civilian authority began on 21 February, the morning after Qadhafi security forces withdrew, in a crowd gathered outside City Hall. Tahir Ba'ur, a fifty-four-year-old technical engineer who would play a prominent role on the eastern frontlines and become the secretary of the Misratan Union of Revolutionaries[25] (MUR) after the war, described the scene:

Seven or eight hundred people congregated outside City Hall discussing what to do. There were judges, lawyers, engineers, and prosecutors. At the beginning they gave the imam a chance to speak to the crowd because people listen to him. A number of prominent people spoke, men like Shahir Ibrahim and Mustafa Manaqiza. They implored the crowd to action. I remember Ibrahim saying, 'Brothers, we must form a committee, we must get organised immediately—this regime will soon fall.'[26]

After lengthy discussions, the assembled individuals formed an administrative committee and groups to guard key sites such as hospitals, electricity plants and the City Hall. Bau'r and a group of sixty or seventy men made their way over to the courthouse while the others discussed and organised the civilian protection groups. They found two or three hundred people gathered outside having similar discussions. After two hours, a group of ten judges and lawyers entered the Courthouse and closed the doors. Thirty minutes later, they came to the window on the second floor and announced they had formed an administrative committee for the city, led by Fawzi Abd al-Al. Bau'r lauded the courage of those early volunteers as the threat of government reprisals against their families was seen as a certainty.

The members of this committee interviewed for this chapter explained that only after three days did they fully realise the immensity of the task before them. In response, they established an administrative committee for the city, nominating Khalifa al-Zwawi, a judge and legal consultant, to lead it. He formed the committee on 26 February, which became the local National Transitional Council (NTC). Zwawi remained its chairman for more than a year, handing over responsibility only after local elections on 20 February 2012. The original committee led by Abd al-Al became the legal committee.

Before committee structures became more formalised, however, the hundreds of Misratans who met outside City Hall each day undertook much of the planning and organisation required to run the city. In interviews with members of the later committees, they explained that their role was usually limited to coordinating the efforts of others or serving as a clearinghouse for information. Over the coming months, a complex organisation structure emerged, with over twenty-six different committees responsible for a range of tasks including food supplies, medical services, internally displaced families, military defence, city finances and utilities.

Community security: Genesis of the armed struggle:

Following the withdrawal of Qadhafi's forces, a dense grid of checkpoints appeared across the city controlling access to every neighbourhood. The majority of individuals manning the checkpoints were youth aged 17 to 28. Usually unarmed, they occasionally carried air rifles or one-shot hunting rifles (most of which were inoperable). The absence of weapons was acute, so anyone approaching a checkpoint with weapons was suspect. Misrata's tight-knit social fabric meant that the youths manning the checkpoints knew everyone in their neighbourhood personally. Consequently, the checkpoints created an instant and effective security blanket across Misrata as 'non-Misratans' were quickly identified. Misratan civilian and military leaders credit the checkpoints with reducing the mobility of prominent Qadhafi officials in Misrata and in securing neighbourhoods by reducing the ability Qadhafi informants (or the 'fifth column') to operate freely within the city.

Misratan civilian leaders described how wealthy businessmen, notables from prominent families, and imams formed local committees. Each group took responsibility for their neighbourhood, including the checkpoints. These groups would later raise and administer the financial resources supporting neighbourhood fighting units. Over time, this relationship matured, as many local committees became the executive committees of revolutionary battalions. This was especially the case with larger groups, where the logistics were managed separately from the fighting.

One of the first actions of the nascent civilian authority was to establish a military working group to prepare the defences of the city. They appointed Muhammad bin Hmaida, a retired army Colonel, as its head. The majority of the other members were either retired army officers or recent defectors. This group would later become the Misratan Military Council (MMC). Initially the group pooled weapons within the city to prepare a defence. Residents donated them after announcements on Misrata FM asked anyone with weapons to bring them to City Hall. In the planning that followed, two individuals on the committee emerged as particularly influential—Salim Jawha and Salah Badi. While personality conflicts between the two men required a reorganisation of the committee, Jawha would, by the end of the war, be responsible for all forces in Misrata, while Badi would go on to form one of the most prominent revolutionary battalions.

The MMC was the central military authority in the city throughout the revolution, but did not exert command or control over the fighting forces. Rather, it facilitated communication between battalions, establishing radio control rooms, which became intelligence repositories. It also coordinated with western and Qatari Special Forces personnel in the city and organised weapon and ammunition deliveries from Benghazi. Though individual battalion members travelled to Benghazi to purchase weapons, their delivery by boat was organised by the MMC. This strengthened its position at the heart of the armed struggle. Later in the war, the group, in partnership with the national NTC, would organise armaments purchases from Sudan.[27]

For five days Misrata was quiet. The calm was broken on 26 February by a pitched battle at Misrata's commercial airport. As residents became aware of the fighting by telephone calls and reports on Misrata FM, men rushed to the airport, usually unarmed, to join the fray. After hours of fighting, the army retreated from the commercial side of the airport into the adjacent military base at 3pm, allowing Misratan fighters to capture their first truck-mounted machine gun. The anti-Qadhafi fighters looted a military food store near the airport, returning its contents to the organising committee at City Hall.[28] The army mounted a counter-attack at 6pm to regain control of the airport terminal. The attack was repelled but at a considerable cost: twenty-seven casualties and over forty injured. While the skirmish resulted in a draw, it demonstrated the resolve of the Misratan side to hold its position despite significant casualties. The skirmish also highlighted a recurring pattern in the uprising: a small group of organised fighters surrounded by a spontaneous force of volunteers. In this case, the military committee sent twenty men to attack the airport using the only 14.5 millimetre machine gun in the city, looted from a security facility abandoned by Qadhafi's forces on 20 February.

The ambush:

On 6 March 2011 at 8am, Qadhafi announced on Libyan TV that his forces had crushed the resistance in Misrata and that celebrations were taking place in the city centre. Most Misratans only became aware of the announcement when friends from across the country began calling them asking whether it was true. At this time, the military committee had less than ten functioning machine guns (14.5 and 12 millimetre) and six RPG launchers with less than a dozen explosive warheads—all looted from the two military bases overrun on 20 February or captured during the fight at the airport.[29]

In the preparations for an attack, the committee organised a force of approximately 150 men to defend the city; with only a handful of weapons, organising a larger force was futile. This did not, however, prevent hundreds of others from joining the fight. Again, the result was a small, organised core hidden among a much larger impromptu group. This mirrored the pattern of organisation at the airport battle and would continue to characterise the military attacks throughout the revolution.

Just after 11am, a column of tanks, armoured personnel carriers, and more than 65 pick-up trucks pushed into Misrata from the base near the airport with almost four hundred troops. The military committee cleared the dozens of checkpoints along Tripoli Street, the main thoroughfare to the city centre, permitting the column to proceed downtown unopposed. As planned, it was met at the overpass at the edge of the city centre by two vehicles mounted with 14.5 millimetre machine guns. Each vehicle fired on the column and then immediately retreated to the city centre. The two vehicles then stopped outside the unfinished central hospital about halfway into the city and engaged the column of military vehicles when it again came into sight. The vehicles retreated again, successfully drawing a small group of pick-up trucks away from the main force. The Misratan vehicles then separated just before City Hall, retreating into two neighbourhoods adjacent to Tripoli Street, drawing the vehicles into an ambush. The military vehicles pursued, entering the narrow streets lined by three-storey buildings where they were immediately hit by youth throwing 'Molotov cocktails'[30] from the rooftops. One group escaped almost unscathed while the second group got trapped, permitting the Misratan forces to destroy three pickups and kill fourteen soldiers.

The main force continued to the roundabout in front of the courthouse. The pick-ups with machine guns fired indiscriminately as they entered the city, targeting cars and buildings along Tripoli Street. The column arrived at the courthouse unopposed. Jawha explained why this point was selected for the ambush: 'The roundabout was the most effective choke point. It was surrounded by tall buildings and there were multiple points of attack. Also, they [the armed forces personnel] did not know the city, so if they retreated they would get disoriented in the surrounding narrow streets, giving us the advantage.'[31]

The group waited for the force to disembark from their vehicles before firing. The subsequent battle went on for hours, ending with the column retreating from the city around 3pm, though not before two of the armed vehicles and six pick-ups were destroyed and over fifty soldiers killed or captured.[32] Individuals present during the fighting explained that the government forces did not expect an attack and that the element of surprise was their most effective weapon. In the aftermath of the attack, videos of the events began appearing on YouTube, contradicting Qadhafi's account of events and his claim that his forces controlled Misrata.

In the days after the 6 March attack, there was substantial back-channel dialogue between senior Qadhafi government officials and members of the communication committee in Misrata. The most high-level initiative involved Abdullah al-Sanusi, Qadhafi's intelligence chief and brother-in-law (who would be indicted for crimes against humanity by the International Criminal Court along with Qadhafi and his son Saif al-Islam). The negotiations quickly broke down as the combination of promised money for development and threats of 'Misrata being returned to the desert' did not alter the committee's insistence that Qadhafi could not longer rule. Local leaders awaited the government's response.[33]

Stage 2: The battle for Misrata

Qadhafi's answer arrived on Thursday 10 March, delivered by the feared 32 Reinforced Brigade, marking a bloody turn in the uprising in Misrata. The 32 Brigade was a mechanised division constituted by a fighting force of approximately three thousand personnel answering directly to Qadhafi's son Khamis. Two days earlier it had put down the uprising in Zawiya, killing nine and wounding more than a hundred.[34] It was among the best trained and equipped fighting force in Libya and committed to carrying out orders such as 'shoot to kill' in defence of the family's rule.

Early that morning, reports trickled into Misrata that the 32 Brigade had arrived at the outskirts of the city. Over the subsequent week, the 32 Brigade bombarded the city with artillery. The promised attack did not begin until the early hours of 18 March 2011. The subsequent fighting was among the bloodiest Misrata experienced. Four separate columns of troops took part in a coordinted attack. The 32 Brigade divided into two, attacking from the airport road and from the coastal highway. A large but less professional contingent constituting of hundreds of 'volunteers' entered from the town of Tawergha, which lay southeast towards Sirt. A fourth grouping of army units based at the airport approached from the south.

Each force met resistance. In the east, the 32 Brigade was able to push to Benghazi Street where it took control of the Science University campus. The victory was short-lived, however, as the Misratan forces began harassing the soldiers with rocket-propelled grenades (RPGs) and sniper fire. Ba'ur described the situation: 'They made a mistake, bringing all the troops into the centre of the city. We only had RPGs and AK-47s. But we moved like birds. We know the streets, we know the paths between houses, so we could attack them from anywhere.'[35]

Misrata's downtown is a dense mass of ten-storey apartment buildings and two-storey walled compounds with ten-foot-tall external retaining walls; passages were cut between compounds so that fighters could move between houses unseen by Qadhafi's military in the street. The labyrinth of passageways allowed Misratan forces to appear and disappear, harassing the highly mechanised security brigades and army unfamiliar with the city's neighbourhoods. Fighting continued over the next two weeks, resulting in the death of more than 350 fighters and civilians. While there are no confirmed figures, eyewitnesses reported army casualties stacked in trucks leaving the city.

On 17 March, the day before the attack, Misrata received its first major arms shipment from Benghazi made up of RPGs, assault rifles, a few 14.5 machine guns and ammunition. It arrived in the middle of the night on a fishing boat that sneaked past the government navy ships blockading the port. One of the men on the ship, Bashir al-Migrisi, recalled the moment, 'I don't know how they did not see us. We cut our engines and drifted by them, we held our breath for ten minutes, but *al-hamdu li-Llah* [praise be to Allah], we arrived.'[36] The passage of UN Security Council Resolution 1973 a week later,[37] and the subsequent bombing campaign, broke the blockade of the port, permitting a steady, if intermittent, stream of weapons shipments largely organised by the MMC and its counterpart in Benghazi. Commanders explained that the shipments were critical to the success of the uprising in Misrata but there continued to be dangerously low levels of ammunition until the fall of Tripoli in August. Jawha, the leader of the Misratan forces by the end of the war, explained: 'There were numerous occasions when we just ran out of ammunition. Sometimes we would get supplies just hours before an attack. If they had attacked any earlier, the lines would have collapsed.'[38]

An earlier shipment on 10 March 2011 helped expand the fighting force significantly as commanders estimated there were only one hundred rifles in the city before this shipment (only a fraction of which were actually military-type assault rifles). Local commanders estimated that only about 350–550 combatants were active in Misrata at that time—a situation that would dramatically change after Tripoli Street was occupied.

The army and security brigades' military superiority scattered Misrata's defences on 18 March, permitting them to occupy much of Tripoli Street. Qadhafi's forces took up strategic positions in the tallest buildings at the centre of downtown, including the 'Insurance Building', which would serve as their headquarters for the coming months. From this vantage point they began indiscriminately shelling the city. The position also granted their snipers an advantage over the Misratan fighters below. The interlocking support of snipers, ground forces and tanks allowed them to wrest control of the remainder of Tripoli Street and the adjacent neighbourhoods. The 'occupation' of the city centre would transform the conflict from one between Qadhafi's forces and a few hundred fighters to a pitched battle against an entire city.

By nightfall, the army and security brigades occupied the downtown core and controlled Tripoli Street out to its airport bases (and by extension Tripoli). Outgunned and outnumbered, Misratan forces fought an urban guerrilla campaign for the next thirty-eight days. The city's residents became galvanised around this cause, supplying food, money and new recruits to the small fighting groups that began to emerge. The dense social networks of Misrata saw residents accommodate as many as 80,000 internally displaced persons (IDPs) affected by fighting, with most families housing two to five other families with them.

The fighting in Misrata pivoted on two supply routes; Tripoli Street for the army and security brigades, and the port for Misratan forces. Retaining control of the port highway became the priority for Misratan forces as it secured access to the deep-water port—the only lifeline for humanitarian supplies and weapon shipments. The neighbourhood adjacent to the highway therefore became one of the most contested battlefields in the subsequent six months of fighting. The ongoing fighting drew a continuous stream of volunteers from across the city.

In July 2011, after four months of fighting, Qadhafi's forces made another unsuccessful attempt to control the port highway. Ba'ur chided them: 'They weren't very smart, they should have taken the port during one of the first attacks ... Either 6 or 18 March. If they had, it would have been a very different war.' He said they had finally recognised their mistake—but it was already too late.[39]

Control of Misrata's downtown centred on the tallest and most imposing building in Misrata—the Insurance Building—which was strategically situated at the beginning of Tripoli Street. Made of steel-reinforced concrete, it was impenetrable to RPGs. It became the menacing symbol of the army and security brigades' control as its vantage point gave their snipers and mortar teams clear lines of sight for kilometres in all directions. Misratan commanders estimated that 10,000 to 15,000 government troops were deployed to Misrata during the fighting, including a significant portion of Qadhafi's elite forces. It is important, however, to distinguish between the professional soldiers like the 32 Reinforced Brigade and the 'volunteers' or reservists, for example in the Popular Guard (*Haras al-Sha'bi*), called up to augment them.

Qadhafi decimated the army in the 1970s and 1980s out of fear of a counter-coup,[40] developing instead a set of private armies, led by either Qadhafi's sons or very close allies. These forces, while well equipped and trained, were usually no more than 3,000 soldiers, leaving the 'volunteer' portion of the army making up the majority of the force. This made the force susceptible to morale problems, especially when the forces began to take heavy casualties. Misratan residents regularly recounted stories of government soldiers abandoning cars, weapons, even tanks, and just running away when coming under fire; this contrasted with Misratan fighters' commitment and willingness to sacrifice. This stark juxtaposition was a cornerstone of the Misrata narrative throughout the war, an emphasis that served to strengthen the morale of the city and provide hope when the situation was dire.

French and British planes began hitting targets near Misrata on 23 March, breaking the blockade of the port and destroying three tanks on the outskirts of the city. But unlike Benghazi, where the initial bombardment destroyed army and security brigade divisions en route to the city, government forces already controlled Misrata by the time the bombing campaign began. Once inside the city limits, NATO military planners, who assumed responsibility for the bombing campaign on 31 March, were reluctant to bomb in heavily populated areas.[41] This would change in April with the arrival of French paratroopers, affording NATO actionable targeting intelligence on the ground. Nonetheless, NATO airstrikes would not play a significant role in the progress of the armed struggle in Misrata until the frontlines were pushed out to the unpopulated outskirts of the city and the arrival of a British forward observer unit in June.

Emergence of armed groups:

During the second stage of the fighting, micro-groups of three to five fighters were continually merging and subdividing at multiple levels: individual fighters 'group-shopped', participating in multiple groups based on familial or previous social relationships (for example, school friends, work colleagues, neighbourhood soccer teams); micro-fighting units also coordinate *in situ* by either merging into larger groups or coordinating as distinct sub-groups to organise and mount an attack. One of the factors encouraging early collaboration between micro-groups was the shortage of weapons. This required ongoing cooperation for larger operations, such as when a group needed an extra 'RPG man' for an operation, 'borrowing' someone from another group.

The size of the fighting force and the membership of individual groups increased exponentially in the following weeks as the operational advantage of larger fighting units became apparent through trial and error. Micro-groups quickly grew to fighting units of 30 to 50 members, even as many as 150 by the time the 32 Brigade and army was driven from the city. During this time, groups established make-shift bases near the frontlines and members no longer returned home at night. Fighters ate, prayed and fought together, graduating into full-time combatants. This change led to less fluid group membership, a more defined group identity and increased cohesion of group bonds.

Two dynamics shaped the group formation process. The first was reliance on a particular neighbourhood or extended family for financing and commissariat throughout the war. All fighting groups interviewed possessed some form of executive committee made up of local notables such as wealthy businessmen or respected community leaders. These community leaders were already influential in their social networks before the revolution; their support, both financial and political, was critical to the acquisition of weapons and vehicles. For smaller groups (for example, 20 to 50 members), these committees were usually less formal, led by a wealthy family member related to the fighters.

The second dynamic was the reputation and capacity of leaders. An individual fighter's choice to remain with a group was a conscious one. Throughout the uprising, individuals fought with different groups, moving from one unit to the next until they found a group and commander they felt comfortable with. These twin dynamics of selective recruitment by groups further stabilised group membership in the third stage of the fighting.

Despite the prominent role of individual commanders in fighters' group membership choices, decision making within a group remained consensus-based. Leaders were one voice among equals, normally older than the fighters in their group, better educated or from a prominent family. But above all, fighters gravitated to leaders they trusted and perceived as strategic. Consequently, battalion leaders had diverse backgrounds—medical doctors, mechanics, imams, and former army officers.

Before the 18 March attack, Qadhafi's armed forces shut down the mobile telephone network in Misrata. In response, local fighters coordinated their actions by setting up designated meeting points at which to meet each day. These meeting points became critical foci for coordination, recruitment and information sharing in different areas in the city during the first few weeks of fighting.

The meeting points forged new relationships and networks between the individuals and fighting units in particular neighbourhoods of the city as they discussed, planned and fought alongside each other. The genesis of the future battalion structures and their leadership can be found in the four major meeting points in Misrata. The gathering points were also information hubs. First-hand accounts, rumours and reports from Misrata FM and international media would be exchanged; stories of bravery of specific commanders or groups were an important currency in these forums. The meeting points created the conditions for larger groups to coalesce around individuals with a reputation for leadership and courage. Stories of the day's fighting were interwoven with tales of the insurgency against Italian colonial authority, supported by images or videos taken during the day by weaponless members of a battalion. This facilitated the contemporaneous way in which images and stories of their grandfather's courage were interwoven into their own narrative and motivation for joining the uprising.

Fighters described their groups as *katiba*, a designation for the military units in Qadhafi's armed forces headed by a colonel. Fighters appropriated the term to describe their own groups, irrespective of whether the group had five or 500 men. A few groups used the term *sariyya* (company, approximately 60 to 180 soldiers) or *liwa'* (division, a military force of as many as 15,000 soldiers). But as a prominent commander of the western front explained, 'We didn't know what any of those military terms meant when we started, so our group used the term *liwa'* because we thought it sounded impressive. That is until we learned it is five times larger than a *katiba*. We only had 15 guys in our group at the time, so we used *katiba* after that.'

The turning point:

In the three weeks following 18 March, the frontlines in Misrata became more defined as government troops attempted to extend their control beyond the Insurance Building and Tripoli Street. Slowed by the guerrilla tactics of the nascent fighting units, the attacks killed an estimated three to four hundred fighters and civilians by early April, with twice that many injured. The situation grew dire as the chronic lack of weapons and ammunition put Misratan fighters at too great a disadvantage compared with the army and security brigades' continuous resupply of weapons and reinforcements from Tripoli. Figure 1 estimates the number of small arms in Misrata during the initial stages of the war.

Figure 1: Number of small arms in Misrata during the first and second stages of fighting.[42]

Date	Number of firearms
19 February: Initial protests	0
26 February: Violence begins	50
6 March: First incursion by Qaddafi forces	150
18 March: Tripoli Street occupied	300
31 March: Fighting escalates	450
15 April: Tripoli Street divided	2,000
31 April: Tripoli Street retaken	2,200
11 May: Liberation of Misrata	3,000
15 May: Three frontlines established	3,500

Sources: Author interviews with commanders and MMC members, Misrata, October 2011.

Yet it was dump trucks filled with sand that would turn the tide of the battle. While accounts differ as to which individual or group first conceived the innovation, the results were definitive. By the middle of April, Tripoli Street was impassable, blocked by huge dump trucks (parked by drivers who were often shot in the process), effectively cutting government supplies to the city centre. The weight and height of the vehicles prevented tanks from running over or pushing them aside. Additionally, the truck's load of sand absorbed tank rounds, making them almost indestructible. A deadly cat-and-mouse game unfolded over the next weeks as Qadhafi's forces brought armoured bulldozers to remove the vehicles, only to see them destroyed, blocking their supply route even further. By the end of April, Tripoli Street was a graveyard of vehicles.

Starved of ammunition, food and reinforcements, the towering buildings occupied by Qadhafi's forces became prisons. Over the next two weeks, Misratan forces slowly encircled the Insurance Building, using the mosques' speakers to play *Allahu Akbar* ('Allah is great', 'God is great' or 'God is the greatest')[43] continuously, boosting Misratan fighters' morale and preventing government soldiers from sleeping. At night, cats and dogs were outfitted with flashlights and released onto the streets surrounding the Insurance Building to draw sniper fire. This tactic wasted snipers' ammunition and revealed their position for counterattacks. Eventually, the futility of wasting further ammunition on a position so well fortified was recognised. The military committee demolished the first floor stairs of the building and directed battalion leaders to pull back, leaving the remaining government soldiers stranded. The remaining soldiers were given the chance to surrender, those who refused were left to starve.

Misratan fighters continued to make advances along Tripoli Street throughout April and early May. Sand-filled dump trucks, and later, when these became scarce, ISO shipping containers, were deployed throughout the city, parsing Misrata into discreet neighbourhood zones. This, combined with the Tripoli Street blockade, starved Qadhafi's forces of supplies, dislodging them from the city centre.

The Misrata Military Council develops:

In early April 2011, the military council established the first radio control centres. Instead of deploying or dispatching fighting units, the control rooms served as a communication bridge between units with radios, and as a central repository for intelligence. Initially, only a fraction of the fighting units had radios, taken from abandoned police stations or dead soldiers. Yet the percentage increased as the war progressed, permitting greater coordination among fighting units. Even in these early stages, the fighting units became explicitly linked to the military council, initially through a registration process. Group leaders registered their weapons and membership by filling out forms and including photocopies of their fighters' IDs. These forms included members' names and the type and serial numbers of weapons in their possession.

While fighting units initially relied solely on the resources of their neighbourhood and extended families to procure weapons and ammunition from Benghazi, as the conflict progressed, the military council began to organise ammunition and weapons deliveries from Benghazi and, later, airlifts from Sudan.[44]

Stage 3: The emergence of Revolutionary Battalions

On 11 May 2011, a fierce battle again erupted at the commercial airport.[45] In contrast to the first skirmish, by the end of the day the Misratan fighters controlled the entire airport base and therefore the city. However, Misrata was still encircled by government forces. As a result, over the next three days frontlines were established in the west (towards Dafniyya), east (towards Tawergha), and along the southern service highway. Critically, the government's batteries of mobile Grad rockets still ranged the city. These Soviet-era missile launchers were notoriously inaccurate, landing indiscriminately across the city, killing hundreds over the coming weeks. Misratan forces therefore prioritised extending the frontlines by 20km to put the city beyond their reach. During this time, army mortar and artillery fire were also used to devastating effect against Misratan forces, which were unaccustomed to this type of warfare. The fighters took weeks to build shelters capable of protecting themselves from heavy weapons fire. The majority of government reinforcements arrived from Tripoli, putting the western front under the most regular military pressure. As a consequence, the 6,000 available fighters were distributed thus: 1,500 fighters in the east, 1,000 fighters along the south and 3,500 in the west.

The fighting groups were radically transformed by the frontlines. Lightly equipped street-fighting units, potent at urban warfare, could not monitor and defend 50km of battle lines. Instead, they had to undergo substantial changes in weapon selection, size of fighting groupings, organisational structures and military tactics. Smaller units merged into larger groups, leading to more defined hierarchies and managerial structures, creating 'revolutionary battalions'. Bau'r described this consolidation process on the eastern front:

We recognised that we would need larger, more coordinated attacks, heavy weapons, a lot more people—and they would need to be organised. This would require field leaders and coordination. So we called all the leaders of the different groups in the east together ... In the first meeting there were twelve leaders and six or seven others—the people who had been organising food supplies, weapons, water.

Seven of the leaders decided to form one group. They called it the Eastern Coast ... this was the first battalion in the east. The other five each remained autonomous, creating individual battalions. Of the seven that combined, there were no family or preexisting personal relationships—we were just of the same mind: we knew that smaller groups were useless—we must grow. The other leaders recognised this too but they said, 'I will find my own guys, collect more weapons and have my own battalion.'[46]

As Ba'ur explained, the frontlines required more fighters, which necessitated more weapons. Over the next two months, both would increase six-fold (see Figure 2). Significant recruitment efforts ensued. To add to the process, the MMC set up training camps along the beach to train and sign up new recruits. By the end of the war, nearly 40,0000 battalion members were registered with the MUR.[47] Approximately 22,000 were fighters in the 236 battalions; the rest were responsible for logistics, managerial, or support functions.[48] Despite this rapid increase, trust networks still mattered, with group members introducing new recruits whom they personally vouched for.[49]

As groups became larger, leaders allocated geographical areas of responsibility for each fighting unit and developed decision making and coordination mechanisms along each frontline. The southern front was the most integrated, functioning almost as a unified force as a result of the fewer groups assigned to this front (approximately 38) and personalities of the battalion commanders and overall coordinator. The eastern front had fewer battalions, but each battalion was generally larger. The frontlines were divided by 1km intervals with groups responsible for one or more depending on the size of the battalion. The majority of the groups established two shifts: one would be on the frontline while the other rested a few kilometres away at a nearby staging base.

On the western front, which had 146 battalions, 15–20 leaders of the largest or most respected battalions would meet each evening to review the day's events and discuss strategic decisions. Smaller battalions were rarely involved in decision making before attacks. Instead, they would be resupplied with ammunition and informed that there would be a 'push' in the morning. The result was that a core group of battalions implemented a strategy within the uncoordinated advance of the remaining 120+ battalions. On occasion, leaders of the smaller battalions would threaten not to participate in an attack unless they were involved in the planning. The threat was usually a bluff as the leader would be inevitably overruled by rank-and-file members who would join the advance out of a desire to participate in the attack and to avoid being seen as cowards for remaining behind.

The shift to static frontlines allowed NATO to more fully engage. The open farmland, devoid of civilians, made the government's tanks, artillery and missile launchers easy targets for NATO airstrikes. The deployment of British forward observer teams in June further increased the tempo of strikes. The army and security brigades hid heavy weapons and trucks mounted with anti-aircraft machine guns under trees and in buildings, deploying long enough to fire and then retreating under cover before NATO's targeting-verification-strike cycle could

Figure 2: Number of combatants in Misrata throughout the uprising

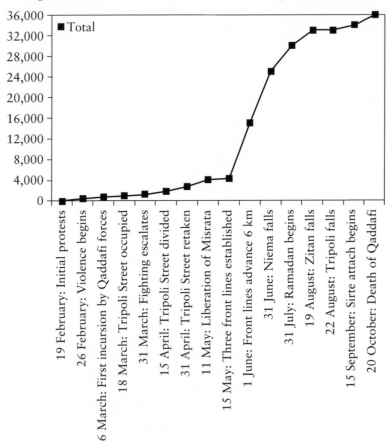

Note: Estimates are dereived from averages provided by senior MMC and-MUR leaders.

Sources: Unpublished MUR registration records as of 15 November 2011; author interviews with commanders and MMC members, Misrata, October 2011.

respond. Their units also began using the same type of civilian pick-up trucks as Misratan fighters to further confuse NATO. Nonetheless, NATO strikes played a critical role in the progress of the fighting, described by fighters as 'the angels in the sky'.

Over the next three months the frontlines would be pushed beyond Dafniyya to the west and Tawergha to the east. The encirclement of

Misrata ended on August 20 when Tripoli fell. The day before, h dreds of Misratan fighters boarded boats to Tripoli to participate i the operation. They joined thousands from the Nafusa Mountains and Tripoli. But Sirt was the final battleground. For two months, fighters from Misrata and Benghazi attacked the last vestiges of Qadhafi's security forces. Previously starved of weapons and ammunition, the Misratans attacked the remnants of Qadhafi's security apparatus fully armed by a sense of destiny and weapons seized from stockpiles in Tripoli. Unaccustomed to fighting a well-fortified enemy, they would drive straight at their targets, becoming bottlenecked on street corners and compound gateways, often with disastrous consequences.

In response, they levelled Sirt's District 2 with their anti-aircraft guns, exacting revenge against a city they felt profited from Qadhafi's largesse. The end came when Misratan fighters captured Qadhafi in a drainage pipe after a NATO airstrike eviscerated half of his fleeing convoy. Qadhafi died en route to Misrata and was later displayed on the floor of a walk-in meat freezer alongside his son, Mu'tasim. Anyone willing to queue could see him. Thousands came, often with their children, to witness what was once unimaginable, heaping verbal, and on occasion physical, abuse upon the corpse of 'Brother Leader'. Human rights groups accused Misratan fighters of war crimes, including the execution of Qadhafi and the individuals travelling in Qadhafi's convoy who survived the NATO airstrikes.[50]

At the time of Qadhafi's death in October 2011, Misratan revolutionary battalions controlled the majority of weapons and fighters in the country.[51] But almost all the battalion members in Misrata, including fighters, mechanics, drivers and executive committees, were civilians based on the registration records of the MMC and MUR: students (40 per cent), private sector workers (38 per cent), public sector employees (11 per cent), professionals such as doctors (8 per cent), or unemployed (2 per cent).[52] The battalions ranged in size from 12 to 1,742 members. Five counted more than 900 members. Approximately 46 groups stabilised at 250–900 members; the remaining 185 groups never expanded beyond 250 members, with the vast majority counting fewer than 100 (see Figure 3).

Conclusion

The duration and intensity of the fighting in Misrata created highly cohesive fighting units that were fiercely loyal to their commanders.

3: The 236 battalions by size of membership[53]

	Number of battalions	Percentage of battalions
	5	2.1 %
--	45	19.1 %
<250	185	78.8 %

Yet the battalions were also integrated with their community and the executive committees that supported them. This created a substantial degree of social control over the fighting units that was further strengthened by the working relationships developed during the war between the local NTC, the MMC and later the MUR. Unlike other cities, which did not play host to sustained fighting in 2011, the legitimacy and integration of these bodies enabled them to provide security for the city after the war. This continued after the death of Qadhafi as the leaders continued to integrate the revolutionary battalions into the MMC and MUR, through, for example, weekly meetings with all battalion commanders to discuss ongoing issues in the city. This incorporation meant that when this group of commanders made decisions, for instance, banning assault rifles carried in public, their members would follow orders. This level of organisation also provided greater influence for Misrata's civilian and military leaders—the MUR, led by Salim Jawha, was pivotal in the creation of the Libyan Shield Force, a parallel security force designed in April 2012 in part to supplant the remnants of the armed forces, which the revolutionaries mistrusted.

The 17 February Revolution defines modern Misratan identity—domestically as well as internationally. Misrata is now known as the besieged city that survived Qadhafi's onslaught and (perhaps more infamously) captured and killed him. To many Misratans, like the young men queued in their trucks outside Sirt, this was their 'manifest destiny', a legacy of Suwaihli's vision for a liberated Libya with Misrata as its nucleus. And it is the legacy of the insurgency against the Italians and their suffering that became an enduring cultural reference in Misrata and Libya more generally. It was interwoven with Qadhafi's repression, creating a contemporaneous narrative of injustice. The narrative of the revolution was similarly contemporaneous, facilitated by the fact that many battalion commanders were direct descendants of Suwaihli. This continuity with past histories of heroism conferred legitimacy and honour on the fighters and tapped into a groundswell of emotion and history. Like Muhammad's comments at the beginning of this chapter, their present experiences were framed in terms of the past. This meant that with Qadhafi's death, much of this history was vindicated, including the insurgency of their grandfathers against Italian colonial rule.

The war also reinforced Misratans' sense of self-reliance. While this narrative is usually described in terms of Suwaihli and the Tripolitania Republic, it was also reinforced during Qadhafi's era. Despite the socialist structure of the *jamahiriyya* economy,[54] Misrata's port was a tax-free zone, contributing to the city's autonomy and reputation for business acumen and wealth.[55] During the fighting, Misrata was cut off politically and militarily from the rest of Libya, requiring it, again, to be self-reliant. Residents relied on each other to house the estimated eighty thousand Misratans displaced within the city during the fighting. While the MMC and revolutionary battalions received arms, logistics and fighting support from Benghazi and surrounding cities, Misratans were left largely on their own to fend off the armed forces. Even NATO's air support, which prevented some reinforcements from arriving from Tripoli, only became critical to the fighting after Qadhafi's forces were pushed to the unpopulated outskirts of the city.[56]

The experience of the war reinforced the city's existing social networks but also fused Misratans to the idea of 'Libya', however ill-defined. When interviewing fighters and civilians alike, Misratans were proud of their city's accomplishments, but they framed these in terms of their contributions to toppling Qadhafi's government and freeing all Libya from his rule. This duality is often misunderstood. Fierce pride in the city is not discordant with an equally intense support for Libya as state.[57] It is with pride that Misratans argued that they 'spilled more of their sons' blood than any other city in Libya'.[58] And it is for this reason that they believe it is not a coincidence that it was Misratan fighters that captured, and killed, Qadhafi.

11

FACTIONALISM RESURGENT

THE WAR IN THE JABAL NAFUSA

Wolfram Lacher and *Ahmed Labnouj* [1]

The 17 February Revolution brought the Nafusa Mountains (*Jabal Nafusa*) from marginality to the core of Libyan politics. Initially neglected by both the Qadhafi regime's counter-insurgency and the NATO intervention, the Nafusa Mountains acquired strategic importance as the war progressed, and mountain fighters played a decisive role in the fall of Tripoli. Libya's post-revolutionary power struggles saw political forces centred on the mountains attempt to convert that decisive role into political influence.

Geography and historical legacies aided the Nafusa Mountains' emergence as a revolutionary stronghold. The mountains are strategically positioned, gradually rising north from the vast rocky plateaus of the Hamada al-Hamra to 900m, then plunging dramatically to sea level. Atop its 400km-long arch, it overlooks the Ja'fara plain west of Tripoli, blocking a main road into the capital at Gharyan. Its towns and villages, sitting at the edge of the cliffs, are accessible only through roads meandering through its rocky canyons. The western part of the mountains formed a natural fortress that Mu'ammar Qadhafi's security brigades were never able to capture, with revolutionary forces relying on the lifeline provided by their control of the Dahiba–Wazin border crossing to Tunisia. The Qadhafi regime's strained relations with several communities in the mountains—particularly the Imazighen (sing.: Amazigh, 'Berber')[2]—motivated their resistance.

Yet the swiftness of the Nafusa Mountains' uprisings, and Qadhafi's inability to recover the area required immense solidarity and cooperation between communities that had historically been at loggerheads with each other. While the mountains' revolutionary strongholds struggled to preserve that cooperation, regime forces rallied support from several marginal constituencies in and around Nafusa. Qadhafi's defeat led to those constituencies' expulsion; unity among the mountains' revolutionary forces also unravelled. The conflict in the Nafusa Mountains was both part of a national uprising, and a local civil war. The dynamics of this local conflict shaped the post-revolutionary era by reinvigorating local identity politics and Amazigh activism, intercommunal conflicts, and sparking the military expansionism of Zintan. Factionalism and identity politics, rooted in history and exacerbated by Qadhafi's policies, were central to mountain communities' role in the war, and defined their stances in the post-Qadhafi era.

Legacies of internal strife

The individual towns and tribes of the Nafusa Mountains that supported the nascent revolution in February and March 2011 responded not only to the Arab Spring, but also acted in the context of their historic local struggles against each other and Qadhafi's central government. These struggles remained remarkably present in their collective imaginations, and gained new relevance during the civil war.[3]

Historically, the key denominator of difference in the Jabal Nafusa, however problematic its definition, was between Imazighen and Arab communities. Its Amazigh communities mostly followed the Ibadi school of Islam, while its Arab communities were mainstream Sunnis. The Imazighen were sedentary (*hadhar*) farming communities from time immemorial, while Arab tribes such as Zintan and Rujban proudly assert their recent past as semi-nomadic pastoralists (*badu*). While Arab communities defined their identity and organisation through tribal genealogy, in Amazigh towns the notion of tribe merely refers to individual villages, and the concept of tribal leadership is not used in local politics. Communities may insist on their Amazigh origin or trace their descent to the Arab tribes that came with the Hilalian invasion.[4] These genealogies have been evolving for centuries, with Amazigh groups associating themselves politically and economically with Arab tribes, often adopting the latter's names and myths of origin. Genealogy and identity remain political matters today. For example, Zintan is a confederation of two large groupings—the Awlad Bu al-Hul and Awlad Dwaib. But while most Zintanis today claim that both descend from the Arab Bani Salim, in the 1950s the Awlad Dwaib were said to have Amazigh ancestors.[5] Amazigh activists argue that Zintan, Rujban and smaller Arab mountain tribes such as the Haraba, are Arabised Imazighen, while Arab communities see 'Amazigh' as a recent, alien concept that replaces the notion of *jbali* ('of the mountains'), which is used partly to counter the idea of an Amazigh history and culture.

Nevertheless, there has been no fundamental Imazighen–Arab divide in the Jabal Nafusa's history—which may also help explain why the lines of conflict during 2011 did not run between Arabs and Imazighen as such. Alliances and conflicts between mountain communities always cut across the Imazighen–Arab divide. For much of the nineteenth and the early twentieth centuries, Tripolitanian tribes and communities organised themselves in tribal alliances (*sufuf*, sing.: *suff*) that remained remarkably stable, since each alliance was based on common interests in land use regimes. In the Jabal Nafusa, Zintan and Rujban formed the core of an alliance against Amazigh communities, who in turn allied with the Arab Mashashiya and Awlad Bu Saif tribes of the Gibla, the region south of the mountains.[6] However, Amazigh communities never acted as a single bloc; towns such as Jadu and Yefren consisted of numerous different tribes, some of which maintained close relations with Zintan and Rujban. Beyond the mountains, Zintan was allied with the Warfalla and Qadhadhfa, who shared Zintan's interest in denying the Mashashiya and Awlad Bu Saif land rights of their own in the Gibla and the Wadian, the valleys of the Sirt region.[7]

These two coalitions repeatedly clashed in the nineteenth and twentieth centuries over land and political preeminence, often allying with outside powers in their struggles. In 1843, Zintan and Rujban sided with the Ottomans against a rebellion of the Arab Mahamid tribe supported by Amazigh communities. During 1911–18, local leaders repeatedly switched their allegiance between the Ottoman Empire and the Italian invaders while battling the same local adversaries. In 1915–16 and 1920–21 an alliance of the Zintan, Rujban and Asab'a again fought Imazighen led by Sulaiman al-Baruni and Khalifa bin Askar, and allied with the Mashashiya. Rifts created by leadership struggles also ran through the Amazigh camp, such as between Khalifa bin Askar of Nalut and Yusuf Kherbish of Jadu, who was leading Amazigh irregulars fighting with the Italians. During the last months of 1921, the majority of the mountains' Amazigh population fled to the Italian-controlled Ja'fara plain to escape a campaign waged by Mohamed Fekini of the Rujban, who claimed to be fighting Baruni's project of an Ibadi–Imazighen state.[8] Raising Amazigh troops through Kherbish, and temporarily drawing on support from the Awlad Bu Saif and Mashashiya, the Italians in 1922 waged war against Zintan and Rujban, who were forced to flee to the Gibla. Deepening their alliances with the Warfalla, Qadhadhfa and Awlad Sulaiman, subsequently joined by the Mashashiya and Awlad Bu Saif, Zintan and Rujban continued the struggle in the Gibla and Fezzan for several years. Defeated, Zintani fighters fled to Algeria and Tunisia in 1930, while their brothers-in-arms from the Warfalla, Qadhadhfa and Awlad Sulaiman fled to Chad and Niger, returning only with the advance of Allied troops in 1943.[9] Perhaps more than any other community in the mountains, Zintanis thereafter maintained a strong oral tradition of poetry and invocations of past battles with the Italians or other enemies. Oral history differs strongly from one town to another on the role of individual leaders, and the struggles of the past continued to shape communities' positions towards each other well into 2011.

The Qadhafi regime adeptly exploited these intercommunal rifts. To build a reliable local support base, it promoted tribes who lacked land rights. The Mashashiya, for example, relied on access to pastures controlled by Zintan and the Warfalla, and had sharecropping arrangements with the Amazigh. In the southwestern Ja'fara, the Ottomans had allocated land owned by Nalut, Kabaw, Haraba and Jadu to the Si'an, who later forfeited their rights by failing to pay taxes; in the mountains' east, the Asab'a worked as shepherds for urban landed families from Gharyan. Under Qadhafi, these property regimes were severely disrupted as land was expropriated for socialist agricultural schemes whose main beneficiaries in and around the mountains were the Mashashiya and the Si'an. These expropriation measures broke the old alliance between the Imazighen, Mashashiya and Si'an and created conflicts that surfaced regularly during the Qadhafi era, and would play a significant role during the revolution. From the 1980s onwards, the regime began recruiting not only among its core constituencies, the Warfalla, Maqarha and Qadhadhfa, but also among smaller and disadvantaged tribes such as the Mashashiya and Si'an, to staff its security brigades and internal security services. One such brigade, the Sahban, established in Gharyan in the late 1980s, was led by Magarha, with significant Asab'a and Mashashiya contingents.[10]

Zintan had close ties with two of these core constituencies—the Warfalla, with whom many family bonds existed, and the Qadhadhfa—and also entered the army and security services, including the Sahban Brigade.[11] Zintan was considered by the Imazighen as the regime's stronghold in the mountains, although Zintan's position suffered somewhat after 1993, when an officer and several soldiers from Zintan were arrested for their alleged links to a coup plot by Warfalla officers.[12] Zintani tribal leaders also mediated in the land disputes erupting throughout Qadhafi's rule, which strengthened their political influence. Mediation, or *ammara*, also served to protect the internal cohesion of Jabal Nafusa communities: in Zintan, forty men, representing each family branch in Zintan and chosen for their integrity, would intervene between disputing parties to negotiate agreements and oversee their implementation.[13] In recurrent conflicts between Zintan and Yefren, as well as Zintan and Riyayna—which during the 1980s and 1990s at times led to confrontations with knives and daggers, given that firearms were strictly controlled—mediation was carried out by neutral parties, such as the Awlad Bu Saif. This capacity for internal and intercommunal conflict management would play a major role during the revolution and after.

Qadhafi's denial of Amazigh history, language and identity also shaped local communities' stance during the revolution. Qadhafi claimed throughout his rule that the Imazighen and Tuareg were of Arab origin and spoke Arabic dialects. His government banned Amazigh language and names, and renamed the Nafusa Mountains as the 'Western Mountains'. Amazigh activists were imprisoned or exiled.[14] Imazighen were prominently represented in the National Front for the Salvation of Libya (NFSL), and after the NFSL plot to attack Bab al-Aziziyya was discovered in 1984, Amazigh members' houses were destroyed and the ruins left as a warning to others; in Nalut, two members were hanged. Though the regime did have its local henchmen, it clearly—and rightfully—considered Amazigh communities as opposition strongholds. During 2006–7, Saif al-Islam al-Qadhafi's outreach to the opposition also included attempts at a détente with the Imazighen. But the regime proved unpredictable and unwilling to reconcile: as late as December 2008, members of the Revolutionary Committees and Saif al-Islam's *Libya al-Ghad* organisation attacked Amazigh activists' homes in Yefren.[15] Unsurprisingly, many of those targeted by Qadhafi's security apparatus would emerge at the forefront of the revolutionary struggle from February 2011 onwards.

Revolution

By early February, events in Egypt and Tunisia had created an expectant mood among Amazigh opposition figures and disgruntled youth in the mountains. Within tightly knit circles in Amazigh towns, intense discussions raged about whether, when and how to rise up. In Yefren, the security services began preemptively arresting possible agitators. The government offered concessions to avert unrest, such as easing housing credit—an offer that triggered a hostile response from some youths in Nalut, who on 12 February tried to set fire to the town's Savings Bank, and were arrested. Opposition activists and community leaders sought to prevent such precocious acts by youth, fearing that Qadhafi would use neighbouring communities—chiefly Zintan—to repress uprisings in the Amazigh towns. Meeting in Tripoli in early February, three longstanding regime opponents from Nalut, Jadu and Yefren who later became leading revolutionaries in their towns—Sha'ban Abu Sita, Fathi Yusuf and Salim Madi—agreed that, should an uprising in the east occur, Amazigh towns would be best advised to wait and see how other communities in the mountains would position themselves.[16]

To the great surprise of its neighbours, Zintan, and not an Amazigh town, on 16 February was the first in the entire west of Libya to join the protests erupting in Benghazi and Baida. As the regime rallied its support base in the west, Qadhafi's popular committees and security apparatus organised pro-regime marches, and in Zintan, emissaries from the Qadhadhfa tribe arrived, invoking their historical alliance with Zintan. On 15 February, Mansur Daw'—head of Qadhafi's People's Guard—requested a meeting with Zintan's elders to solicit their support, given that Zintanis were heavily represented in the army and security services. The first meeting, with Zintan's Popular Social Leadership[17]—a regime body that included tribal leaders—ended inconclusively, and another meeting was held the following day with a wider group of Zintani notables.[18]

Five members represented each tribal branch of Zintan at the meeting. According to two of those, Daw' requested 1,000 men to fight alongside Qadhafi's security brigades, and 3,000 more to organise a public show of allegiance.[19] Heated debate ensued between those who prioritised Zintan's alliance with the Qadhadhfa, and those who opposed it, invoking Zintan's tradition of fighting injustice and oppression. Normal decorum and deference to authority was abandoned; some present even threatened to go to war with each other rather than join the clampdown.[20] A significant proportion of those present refused to acquiesce to Qadhafi's request, and some noted how doing so would have a devastating effect on Zintan's unity and social cohesion. This latter point, the threat to Zintan's unity posed by repressing the eastern protests, appears to have been decisive in tribal leaders' considerations. Nevertheless, it remains unclear to what extent Zintani tribal leaders acted out of genuine frustration with the regime, or tactical calculations to raise the price for Zintan's support.

Meanwhile, outside the room, Zintani youths made their opinions known. A group of protesters interrupted the meeting, bringing it to an end. Several attendees joined with the protesters to move towards Zintan's central square, where a crowd of demonstrators was rapidly growing and began to shout slogans for the fall of the regime.[21] At mid-afternoon prayer, a well-respected Zintani imam, Shaikh Tahir Jdi', delivered a fiery speech urging the whole community to stand against Qadhafi. Shortly afterwards, protesters looted and burned down the police building and the *Mathaba*, the local branch of the Revolutionary Committees, providing Zintanis with an initial stock of weapons. Sheikh Tahir's speech and the ensuing protests were broadcast on YouTube and satellite channels at the same time as protests in Benghazi and Baida reached unstoppable momentum. A convoy of Central Security (*al-Amn al-Markazi*) forces arrived that night in Zintan and arrested several people in the main square, but then left again, apparently fearing reprisals. The same evening, another delegation of emissaries arrived in Zintan, offering 160,000 Libyan dinars (LYD) for every Zintani male between the ages of twenty and forty in exchange for abandoning revolutionary agitation. Zintan refused the offer. The emissaries returned later that night with an even more extravagant offer of 300,000 LYD for every Zintani family, in addition to a house on the Tripoli airport road. Qadhafi further asked for a delegation of Zintani elders, including Shaikh Tahir, to speak to him personally.

But Zintan's leaders rejected these and all subsequent offers over the following days, and from 17 February onwards, government forces began establishing checkpoints on the town's outskirts to cut off supplies. Following Zintan's lead, communities across the mountains joined the uprising. Small protests had already erupted in Kikla on 16 February. In Rujban, with its close relations to Zintan, a group of young protesters on the evening of 16 February sought to prevent a convoy of forces led by the Gharyan-based Sahban Brigade from reaching Zintan via Rujban's access road. Later that night, protesters burned the *Mathaba* and Internal Security Service's office in Rujban, meeting resistance from security forces when they tried to storm the police office. In the event, a young protester, Usama al-Tubbal, was killed— the revolution's first victim in the mountains. The following day, both Rujban and al-Qal'a joined the revolt.[22]

As in Zintan, many community leaders in the Amazigh towns were initially wary of entering into open rebellion, but were forced to take a stance by their youth. Small, spontaneous protests by youths erupted in Yefren, Jadu, Nalut and Hawamid—an Arab community with close ties to Nalut—on the evening of 18 February. In Jadu, a Central Security force that had arrived in the town the previous evening arrested several protesters, prompting community leaders to press for their release—successfully, though one prisoner disappeared, causing raging protesters to burn the local base of the Revolutionary Committees.[23] In Nalut, a small group of protesters burned the local *Mathaba* on 19 February, but stopped short of attacking state institutions such as the police or customs offices. When a Border Guards unit arrived in Nalut the following day, members of the town's Popular Social Leadership and police officers convinced the unit's head, an officer from Surman, that the situation was under control, warning of bloodshed if the force did not withdraw—which it did.[24] In Yefren, Sasi Grada, head of Libya's Oilfield Guard and a leading regime enforcer, and his relative Rustum Grada began distributing weapons to regime supporters, deterring protesters from attacking regime institutions on 19 February—but the following day, the crowd had grown and finally burned the *Mathaba*, as well as the International Security Service's office.[25]

In some towns, retired military officers were among the very first revolutionaries—most prominently Muhammad al-Madani in Zintan, a retired army colonel and well-respected local preacher. In Nalut, both acting and retired military officers joined in the first few days, led by the head of the Nalut border section, Col. Yahya al-Qut'i from Hawamid, and the retired officer Muhammad al-Tamtam. 'They were more Nalutis than military officers,' one former revolutionary said.[26] But for many members of the army and security forces in the mountains, the first days were a period of ambiguity and hesitation. Formal defection to the rebels would prevent officers from moving across the region to organise arms supplies, or mediating between their communities and regime forces. Though developments in Zintan still provoked incredulity in Amazigh towns, Zintan's uncompromising stance was crucial in encouraging Amazigh community leaders and members of the security forces to join the revolt. Early contacts between towns were instrumental: Madani led early outreach from Zintani revolutionaries to Rujban and Jadu—both of which were historically closely tied to Zintan—and established ties with Ibrahim Madi from Yefren and Qut'i and Tamtam from Nalut.[27] Through these emerging networks, the towns that joined the revolt assured each other of mutual support, and planning for common defence began. For Zintan, Nalut was crucially important for the Wazin border crossing to Tunisia, as a supply line and potential exit route. For Amazigh towns, Zintan had privileged access to weapons and ammunition, due to arsenals in Zintan or its vicinity, as well as the large number of Zintani army officers. Starting with the very first contacts established by Madani, Zintan provided arms to its Amazigh neighbours, often in exchange for food and medicine. Qut'i was arrested when returning from the first such mission to Zintan, on 24 February.[28]

From the beginning, the Nafusa Mountains' uprisings took the character of an armed revolt against the regime—and Zintan led the way. At the outset, most communities across the mountains only possessed a handful of old weapons, such as Mauser rifles supplied to the anti-colonial resistance by the Germans during the First World War, or Italian rifles dating from the 1930s. Communities rapidly armed themselves through a combination of forceful seizure, defections and complicity within the security forces. They were helped by the confusion of the first week, when nobody could be sure whose side one's counterparts were on. In Nalut, Qut'i distributed dozens of assault rifles in the uprising's very first days, and ensured that his subordinates in an army base at Sinaun (100km south of Nalut) handed over weapons and ammunition to Tamtam. In Jadu, revolutionaries on 19 February negotiated in vain with Jadu officers to hand over their weapons storage, and eventually took the facility by force, seizing over a hundred rifles.[29] Zintani efforts, however, were of a different order. In the days following the uprising, Zintani fighters began hit-and-run attacks on checkpoints surrounding the town to seize arms. Zintan's revolutionaries on 19 February formed a local committee, led by Madani, to prepare the town's defence and manage the consequences of the cessation of all government services. At the same time, defected army officers in Zintan could draw on the complicity of Zintanis still in active military service. Inside information enabled Zintani assailants on 20 February to briefly seize the major weapons storage at Qariyat, 300km southeast of Zintan, and carry away significant quantities of arms and ammunition. Around the same period, Zintanis also negotiated the surrender of army bases in Yefren, Shqiqa and Mizdah, allowing not only themselves, but a diverse group of people from Yefren, Jadu, the Mashashiya and the Quntrar to arm themselves.[30]

Clearly, by this time, Zintan's insurrection had already reached the point of no return. But still, throughout the first weeks, ambiguity prevailed in relations between communities, as well as between rebels and security forces. Members of the armed forces and security services kept deserting and returned to their communities with weapons. Col. Mukhtar al-Firnana of Zintan, who later became a key intermediary with NATO, left his post at Sabratha on 17 February to go to Zintan, but went back the same evening, finally announcing his defection upon his return to Zintan on 25 February.[31] Weapons were handed out to supposed loyalists through the Sahban Brigade in Gharyan, some of which were then channelled to rebels.[32] In late February, Yefren rebels bought twenty assault rifles from their Mashashiya neighbours, with whom they would soon enter into conflict. In the Nalut area, an army unit arrived in late February to seize control of the Wazin crossing, but the defected Naluti army officers Col. Ahmad Yarro and Khalid al-Azzabi negotiated with the unit's commander that it would remain in its base and allow unimpeded movement across the border for supplies and the evacuation of wounded rebels.[33] (The arrangement only ended with the arrival of a new unit in mid-March, which heralded the beginning of war in the area.) In early March, Nalut's revolutionaries successfully negotiated with the small group of soldiers guarding the nearby Juwaibia base hosting a battalion of around 300 Soviet-made tanks. The soldiers evacuated the base without a shot being fired.[34] However, the majority of the tanks had been rendered unusable by the removal of key parts, and had essentially been left to rust since the mid-1990s; moreover, there was no ammunition at the base.

Each community also began activating wider networks and historical alliances in the uprising's first weeks. In the greater Tripoli area, descendants from the Amazigh towns began making their way back to help defend their communities. Zintan activated Tuareg and Tebu connections in southern Libya. While the town of Zintan was considered their 'homeland' (Zintan al-Watan), the tribe had historically nomadised across the area southeast of the mountains—the Gibla—and settled in Mizda, Dirj and the western Wadi al-Shati'. In early March, Zintani emissaries met with the Tuareg leader Ufnait al-Koni to convince the Imanghassaten Tuareg to join the revolt, but failed after they did not concede to Tuareg demands for weapons.[35] Around the same time, Zintanis in Ubari contacted Tebu leaders with whom they had close relations in the smuggling business. One former leader of a Tebu rebellion in Niger, Barka Sidimi, had just joined the revolt with weapons and vehicles given to him by Mas'ud Abd al-Hafiz, the military governor of Sabha. Though the weapons Barka gave to a Zintani army officer at the Wigh base were negligible, the gesture renewed a longstanding alliance that would outlast the revolution.[36]

Community leaders from revolutionary strongholds and neighbouring towns who were ambiguous or hostile towards the uprising also reached out to each other. A first delegation from al-Qal'a visited the Mashashiya on 18 February, invoking the two communities' historical ties to persuade the Mashashiya to join the revolution. The Mashashiya rebuffed these advances—as one attendee put it, primarily because they refused to side with Zintan, their longstanding adversaries.[37] Another delegation from Yefren and al-Qal'a met with Mashashiya elders three days later, and another one shortly after that—to no avail. Zintani elders engaged in similarly unsuccessful efforts, requesting in vain that the Mashashiya in al-Awainiya and Zawiyat al-Baqul stay neutral and keep the road open to Zintani movements.[38] A delegation from the Si'an in late February assured Nalut that none would harm the other, regardless of political differences—but encountered suspicion in Nalut, given reports that the regime was arming and recruiting among the

Si'an.[39] Kabaw was initially split, but joined the revolution from 23 February onwards. The small Amazigh town of Tamzin and the Arab Haraba community did not join the revolt, and were eyed with suspicion by neighbouring Jadu, Kabaw and Nalut, who barricaded both towns' entry roads.

These divisions were partly caused by the regime's two-pronged strategy of coaxing rebellious towns into abandoning their stance, while mobilising its own constituencies against their neighbours. In Ruhaibat, the mixed Arab-Amazigh population split along ethnic lines, with Amazigh joining the revolt, while Arabs were prevented from doing so through a combination of inducements and pressure by the community's leading regime figures—the former head of the external intelligence service Abu Zaid Durda, and Gen. Muhammad al-Issawi, who later led military operations in the western part of the mountains.[40] General Misbah al-Arusi, a senior army commander from Kikla, sought to recruit volunteers in Qawalish.[41] Nasir al-Mabruk, deputy interior minister and a leading Riyayna figure, caused his town to split between its west—which did not join the revolt—and its east, which did. Regime emissaries to the Si'an and Mashashiya successfully exploited these community's fears that they would lose the land rights they gained during the Qadhafi era should the revolt by Zintan and the Amazigh towns succeed. Among both communities, the regime began recruiting volunteers for the People's Guards (*Mutatawwi'un al-Hars al-Sha'bi*).

At the same time, the regime attempted negotiation with rebellious towns. With Kabaw community leaders acting as intermediaries, General Issawi unsuccessfully reached out to Nalut in late February, offering cultural rights for the Imazighen.[42] On 5 March, regime functionaries from several Amazigh towns, including a delegation of eleven figures from Yefren—led by the aforementioned Sasi Grada and Sulaiman Gjam, national head of the Agricultural Police—accepted Qadhafi's invitation to meet at his compound at Bab al-Aziziyya.[43] But these figures had already lost their sway in Amazigh towns, now irreversibly aligned with the revolution. Accordingly, Qadhafi focused on winning back Zintan. In his famous 22 February televised speech, Qadhafi spoke at length about the impossibility that Zintan could be traitors, given their glorious past as leaders of the anti-colonial struggle. On 8 March, Qadhafi held a large meeting with Zintan representatives at Bab al-Aziziyya, with his hour-long speech at the event being televised. But by this time, Zintan was already being attacked, and the attempted rapprochement failed.

By early March, then, a large section of the mountains were counted as 'liberated'. Each mutinous town had barricaded its entry roads and the first Amazigh flags made their appearance. But east of Kikla, the regime retained support in Qawalish and Asab'a, and quickly reestablished its hold over Gharyan, the seat of two large army units, after major and sustained protests. Kikla, al-Qala'a, Yefren and Zintan were cut off from each other by towns in which government forces established checkpoints. The Mashashiya towns of Zawiyat al-Baqul and Awainiya, the Si'an towns of Tiji and Badr, as well as Qawalish and western Riyayna, would soon become bases for regime forces' onslaught against the rebels. (Qadhafi would later appeal to the Si'an, Mashashiya and Asab'a to 'cleanse' the mountains from 'the traitors and rats').[44] For now, however, Qadhafi's efforts to stifle the revolt centred on the capital and the coastal cities of Misrata, Zawiya and Zuwara. During late February and early March, Khamis al-Qadhafi's 32 Brigade's ruthless recapture of Zuwara and Zawiya—cities with which Amazigh communities had close and extensive ties—further underlined to mountain rebels that military defence was the only viable option.

The war for the mountains

The regime's campaign to subdue the mountain revolts began on 1 March with the army's 9th Brigade, Sahban, crushing protesters in Gharyan and moving towards Zintan, encountering resistance in Kikla and al-Qal'a on the way. Mashashiya women sang and celebrated when they entered Awainiya.

Revolutionary strongholds' efforts to coordinate a common defence intensified. Zintan's defence was led by former military officers and reservists, who formed a Military Council under Usama Juwaili, a former major in the army's electronic support unit who had left the army in 1992. But it was the head of Zintan's local council, Colonel Muhammad al-Madani, who had served in Qadhafi's Special Forces (*Sa'iqa*), and had fought in the Chad war, who guided military strategy. With Juwaili, he activated a network of friends and former army colleagues across the Nafusa Mountains, including Colonel Ahmad Yarro in Nalut, Abd al-Rahman Abu Rihana and Colonel Sa'id al-Aribi in Jadu, as well as Ibrahim Madi in Yefren and Hussain Grada in al-Qal'a, which did much to ensure unity among those towns.[45] On 7 March, when a Sahban unit approached Yefren from its eastern entry road at the foot of the mountains, Yefreni elders asked for time to discuss the town's possible surrender. This gave Yefren's fighters time to call reinforcements from Zintan and al-Qal'a, who, under Madani's command and with support from Naluti revolutionaries, launched a preemptive dawn attack on the force and seized its heavy weapons.[46]

A major new offensive began from 17 March onwards on Zintan's outskirts, led by the Sahban and commanded by General Abd al-Salam Bashir, but drawn from a variety of army units, including tank and artillery battalions from Tripoli and Khums.[47] Zintan's defence against this force was a joint victory of fighters from across the mountains, in what became known as the battle of Kshaf, towards Zintan's east, from 19 to 22 March. Zintanis received major support from Rujban, Jadu, Kabaw, Nalut, as well as Yefren and, under Madani's command, blocked the Sahban from entering Zintan, then gradually pushed the force back towards the east, making important seizures of small and heavy weaponry.[48] All the while, Zintan remained cut off from electricity, and was bombarded by Grad rocket launchers from forces based at Western Riyayna.

With the Zintan offensive stalled (though Grad bombardment continued) the Sahban Brigade and People's Guards launched a major assault on Yefren, al-Qal'a and Kikla on 28 March, after a Yefreni army colonel, Ali al-Ammuri, attempted and failed to negotiate Yefren's surrender.[49] The vast majority of the towns' civilian population left for the Tunisian border; remaining fighters in each town were dependent on the other two towns for their defence. Over the next days, the Sahban Brigade, supported by the Gharyan-based 8 Brigade and volunteer forces based in Awainiya and Qawalish fought their way into Yefren and Kikla, with al-Qal'a coming under heavy bombardment. On 6 April, taking heavy losses, the Sahban and People's Guards occupied Yefren's centre, Mashashiya volunteers chanting and waving green flags.[50] Yet until its liberation in early June, Yefren's heights remained held by revolutionary fighters carrying out hit-and-run attacks, while al-Qal'a rebels held their town despite continuous shelling from the Sofit heights, north of Kikla. The three towns were largely cut off from supplies reaching Zintan from the Tunisian border, since the towns of Awainiya and Riyayna blocked access to Zintan. Donkeys were used to supply weapons and ammunition, and diminishing supplies of water were available from household water tanks and wells—though electricity cuts made operating many wells difficult.[51]

In the Nalut area, fighting began in earnest in mid-April. Naluti fighters had won an important victory in an attack on a Border Guards unit at the Ghazaya base on 18 March, capturing 24 prisoners who were released shortly afterwards. From 11 April onwards, however, major force contingents entered the area via Tiji and Badr. As in the Zintan and Yefren offensives, regime forces in the Nalut area were a combination of regular and irregular units commanded by the Sahban Brigade, including units organised on tribal lines, recruited from Si'an, Nuwail and urban soldiers and irregulars, supplemented by volunteers from Tamzin, Kabaw, Haraba and Awlad Mahmud.[52] In addition, contingents of the 32 Brigade were deployed to al-Ghazaya to control the Wazin border crossing, choking the revolt's supply lines.[53] South of Nalut, Tuareg contingents from the Ubari-based Maghawir Brigade had been deployed to Sinaun. This combination of regular and irregular units did not always work to their advantage: regular artillery units charged with shelling Yefren, Jadu and Nalut often disabled their projectiles so they would not explode, or even notified rebels in advance of areas to be bombarded.[54] Naluti revolutionaries established communications with Mustafa Hammadi, who commanded the Tuareg unit based at Sinaun and, invoking their *Tamazgha* (their common identity as Imazighen), dissuaded Hammadi from moving against Amazigh towns.[55]

The arrival of reinforcements and onset of shelling in the Nalut area prompted a mass evacuation of Naluti families from 11 April onwards, via desert tracks. Whereas civilians from Kikla, al-Qal'a, Yefren and Zintan fled the shelling of these towns, Nalut's decision to evacuate Naluti families was a deliberate political signal intended to alert the international community.[56] At Tatauine in Tunisia, a refugee camp and a hub for humanitarian supplies to the mountains emerged, with Qatari support. But the arrival of regime forces made evacuating civilians and ensuring food, fuel and medical supplies through Tunisia increasingly dangerous and supplies became scarce, creating intercommunal tensions. Zintan and Nalut disagreed over exchanging Naluti tanks for Zintani ammunition, with Nalut accusing Zintan of short-changing it.

Meanwhile, the NATO air campaign almost entirely neglected the Nafusa Mountains during its first two months, concentrating on the Misratan and eastern Brega–Ra's Lanuf fronts, command-and-control centres, and major coastal military facilities. Excluding a raid on the Qa'a weapons storage facility 50km south of Zintan on 8 April, the first NATO strikes in the mountains targeted government forces around Zintan on 25 April, and again three days later. No strikes occurred in the Nalut and Yefren–Qal'a-Kikla areas until early June.

Without NATO support, cooperation among the fragmented rebel forces to open up supply lines became ever more critical. Having jointly repelled an attempt by regime forces commanded by General Issawi to reach the mountains via Ruhaibat's access road on 13 April, fighters from Zintan, Rujban, Jadu, Ruhaibat, Kabaw, Hawamid and Nalut began planning to seize the Wazin border crossing,[57] which under Madani's leadership, they did on 21 April.[58] Four days later, a joint rebel force won another significant victory at al-Mujabra, where regime forces had reached the mountains, but were beaten back.

Rivalry among rebels, conflict between communities

By April, military councils dominated by defected army officers had emerged in Zintan, Nalut, Jadu and Rujban, primarily to centralise the distribution of heavy weapons, ammunition and logistical supplies; in addition, they provided training in the handling of heavy weapons. Defected or former officers such as Madani, Aribi and Major Ali Amlish from Jadu, or Tamtam from Nalut also played a major role in shaping military strategy, particularly in joint operations. But other towns, such as Kabaw or embattled al-Qal'a and Yefren, entirely lacked professional soldiers, and across the mountains the vast majority of fighters were civilians operating largely autonomously from the military councils, gradually coalescing into small armed groups whose leadership slowly emerged through particular displays of courage, charisma or military skills.[59]

The leader who could unite these different constituencies, both within Zintan and across Nafusa towns, was Madani, who with his strong preacher's charisma was a towering influence on Zintan's revolutionaries, imposing moral discipline and taming the impulses of volunteers who would flock to the front upon news of the enemy's approach. Madani also successfully curtailed the ill-treatment of detainees and the theft of private property as war spoils by Zintani youth.[60] His military credentials and deeply pious demeanour made him a consensus figure for everyone from army officers to Islamist civilian fighters in Zintan and Nalut alike. Former members of the Libyan Islamic Fighting Group (LIFG) from Nalut still see Madani as 'a sheikh for the entire Jabal Nafusa'.[61] From Nalut to Yefren, former revolutionaries agree that with Madani's death in battle on 1 May, his unifying influence disappeared, and Zintan's relations with its neighbours changed.[62]

In Zintan itself, tensions over military leadership surfaced immediately after Madani's death. Two rival camps had emerged; Juwaili's Military Council, which combined retired army officers and civilians, and the 'Western Mountains Military Council', led by Colonel Mukhtar Firnana and formed by Zintani officers who had been in active service at the outbreak of the revolution. Despite its name, Firnana's council included some officers from Jadu and Rujban, but excluded other towns; Naluti officers refused to join, seeing the initiative as an attempt by Firnana to centralise control.[63] The day after Madani's death, Firnana and his fellow defected officers claimed military leadership, but were opposed by Juwaili and his civilian revolutionaries, who remained suspicious of Firnana's group. Within Juwaili's Military Council, seven separate battalions emerged, led by former army officers and civilians, and military decision making went from guidance by Madani to collective leadership by battalion commanders.[64]

However, such rivalries were not only a consequence of Madani's death or individual interests, but of the rebellion's growing success. Improved supply lines from Tunisia slowly began to change the balance of power in the mountains, but also fomented discord among the mountain towns. As foreign support entered from Tunisia, each town associated itself with different sources and hosted competing groups of external volunteer fighters.

From their logistics hubs in Tataouine, Qatar, the Emirates and Oman provided assistance to different local partners. Whereas the UAE tended to deliver its aid to Zintan and Qatar favoured Nalut, Oman supported other Amazigh localities with whom it shared Ibadism and associated historical connections—particularly Jadu.[65] Qatar had provided assistance and training to Naluti revolutionaries as early as April 2011. Later, Qatari arms supplies arrived via Tunisia, secured by the Tunisian army; in Nalut, Qatari officers distributed the weapons both to local groups and commanders across the mountains, in coordination with Nalut's Military Council.[66] Nalut's position was boosted by its hosting of the Martyrs of the Capital (*Shuhada' al-*

Asima) Battalion, led by former LIFG members, as well as Mahdi al-Harati's Tripoli Revolutionaries' Battalions, which arrived through Wazin in early May. A former LIFG member of Naluti origin, Murad Zikri, facilitated both groups' entry into Nalut; in turn, their presence helped channel further Qatari training and other assistance. Almost simultaneously, French and Emirati ground advisers arrived in Zintan, with the US and Emirates supporting the construction of an airstrip near Rujban, close to Zintan. Teaming up with Firnana's 'Western Mountains Military Council', the Emiratis set up an operations room that became the region's key liaison with NATO.[67] When Qatari advisers arrived in Zintan in mid-June, they set up an operations room separate from the Emiratis. Yefren, al-Qal'a and Kikla had no representatives in the operations rooms in Zintan; Yefreni leaders communicated directly with Abd al-Salam al-Hasi in the Benghazi operations room, but their pledges for air strikes at regime forces were in vain. In Nalut and Yefren, frustration grew over NATO's neglect of their areas, and Al Jazeera's rare references to their towns and description of military developments as east or west of Zintan.[68]

The National Transitional Council (NTC), meanwhile, played a marginal role other than providing a framework of legitimacy for the mountains towns' interaction with NATO and its allies. Though most towns had their NTC representatives, they derived little influence from their membership in the council. For the first three months, the overall local perception was that the Nafusa Mountains towns were left to fend for themselves. Mahmud Shammam was the first member of the Executive Committee to visit the region in mid-June and facilitated the Qatari chief of staff's visit.[69] Ali Tarhuni followed in mid-July offering financial aid to the towns, and NTC Chairman Mustafa Abd al-Jalil at the end of that month. The NTC's visit—as with the initial Qatari and Emirati forays—betrayed substantial unfamiliarity with the mountains' history and politics, and concerns of mounting tensions between Nalut and Zintan over the distribution of weapons coming through Tunisia or via the newly constructed airstrips.

On the ground, however, rebel forces gained momentum. As greater supplies of weapons became available through external support and raiding government forces' supplies, and as rebel ranks gradually expanded with volunteers reaching the mountains via Tunisia, their forces began to coalesce into individual battalions (*kata'ib*). In Nalut, Jadu, Rujban and Zintan, fighters from elsewhere in Libya set up camps—in Nalut alone, the two Tripolitanian battalions were joined by camps of fighters from Zawiya, Zuwara and Sabratha. They gained the trust of local communities through courageous behaviour in the battlefield, which dispelled fears that they could be infiltrators.[70] Nevertheless, incoming strangers were at times met with suspicion from the tightly knit mountain communities, and recommendations from local contacts were indispensable for newcomers. Not all external contributions were welcome in every town: when a group of rebel leaders from Jadu went to seek arms supplies from the Qatar-based religious scholar Ali Sallabi in Benghazi, in June, they were promised weapons deliveries if they agreed to host a contingent of Islamist fighters. The group from Jadu refused and, upon their return, a Qatari officer was beaten up in the town because his country was seen as favouring Islamists in its arms supplies. Even so, the number of fighters in Jadu increased from around 200 in March to 1200 in August.[71] Contingents in Zintan and Nalut were several times that size. Even in besieged Yefren, the number of revolutionaries went from around 250 in late March (of whom 75 were fighters) to around 500 in late May.[72]

With such strengthened forces, the capture of Shakshuk (at the foot of the mountains, north of Jadu) on 1 June marked the turning point of the war from a defence of mountain strongholds to an offensive against regime forces. With rebel forces from Yefren and Jadu meeting for the first time since late March, the victory at Shakshuk enabled Jadu to channel crucial supplies to the Yefren front.[73] There, fighters from Yefren, Kikla and al-Qal'a began an assault on government forces, freeing Yefren on 2 June. Kikla rebels moved on, seizing their town by 5 June.[74] Together with Zintan, forces from the three towns eventually dislodged regime forces from the Sofit heights on 16 June, ending the artillery bombardment of al-Qal'a. When Zintani forces seized the major weapons depot at al-Qa'a, 50km south of Zintan, on 28 June, they called their comrades from Rujban and Amazigh towns to share in the bounty.[75]

During the advances of June and July, which now were increasingly supported by NATO strikes, conflicts surfaced between rebels and the communities that had permitted government forces to use their towns as bases. In mid-May, already, Zintanis had clashed with armed irregulars from Western Ryayna, and the Mashashiya population of Zawiyat al-Bagul had escaped before Zintan captured the town.[76] When Awainiya and Western Ryayna were taken, in mid-June, the entire population fled, and rebel forces from Zintan, Yefren, al-Qal'a and Kikla looted and burned their homes. In early July, the town of Qawalish met the same fate, the population fleeing to Tripoli the day before rebels arrived.[77] Many Mashashiya initially fled to Asab'a and later to Tripoli, Shqiqa, Mizdah, Sabha, Tarhuna, Bani Walid and Sirt. Forces from Zintan and Amazigh towns pushed on, eventually taking Gharyan and Zawiya on 16 and 17 August, now heavily supported by coalition air strikes.

Conflicts also surfaced between rebel forces. Nalut sought to coordinate with Zintan, Rujban and Jadu to advance on Tiji and Badr, since an advance purely by Nalut and Kabaw would complicate the surrender of the Si'an towns. Naluti fighters dislodged regime forces from Takut and Ghazaya on 28–29 July, their firepower boosted by the successful repair of several aging tanks from the Nalut base and coalition air strikes. But when Nalut lost several fighters during a failed offensive by Zintani and Naluti forces towards Tiji, each side blamed the other for the failure, and the two groups almost turned their guns on each other. The joint offensive was delayed. Eventually, Nalut and Kabaw captured Tiji and Badr in mid-August, driving out the remaining population, and looting both towns.[78]

Spoils and power

As rebel forces descended from the mountains, their paths and interests diverged. In Tripoli, battalions from the mountains and Misrata took over state buildings and private homes of senior officials, engaging in widespread looting and car theft. Heavy machinery from construction sites was hauled off to the mountains, as were great quantities of weapons and ammunition from arms depots across the greater Tripoli area. Zintani forces acquired particular notoriety for these acts, which Zintan's neighbours were quick to attribute to the tribe's historical reputation for raiding.

The ranks of Nafusa Mountains rebels swelled dramatically in the weeks after the fall of Tripoli, with thousands of Tripoli residents joining groups from their town of origin, and dozens of smaller armed groups emerging over which the military councils of the mountains had virtually no influence. From its initial seven, Zintan's battalions went to 35 distinct groups by October 2011.[79] The largest were the Qa'qa' and Muhammad al-Madani Battalions. The Qa'qa' Battalion, then led by the Zintani businessman Abd al-Majid Mliqta, also provided security to Mahmud Jibril and his associates in Tripoli, establishing a connection that would later result in close ties between Zintan and Jibril's National Forces Alliance. Disillusioned with the excesses of so-called revolutionaries, units from Yefren and Nalut were the first to withdraw from Tripoli in November 2011, with Nalut's Military Council apologising for any wrongdoings Nalutis may have committed in Tripoli.

Another point of divergence was over dealing with the former regime and government officials fleeing Tripoli to Tunisia. The Zintanis quietly assisted the escape of senior regime officials, providing safe passage to exit the country via Zintan and Rujban. It remains unclear whether this was done on the basis of Zintan's tribal alliances, lucrative financial deals, arrangements with western intelligence services, or a combination of these factors. General Abd al-Salam Jallud, who had been among Qadhafi's closest associates from the 1969 coup until his fall from grace in 1995, escaped to Zintan on 19 August, and was subsequently able to leave the country.[80] Bashir Salih, Qadhafi's cabinet chief and head of the Libyan African Investment Portfolio, escaped via Zintan to France, and from there to South Africa.[81] Al-Tuhami Khalid, head of Internal Security, was seen boarding a French military helicopter in Rujban.[82] The Nalutis, however, were less tolerant, and along with the Tripoli battalions whom they had hosted, sought to arrest as many as possible. Less prominent or well-connected figures who attempted to flee via Wazin, some bearing letters of safe passage from the Zintan Military Council, were arrested by Nalut forces and handed to Abd al-Hakim Bilhajj's Tripoli Military Council—reflecting the links between Naluti revolutionaries and former LIFG members established during the war.[83]

Zintan also parted ways with the Amazigh towns in being far more expansionary, seizing strategic locations across Tripoli and southern Libya. A Zintani unit led by Colonel Mukhtar al-Akhdar had taken the airport and surrounding area on 21 August, establishing a sphere of influence that Zintani forces would maintain long after the war. In parallel, Zintan set about occupying what its leaders saw as the tribe's historical territory, stretching to the Algerian border and the south. Until August, the area between Nalut and Ghadames had been controlled by forces from the Ubari-based and Tuareg Maghawir Brigade under the control of Hammadi. Juwaili negotiated their departure in late August 2011, providing Hammadi with fuel to withdraw to Ubari, from where Hammadi's deputy, Colonel Muhammad Ag Najim, continued on to northern Mali, sparking a chain of events that would lead to the collapse of state control over Mali's north.[84] The Maghawir's withdrawal allowed two Zintani units to establish themselves in Ghadames from whence they controlled the Algerian border from Nalut south to Ghat.

Through the first six months of the transitional era, Zintani units continued their expansion in the southwest. This was aided by Juwaili's appointment as defence minister in November 2011 and his formalisation of Zintan's control of the western borders and southern oil fields. Zintani groups led by Colonel al-Ujmi al-Uthayri established a significant presence in Wadi al-Ajal during November 2011, and obtained government decisions granting them control of major oilfields, such as ENI's Elephant field near Murzuq, which until then had been secured by forces from Yefren. Zintani battalions in the south quickly recruited Tebu and members of the Arab Hutman tribe to cement their local positions.[85] In addition, they drew on Zintan's well-established ties with the Imanghassaten Tuareg to lobby the government—unsuccessfully—to dissolve the Maghawir Brigade, recruited from Malian Tuareg, which remained largely intact in its Ubari base.[86] When this failed, Juwaili began channelling salaries to the Maghawir—now renamed the Tendé brigade—through Zintani commanders, turning it into a Zintani client force. This effectively shifted Zintan's alliance in the region from the Imanghassaten to the Tuareg of Malian origin who formed the bulk of the former Maghawir Brigade.[87] Through such links with Tebu and Tuareg militias, the basis was laid for a permanent Zintani presence across an area the town's leaders had long seen as their natural sphere of influence.

On a smaller scale, the Imazighen too moved south, creating new relationships with the Tuareg. Since June 2011, three defected soldiers from the Tuareg Maghawir Brigade had fought with Yefren rebels, having arrived via Tunisia. After Tripoli's fall, they persuaded dozens of their comrades to defect from Sirt, or gathered them as Colonel Hammadi's Tuareg brigade disintegrated. This now-emerging Ténéré Battalion, together with 150 fighters from Yefren and Kabaw, took Ubari and Ghat on 21–23 September.[88] With that initiative came renewed solidarity with the 'Imazighen of the Sahara', as Amazigh activists now called the Tuareg. Prior to reaching Ubari, groups from Yefren, Jadu and Kabaw fought in Sabha, and retained a presence in the city for several months afterwards.

The final point of divergence came over the treatment of 'pro-Qadhafi' towns and neighbours. Here Zintan's tribal alliances took precedence over the revolutionary struggle, which the Imazighen still pursued. Zintani forces, excepting some individuals and smaller armed groups, participated neither in the siege and sacking of Bani Walid, nor in the capture of Sabha—in contrast, Amazigh fighters played a major role in both battles. Entering Bani Walid would have spelled the definitive rupture of Zintan's relations with the Warfalla, and fomented internal tensions in Zintan. The efforts of Zintan's leaders to mend their damaged ties with historical allies whose leaders mostly sided with the regime, such as the Warshafana and Warfalla, isolated the town within the camp of revolutionary forces. These choices led Zintan to become a political and military counterweight to both Misrata and the Amazigh towns in the post-revolutionary era.

The mountains in the new (dis)order

Three main factors shaped politics in the Nafusa Mountains in the early post-revolutionary period: the rifts of the civil war; competition over the redistribution of power and resources in the postwar disorder; and Amazigh activism.

Intercommunal conflicts fuelled by the civil war continued to rear their ugly heads. Communities across the mountains remained heavily armed, while the social control exerted by community leaders over individuals and groups carrying weapons steadily eroded. Major fighting erupted between Zintan and the Mashashiya in Shqiqa in December 2011, and again in June 2012 after the killing of a Zintani field commander. More than seventy people were killed in the second Zintani attack on Shqiqa, and several hundred Mashashiya families were forced to flee yet again.[89] While smaller communities, such as Ghana'ima near Yefren, had been allowed to return in the months after the conflict, Awainiya and Qawalish remained ghost towns at the time of writing.

Qawalish residents, attempting a first return without prior agreement from Kikla, were immediately forced out again in September 2011. Talks that included the two parties as well as al-Qal'a, Yefren and eastern Riyayna produced a first agreement to permit a return to Qawalish in January 2012, premised among other things on the establishment of one local council for both communities, which meant political predominance for Kikla. However, the same month, two successive attempts by Qawalish residents to return met with armed resistance from Kikla, and after that, attempts at conflict resolution remained unsuccessful.[90] The Mashashiya opened separate talks with Zintan and Amazigh communities—particularly Yefren—since contentious issues differed between the two: Zintan's demands were largely confined to resolving conflicts related to the civil war, and land issues played a minor role. Yefren's demands to permit the Mashashiya's return to Awainiya not only included a formal demand for pardon and the withdrawal of tribal protection from suspects, but also a formalisation of land rights based on the recognition of Yefreni privileges.[91]

The return of some Si'an to Tiji and Badr shortly after the towns' capture, bringing with them weapons from their volunteer service for the regime, created tensions with Nalut, Hawamid and Kabaw. When a fighter from Nalut was killed in Tiji on 1 October 2012, Nalut forces shelled and then rampaged through Tiji and Badr with tanks, destroying property and killing at least four people. Both Si'an towns and their adjacent agricultural projects were further looted by Nalut, and their population was warned not to return.[92] Neighbouring communities mediated a tense calm in the area, but in March 2013, renewed clashes between Hawamid and the Si'an town of Ziqzaw quickly escalated into heavy fighting that again drew in Nalut.[93]

Communities in the Jabal Nafusa displayed a remarkable capacity for managing such conflicts in the absence of state authority. Local actors considered neutral by the conflicting parties invested substantially in mediating and overseeing the implementation of tenuous ceasefire agreements, such as leaders from the Awlad Bu Saif between Zintan and the Mashashiya, or Jadu and Rujban between Nalut and the Si'an. A regional reconciliation committee was formed that included widely respected figures from Arab and Amazigh communities, and was highly active in mediating across the Jabal Nafusa, but also in other conflicts from Kufra to Zawiya. Conscious of its growing isolation in the mountains, Zintan during 2013 began reaching out to neighbouring communities, gradually releasing its Mashashiya prisoners and paving the way for the return of residents to Western Riyayna in October.[94] However, Western Riyayna was a rare exception in that mediation efforts produced a genuine resolution for this conflict, instead of just a temporary ceasefire arrangement. This success was possible primarily because Zintan's differences with Western Riyayna were largely confined to the community's hosting of Qadhafi's security brigades during the war, and did not include the complex land issues and historical legacies that bedevilled other local conflicts.[95]

Rivalries over redistributing local power and privileges compounded the rifts of the revolution in some cases, but also produced alliances that cut across its divides. This was particularly evident in competition over black market trade with Tunisia. During the Qadhafi era, smuggling of agricultural and construction equipment and materials through Nalut to Tunisia had been tightly controlled by Si'an and Nuwail networks, through both communities' military officers based in Nalut, while the Amazigh population had played a subservient role.[96] With the regime's collapse, armed groups from Nalut began exploiting their control over the border crossing to expand their share in smuggling. The town became a major hub for alcohol smuggled from Tunisia, as well as vehicles imported duty-free through militia-held Libyan ports for export to Tunisia, from which the Nuwail and Si'an were now excluded.[97] This burgeoning business awakened the interest of Zintani groups, and in August 2012, Defence Minister Juwaili gave formal authority over the border section from Nalut to Ghadames to a Zintani unit—which was promptly sent back by Nalutis. Zintani factions subsequently established themselves in Nuwail and Si'an territory along the border, and in parallel, the Zintani transport minister in the Zaidan government, Abd al-Qadir al-Ayid, began lobbying for the establishment of a separate border crossing for the Si'an to use. Nalut fiercely—and successfully—opposed the plans, which were perceived in Nalut as a Zintani conspiracy with the former regime's constituencies in the area.[98]

Elsewhere, Zintani factions used their military power to expand their share of the smuggling flows traversing southern Libya and obtain political concessions to do so. Through their ties with Tuareg and Tebu militias, Zintanis networks played a key role in the trafficking flows between the Sahel and northern Libya, and smuggled weapons to armed groups in northern Mali.[99] Zintani groups also maintained their presence at Ghadames and cemented control over Tripoli International Airport. Zintani forces briefly relinquished control over the airport following a deal in April 2012 that saw Zintanis taking over many civilian positions at the airport. After a disgruntled battalion from Tarhuna briefly seized the airport in June 2012, Zintani units regained control, and subsequently retained a permanent though unofficial presence. The airport presence served a key function for the smuggling of contraband goods.[100]

Zintani factions' economic and military ambitions combined with the formation of political alliances, with Zintani outreach to political and tribal constituencies associated with the former regime alienating many of Zintan's former revolutionary allies. After counter-revolutionary forces took control of Bani Walid in early 2012, Zintani networks began smuggling former members of Qadhafi's security forces to the town from Tunisia.[101] The aforementioned Qa'qa' Battalion, which by early 2013 had a presence in Tripoli, along the Algerian border and in southern oilfields, even recruited former members of Khamis al-Qadhafi's 32 Brigade and the Tuareg Maghawir Brigade to fill its ranks in the Tripoli area.[102] The Mliqta brothers, who controlled the Qa'qa', also cemented Zintan's political alignment with Jibril's National Forces Alliance, which from late 2012 onwards promoted a conciliatory approach towards former regime officials in the struggles surrounding the 'Political Isolation Law'.[103] Zintani elders also sought to mediate between Bani Walid's revolutionary and counter-revolutionary camps. When this failed, Zintan's leaders—including Defence Minister Juwaili—voiced strong opposition as a coalition of revolutionary forces from Misrata, Zawiya and Gharyan captured Bani Walid yet again, in October 2012. By this time, the unity between the Imazighen and Zintan during the revolution was but a faint memory. When fighters from Amazigh towns joined with former revolutionaries from Zawiya and Sabratha in September 2012 to create the National Mobile Force (*al-Quwa al-Wataniya al-Mutaharrika*), charged with securing Tripoli's southwestern outskirts, Zintani leaders saw this as a direct challenge to their own military forces.[104]

Facing growing hostility from the revolutionary camp, Zintani armed groups adopted an increasingly aggressive approach. After the Zaidan government in June 2013 conceded to Tuareg and Tebu demands for a greater share of guarding posts at the Elephant and Sharara oilfields in the southwest, to the detriment of the Zintani forces at the fields, Zintani groups attacked the headquarters of the Oilfield Guards in Tripoli.[105] The attack turned into a major confrontation with Tripoli-based forces from the Supreme Security Committees. A week later, Zintani forces occupied a major interior ministry facility on Tripoli's airport road. Such brazen acts deepened resentment against Zintan among revolutionary forces from the mountains, Zawiya, Tripoli and Misrata, who now joined forces to curb Zintani action. Feeling ever more isolated, and increasingly unable to rein in the various armed groups associated with their town, Zintani leaders convened a big 'forum of Libyan tribes and cities' in July 2013, at which many of the former regime's constituencies were well-represented, but Zintan's Amazigh neighbours were missing—except Jadu, which now increasingly acted as an intermediary between Zintan and the Imazighen.[106] The Imazighen's increasingly assertive activism in pursuit of cultural and language rights also heightened tension with Zintan. With the confidence that flowed from their crucial role in the revolution, Amazigh activists forcefully pushed their demands, threatening to block the transitional political process if they were ignored. Such activism represented an important departure from the localism that had dominated politics and military organisation during the civil war. Many in Zintan, however, saw the ubiquitous Amazigh flags as a symbol of secession, and were irritated about what they perceived as the 'extremist' discourse of Libyan figures in the pan-Amazigh movement, such as Fathi N'Khalifa of the World Amazigh Congress.[107] Amazigh politicians, in turn, increasingly interpreted Zintan's outreach to former regime constituencies as attempts at building an Arabist alliance to counter the demands for Amazigh cultural and language rights.

As early as September 2011, the 'National Libyan Amazigh Congress' convened in Tripoli to denounce the NTC's failure to explicitly recognise the Amazigh language in its constitutional declaration.[108] Further angry reactions followed the creation of Abd al-Rahim al-Kib's interim government in November 2011; whereas the interior and defence ministries were held by figures from Misrata and Zintan respectively, the government did not include any Amazigh representatives. Imazighen fears of discrimination deepened when Abd al-Jalil publicly suggested that Amazigh activism was being fanned by foreign powers,[109] and again when the Zaidan government included only one Amazigh minister—al-Hadi Hinshir from Yefren as the minister of water resources. As the politicking around the constitution-drafting process began, Amazigh mountain towns in January 2013 joined with Zuwara and Tuareg communities to form the High Council of Libyan Amazigh, which focused on demanding guarantees that ethnic minorities' cultural and language rights be protected in the constitution.[110] But beneath the surface of unity, the mountains' Amazigh communities were divided over the nature of their demands and the means to achieve them. Tactics such as the closing down of a gas pipeline or the rampage at the seat of the General National Congress (GNC) by Amazigh activists damaged the Amazigh movement's reputation in the mountains and across Libya. Moreover, the growing influence of Salafi movements, another legacy of the revolution, directly contested the Ibadi tradition of Amazigh communities—particularly in Nalut, the only Amazigh town with a nucleus of former LIFG fighters.[111]

Conclusion: Factionalism resurgent

Amazigh activism and Zintani expansionism show how Nafusa Mountains communities have given rise to national-level political and military forces in the transitional era. But these forces also played a major role in ensuring that Libya's post-revolutionary scene was essentially defined by localism and—in the case of the Amazigh movement—identity politics. Not unlike the alliances (*sufuf*) of the Ottoman and colonial eras, mountain communities' rifts and alliances are shaping national level politics in the transitional period, and Tripoli politics feeds factionalism in the mountains.

Another parallel emerges between current and historical patterns of factionalism in the mountains. As over the past century, each mountain town is now writing its own history of the war.[112] The accounts of each community's contribution to the revolution differ sharply from one town to another, as do perceptions of each group's involvement with the regime during the war. Downplaying other communities' role has become an integral part of these struggles over the history of the revolution. For Nafusa Mountains communities to overcome the problem of factionalism, they will have to negotiate a common history of the war.

12

BANI WALID

LOYALISM IN A TIME OF REVOLUTION

Peter Cole

Bani Walid's revolts

'We've been here before,' said the former employee of one of Mu'ammar al-Qadhafi's security services, hiding in the town of Bani Walid as the revolutionary battalions surrounded his town. 'This is not the first time Bani Walid has resisted the coastal tribes and their foreign alliances with foreigners.'[1]

As did pro-revolutionary towns, loyalist communities underwent a process of rediscovering their own histories and narratives to boost morale and interpret the events of 2011. Bani Walid was one such community, which, though impoverished under Qadhafi, fought consistently against the revolutionaries until Qadhafi's death. Understanding why they stayed loyal requires an understanding of their stories. Qadhafi himself visited the townships of the west during the revolution and retold the same stories, mixing them for good measure with the anti-imperialist and anti-colonialist rhetoric that his audiences appreciated.

The spook hiding in Bani Walid recounted the same historical narrative shared among his townsmen, perhaps selectively remembered;

285

casting Bani Walid's loyalism as the latest iteration of a historical cycle in which they repeatedly faced down foreign powers attempting to dominate Libya's coastal population centres, and western tribes they manipulated against them.

This simplified narrative privileged Bani Walid as the head of the Warfalla, a large community of related families and lineages spread across western Libya, all of whom trace their ancestry back to the town, which has tremendous cultural resonance with many Warfalla even today. The narrative began in the Ottoman era and continued in its themes of resistance and alliance until 2011. The Ottoman Empire in Libya had historically shared power with great tribal confederations or states that paid tribute to the empire, but in the nineteenth century it tried to build the state by collecting taxes, while also attempting to forcefully control Saharan caravan routes in Fezzan. Coastal communities largely sought tax exemptions in exchange for becoming tax collectors. Southern Tunisia and the Nafusa Mountains were split. But southern tribes and towns, which had more economic independence from the Saharan trade, resisted. Bani Walid and the Warfalla revived an old tribal confederation—al-Suff al-Fuqhi—with its southern neighbours the Awlad Sulaiman and Qadhadhfa—both semi-nomadic, militarily inclined peoples—who together controlled the vast central-western deserts and oases of Hun, Waddan and Sabha. Under the leadership of Abd al-Jalil from the Awlad Sulaiman, the alliance revived a sultanate in Fezzan from 1830–1842, which opposed the coastal communities and the new tax system. The Ottomans levied other Libyan tribes—the Awlad Bu Saif and Maqarha, who were threatened as much by the sultanate as by the Ottomans—against them, and in 1842 Abd al-Jalil was killed.[2]

The rebellion of the Fezzan sultanate against the coast was revived by Bani Walid during their fights against Italian-backed Libyans in 1923, and NATO-backed Libyans in 2011. But during the latter, another footnote of tribal politics from this era resurfaced. While the Warfalla were fighting the Maqarha and Awlad Bu Saif, their neighbour—Zintan—was engaged in its own civil war against the Awlad Bu Saif, while allied with another tribal confederation revolting against the Ottomans. This led to a verbal pact between Bani Walid and Zintan called *khutt al-jadd*—literally 'brothers of the same grandfather'—that the two communities would never fight. In 2011 the two towns would revive that pact.[3]

By the late nineteenth century declining Saharan trade due to European competition, and the gradual expansion of the Ottoman state, pushed Bani Walid into accommodation with the Ottomans. Ottoman state bureaucracy was the best way of generating trade, wealth and status, and generated a new class of notables[4] and state bureaucrats. It also kept competition between towns alive. Bani Walid's undisputed leader was Abd al-Nibi Bilkhair, an Ottoman tax collector who reached that position through generous patronage. For Bilkhair, his people's interests, and the threats posed to them by Misrata and Tripoli, trumped remote ideological concerns.[5]

When the Ottomans withdrew from Libya in 1912 following Italy's military invasion in 1911, Bilkhair and Bani Walid's main revenue stream was threatened. Accordingly, Bilkhair in 1913 became an adviser to Italy's military as it moved south to occupy Fezzan, which it did in 1914. When the Libyan resistance crushed the Italians at Qardabiyya on 18 April 1915, Bilkhair switched sides and looted the Italian garrison at Bani Walid. But by 1918, Bilkhair and Bani Walid saw their main threat as emerging from Misrata, where Ramadan al-Suwaihli, absorbing Ottoman and German aid that arrived through Misrata's port, had also grown rich from raiding Italian garrisons. Bilkhair thus again began taking money and arms from the Italians, and with Suwaihli encroaching on Bani Walid's borders, civil war between Bani Walid and Misrata became inexorable. Suwaihli invaded Bani Walid in 1920; Bilkhair blocked up the wells that Suwaihli's fighters needed to progress and according to Bani Walid's account tricked Suwaihli by inviting him deeper into his territory for talks, and Suwaihli's depleted forces were ambushed and killed en route.[6] The rift was never healed. Misratans in 2011 refused to enter Bani Walid for fear of reviving the irresolvable feud; when Misrata's Libya Shield division finally did, in 2012, they bore pictures of Suwaihli and posted them onto Bani Walid's houses.

The Bani Walid-Misrata conflict, along with the Nafusa Mountains' collapse into civil war in 1920, enabled Italy to reoccupy Libya in 1923. This drove the Bani Walid and Warfalla inland and into insurgency with the Awlad Sulaiman and Qadhadhfa. While communities did switch allegiance for and against the Italians, Turks and other powers, their relations among each other remained largely constant based on the *sufuf* alliances or competition with other communities, which themselves were based on older patterns in land and pasture use regimes.[7] Even the leaders of the western resistance—Bilkhair and Abd al-Jalil Saif al-Nasr of the Awlad Sulaiman—were descendants of the founders of the sultanate of Fezzan. The Italians, like the Ottomans, sponsored Libyan tribes—the Maqarha and Riyya—to fight them, and worked with a cooperative notable, Khalifa al-Zawi, who ruled from Murzuq from 1916 to 1926. The Awlad Sulaiman and Warfalla led a hit-and-run campaign against Italians for four years, flushing Zawi from Murzuq in 1926, but by 1930 had lost to Italy, which used poison gas and planes. Saif al-Nasr and his followers among the Awlad Sulaiman fled to Chad and Egypt; Bilkhair fled to Tunisia and Algeria, where he died in 1932.[8]

As Libya entered independence in 1951, these communities returned from exile and formed part the bedrock of the Libyan state in the west. Another scion of the Saif al-Nasr family, Muhammad Saif al-Nasr, became ruler over Fezzan. Tribal identity again ceased to have real meaning in determining individual political affiliations. But socially, it was a different matter. State mechanisms were so rudimentary that institutions such as the police, which grew to 12,500 under King Idris,[9] had to depend on the participation of the predominant majority tribes like the Warfalla. Just as in the east, where King Idris promoted and utilised eastern tribes such as the Sa'da confederation in the police and armed forces, in Fezzan, 'the Warfalla followed the Awlad Sulaiman into government under Saif al-Nasr. They did not challenge Saif al-Nasr's political position, but in turn he depended on and utilised the Warfalla, who entered his security services and police.'[10]

According to one Bani Walid police officer, by Qadhafi's coup in 1969, 'nearly all those who enforced it in the secret police were Warfalla. At that time they dominated the security services, and though this lessened over time, Qadhafi's interest was always in using the Warfalla to control other tribes.'[11] In Bani Walid's eyes, Qadhafi's revolution meant little more to them than the passing of power and patronage from one of their neighbours to another—from the Awlad Sulaiman to the Qadhadhfa.[12] In a key event in 1975, Qadhafi visited Bani Walid to receive a bay'a (oath of allegiance) from Warfalla leaders—a major event signifying his switch to explicitly basing his rule on tribal loyalties and allegiances—including on the basis of historical sufuf, but also cross-cutting some of the historical relationships.[13]

Qadhafi sought to eradicate tribalism in Libya, writing that 'when the tribes of a nation are in conflict and only watch out for their own interests the continuation of the nation is at risk'.[14] But as Libya's modern state institutions grew, its officials still followed patterns of patronage, particularly via the placing of infrastructure and facilities that dictated employment options available to the local community. Bani Walid had a university, technical colleges, military bases and an airport; an 'electrical office' employee gave a personal account of the natural progression into the state apparatus that these allowed; 'I went to Bani Walid's electrical engineering college. Students came from all over Libya, but the majority were from Bani Walid. Graduates found it very easy to find employment in the state communications industry, post office, electrical office, and so forth. I went into the electrical office.'[15]

Sometimes the bias was personal and overt, though not exclusively 'tribal'. Promotion within the security services was subject to patronage by senior officers. A Warfalla internal security officer from Sirt described his progress:

I was an Air Force airplane mechanic in Sirt, but in 1982 was put on medical leave after a neck injury. A panel declared me unfit for duty, but after appeal sent me one of Qadhafi's representatives in Jufra. His assistant recognised me—we had studied at the same school. He was impressed with my form and bearing, and transferred me to a naval job near Zuwara; then, when Qadhafi decided to recruit five hundred from the military into security services, I joined the programme. I then moved on to monitoring the commercial and private sector.[16]

Bani Walid, then, treasured two impulses at the heart of their identity; their resistance to Italian and Ottoman incursion in Libya, which had caused western tribes to fight each other, and their status as protectors of independent Libyan statehood.

Bani Walid's coup

Despite their numerical dominance in Qadhafi's state security apparatus, Bani Walid saw little material reward. Aside from those few Warfalla in Qadhafi's political circles, such as Ahmad Misbah,[17] the town's prominence among the mid-to-lower tiers of government did not promote social mobility. 'We are Bedu,' a police chief reflected, 'Bedu make for good soldiers but they are not so good at being in charge.'[18] A son of a former minister from Bani Walid said: 'I counted only 385 people throughout Qadhafi's entire forty-two years who were rotated between positions of power, and of those, the Bani Walid only had three—a minister for justice, for education, and electricity. Misratans had eleven. While the peasantry and uneducated were quite happy, the educated of Bani Walid became disgruntled.'[19]

By 1993, this disgruntlement encouraged forty-two officers from Bani Walid families in the army to attempt a coup in collaboration with the opposition National Front for the Salvation of Libya (NFSL). The coup failed when the senior officers in Tripoli were arrested a few days before the planned attack; the forty-two leaders were later executed and many of their relations fled into exile.

The failed 1993 coup, paradoxically, set in motion a chain of events that led Bani Walid to stay loyal in 2011. One consequence was Bani Walid's ostracisation within Libya. A law professor from Bani Walid university said:

Qadhafi visited our neighbours—the Warshafana, Zlitan, Tarhuna—demanding that they punish Bani Walid as traitors and spies. He would provoke them—for example, a student from Tarhuna was shot[20] at Tripoli's al-Fath University. The gunman was never identified, but a Bani Walid student was accused and Tarhuna was encouraged to retaliate.[21]

This manipulation of community dynamics stirred Bani Walid's sense of independence and resistance. A student at Bani Walid university who had volunteered with Qadhafi's troops gave the narrative: 'When the coup failed, other Libyans called the Warfalla "rebels" and "betrayers". Some wrote satirical poems that read like verbal abuse.'[22] Bani Walid bitterly resented their degradation and in 2011 when their neighbours—Misrata, Zintan, and others—called on them for help, the bitter memories flooded back. One Zintani commander, involved in outreach to the Bani Walid during the revolution, noted: 'Leaving aside those who genuinely loved Qadhafi, those who stayed loyal had a grievance against the Libyan people because of this treatment in 1993, saying "Why should we support them now?"'[23]

The coup set off two other chains of events affecting Bani Walid and other loyalist communities in the revolution. The first was Qadhafi's creation of a professional corps of 'security brigades,' designed to coup-proof the armed forces, and on whom Qadhafi relied to repress the 2011 revolution.[24] Qadhafi had previously created civilian paramilitary armed units for political purposes such as the People's Guard (al-Hars al-Sha'bi), a volunteer force created in 1990 to control mosques and Islamist agitation, and the Revolutionary Guard, the security arm of the Revolutionary Committees developed following an earlier army coup effort in 1985,[25] all of which fought in 2011. But the security brigades which emerged after 1993, and which recruited from these organisations and the armed forces, were professionalised on a far larger scale. 'After the Bani Walid coup, Qadhafi increased the size and number of security brigades over the army. The army reported to Abu Bakr Yunis Jabr, the chief of staff, and our training was to serve and defend the state. But the security brigades were trained to defend Qadhafi's revolution.'[26] The brigades also technically reported to the chief of staff, but also sat on the 'permanent security committee' hosted in Qadhafi's Leaders Office alongside the internal security division of the Central Intelligence Bureau headed by Abdullah al-Sanusi.[27] Over time, the armed forces became little more than a supplier of services and training to the security brigades, who were better paid and equipped.

Between 1993 and 2011, the security brigades, which recruited explicitly on a tribal basis, developed in western and southern Libya. The Imhammad Imgharyif Brigade was based in central Tripoli while the 32 Reinforced Brigade, headed by Qadhafi's son Khamis, occupied three bases covering entry roads to the capital. Both recruited from the five major western tribes—the Warfalla, Zintan, Qadhadhfa, Maqarha and Hasawna—and the town of Tarhuna near Bani Walid.[28] Other brigades mushroomed across the west and south. Tuareg fighters were drafted into the Maghawir Brigade in Awbari and Ghadames, and granted temporary limited Libyan citizenship in 2005 to do so; Tebu, Qadhadhfa and Awlad Sulaiman into the Faris Brigade with minor tribes from Sirt.[29] But the brigades never took root in the east, excepting in Benghazi where the Fadil Brigade, which drew from the five major western tribes listed above along with eastern Ubaida, Awlad Ali, Zway and Qut'ani tribes, was stationed. This fact had much to do with why Libya's east defected to rebels in a matter of days, while the west, where the brigades were much stronger, held fast.

In Bani Walid, a small battalion appended to the brigades grew under the command of one Jibran Hussain. Jibran's rise to this command position was the result of another chain of events flowing from Bani Walid's coup: Qadhafi's subversion of Libyan tribes. 'The 1993 coup was not a tribal coup, for sure,' noted a family member of Khalil al-Jadak, one of the coup's ringleaders, 'but it was certainly their tribal background that allowed the forty-two officers to trust each other. Qadhafi noticed that, and wanted to destroy it.'[30]

The first step in coopting the tribal structures was to understand them. Part of the legacy of Warfalla Ottoman bureaucrats and tax collectors such as Bilkhair was they had codified, for tax purposes, a fairly rigid social organisation centred around five branches or 'fifths' (*akhmas*) based in Bani Walid—three in the highlands, two in 'lower Bani Walid' which stretched northeast towards Misrata.[31] Social or tribal affairs were decided through the heads of fifty-two 'houses' or *lahmat*, which met regularly in Bani Walid to do so (and the interviews in this chapter were partly conducted on the sidelines of those meetings in February 2012). The 'upper' three branches formed a loose alliance called the *Ajalsa*, which assumed the political leadership (*hukama'*) of the tribe. One branch, the *Sa'dat*, had historically predominated, and prominent officers and ministers hailed from among them; the other two branches were the *Jamamla* and *Sabayi'*. Meanwhile the two 'lower' branches—the *Faladna* and *Awatin*—had opposed and alternated power with the upper three.[32] Across modern Libya, the machinations and views of the fifty-two families and their heads no longer always counted for much to Warfalla—some ignored it, others saw it as quaint but important to their cultural identity. But in Bani Walid, the system was tremendously important in forging opinion.

Qadhafi's punishment of the coup ringleaders was done so as to feed in to these historical divides and destroy trust between the Bani Walid 'houses'. 'He made us carry out the punishments ourselves,' said the governor of the town at the time, 'which is much more shaming than if the government punishes you, and it created real hatred within the Bani Walid.'[33] Those punishments were remarkably severe. While the ringleaders themselves were executed by the people's courts and military, their children were forbidden from study, their houses demolished, electricity to homes cut, salaries withheld, and Qadhafi even encouraged the families of the ringleaders to leave Bani Walid altogether.

Qadhafi first asked the Bani Walid to kill the coup ringleaders themselves but the town's leadership refused. Thus began the process of determining loyalty, by which those who did not demonstrate their loyalty to Qadhafi by punishing their kin were themselves punished. Most Warfalla in senior regime positions were sidelined or removed. The Warfalli minister of justice and interior from 1978–81 and head of the Supreme Court since 1981 was fired in 2001, according to his son 'because he refused to prosecute other Warfalla or Bani Walid'.[34] Likewise the heads of Bani Walid's houses refused to comply, so Qadhafi, in one head's words, 'put Bani Walid under siege economically, with a total development blockade (*hisar tanmiyya*). There was no money, jobs, construction, no roads; no water, while the rest of Libya developed.'[35]

Meanwhile from 1994–96 Qadhafi formed a new nationwide system of People's Social Leadership Committees (PSLC, abbreviated in modern discourse as 'social leadership', or *qiyada ijtima'iyya*)[36] intended to bring tribal structures into Qadhafi's decision-making chain.[37] For Bani Walid, the system was 'modelled exactly on our tribes'.[38] For each of the fifty-two families, he appointed a coordinator (*munassiq*) whom he paid to carry out decisions enacted at the Leaders' Office. The coordinators chosen were those who enthusiastically participated in the collective punishments against the coup plotters. Bani Walid residents vividly recalled those coordinators who cheered on the bulldozers destroying families' houses, and were willing to be seen doing so, to demonstrate their loyalty and thus receive benefits. Coordinators 'didn't have executive power like government ministries, but they had legal powers (*sulta tashri'iyya*) over ministries in their land area. They could get people jobs on recommendation. Their word could get people fired.'[39]

Qadhafi's new coordinators elected one senior representative for each of Bani Walid's five branches, who then elected one head, Ali Fituri, who in fact was not even from Bani Walid but from the neighbouring Awlad Sulaiman, his 'election' controlled through a public voting process (*tas'id*) observed by government officials. Bani Walid despised Fituri as the man responsible for their collective punishment. In 2011, Fituri fled to Zintan who sheltered him there; his presence became another key element of the Bani Walid's resistance to and distrust of rebel intentions.[40]

One critical part of the imposing of the PSLC was annulling all historic bonds and agreements between the fifty-two houses, called *tabarri*. This dissolution was so upsetting and controversial that even the new social leadership would not do it. Eventually, a candidate was found—Jibran Hussain—who dissolved all other forms of social representation other than the new 'social leadership'. Jibran Hussain was rewarded with command of the small battalion appended to the security brigades, which was stationed in Bani Walid and recruited several hundred of its youth, symbolising the extent to which Qadhafi had reestablished his influence over the Bani Walid. The benefits Jibran received in money and power for doing so 'made many regret that they had not done so themselves when asked. Frankly, that was when all of Bani Walid started working with Qadhafi.'[41]

Bani Walid's revolution

Bani Walid thus entered the 2011 revolution with the living memory of 1993 and its aftermath. Other Libyans who had distanced themselves from and condemned Bani Walid's coup effort, including the National Front (NFSL), now enthusiastically supported the National Transitional Council (NTC). But, in one security services employee's words, 'the fifty-two people governing [Bani Walid's] social affairs were Qadhafi's same social leadership. Some had participated in the punishment of the Bani Walid, or indirectly supported it.[42] Another fighter in the security brigades concurred; 'It wasn't like they were driving the bulldozers through people's houses, but they were complicit [*mutawarritin*].'[43]

At the revolution's outset, Qadhafi sent prominent Warfallan members of his inner circle, such as Salih Ibrahim, or Umran Bu Kra, to Bani Walid to woo notables with cars and distribute cash.[44] One member of that social leadership, who appeared regularly on Libyan state television to support Qadhafi, described the impact the revolution had on Bani Walid's youth, and the role the social leadership had in encouraging quiescence.

When the revolution began, the Bani Walid split—in every family or house [*lahma*], one would go off in this direction, the other in that. Us elders were most concerned that the town not fight each other and factionalise, so we said "If you want to fight with Qadhafi, go to Sirt or Tripoli; if you want to fight against him, go to Zintan. But no fighting here."[45]

Other Libyans used the Libyan proverb 'holding the stick in the middle' to describe this position.

In early March the social leadership reached out to their neighbours for solutions—but only demonstrated the limitations of influence through tribal mechanisms. One member said: 'We sat with the social leaderships of western tribes, including the Qadhadhfa, Maqarha and Awlad Sulaiman, and discussed peaceful options for addressing the cause of reform. The west agreed but the east refused.'[46] Another said, 'Zintan was amenable in the beginning, but after it secured its own weapons supplies it rejected the offer.'[47] The speed of events in the east, and most likely Qadhafi's own rejection of reform, drowned out these efforts.

Jibran Hussain's battalion was called up to Sirt soon after the protests in Benghazi erupted, and was a part of the column that marched to Benghazi on 17 March 2011, where it perished on 19 or 20 March in the initial French airstrikes protecting the town under UNSCR 1973.[48] Bani Walid heads say it did not demonstrate their loyalism as a community at that stage, when the people themselves were more neutral. One said, 'We were against sending the army to Benghazi at the beginning. Jibran went, but he was a regime man. He didn't represent us, and most of us didn't like him. There was no Bani Walid council ordering him to go to Benghazi.'[49]

But the foreign intervention that caused Jibran's death, and the NATO no-fly zone that followed, drew Bani Walid into a conflict previously seen as localised. A more hardline family head said: 'NATO's intervention changed our position from staying neutral towards protecting Libya's unity. I think Western policy is about colonial domination and oil. And so we held out fighting against Libya's division and colonialism.'[50]

Bani Walid's youth were galvanised. Significant numbers signed up with the reservist People's Guard and People's Resistance Forces, reintroduced to fight alongside the security brigades and to police Tripoli; the recruitment process was explicitly 'tribal' and required groups of ten from the same town to join as a bloc to vouch for each others' loyalty.[51] Armoured vehicles bore the names of the community operating them, including, but not limited to, Awlad Sulaiman, Qadhadhfa, Maqarha and Warfalla.[52] This was in part a manipulation of communal identity by the security brigades, conflating the ideal of fighting for the community, for the 'state', and for Qadhafi.

Many interviewees who fought for the government saw their actions as continuing the narrative of their community. Their history, selectively remembered, of resisting foreign-allied coastal communities, dovetailed with a feeling that they had shaped and built the state that was now under threat. These ideals trumped personal feelings toward Qadhafi's punishment of Bani Walid. In one fighter's words, 'Some people here love Qadhafi personally, but some also want to serve the state even if it they don't agree with everything it does.'[53] Others saw in Qadhafi the same narrative of resistance and independence they identified with: 'Do you remember in 2009 when he tore the UN charter up in front of all of the world? Qadhafi spoke the truth when no one else would.'[54]

The more nuanced state employees distanced themselves from Qadhafi but saw the revolution as destroying the state with which they identified. An electrical company employee said, 'In Libya, Qadhafi *is* the state, and you cannot stand against Qadhafi without standing against the state itself.'[55] A fighter said, 'Qadhafi's forces rallied after Benghazi was taken, not because they liked Qadhafi, but because when you get rid of Qadhafi, you get rid of everything else.'[56] One notable said, 'Benghazians wanted change fast as lightning. They went in four days from protesting compensation for Abu Slim prisoners to toppling the state. Then they brought up the new flag and anthem. That is not protest—they were against the state itself.'[57]

Revolutionary forces began seeking out and promoting any hint of support within Bani Walid. Rebel media reported celebration over Jibran Hussain's death,[58] and soon afterwards an anonymous announcement was circulated to the NTC and rebel media in the name of the 'Bani Walid Crisis Administration Committee' supporting the revolution.[59] In April, the NTC's Arif Ali Nayid (himself originally from the Warfalla), attempting to source representatives from the country's west and south, identified one of the coordinators of Qadhafi's PSLC, Mubarak Salih al-Futmani, who was flown to Dubai, Doha and Benghazi and nominated as Bani Walid's representative to the NTC. Futmani and his supporters—as had some of the families behind the 1993 coup which backed Futmani—hailed from the Awatin and Faladna branches of 'lower' Bani Walid (the Lawtiyin), close geographically to the town of Misrata, which had traditionally opposed and alternated power with the 'upper' branches (the Fawqiyin) who had prospered under Qadhafi and the PSLC; in this way calculations of support or opposition to the rebels mirrored existing divisions within Bani Walid's houses.

On 28 May 2011, Futmani's family organised a small protest supporting the revolution at the central vegetable market in the town centre, along with families of the 1993 coup participants, such as the al-Jadak and Tu'ti families. It was immediately confronted by loyalist youth from other Bani Walid families. The protestors scattered; some were chased into a nearby school, where around twelve of their leaders—including Futmani's brother and son—were executed. The social leadership allegedly attempted to mediate, but the majority's sympathies lay either with the loyalists, or else wished to remain out of the conflict. One notable said: '28 May was the beginning of the problem. When those youth were killed, the Bani Walid split into two camps. The minority who supported the revolution left. Qadhafi's supporters stayed.'[60] The remainder of the 28 May movement fled to Zintan.

By 20–27 August, as Tripoli fell, Bani Walid became a critical refuge for fleeing loyalists. By the fall of Qadhafi's compound at Bab al-Aziziyya on 23 August, most loyalist brigades had been ordered to stand down, or like Khamis al-Qadhafi's 32 Reinforced Brigade, down to its last two hundred fighters, fled on 24 August through Abu Slim towards Bani Walid.[61] Significant numbers of state employees also fled, fearing the oncoming barrage of ordnance unleashed against the vanguard of loyalist fighters stationed in Abu Slim. Streams of civilian cars and families fled the Abu Slim and Hadba neighbourhoods, which were heavily populated with Bani Walid and Warfalla migrants, towards Bani Walid.[62]

NATO and its member states' ability to coordinate the rebels as they pursued the loyalists was somewhat weakening. The Misratan forces, after an initial loss of contact due to domestic cellphone coverage issues, had reorganised once their operations room had relocated from Misrata to Tripoli, and their forces fanned out southeasterly towards Tarhuna and Bani Walid.[63] The intermingling of civilians and fighters prevented NATO from targeting the fleeing forces, with the exception of one strike targeting, and allegedly killing, Khamis near Tarhuna on 29 August.

The sheer number of recently liberated Tripolitanian and coastal armed groups also defied organisation. These groups had neither the experience nor entirely the connections to effectively coordinate with each other or with NATO operations rooms. Internal political considerations made the situation worse, since neither Zintan nor Misrata wished to enter Bani Walid. Zintan had little motivation to break the *khut al-jadd* nonaggression pact sealed by their grandfathers; they had good relations with Bani Walid, and Zintan's interests lay in in Tripoli and towards the south and west.[64] Misrata did not wish to reawaken the conflict that they fought with Bani Walid during the Italian occupation, and were more focused on their slow progression towards Sirt.[65]

The NTC positioned Futmani and the pro-revolutionary faction of the Bani Walid to lead the approach to Bani Walid. Futmani had formed a small '28 May' battalion in Zintan, backed up by small and inexperienced militias from the recently liberated towns of Zawiya, Suq al-Jum'a, Gharyan, and Tripoli and the east.

Futmani and the 'social leadership' put themselves on a collision course. On 1 September at the 'Malti' mosque on the Tarhuna–Bani

Walid road, Futmani and the 28 May faction, with other Warfalla representatives appointed by the NTC demanded that they be allowed to enter, raise the new flag, and form a local and military council. Heads of major houses compromised by their association with Qadhafi did not attend, leaving them represented by heads of smaller houses such as Muhammad Abd al-Karim al-Tani, Miftah al-Baghul, and Miftah al-Rabbasi.[66] They insisted that the revolutionary battalions enter only on condition of surrendering heavy weapons and not making *ex judiciae* arrests[67] of those sheltering in the town. A relative of a senior family head said: 'They were scared, that's half of the truth. But it is also part of our identity as Bedouin that we offer protection when asked. Even if you killed my father, I would die before you if you asked for it.'[68] 'We call this *labid alayya*,' said a member of a Bani Walid political family.[69]

The arrival of Saif al-Islam al-Qadhafi in Bani Walid complicated everything. He had recently arrived in Bani Walid and received condolences there on Khamis's death over 29–30 August. While the negotiations were ongoing, he had moved on, according to one notable; 'He passed through Bani Walid on his way to Jufra, getting there around 12 September.'[70] A state TV employee who fled Abu Slim was among those who ended up with his entourage. 'It was pure luck. He never intended to stay in Bani Walid—but when he tried to enter Sirt, the Misratans and east had surrounded it. So he went back to Bani Walid.'[71]

By that point, negotiations with the social leadership had broken down acrimoniously, and on 7 September Futmani and the rebels tried to force their way in. That provoked the town itself to fight the rebels, creating a true Libyan-on-Libyan conflict at Wadi Dinar, at the northern entry to the town, where the disorganised rebels became caught in a chokepoint and became sitting ducks in a messy and bloody fight.

Bani Walid's young fighters were by this point motivated by pride and local grievances more than any lingering loyalty towards Qadhafi. They were encouraged by their wives and mothers. 'You really should have heard our women,' one fighter said. 'They told us they would go and fight and questioned our manhood.'[72] They were supplied and encouraged by the few sheltering fighters in the town, including Saif al-Islam's entourage. Another said, 'Maybe eight or ten of those who supported the previous government and loved Qadhafi had money and weapons. They distributed them to small boys and teenagers and said "Fight for your dignity, fight for your land!" I remember one boy whose father was in Tripoli and mother in Misrata. They said to him, "We will give you a gun, and supplies, and you can fight for your land, dignity, sisters and families." They manipulated them to fight in this way.'[73] Further negotiation failed. 'During the fighting, the negotiations were continuing, but without any use. Groups of notables came from Tripoli, Tarhuna and Zintan came and sat with us. Our demands were to not kill or arrest anyone or take our weapons until the state is stable.'[74] Some of the social leadership, caught in the middle, appear to have tried to negotiate with Saif al-Islam and the loyalists to leave the town. 'Three or four times the social leadership offered a ceasefire which would allow Saif to leave'[75] but the rebels rejected this option. Loyalist hardliners also prevented ceasefire: 'whenever the social leadership reached a deal, the ones distributing guns and money said "No! We will fight!' Come on, pick up a few bullets!"'[76]

The fighting took until 17 October to die down, and was only truly resolved once the remaining loyalists fled and Bani Walid ran out of ammunition.[77] The last week saw the rebels mount a renewed three-pronged assault on Bani Walid from the north, west, and east.[78] The loyalists scattered into nearby farmsteads and villages or went south.

Conclusion

The shortcomings of the NTC's approach to post-conflict reconciliation had graver consequences in Bani Walid than anywhere else. While Sirt had likewise seen dozens of extrajudicial executions and local and military councils dominated by Misratan residents of Sirt, most Sirtawi civilians were allowed to flee before the rebels finally flushed out Qadhafi's last entourage. In Bani Walid, the manner of the rebels' entry pitted the town against the new order, as did the NTC's backing of a few pro-rebel families in what had become an intra-town feud. The fighting groups from Tripoli, Zawiya and the mountains entered by force, moving house to house searching for loyalist elements. They conducted sweeping and arbitrary arrests, including against those who resisted or refused access to their homes. Gold, jewellery, and furnishings were stolen.[79]

As elsewhere in western Libya, the NTC requested its representatives to set up local and military councils. In Bani Walid's case, the local council, formed by Muhammad Bashir Tu'ti, and the military council formed by Mubarak al-Futmani immediately tried to arrest a list of 300–400 wanted people (*matlubin*) sheltering in Bani Walid whom they accused of crimes committed during the revolution—including those who allegedly executed Futmani's family on 28 May. The 28 May battalion, itself comprising fewer than 200–300 men, threw its weight around town as it carried out arrests and disappearances. Bani Walid acknowledged hiding and protecting fleeing officials, and stockpiling weapons to do so. But they felt that Futmani's arbitrariness and the evident lack of any judicial proceedings or police force justified their being protected. They compared Futmani's military council to Qadhafi's Revolutionary Committees or Revolutionary Guard, and felt that Futmani himself was emulating those of Qadhafi's People's Social Leadership Committees who had been amply rewarded for showing ruthless loyalty. 'He wants to be another Hussain Jibran,' said one resident.

Because Futmani did not have sufficient numbers to police the town, in early December its leadership asked other revolutionary battalions for armed support to carry out an arrest. Suq al-Jum'a responded, sending a small armed group to the town. The impact was disastrous; Bani Walid's social leadership asked friends in the neighbouring town of Tarhuna to stop them entering; those from Suq al-Jum'a who made it through were attacked by Bani Walid, who killed sixteen and imprisoned eleven. In the end a prisoner swap was negotiated, but Suq al-Jum'a's dented pride caused them to continue their own arrest campaign in Tripoli itself; some even stormed Tripoli's airport in early December to try and force the NTC to resolve the issue in their favour.[80]

Conflict resolution efforts stalled because of the NTC's inability to settle national questions over transitional justice and control of security forces. A reconciliation committee of elders from throughout western Libya, led by Zintan and Tarhuna, negotiated a prisoner exchange, followed by attempts to set up a power-sharing agreement throughout December and January.[81] But the key sticking point was over 'wanted individuals'[82] particularly from the 28 May and Suq al-Jum'a attacks.[83] Bani Walid also desired to choose the head of the local council. Though Zintani and Bani Walid negotiators eventually proposed to split the council 16–14 between the Bani Walid houses and Futmani and Tu'ti's faction (with a council head, Mu'adil al-Kish, chosen from the latter camp), neither side had an interest in implementing the agreement, and the NTC also neglected to do so.[84]

Both sides lacked interest in a settlement. The 28 May movement reduced their military presence in Bani Walid by wearing plain clothes and avoiding using armoured vehicles, but continued their arrest activities.[85] When in January the military council arrested a young man named Muhammad Bu Shlaibta, tempers snapped. Former loyalists and residents who had quietly been stockpiling weaponry for just such an event stormed the 28 May headquarters and drove Futmani from the town. An alternative battalion—totally rejected by the new authorities—was installed, commanded by Salim al-Wa'ir, who claimed descent from the leaders of the 1993 coup. Originally named 'the Martyrs of Wadi Dinar'—which provocatively recalled their fighters' defence of the town in September 2011—it was eventually named 'Warfalla 1993' battalion,[86] which laid further claim Bani Walid's revolutionary heritage.

Bani Walid, which was utterly isolated both politically and in terms of government services, reengaged by reviving 'tribal' or communal agreements over a succession of meetings in Bani Walid with community notables from among its old allies, such as Zintan, the Awlad Sulaiman, Tarhuna, Warshafana and Sirtawi tribes, in early 2012. Bani Walid also created the 'Warfalla Social Council'—an eighty-strong body, with sixty from Bani Walid and twenty from across Libya, intended to represent the interests of the community across Libya. A major meeting on 5 February 2012 brought together Warfalla representatives from across Libya, which led to signed alliances (*tahalufat*) in early February 2012 with the Warshafana, Si'an, Mashashiya, Tarhuna, and Ajalat tribes, agreeing 'to cooperate in voting for figures in the elections, to defend one another in case of attack, and share resources'.[87]

The Warfalla Social Council, and its various coordinations with neighbouring tribes seemed anachronistic as a political body. Though the old narratives of the tribal confederations and resistance movements of Bani Walid during the Ottoman and Italian occupations had been revived as a result of the revolution, on no level was being Warfalla a barometer of political opinion. Warfalli Libyans had been in the vanguard of the '17 February Revolution' in Benghazi, and ran the gamut of political opinion from loyal Revolutionary Guards officers such as Hussain Jibran, to members of the former Libyan Islamic Fighting Group such as Tariq Durman, a commander in Futmani's 28 May battalion.

But this analysis was not shared by the social leadership of Bani Walid, for whom the town remained the figurehead of vaguely counted Warfalla communities across Libya; 'over a million, across Libya' according to one, 1.7 million according to another.[88] This belief in their numerical weight dovetailed with the belief that they were integral to the continuity of the state; another family head said 'you cannot build a strong state without the Warfalla. They are too numerous'.[89] One Social Council organiser expressed the belief that the Social Council could 'guide and shape how people vote', another felt that registration and electoral boundaries could be manipulated to convert the Warfalla into an effective voting bloc. By May 2012, the Council, and its shared meetings with Zintan, Warshafana, Si'an, Mashashiya, Tarhuna and Ajalat elders, had collectively decided to put their weight behind, and elect independent candidates on behalf of, the National Forces Alliance—a political body represented by Mahmud Jibril that supported the swift reestablishment of the army and police, and opposing actual and perceived excesses of the *thuwwar*.[90] This support, given the demographic weight of the western tribes, gave Jibril's organisation an enormous boost in the party lists, helping it to become one of the largest single groupings within the General National Congress.

By the elections of July 2012, Bani Walid had yet to resolve the challenges and consequences of 2011 in its favour. The 2011 revolution had swept away the state and system that it had built since the dawn of Libya's independence. But in place of this narrative, a far older communal identity arose based on its relationships with its neighbours and shared history of colonial resistance. The immediate injustices of the post-revolutionary era fostered this new sense of identity among a wide number—though by no means all—of Warfalla in Libya, and gave the community a sense of political direction. They could not solve the issues created by a lack of any national reconciliation programme, and an equal lack of state control over the justice sector—and Bani Walid members were to find themselves under further pressure as the debates around 'political isolation' grew into 2013. However, the continuities in their identity and history had ensured for them a place, however precarious, in the post-Qadhafi political order. In doing so, they negotiated the complex question of tribe, community and identity in modern Libya.

13

LIBYA'S TEBU

LIVING IN THE MARGINS

Rebecca Murray

'Our forefathers came here hundreds of years ago. When we hold the sand, even in the night when the moon is shining, we know where we are.'

– Ibrahim Abu Bakr, Tebu archeologist, Awbari[1]

The indigenous Tebu people have long been marginalised in Libya. Decades-long victims of state-sanctioned discrimination under Mu'ammar al-Qadhafi's 'Arabisation' campaign, they were swift to join the revolution against his rule in 2011. With Qadhafi's overthrow they hoped to attain the full rights as citizens they had long struggled for.

Tebu fighters were valuable desert allies for the coastal rebels. With communities ranging some 1600km across Libya's vast southern Sahara, the Tebu rallied behind the banners of their military leaders, most prominently Baraka Wardaku in the west, and Hasan Musa and Ali Ramadan Sida in the east. The revolution did not, however, immediately bring the gains the Tebu sought, leaving them disillusioned with

Libya's transitional politics. In the power vacuum after Qadhafi's fall, they became embroiled in conflict with neighbouring Arab tribes in the south that cost hundreds of lives.[2]

This chapter focuses on Libya's Tebu community, and the crucial role they played during Libya's 2011 revolution. Told mainly through the voices of Tebu military and civil leaders, it traces the Tebu's origins and way of life, their systematic discrimination under Qadhafi, involvement in the Libya–Chad war and their revolutionary ambitions leading up to Qadhafi's overthrow. The chapter follows the Tebu's battle against Qadhafi in 2011, and their role in securing victory for the revolution in Libya's south. Finally, the chapter examines the long-simmering conflicts the Tebu remain embroiled in across the south, their ongoing struggle for civil rights, and their prospects for a peaceful future.

An uncertain identity

Libya's immense desert is home to oil, rare minerals and Qadhafi's ambitious 'Great Man Made River' project, which pipes underground water to Libya's thirsty coast where over an estimated 80 per cent of the country's six and a half million people live.[3] It is also prime smuggling territory, with weapons, drugs, alcohol and migrants ferried in, and arms and Libya's heavily subsidised fuel and food supplies driven out.[4]

I first met one Tebu leader, Isa Abd al-Majid Mansur, in September 2012. He was resting with his Tebu Border Guard unit, with its mismatched fatigues, battered weapons and dirty pick-up trucks, at dusk on the outskirts of Zuaila, an ancient stop along the historic slave trade route. The National Transitional Council (NTC) had controversially awarded the Tebu control of the southern borders, including to Mansur in the southeast, to the detriment of local Arab tribes[5] who, like the Tebu, made their living on illicit cross-border trade.

Having fallen out of favour with Qadhafi during Libya's long war with Chad, the charismatic Mansur fled to exile in Norway for almost a decade, where he became an outspoken rights advocate for the marginalised tribe in the international media, and established the Front for the Salvation of the Libyan Tebu in 2007. He said Qadhafi offered him up to five million US dollars to keep quiet.[6] A month after Libya's revolution began in February 2011, Mansur returned a hero to the country's Tebu community. But he eschewed the NTC's politics in Benghazi.

Instead, he drove nearly 1000km south into the desert to his remote childhood home of Ribyana, near the trading hub of Kufra, to raise a Tebu fighting force. At that time Mansur expected the revolution would prove a turning point in the struggle for Tebu rights. In his words, he said he personally received instructions from NTC head Mustafa Abd al-Jalil in March 2011 to secure the southern borders near Sudan and Chad with his Tebu fighters, which the NTC spelt out in an official letter. His optimism was reinforced near the end of the war when he accompanied Tebu leaders from Kufra to a meeting with Abd al-Jalil at the Benghazi airport in October. He claimed that Abd al-Jalil assured them of Tebu representation in the new government and promised to form a committee to determine Tebu identity and rights. 'He said we played a key role in the revolution, and that we would get our rights,' said Mansur.[7]

The Tebu are not strangers to Libya. For centuries, Libya's south has been home to the dark-skinned semi-nomadic traders, whose cargo once included sub-Saharan slaves. Scattered across the nation state borders of Libya, Chad, Niger, and to a lesser extent, Sudan, the Tebu regard the rugged Tibesti mountain region along the Libya–Chad frontier as their spiritual centre.[8] They are divided into two main groups— the smaller Teda, who from their homeland in the Tibesti mountains straddle Niger, Libya and Chad, and the more populous Daza based to the south and east of the Tibesti in Chad and in Kawar in Niger.[9] Estimates of the Teda and Daza range between 100,000 to several hundred thousand.[10] They share a unique language and customarily marry outside immediate family circles, thus knitting Tebu tribes together across a wide geographical expanse.[11]

In Libya, the question of the Tebu's citizenship status and decades of state-sanctioned discrimination in housing, education, employment and freedom of movement stem from the citizenship law number 17, passed in 1954.[12] Libya's courts demanded written identification in 'family books' as proof to determine Libyan nationality. The Sanusi ruler, King Idris, governed the then-impoverished state, with Tebu serving as his personal bodyguards. But the Tebu's semi-nomadic lifestyle, the Arabic language barrier, their high illiteracy rate and ignorance of government legislation conspired to keep them disenfranchised.[13] Muhammad Lino, a journalist from Murzuq, succinctly summed up the mentality of Tebu elders. 'They didn't know anything except the desert and had lived here for hundreds of years. So they asked—what do these papers have to do with me?'[14]

In 1969, Qadhafi's push for Arab nationalism undermined Libya's indigenous populations. 'When Qadhafi came to power things changed,' said Adam Arami al-Tibawi, the head of the Tebu National Assembly who risked his life as a secret activist under Qadhafi's government.[15] 'He had a strong belief the land was for Arabs only— the Socialist People's Libyan Arab Jamahiriya. That's the reason the Tebu were marginalised.'[16]

The Libya–Chad war and its legacy

Qadhafi's military occupation of northern Chad from 1972 to 1994 wreaked further havoc on the Tebus' legal status. Major droughts in 1973 and 1983–4 forced large numbers of Tebu from Chad and Niger to abandon their dying herds and flee to Libya—as did many other Arab and Tuareg pastoralists in the Sahel—creating the first Tebu shanty towns in Kufra and Sabha. Qadhafi manipulated these demographic changes to help consolidate Libya's outstanding claim, first made by King Idris, on the mineral-rich Ouzou Strip that runs parallel to Libya's southern border and includes the Tebu-populated Tibesti mountain range.[17] Qadhafi placed the area under Libyan civil rule, administered from Kufra. He encouraged paperless Tebu to register for their Libyan identification there, and induced them to join Libyan army ranks in return for eventual Libyan naturalisation.[18]

Libya attempted to overthrow Chad's ruler, Tebu President Hissene Habre, in 1980 and usurp the Ouzou Strip with the aid of another Chadian Tebu leader and former Habre ally, Goukouni Oueddei.[19] Many Tebu commanders during the 2011 revolution came to prominence as bit-actors in these events. Libyans built roads, military bases and shipped in tanks and thousands of troops. But with robust French and US intervention, Habre beat back the Libyan military initially from the capital, and eventually expelled them from Chad in 1987. Qadhafi's tumultuous relationship with Oueddei—a popular leader among Libya's Tebu who had fallen out with Habre over political rivalries—ultimately doomed the enterprise. Qadhafi's military adventures in Chad during the mid-1980s triggered conflicts with Oueddei. In 1986, reports of Oueddei being 'accidentally' shot in the stomach by one of Qadhafi's officials in Tripoli incensed the Tebu community.[20] 'Then the Tebu realised that Qadhafi wasn't with them, and joined the opposition,' explained Isa Abd al-Majid Mansur.[21] 'The reason Qadhafi lost the war was because he lost Tebu support.'

In 1994, to Qadhafi's surprise, the International Court of Justice (ICJ) awarded the Ouzou Strip to Chad.[22] Under international pressure to accept the court's ruling, Libya reluctantly acquiesced. Ali Ramadan Sida, who later became a prominent Tebu commander in the 2011 revolution, was the government's official Tebu eyewitness to the historic handover of the Strip to Chad.[23] He was one of a handful of Tebu who served as high-ranking officers in the Libyan army. Although from Kufra, Sida said he advanced because of his education in the northeast town of Baida, where he was not categorised as Tebu. 'During the ceremony the Tebu from the Ouzou Strip were sad and offered to fight for the Libyan government,' Sida remembered. 'We said the ICJ decision was final, but we did try and negotiate their move to Libya.'[24]

However, Qadhafi's obsession with Chad ground on. In 1998, the opposition Movement for Democratic Justice in Chad (MDJT), founded by former Chadian Defence Minister Youssouf Togoimi and backed by Libya, mounted an unsuccessful guerilla war from the Tibesti region to topple Chad's President Idris Deby, who assumed power after a 1990 coup ousted Hebre.[25] After the defeat of the MDJT by Chad in 2003, Qadhafi distanced himself from the defunct movement.[26] His police rounded up former MDJT supporters, many of them Tebu, and threw them in jail. Among them was the army officer Baraka Wardaku, who had fought for Qadhafi in Chad, and in the 1990s headed a Tebu rebellion in Niger, sponsored by Qadhafi. Wardaku, who went on to head Murzuq's military council following the revolution, and Kufra's venerated elder statesman, Hussain Shakki, were both detained in Abu Slim and Tajura prisons respectively.[27] Hasan Musa, an influential Tebu rights advocate from the Ribyana oasis, quietly kept his head down to avoid arrest. Mansur, who then worked for the government, fled to Norway in 2000.[28]

Qadhafi's sudden crackdown was another seminal moment for the Tebu. It nurtured their leadership and planted the seeds for the Tebu's joining the 2011 revolution. Bazinga Mawlami, a Tebu fighter with the MDJT who was imprisoned in Abu Slim, fought under Baraka Wardaku's command during the 2011 revolution in west Libya. 'They kept asking me if we wanted a Tebu state,' he recalled about the time he spent in jail.[29]

Libya's decades-long war with Chad and withdrawal from the Ouzou Strip left its mark. All Tebu who were encouraged to register as Libyan citizens in the Strip, as well as those Chadian Tebu rebels who fought for Qadhafi against their own government, found their Libyan citizenship status frozen, with devastating consequences. Many Tebu had their papers confiscated after the withdrawal, or never had them at all because they were without the required 'family books'. Classified as foreigners, their entitlement to state education and healthcare was gone; they were harassed at checkpoints and eked out a subsistence living as guards or smugglers.[30] A mix of chronic unemployment, lack of opportunity and stigmatisation all stirred the pot of discontent.

Salah Arzai from the southwest outpost of Qatrun, who became a Tebu aide to the NTC, said that despite possessing Libyan papers he was barred from powerful positions in the national government, military or business. Complex questions over citizenship meant that in practice, 'all Tebu were [treated] on the same level.'[31] After graduating with a Masters degree in business administration, Arzai embarked on a fruitless three-year job hunt, where would-be employers shelved his resume once they realised he was Tebu. When the revolution arrived he was one of the first to fight.[32]

Libyan towns with Tebu communities illustrate this inequity. The southwest city of Sabha, for example, is a study in contrasts. Its population of over 200,000 include the Tebu and Tuareg alongside Arab Warfalla, Awlad Sulaiman and Qadhadhfa tribes. These Arab communities, which historically had extended south to Niger and Chad, were encouraged to resettle in the town in large numbers under Qadhafi during the aforementioned population migrations caused by droughts and the Chadian and Nigerien wars during the 1970s and 1980s. But outside Sabha's bustling downtown commercial strip and terraced homes are shabby residential blocks and hundreds of homeless sub-Saharan migrants, seeking day labour to bring them one step closer to their next ride north. On the outskirts, an unpaved road runs to the Tuyuri shantytown, shared by Tebu and Tuareg residents who were mainly also refugees from drought and war in Chad, Niger and Mali. They feel that Qadhafi's pro-Arab politics and resettlement was at their expense, and they are excluded from the wealth of the oil-rich state. 'The housing ministry did not give people building certificates, and tore homes down because they were temporary,'[33] Adam Ahmad, the local council head, said. A cow-barn had been converted into the area's local clinic, and the overcrowded, cinderblock school held fifty children in a class. Power cuts in the sweltering heat are endemic, and there is no running water or sewage system.

The physical features of other Tebu communities across the country are similar.[34] In Murzuq, Qatrun, Kufra, and a chain of isolated desert outposts, ubiquitous shacks built with a mixture of mud, rusted corrugated iron and cardboard line the dusty roads. Nearby, livestock enclosures of woven sticks coexist with discarded fuel canisters, rebar, and heaps of waste.

In Kufra, an oasis tucked into a desert corner bordering Egypt, Sudan and Chad, communal conflicts simmer dangerously. The area has produced several prominent Tebu revolutionary leaders, including Musa, Sida, Shakki and Mansur, some of whom contributed to the town's integral role in the Libya-Chad war.

The Tebu make up 10 per cent of Kufra's population of 43,500.[35] They live in the segregated, hemmed-in communities of Gadarfai and Shura, which resembles Tuyuri in Sabha, with high unemployment, ramshackle homes, rubbish piles, brackish drinking water and a dearth of public services. Their uncertain fate was bound up with the sweeping demographic changes the remote oasis saw over the past century. The Tebu saw themselves as Kufra's original inhabitants, but in the mid-nineteenth century, the (Arab) coastal Zway community migrated south, settling the town of Tazerbo (a Tebu phrase meaning 'Great Kufra') and the green oasis chain of Kufra in the 1840s, creating powerful social ties stretching from Kufra to the seaport of Ajdabiya. Members of the Muslim Sanusi order raised Kufra's profile at the end of the nineteenth century, seeking refuge there from their conflict with the Ottomans. They made a strong impression on the region's inhabitants as they fought against European powers, including the Italians who ruled the territory from 1911 until 1943, when German and Italian forces abandoned Libya.[36] The Zway dominated the cross-border economy in the Kufra region until the revolution,[37] as well as its civil and military councils, businesses and natural resources. The inequitable distribution of wealth and status was a key instigator for the political earthquake ahead.

From discontent to revolution

By December 2007, the government's ill-treatment of Tebu in Kufra (primarily those registered in Ouzou, branded 'returnees' (*a'idin*)), such as confiscating their Libyan documents, denying them birth certificates and branding them 'foreigners' from Chad, grew more pronounced.

Despite widespread protests in Kufra, bulldozers moved in and homes were systematically demolished over the next two years.[38] In November 2008, anger exploded when Kufra's Tebu students were barred from taking examinations. With both tribes armed, the Zway appealed to Qadhafi's army for help. 'The Zway told them the Tebu were waving Chadian flags, and that Isa Abd al-Majid Mansur was on TV planning to return and declare a Tebu state,' said Yunis Isa, a Tebu resident from nearby Ribyana.[39] The military moved in to seal the Tebu neighbourhoods, and an army helicopter gunship hovered above as troops started firing. The United Nations (UN) recorded thirty-three dead in the small town from the five days of violence.[40]

'When Qadhafi visited Europe in 2009 I felt hopeless,' said Mansur, who was still in exile in Norway.[41] This was the time of Libya's triumphant reconciliation with the West, spearheaded by Qadhafi's son Saif al-Islam. But Mansur breathed a sigh of relief as he watched Qadhafi's rambling, controversial speech at the UN General Assembly in September that same year. 'I saw how he was treated and realised he wasn't loved.'[42]

Back in Libya, the seeds were being planted for a Tebu revolt. In 2009, Benghazi-based Adam Arami al-Tibawi and Kufra-based Hasan Musa secretly formed what would be the first organised Tebu resistance directed against Qadhafi's rule—the Libya Change Movement.[43] 'We prepared our Tebu revolution against Qadhafi,' Tibawi recalled, counting on a groundswell of anger at the dictatorship to trigger a larger revolt.[44] Some Zway, as well as the Tebu, had suffered under Qadhafi's brutal rule. 'I was the political side,' he said. 'I had indirect contact with Musa, who was the army commander and go-between with the Zway in Kufra.' Tibawi focused on raising money to buy smuggled weapons from Sudan and Chad. They had about 200 trained men working in anonymous small groups, and planned to target army bases.

'In the beginning only Tebu participated. We stored our arms in secret places,' said Musa. 'Then we contacted the Zway to join. I only asked close friends who I trusted.'[45] Once he was released from jail, Hussain Shakki was asked to serve as a liaison between Kufra's elders and select Zway leaders. Ali Ramadan Sida's brother, Rajab, another Tebu fighter based in Kufra, was assigned to gather intelligence on military camps. 'After 15 February 2011 I saw how strong Qadhafi was, and the mistakes we made,' Rajab Ramadan said.[46] Tibawi laughed in retrospect. 'We were supposed to start in July 2011. But we were lucky. The revolution started in Benghazi and we joined them. This was our opportunity to get our rights.'[47]

They received assistance from Sudan. Alex de Waal, director of the World Peace Foundation at Tufts University's Fletcher School of Law and Diplomacy, explained that the neighboring Sudanese government was tired of Qadhafi's internal meddling, and his backing of the rebel Justice and Equality Movement (JEM), based in Darfur.[48] 'For obvious reasons the Sudanese were very keen to see Qadhafi's removal and had actually been preparing forward defences against Qadhafi's destabilisation, particularly by JEM, in 2009 and 2010.'[49]

When the 'February 17 Revolution' sparked in Benghazi in February 2011 Sudan was swiftly able to coordinate the supply of weapons, training, logistics and intelligence support to the Tebu and NTC.[50] It also tightened its border to prevent JEM from coming to Qadhafi's aid and set up a military support base in Jabal al-Uwainat, strategically straddling the Libyan, Egyptian and Sudanese borders. 'That was the major supply route used for supplying the NTC for the next few months,' said de Waal. 'The Sudanese filled a particular gap, turning enthusiastic volunteers into an army that could actually mount operations.'[51]

Meanwhile, in Libya's southwest town of Murzuq, Wardaku reached out to Tebu in Sabha, Qatrun and as far west as Tuareg-dominated Awbari, and quietly built a Tebu military force using cars fuels and weapons surreptitiously acquired from Qadhafi's armed forces and security brigades in Sabha. One of his first recruits was journalist Muhammad Lino, then an oil worker, who followed the Tunisian and Egyptian revolutions closely from his office. 'I realised Qadhafi was finished,' Lino said.[52] He resigned from his job on 15 February 2011, the day the protests first roiled Benghazi, and enlisted with Wardaku's men. They used their Tebu desert expertise to rescue northeastern Libyans stranded in Tripoli. 'We organised their escape. We drove them down to Sabha, across to Kufra and up to Benghazi.'[53]

Like Lino, Adam Sidi Abdullah, a military explosives expert, quit his Tripoli-based job and joined the rebellion. At his hometown of Awbari, 100km west of Sabha and the last in a chain of desert oases before the Algerian border, a longstanding nonaggression agreement between the semi-indigenous and marginalised Tebu and Tuareg—the so-called *midi midi* agreement—held. 'The Tuareg in Awbari joined Qadhafi, because he promised them rights,' he explained.[54] 'But when Qadhafi wanted the Tuareg to fight the Tebu, they refused. The Tuareg didn't want war between the two tribes—we are close.'[55]

Libyan army officer Ali Ramadan Sida also realised that the uprisings in neighbouring countries could catalyse change at home. 'When the revolutions in Tunisia and Egypt happened, all the people inside the army liked it, but were scared to say so because intelligence was watching us,' he said.[56] 'On 24 February I defected from the army. It was like we were inside a jail, and suddenly someone opened the door for us to leave. That's what the 17 February Revolution was like for everyone.'[57] Sida joined five high-ranking Zway officers in Kufra on 23 March to televise their joint allegiance to the revolution. Two days later they raided the Sarrah military base 300km south of Kufra, confiscating all the weapons and cars. The army troops surrendered, and joined the rebel cause.[58]

But not all Tebu initially wanted to take part. When Musa talked with the Tebu community in Kufra, the youth were excited about the revolt, but the elders were less enthusiastic. They thought the town was too isolated, that food would be cut off, and they would not withstand the military. They also feared fighting would erupt between the local tribes. But despite this reluctance, local Tebu and Zway leaders went to Benghazi's Freedom Square and declared their support of the revolution.[59]

In March, government representatives sent money and Kalashnikovs to Kufra to persuade the town to fight on Qadhafi's side. Two months later Qadhafi revoked the Tebu's citizenship ban, nervous about a Tebu rebellion. 'But the Tebu said it was too late. They realised Qadhafi was always telling lies,'[60] said Sida. Instead, the Tebu took Qadhafi's gifts, and turned them against him.

Musa said in April 2011 that NTC head Abd al-Jalil promised him and Tibawi full citizenship rights for the Tebu after the revolution.[61] This was a full six months before Abd al-Jalil reiterated his vow to the Tebu leadership at Benghazi's airport when the revolution was almost won. 'I reminded him then, if you break this promise you have full witnesses,' said Tibawi.[62] 'We want justice, freedom, respect and dignity.'[63]

The Libyan Tebu had grasped the historic opportunity to fight. Given their tight-knit marriage and social connections, Tebu on both sides of the border with Sudan, Chad and Niger fell into line. Musa and Sida formed the Ahmad Sharif Battalions, named after a fighter against the Italian resistance from the Sanusi order, and eventually cordoned off much of the vast frontier, with the exception of the Tuareg's southwest corner.

With the help of the Sudanese government and aided by the NATO-enforced no-fly zone declared in late March, Tebu forces stemmed the cross-border flow of mercenaries and arms reinforcements to Qadhafi, and captured loyalists who fled. Providing a solid rear-guard to the rebel forces fighting along the coast, Wardaku and his recruits joined up with Musa in Kufra. They ferried in weapons from Sudan, then up to Benghazi, as well as across the desert to arm the Tebu in the west.[64]

As one of the NTC founding members, Benghazi-based Fathi al-Ba'ja vigorously worked to enlist support for the revolution from foreign governments, and coordinate the new and dynamic civil society movement. But Ba'ja had reservations about the resistance in the south. 'At the beginning of the revolution the Tebu had a chance to strengthen their position,' he said.[65] 'The Zway were undecided for us, even in Kufra. Some came to us, and then a week later would change sides. They had different flags.'[66]

Starting in April, the Tebu played a role in the battles against Qadhafi's military for the expansive Sarir oil fields, run by the Arabian Gulf Oil Company (AGOCO) in the Sirt desert basin.[67] It was a crucial funding source for the revolutionaries. Sida remembered tipping off the NTC to a pending attack on 30 March.[68] But promised weapons didn't materialise—neither from his former Zway army colleagues, including Kufra's current military council head, Sulaiman Hasan, nor from the NTC in Benghazi—and Qadhafi's military grabbed the oil fields on 4 April. Ten days later, when Tebu fighters from Kufra, Murzuq and Qatrun finally joined forces with arms from Ajdabiya, they captured the oil fields. They battled over Sarir again two months later, with Mansur's troops now joining the fight.[69]

On 28 April, Qadhafi's army finally rolled into isolated Kufra, in a convoy of about sixty armed pickup trucks. Some rebels scrambled south to the Sudanese border to get weapons, while others hid near Sida's house in Kufra's Shura neighborhood.[70] 'About two hundred came to the courthouse and had a gunfight,' remembered Kufra's Zway local council head, Muhammad Abu Sadana.[71] 'They drove a bulldozer through the building. The Libyan Tebu came to rescue me and brought me to the hospital.'[72] For one week Qadhafi's troops conferred daily with the residents, reflected by the conversational array of banners, with Qadhafi's green flag mixed in with the NTC's new red, black and green design. The loyalists played both sides, warning the Zway that Tebu fighters had been infiltrated by al-Qa'ida, while they promised the Tebu residents citizenship and asked them to join the government's fight.[73]

Ramadan Sulaiman, a Tebu military leader from Awbari, was part of the group that sped to the Sudanese border for reinforcements. 'We got nearly forty cars with anti-aircraft weapons and RPGs,' he said. 'Then we went to liberate Kufra.'[74] On 5 May, sufficiently regrouped, the Tebu, joined by some Zway and northern rebels, mounted a ferocious armed assault that liberated Kufra within a day.[75] 'There is no question the Sudanese played a decisive role in liberating Kufra,' said de Waal.[76]

Tebu communities in western Libya took longer to assert themselves. Threatened by the government's stronghold of Sabha, the Tebu-populated towns of Murzuq and Qatrun were quiet through the spring months of the revolution. Qadhafi had also sent emissaries there, offering guns and money, backed up with promises to solve the Tebu's citizenship status. Tahir Muhammad Makni, now the new Tebu representative to the Tripoli-based General National Congress (GNC), moved quietly as a civilian activist within the western desert triangle of Awbari, Qatrun, Murzuq and Sabha to encourage revolutionary support. 'We were working in secret because Qadhafi had full control of Sabha. Even our committee was infiltrated with spies, and they put my name on the wanted list,' he said.[77] 'People were saying this was not a good time to revolt, because Qadhafi forces were here, and it was not under NATO's area of operations. There were many fears.'[78]

Baraka Wardaku was also cautious. 'It was very dangerous to communicate then,' he said.[79] '[Our car] broke down by a military base and we gathered intelligence. Then we attacked all the surrounding army barracks in the early morning of 17 July and captured their cars and weapons.'[80] Qatrun, the nearest town to the border army base of Wigh fell quietly, but was briefly recaptured by loyalists just over one month later. This was short lived: the revolution's momentum had finally pushed Tebu fighters up to Murzuq on 17 August. There they planned for a final assault on Qadhafi's last southern front in Sabha.[81]

Although Qadhafi's promises for citizenship and rewards fell on deaf ears among the Tebu, many Tuareg of Malian and Nigerien origin gambled on Qadhafi's victory. After signing up to fight for the government, they were sent to reinforce the battlefields along the coast. The void they left with their migration and the liberation of most of Libya left Sabha vulnerable to a rebel takeover, from the north and the south.

The fall of Tripoli on 20 August hastened the revolution's end. As Qadhafi fled east to Sirt, northern rebels from Tripoli and the Nefusa Mountains drove south. They walked into Sabha a month later, on 22 September, without much of a fight. The Tebu were euphoric. 'At this time we thought in a free Libya we would get all our rights,' Wardaku told me.[82]

Sida summed up the mood best. 'During the revolution, people were perfect, excellent, and even the Zway and Tebu were close friends,' he said. 'But when we returned to normal life, we found all the same people in their old positions.'[83]

Fighting over the spoils

Since the revolution, not only have the Tebu dominated trade routes and the borders; they also guard checkpoints, oil fields, prisons and weapon stockpiles. Although their official remit for policing expired with the newly elected Libyan government, they still fill the security void patrolling the extensive area in armed pick-up trucks—from the southwest outskirts of Sabha, Awbari and Murzuq across to Kufra's small oasis, 900km east.

A few paved roads run to border crossings with Niger, Chad and Sudan. At remote checkpoints manned by Tebu fighters, commercial trucks idle along the road, heaped with fuel canisters, household goods, migrant labourers, and usually buried beneath, a more illicit trade.

But most travelled routes across Libya's Sahara are off-road, where it is common for Tebu families, border guards and smugglers along the way to trade greetings, directions or help repair vehicles.[84] There are also 'medical tourists'—predominantly elderly or handicapped Tebu with crutches and wheelchairs—headed to remote hot, sulfuric springs to treat their ailments.

I travelled the Sahara in the summer of 2012 with Ahmad, a border guard, who frequently drove the twenty-four hour cross-country trek to the Ribyana oasis. Dressed in a bright white *dishdasha* and aviator sunglasses, he expertly surfed towering sand dunes at gut-wrenching speeds, rattled over volcanic rock and in the dark, navigated an old minefield from Libya's war with Chad. Lacking expensive satellite equipment, Ahmad followed an almost invisible path through the Sahara marked with small piles of stones, empty fuel canisters, and the night's stars.

The fertile village of Ribyana—the hometown of Tebu leaders Musa and Mansur—is wedged between the monotonous rolling dunes and appears lost in time. Simple homes crafted from baked mud and woven palm fronds shelter the population of around 4,000. They are mostly Tebu, with a sprinkling of Zway families. Cut off from mobile networks and public infrastructure, restless youth look for education and work in nearby Kufra, 130km to the east, or in the northern coastal cities of Ajdabiya and Benghazi.

Those left behind, like Ahmad, have few options. The piecemeal work of smuggling fuel and migrants is grueling and dangerous, but can net a monthly income of over 9,000 US dollars. Since the revolution however, Ahmad chose to join the Border Guard.

After the revolution, the Tebu found themselves in a conflict with local Arab tribes over trade routes, resources, and proving their Libyan identity. They are also challenging the political prestige of the Arab status quo. In Kufra that struggle soon grew violent, as the town experienced a deadly turf war in a post-revolutionary power vacuum.

At stake are the lucrative cross-border trade routes that have made both tribes fortunes, in fuel, food, alcohol, drugs, weapons and migrants. The Zway accuse the Tebu of being 'foreign', while the Tebu call the Zway racist.

Kufra's neighborhoods are strictly segregated along tribal lines.[85] Qadhafi's favoritism towards many Zway is reflected in their relatively prosperous neighborhoods. But since the NTC asked the Tebu to enforce border and desert checkpoints during and after the revolution, most of the Zway's commercial trucks in Kufra are now parked at a standstill, with only the Tebu's small Toyota pickup trucks freely crossing.

However, Tebu residents inside Kufra remain confined to the impoverished ghettoes of Gadarfai and Shura, cordoned off by checkpoints manned by the army's special forces, who took over from the government-sanctioned Libya Shield Forces. Families live in damaged shacks among heaps of waste, unexploded ordnance, and scorched earth.

Two months after the revolution's end, intertribal fighting broke out in November 2011 at an official desert checkpoint 30km away, manned by Mansur's border force. The town's Zway tried to erect their own checkpoint, just metres away. An argument escalated and shots were fired, leaving dead and injured.[86]

'This was not a big problem, it could have been solved,' insisted Sida.[87] But the wounded Tebu were shot at again outside Kufra's downtown hospital. 'I was going to secure the hospital and conduct negotiations, but was ambushed on the way'.[88]

Khadija Hamid Yusuf had been a nurse at Kufra's hospital for ten years. Now the Tebu medical staff were threatened. 'The Zway security guard and ambulance driver came in with Kalashnikovs and warned: "This is your last day or we will shoot you."'[89]

An unhappy NTC delegation flew south to Kufra, brokered a ceasefire and said they would investigate. But they did nothing, Sida said, and the sporadic acts of violence erupted into widespread conflict in February 2012, which killed nearly 200, and injured hundreds more.[90]

In the full-scale fighting that followed, mortars were indiscriminately lobbed into the cordoned-off neighborhoods. Tebu medical staff hastily set up two makeshift clinics in Shura and Gadarfai after their expulsion from Kufra's hospital. But they lacked skills, equipment, medicine and clean water to treat critically injured patients, and were forced by power cuts to perform surgery by flashlight. The Gadarfai medical staff were too afraid to bury bodies outside their besieged compound, so they stacked them up in the guardhouse instead, where they decomposed in the desert heat.

'I was in Benghazi when I heard that Chadians were invading Libya,' said Rami Al-Shabaibi, a Libyan journalist with Associated Press.[91] 'When I got there, there were no Chadians, only Tebu. I kept asking people for their identification.'[92] He believes the Zway's satellite equipment and media savvy played a pivotal role in convincing the auxiliary Libya Shield Forces, loosely affiliated with the Ministry of Defence, to drive down and keep the peace (though the fact that Hafiz al-Aquri, one of its leaders, had Zway family also played a role). The undisciplined force soon turned their weapons on the Tebu. Fighters from as far as Misrata came to fight 'the foreigners' reported in the media, with little idea of the terrain or the enemy they were shooting at. Meanwhile, the Zway had a grip on the airport and the transport, including humanitarian aid, going in and out.[93]

Sida was at the Sarir oil fields when he saw eighty armoured cars trundle towards Kufra. 'They told me there were mercenaries in Kufra, and they were going to fight them. I told them I was Tebu, and that there were only Tebu in Kufra. I invited to show them our neighborhoods first-hand. They agreed, and we travelled down together,' said Sida. 'When they realised there were no foreigners or mercenaries they became very angry with the commanding Libya Shield Forces.'[94]

After hundreds were killed in the spring of 2012, the Ministry of Defence backed down in its support of the armed groups sent down to be 'peacekeepers', and a ceasefire between the Tebu and Libya Shield was hammered out in June. Subsequently, the Tebu and Zway, exhausted and reeling from such a high body count for their small communities, warily signed a separate ceasefire on 20 July 2012, the first day of the Islamic month of Ramadan.

Looking towards the future

No sooner was the ceasefire signed, than the Zway-dominated municipal government encircled Kufra with a large barrier, effectively cutting off the Tebu's approach from the western desert, and putting the bitterly divided oasis under siege.

Ceasefires, often brokered by 'neutral' elders, are notoriously weak in post-revolutionary Libya because of vague language and the absence of strong, centralised institutions to back them up. 'The wise people are together, but the young people are separated now,' lamented Muhammad Sidi, a principal Tebu peace negotiator from Qatrun. 'How do we bring those people together?'[95]

Libyans invested a lot of goodwill in the national election day on 12 July 2012, and enthusiastic Tebu and Tuareg voters turned up at the polls in Sabha's Tuyuri neighborhood. They professed their wish for citizenship, rights and dignity.[96] But kilometres away in the burnt-out shantytown of Hajara, few Tebu had identification, or intended to vote.

The town's Hajara and Tuyuri neighbourhoods had suffered a fierce attack on 26 March 2012, after an argument between Tebu and the local Bu Saif and Awlad Sulaiman tribes triggered a battle over power and trade.[97] Tebu fighters sped north from Murzuq and Qatrun to the defence of their tribesman as neighbourhoods were shelled. When Prime Minister Abd al-Rahim al-Kib finally arrived one week later, nearly 150 had been killed and over 500 wounded before a ceasefire was declared.[98]

Tayuri survived. But for the disenfranchised Tebu in the now-ruined and impoverished Hajara—a cluster of old Arab mud brick homes abandoned by previous residents for Qadhafi's new housing projects—the elections were an afterthought. Camped out with relatives or living in tents, their dire situation had just got worse.

Muhammad Ali, a Sabha University student, was one of the lucky few with papers among his friends. They sat at dusk at the entrance to Hajara and described the assault by armed men from the Awlad Sulaiman tribe. 'There was no advance warning of the attack. They went door to door, and stole my car.' He added, 'Even with identification we have trouble at checkpoints, because people think we are from Africa.'[99]

After accusations of fraud and a delay in the Kufra and Ribyana elections—including 1,000 Tebu being struck from the election rolls— only two Tebu representatives won seats in the 200-member GNC.

'The picture is not clear right now,' Tibawi told me after the elections.[100] 'We in Libya never talk about trust. We need trust before we can talk about reconciliation. How can we have peace with no trust?'[101]

Although at the time of writing the UN and international community are pushing the new elected representatives to include constitutional minority rights for indigenous populations like the Tebu, Amazigh and Tuareg, independent Tebu representative Tahir Muhammad Makni is not sure this will happen. 'I'm not optimistic about getting what we dream for,' he said.[102]

On 17 December 2012, Libya's prime minister, Ali Zaidan, declared southern Libya a closed military zone subject to martial law, with the border policed by warplanes, and plans to send in troops.[103] The act was framed within the context of the war in Mali, the fight against al-Qa'ida in the Maghreb (AQIM), and the international 'war on terror'.

Tebu leaders from Kufra, to Murzuq, to Awbari view themselves as a valuable asset to the Libyan government, and the US Africa Military Command in their regional war against al-Qa'ida, and imply they could be forced to prove the power of their desert tribal networks if their rights are swept off the table.

'The stability of the south depends on Tebu rights,' said Musa. 'And Libya's stability depends on the south's stability.'[104]

14

TUAREG MILITANCY AND THE SAHELIAN
SHOCKWAVES OF THE LIBYAN REVOLUTION

Yvan Guichaoua[1]

The Sahara is neither a political void, nor an economic no man's land. Its populations actively trade, share views and behavioural norms. The survival of these networks depends on relationships with regional state and nonstate actors, among whom Mu'ammar al-Qadhafi's government in Libya used to feature prominently. His government offered economic support as well as political attention to Saharan communities. Qadhafi was driven by opportunism, yet his interventions provided some predictability to the vulnerable lives of Saharan communities.

Qadhafi's removal changed Saharan transnational political networks profoundly, and affected a system of governance involving heterogeneous actors, including Tuareg, Arab and Tebu but also Songhai, Hausa or Fulani communities, their nonstate armed protectors, as well as al-Qa'ida-affiliated armed groups originating in Algeria. Its echoes reverberated violently from Libya to Mali, then, after the French military intervention there in early 2013, to Algeria, as epitomised by the attack on a gas plant at In Amenas in January 2013, and Niger, where deadly attacks hit Arlit and Agadez in May 2013. These attacks seem to have been perpetrated by groups relocated in southern Libya after a spell in Mali, indicating the continuing interpenetration of the Sahelian and North African spaces and their unfinished political reconfiguration since the Libyan Revolution.

For the Tuareg communities in particular, the 2011 revolution in Libya created a complex chain of events that drew in their kin in Niger, and Mali.[2] While many Sub-Saharan African migrants in Libya headed south to flee the combat zones,[3] others, notably Tuareg fighters from Niger and Mali, entered Libya to offer support to Colonel Qadhafi's military campaign.[4] When Qadhafi's government was defeated, the same combatants eventually returned to their home countries along with other Tuareg who had settled in Libya previously, in turn triggering the collapse of northern Mali. A Tuareg separatist movement, the *Mouvement national de libération de l'Azawad* (National Movement for the Liberation of Azawad,[5] MNLA), making extensive use of weapons and fighters from Libya, conducted a blitz offensive against Malian troops stationed in northern garrisons on 17 January 2012, provoking an unintended coup against President Toure in the south-based capital Bamako and the subsequent de facto secession of Mali's north, roughly comprising two thirds of the national territory. But the MNLA ran out of resources soon after it declared the independence of Azawad on 6 April 2012, and was driven out by yet other recipients of Libyan weaponry,[6] namely Mali-based Islamist groups closely connected to al-Qa'ida in the Islamic Maghreb (AQIM).[7] AQIM, a jihadist outfit born out of a process of factionalisation among Islamist forces during the Algerian civil war in the nineties, had found shelter in north Mali in 2003 and had enjoyed relative impunity since. Its local influence grew after it made the kidnapping of Westerners a prosperous money-making industry. When MNLA forces swept north Mali and defeated the army, AQIM dismissed its nationalist stance, rallied Tuareg combatants committed to jihad and capitalised on anti-Tuareg sentiment among Songhai and Fulani northern communities. The Islamist coalition eventually vanquished the MNLA and imposed a nine-month Islamic rule over north Mali before France launched a military intervention to oust them.[8]

The Libyan revolution gave its Malian Tuareg participants and their local nationalist counterparts the firepower they had previously lacked to destroy Bamako's 'hegemony on a shoestring'[9] in northern Mali.[10] How do the stories of Libya and Mali intertwine?

This chapter firstly describes the long-lasting interconnectedness of the Tuareg Saharan political economy, perpetuated over centuries by long-distance travellers exchanging a wide range of licit and illicit commodities, building networks, accumulating social and financial capital, and, more recently, exploiting the economic and political opportunities afforded by Qadhafi in Libya. Secondly, the chapter details the interference of Qadhafi's regime with Niger and Mali's management of domestic Tuareg insurgencies. It then explains the Tuareg's nuanced support of Qadhafi's defence against the rebels' offensive in this context.

Libya and the political economy of the Sahara

Moussa T. is a young Tuareg who I interviewed in May 2009 in Djanet,[11] in southeastern Algeria: 100km from the Tenere desert, Niger; 50km from Ghat, Libya. From October to April, Moussa is employed as a guide for tourists in the stunning scenery of the Tassili n'Ajjer, driving the 4x4 loaned to him by his boss Issouf H., a Tuareg travel agent from Niger who lives in Djanet. In the hot season, depending on the opportunities that arise, Moussa travels to Libya to buy spare parts for four-wheel drives, which he resells in Djanet, or in nearby Tamanrasset. When short of money, however, he organises convoys of sub-Saharan migrants wishing to enter Libya. Some of these migrants have been dropped at the Algerian border by Tuareg drivers from Niger after a long trip from Agadez. Others arrive in Tamanrasset first, via the mining town Arlit and Tenere, before being driven to Djanet by Moussa or his friends. When numbers of migrants in Djanet are high enough, Moussa assembles large groups of them and guides them on foot on the long rocky trail towards Ghat. The three-day trek is dangerous, sometimes deadly, as 'Africans don't know how to walk in the rocks' and cannot keep pace with their agile guide.

Moussa is relatively young for a *chifor* (driver) and admits he could make much more money by transporting other 'cargoes' (*chargements*) instead of migrants or tourists. In Djanet's economy, young *chifors* transport migrants when they lack the requisite experience and connections to transport arms or illicit drugs, which yield larger profits. Arms and drugs trafficking is controlled by a few politically connected patrons who own cars 'as fast as little planes', which cause amazement among those who see them pass by in the dunes. The two types of convoy—Moussa's slower trucks, and the fast 4x4s of the narco- and arms traffickers, indicate the two separate networks and economies that overlap in these same spaces.[12] Entry into the most profitable segment of trade also faces a moral barrier: illicit drugs are forbidden by Islam (*haram*) and transporting them exposes traffickers to social stigma.[13]

The geography dictates that arms and drug traffickers use few routes, the most well known of which is the 'Salvador pass', south of Djanet, a narrow corridor between the mountains bridging Libya and Niger. Most of the arms smuggled out of Libya during the 2011 civil war entered Niger there—as well as other goods, including construction material, to be sold in Agadez.[14] The Salvador pass is also the point where Qadhafi's former chief of intelligence Abdullah al-Sanusi left Libya in October 2011, with the help of former Tuareg rebels from Niger.[15]

While not rich, Moussa occasionally manages to save money, which he immediately invests in building a house, brick after brick, as a way to speed up his marital prospects. Moussa is better off than most of the other Tuareg young men that cross his path in Djanet. Every night, a large warehouse in Issouf's family compound, which normally stores trekking equipment for tourists, hosts young Tuareg travellers heading to Libya to occupy seasonal jobs in gardens or construction sites, or returning to Niger. Issouf hardly knows them; they were recommended to him by common acquaintances.

Djanet is a node of the trans-Saharan trade whose economic success largely depends on the activities in which Moussa and Issouf engage. Djanet is connected to other distant Saharan nodes similarly sustained by this transnational network of trade: Timbuktu, Kidal, Gao or In-Khalil in Mali; Agadez or In-Gall in Niger; Ghat, Awbari or Sabha in Libya. While the people and commodities travelling between these places change, the trading routes as well as the 'connectivity' that makes them parts of a coherent political economy are deeply rooted in history. Convoys of people (slaves, caravaners, migrants), animals (camels) and goods (gold, salt, textiles, cowries, tanned leather, dates and other foodstuff; more recently petrol, perfume, electric appliances, cigarettes, drugs, firearms) have been crossing the desert for centuries. Oases towns are inherently fragile ecologically; therefore trade connections are necessary for their survival.

These trade connections have been sustained over the centuries by Islamic law and carefully maintained social capital. Trans-Saharan trade began well before the spread of Islam. But Islam, entering Africa in the seventh century, homogenised and strengthened the legal regulations governing long-distance commerce.[16] Social capital, notably via marital strategies, and cosmopolitanism—that is, aptitude for navigation across diverse linguistic and institutional settings[17]—combined to ensure the cohesion of trading networks. Success was made sustainable through constantly negotiated alliances, and involved subtle social hierarchies. As a consequence, trans-Saharan trading networks tend to form a vast dynamic moral economy requiring careful maintenance.[18]

Crucially, state actors—local customs officers as well as politicians—play a role in this economy. An oft-observed truth of the Saharan political economy was that for governments, controlling men is far more important than controlling territory. State officials' activities thus ranged in scope from collecting bribes to running entire trafficking networks. The booming cigarettes trafficking between Niger and Libya in the 1990s was controlled by Libyans from the Qadhadhfa tribe, raising the strategic value of the connection between Libya and Niger[19]—demonstrated later by Qadhafi's officials' choice to head to Niger at the end of the war.[20] These examples, from Moussa to the Qadhadhfa, demonstrate that the Sahara is anything but the 'ungoverned space' classically conveyed by the Western media.[21] How resilient this economy is to shocks such as the rise of narco-trafficking, the collapse of Qadhafi's government in Libya, and the subsequent Islamist takeover in Mali is explored further below.

Libya's importance in the Saharan economic space had mounted gradually since the 1960s. Pastoralism and long-distance caravanning, the traditional economic specialisations of the Tuareg, faltered under French colonial rule.[22] After Mali and Niger became independent in 1960, recurrent rebellions, the ensuing waves of state repression, the opening of new trading routes by air or sea, as well as droughts, accelerated the economic decline of their northern provinces.[23] Tuareg rebellions hit Mali in 1963, the 1990s, 2006 and then again in early 2012. Niger witnessed two periods of rebellion; in the 1990s, then again between 2007 and 2009. These insurgencies took place in the backdrop of Tuaregs' social and economic marginalisation in the postcolonial power systems privileging southern elites in Bamako and Niamey, respectively. The response by Niger and Mali's governments (including the use of violence) has varied greatly in the two countries. In 1963, during the first rebellion, Malian authorities used blind repression. The second rebellion in Mali also turned into bloody communal violence perpetrated by proxy militias controlled by the

government. Significant killings of Tuareg civilians were also perpetrated by governmental forces in Niger, such as the 'Tchintabaraden
massacre' in 1990, leaving a durable imprint on collective memories
and subsequent nationalist narratives. Successive peace deals were
signed in the 1990s in Niger and Mali but were poorly implemented,
perpetuating resentment.

This resulted in the disenfranchisement of large numbers of young
Tuareg men, who, in response, migrated north to Algeria and Libya.
Migration created a new trans-Saharan identity, that of the *ishumar*
(from the French word *chômeur*, meaning unemployed). The *ishumar*
were itinerant young men moving from one economic opportunity to
the next. They began to question traditional tribal order, developed an
ethos of solidarity and autonomy, and all the while tightened the social
and economic connections in the towns between which they travelled.
The globally acclaimed blues band Tinariwen sang the refrain
'Aujourd'hui je suis là mais demain je ne sais pas' ('Today I'm here,
tomorrow I don't know'), popularly sung among the *ishumar*, which
essentially encapsulated their worldview and lifestyle.[24]

Libya became the Eldorado of the *ishumar* and their remittances
were a source of financial assistance for their relatives at home.[25] While
not offered full citizenship by the Libyan government—with the exception of some that became fighters in Qadhafi's security forces—they
could live and run businesses in Libya unhindered by the authorities.

Ishumar were the forerunners of a larger wave of migration into
Libya from sub-Saharan Africa in the 1990s, which they in turn supported as drivers and transporters. This wave of migration was largely
demand-driven. Libya faced a labour shortage and was cash-rich, triggering demand for unskilled foreign workers.

Hospitality towards Sub-Saharan Africans also stemmed from diplomatic considerations. Failed attempts at building pan-Arab solidarity,
as well as diplomatic and economic isolation following the embargo
declared after the Lockerbie attack in 1988, pushed Qadhafi's government to develop ties with sub-Saharan Africa. The process resulted in
massive Libyan investments in diverse productive sectors of sub-
Saharan countries, as well as spectacular displays of generosity, such as
Bamako's Libya-funded administrative district, housing all of Mali's
main ministries and inaugurated in September 2010.[26] These diplomatic
efforts culminated in Qadhafi's creation of the Community of Saharan
and Sahelian States (CEN-SAD) in February 1998.[27] CEN-SAD was a

free trade area initially founded by Libya and five Sahelian countries (Burkina Faso, Niger, Mali, Sudan and Chad), subsequently expanding to 28 members. One of its primary goals was to encourage the circulation of people. CEN-SAD's creation coincided with a spectacular increase in the proportion of sub-Saharan migrants working in Libya.

But Qadhafi was careful not to make immigration irreversible. The migrants were closely monitored in the towns in which they registered to work. When domestic political or economic pressures dictated, migration could be curtailed. In 2004, for instance, 5,000 Nigeriens were expelled from Libya.[28] Similarly, in the mid-2000s, Qadhafi complied with the European Union's new strategy for controlling immigration by allowing the guards from the EU agency Frontex to patrol its borders.

Qadhafi's Libya did not only enhance its political influence on the African continent through immigration policy and economic investments. Qadhafi also intervened directly in the national affairs of his neighbours, as epitomised by his mediation of the recurrent Tuareg rebellions in Niger and Mali. The political capital accrued in these interventions, would translate into ready Tuareg military support to Qadhafi at the onset of the 2011 uprising.[29]

Qadhafi's role in shaping Tuareg regional politics

Libyan support for Tuareg rebellion in the Sahel is not new. During World War I, the Tuareg leader Kaocen united several Tuareg tribes from the Aïr region, north of Agadez in Niger, and challenged the French colonisers militarily with the support of the Cyrenaica-based Sanusi order, which shared control of what is now Libya with the Ottomans.[30] Kaocen's alliance with Cyrenaica was the first example of what became a recurrent feature of Tuareg rebellions'—their using foreign alliances to gain advantage in local power struggles. In this way, Qadhafi's apparently whimsical agenda simply fitted a preexisting political dynamic.

In the 1970s, Qadhafi recognised a political opportunity in the disenfranchised young Tuaregs fleeing droughts and political repression in Niger and Mali. Posturing as a flag-bearer of a revolutionary, anti-imperial struggle, he created the Islamic Legion in 1979, an auxiliary armed group that enlisted up to 8,000 combatants from Egypt, Sudan, Niger and Mali. This force served in various and generally disastrous military campaigns in Chad, Uganda and Lebanon.[31] It also served domestic purposes, since unlike the regular army, it was exclusively dedicated to Qadhafi's protection and safeguarding him against potential military coups.[32]

Testimonies and narratives of Tuareg ex-combatants acknowledge the Islamic Legion played a central role in the rebellions that hit Niger and Mali in the early 1990s. Most veteran rebels of the 1990s I interviewed since 2007 root the immediate causes of the insurgency in the economic and political marginalisation of the Tuareg after independence, but insist that its military translation was permitted by the experience of combat acquired under Qadhafi's auspices, as part of the Islamic Legion. In the eyes of the Tuareg who stayed in Niger and Mali at the time, the rebellions were started by 'Libyans'.[33] Most Tuareg leaders of those rebellions had fought in the Islamic Legion in the hope that Qadhafi would support their struggle in turn. This tacit promise was not fulfilled, however, as Qadhafi wanted to avoid a direct confrontation with Libya's neighbours. This created resentment among Tuareg rebels, who, in the 1990s, fought the central authorities of Mali and Niger 'without a single bullet from Qadhafi',[34] relying instead on arms raided from Malian and Nigerien military depots. Qadhafi's relationship with the Malian and Nigerien Tuareg, therefore, was ambiguous: the Tuareg had developed relatively commercial prosperous exchanges thanks to Libya's openness, yet these ties enhanced Qadhafi's capacity to manipulate Tuareg political aspirations and militancy.

In the 1990s, Qadhafi offered Tuareg rebels sanctuary in Libya and was, a decade later, instrumental in negotiating a ceasefire between the rebels and Mali and Niger. Qadhafi became the mediator of the regional tensions he had fuelled, garnering him international legitimacy in the region. Qadhafi held this position because of Libya's economic regional power. He could negotiate an end to fighting by coopting rebel leaders and promising military integration to their followers; he could also sponsor longer-term post-conflict policies aimed at preventing the resumption of conflicts such as the UNDP-run *Programme de Consolidation de la Paix dans l'Aïr et l'Azawak* (Programme for Peace Consolidation in the Aïr and the Azawak, PCPAA) in Niger in 2005 aimed at turning ex-combatants into small entrepreneurs. By doing so, Qadhafi became a crucial power-broker between the weak governments of Niger and Mali, and the armed actors in the remote periphery of their national territory.[35] The different ways in which these political processes unfolded had direct consequences for the Tuareg's positions in the 2011 revolution in Libya.

Libya and the Tuareg rebellion in Niger (2007–9)[36]

On 9 February 2007, the military post of Iferouane, located in the north of Agadez, was attacked by armed men claiming affiliation to a new movement: the *Mouvement des Nigériens pour la justice* (Nigerien Movement for Justice, MNJ). This was the start of a two-year rebellion based primarily in the Aïr Mountains, led by Aghaly Alambo, a mid-ranking officer of the *Front de libération de l'Aïr et de l'Azawak* (FLAA), the leading insurgent movement of the 1990s. After his time in the FLAA, Alambo took on the position of *sous-préfet* in Iferouane, north of Agadez, and ran a profitable travel agency—a business often associated with cross-border trafficking. Allegedly, Alambo took the leadership of the MNJ because of the involvement of his brother, an army deserter, in the MNJ's first attack, which made him a wanted man. His reputation as a brave combatant of the late FLAA and the early death in combat of the charismatic Capitaine Acharif ensured he was not initially challenged.

Within a few months, the MNJ amassed over a thousand combatants. The MNJ denounced the unfulfilled promises of the peace agreements signed in the late 1990s, which called for the economic development of Agadez and its region, greater regional autonomy through decentralisation, and an ambitious programme of integration of ex-combatants in national security forces and public administration. The MNJ also demanded better redistribution of wealth from uranium mining, Niger's principal source of government revenues, which is extracted in Arlit, north of Agadez.

By late 2009, however, the MNJ had collapsed, due not only to exhaustion of resources but also a Libyan intervention, which consisted in coopting part of the MNJ leadership into a new faction that accepted disarming. We detail below how Libyan authorities were instrumental in the launch as well as the demise of the MNJ.

In 2005, France, the US, and Libya sponsored the PCPAA, an economic package that was negotiated in the 1990s peace agreement between the Nigerien government and the Tuareg rebels. Coordinated by the United Nations Development Programme (UNDP), PCPAA supported 3,000 ex-combatants in starting micro-enterprises.[37] Also in

2005, Libya, as a favour to the Nigerien authorities, arranged resi-
dence permits and positions in the Libyan security forces for 500 ex-
combatants of the FLAA.[38] But the Libyan efforts—along with those
of other donors—proved inadequate. The PCPAA started late and
offered too little (typically small onion-growing businesses) to its recipients, who rejected the strictly economic scheme. Similarly, the informal integration process of ex-combatants into the Libyan and Nigerien
armed forces, and its overreliance on the discretionary power of FLAA
leaders, proved unworkable as too many FLAA combatants ended up
side-lined. It was eventually ex-FLAA members who triggered the next
rebellion in 2007, choosing Alambo to lead them and rebranding their
movement MNJ.

MNJ's low-intensity guerrilla war ensued, logistically supported
from Algerian and Libyan territories. Unable to handle the situation,
Nigerien authorities appealed again to Qadhafi, who, in 2009, summoned the MNJ leaders to Tripoli. The negotiation degenerated into
bargaining, in which the end of hostilities was simply bought for cash.

This buyoff factionalised the Nigerien Tuareg militants into three
main groups. Two new groups split off from the MNJ: the *Front des
Forces de Redressement* (FFR) and the *Front Patriotique Nigérien*
(FPN). The cause of the breakdown was not ideological but stemmed,
instead, from personal rivalries among the leaders driven by Libya's
intervention. Parochial, self-interested considerations replaced the original nationalist claims and killed the insurgency.

The FPN tried to claim priority access to the funds offered by
Qadhafi. Meanwhile Alambo, the MNJ president, negotiated with
Libyan authorities on behalf of the MNJ. The prospects of the MNJ at
the time are summarised by a MNJ fighter: 'our resources were
exhausted and we were tired. The best thing to do was to sell our
rebellion at a good price. Alambo obtained a good price and the great
bulk of the combatants supported his option.'[39] According to the same
combatant, the negotiated payment only covered disarmament. A second phase, consisting of employment for ex-combatants, was expected,
but never transpired as Qadhafi was toppled in 2011.

Even the disarmament process did not run smoothly, as low-level
fighters accused their leaders of deceit. According to ex-combatants
interviewed in March 2012, they only received payment of $1,000 in
Sabha, southern Libya just prior to returning to Niger, instead of the
$6,000 payment per combatant it was rumoured the leaders received

from Qadhafi. With no documentation of the agreement there was no way of verifying the claims. Rumour became fact and Alambo was disavowed by many MNJ members and his house in Agadez ransacked. Alambo stayed in Tripoli, under Qadhafi's protection, until the revolution kicked off.

In 2011, Alambo became a recruiter for Tuareg fighters for Qadhafi's security brigades. In an interview given in Niamey in September 2011, Alambo narrates how, in June of the same year, he was asked by Qadhafi to help him fight the rebels.[40] Endowed with Qadhafi's resources, Alambo activated some of his loyal MNJ ties to recruit some of his past followers as fighters to Libya. This recruitment drive lasted approximately two months and was supplemented by spontaneous volunteers from disenfranchised MNJ ex-combatants. Some of those former MNJ combatants, interviewed in Niamey in March 2012, described both routes: 'The first option consisted in riding to Djanet from Arlit with smugglers. Then from Djanet I would go to Ghat, Awbari or Sabha and find a welcoming brigade there; there were plenty of them and it was easy to find a relative with whom to travel at no expense.' Alambo's system, by contrast, was far more organised. 'The second option consists in joining one of the periodical convoys leaving the Aïr Mountains. What you need to know is when it leaves; then you just show up and everything is taken care of: food and transport.'[41]

No more than a few hundred[42] fighters from Niger—some of whom had remained in Libya as *ishumar* for years—fought for Qadhafi, partly out of sympathy for the man who made Libya an eldorado for the young Tuaregs, partly for the money, but also for the guns and other items they expected to bring (and sell) when returning home. Testimonies of their experience as mercenaries are scarce because interviewees were reticent to be associated with the fallen leader. Those that did talk were bitter. An elderly veteran of the Tuareg rebellions in Niger told the magazine *Jeune Afrique* that he and around 200 other men left Agadez in 2011, after a call from Aghaly Alambo, in the hope of making 5,000 Euros. They, and those others who survived, came back with nothing.[43]

Alambo's last feat of assistance to Qadhafi was to facilitate the escape of senior government figures through Niger in early September 2011 with the support of Nigerien authorities,[44] who only required that they disarm on entry. Ali Qana, Qadhafi's Tuareg military commander of the southern zone was among those Alambo helped smuggle south. The Niger government's support may have been a result of past allegiances, but one may conjecture it was also tolerated, if not arranged, by the French government in order to accelerate the fall of the Libyan government. Providing further evidence to this suggestion, Niger issued a diplomatic passport to Bashir Salih, Qadhafi's former chief of staff and head of the opaque financial institution, Libya African Investment Portfolio, who despite being wanted by Interpol resided in France until early 2012, when he was allowed to flee, when opinion and media pressure for his arrest mounted.[45]

Alambo became special adviser to Amadou Hama, President of the Niger National Assembly. The agreement granted Alambo state protection and, for Niger authorities, it kept a potentially dangerous troublemaker in check. This (provisionally?) put an end to Alambo's privileged venture with Qadhafi's inner circles.

The 2011 revolution affected the personal trajectories of Nigerien Tuareg *ishumar* and fighters, and temporarily distorted the economy of northern Niger's Agadez region. Yet unlike Mali, the integrity of the Nigerien territory was left unscathed. In Niger, the structural imbalances between the north and south are less pronounced than in Mali. Secondly, the history of violence between Malian Tuareg rebels, the Malian army and its allies was far more severe than in Niger.[46] Thirdly, AQIM's presence in northern Mali inflamed political tensions and relations between communities. Fourthly, a high concentration of disputes over the control of narco-trafficking from West Africa through Mali to the Mediterranean coast made northern Mali particularly vulnerable to resumption of violence and state collapse. Finally, there were more Malian than Nigerien Tuaregs among those enrolled in Qadhafi's security brigades stationed in Sabha or Awbari who were compelled to leave Libya following Qadhafi's fall.[47] As a consequence, the aftermath of the Libyan revolution only exacerbated an already deteriorating political situation in northern Mali.

The MNLA's Libyan connection

Between 2006 and 2009—almost concomitantly with the MNJ in Niger—a young Tuareg officer, Ibrahim Ag Bahanga, led a low-intensity guerrilla war in Kidal, Mali's most northern province. Ag Bahanga, was a mid-ranking Malian army officer, an ex-rebel of the 1990s, who was then integrated into the Malian army. Despite being uneducated and not particularly articulate, his military prowess and charisma made him a potent leader. As in Niger, the poorly implemented peace agreements and integration programmes for Tuareg ex-combatants into the regular army, as well as rivalries between Tuareg groups treated differently by the regime, produced a renewed wave of insurgency. However, Ag Bahanga, unlike Alambo, refused to be bought. Despite signing a peace accord under Algerian auspices, he and his men fled north, becoming 'social bandits', righting wrongs by attacking army posts and drug convoys (a trade largely controlled at the time by specific Arab clans in the Gao region). The state armed local militias in response. Composed of fighters belonging to subaltern communities of northern Mali, including Arabs, Tuaregs, Fulanis and Songhaïs, these militias successfully pushed Ag Bahanga into exile into Libya in early 2009. He and his men remained there until the outbreak of fighting in Libya in 2011.

Libya's 17 February Revolution presented Ag Bahanga with an opportunity to recruit fighters to return to Mali.[48] Instead of becoming Qadhafi's recruiter, Ag Bahanga initiated talks between the young activists in Mali that in his absence had formed the separatist *Mouvement National de l'Azawad* (National Movement of Azawad or MNA) and Malian Tuareg soldiers serving in Libyan security brigades in southern Libya. These units were headed by Mohamed Ag Najim. Ag Najim's father had been killed by the Malian military in the Adagh Mountains (Kidal province) in 1963. He typified the kind of dedicated Saharan combatants that Qadhafi had recruited into the Islamic Legions, and later, the mostly Tuareg Maghawir brigade.

Ag Bahanga, his men in Mali, and those he managed to convince in Libya, frantically transported military equipment, cars or petrol from Ag Najim's open stockpiles, into Mali, via Algeria and Niger in July and August 2011. The armaments that crossed the borders included AK47s, grenades, mounted machine-guns, vehicles,[49] but also anti-tank missiles, rocket launchers and MANPADS (Man Portable Air Defense Systems, equipped with SA-7 or SA-24 missiles).[50] Strikingly, the constant long-distance travels back and forth of convoys of arms between Libya and Mali were hardly stoppable. Although governmental authorities of Niger made some sporadic arrests, these interdictions were more often provoked by self-interested coincidental denunciation than rigorous and permanent monitoring of the borders.[51]

The product of Ag Bahanga's hectic networking between the Mali-based youth activists of the MNA and Ag Najim's fighters became the *Mouvement national de liberation de l'Azawad* (MNLA) formed in late 2011, soon after Ag Bahanga's accidental death in a car crash in August 2011. The MNLA first hit the Malian army on 17 January 2012 in Menaka, in the Gao region, with a firepower no Tuareg rebellion in the past had managed to gather. The Malian army did not resist the offensive, and AQIM units as well as local government-sponsored proxy militias that had ousted Ag Bahanga in 2009 were forced to reconfigure their complex alliances.

The MNLA's original attack was only the first in a series of events that dramatically changed the Saharan political landscape. Using French-based media and articulate Paris-based propagandists, the MNLA postured as a pro-West, anti-AQIM, secular force, in the hope of receiving support from France and other Western powers. The support did not come; the MNLA's pro-West extraversion tactic failed and its resources shrank. At the same time, AQIM, whose bases were located in northern Mali, managed to capitalise on the anti-MNLA sentiment among northern non-Tuareg communities (Songhaï, Fulanis or Arabs). After the rout of the Malian army, the rule of northern Mali was contested by the MNLA and an Islamist coalition whose backbone was formed by AQIM cells. And it is the Islamists who eventually won.

They took control of northern Mali through a formidable reversal of alliances, as influential, formerly state-sponsored non-Tuareg militias and youth groups present in the northern cities of Gao and Timbuktu aligned with what they considered the lesser of two evils. The inclusive discourse of Islam and the harshness of Islamist groups against criminals were preferred to the nationalist stance of the MNLA and its inability to discipline troublesome—when not criminal—followers. AQIM's other master strategic move consisted in coopting Iyad Ag Ghaly, a former prominent Tuareg nationalist rebel. Ag Ghaly had followed a personal trajectory towards Salafism and his leadership was dismissed by younger activists in the consultative process that led to the formation of the MNLA. Ag Ghaly's later alliance with AQIM marked his revenge against those who had sidelined him and incapacitated the MNLA in its opposition to AQIM; confronting Ag Ghaly would have triggered deadly internecine conflicts and annihilated the chance of actualising the project of an independent Azawad.

The intention of the Islamists to push their territorial control further south in January 2013 triggered an immediate and heavy French

1. LIBYA'S UNCERTAIN REVOLUTION

1. Binder, Leonard, *In a Moment of Enthusiasm: Political Power and the Second Stratum in Egypt*, Chicago: University of Chicago, 1978.
2. See Vandewalle, Dirk, 'After Qaddafi: The Surprising Success of the New Libya', *Foreign Affairs* 91 (2012), pp. 8–15.
3. I am grateful to my colleagues Dr Amal Obeidi and Dr Zahi Mugharbi for a fascinating debate on the subject at the inaugural conference of the Center for Maghrib Studies in Libya, Tripoli, 30 Sep.–2 Oct 2013.
4. Qadhafi's invented term, roughly translated as 'state of the masses', which articulated his vision of stateless government. See Vandewalle, Dirk, *Libya Since Independence: Oil and State-building*, Ithaca: Cornell University Press, 1998, Chapter 4.
5. Boduszynski, Mieczyslaw, and Duncan Pickard, 'Libya Starts From Scratch', *Journal of Democracy*, 24, 4 (2013), p. 89.
6. See Vandewalle, 'After Qaddafi'; and *A History of Modern Libya* (2nd ed.), Cambridge: Cambridge University Press, 2012.
7. Boduszynski and Pickard, 'Libya Starts From Scratch', p. 87.
8. Lacher, Wolfram, *Fault Lines of the Revolution. Political Actors, Camps and Conflicts in the New Libya*, SWP Research Paper, Berlin: German Institute for International and Security Affairs, May 2013.
9. The best account of this tension remains Lisa Anderson's *The State and Social Transformation in Tunisia and Libya, 1830–1980*, Princeton: Princeton University Press, 1987.
10. Pelt, Adrian, *Libyan Independence and the United Nations: A Case of Planned Decolonization*, New Haven: Yale University Press, 1970.
11. For the most poignant novellic depiction of the consequences to opposition, see Matar, Hisham, *In The Country of Men*, New York: Dial Press, 2008.
12. Amidst numerous incidents, the taking of public park land in Benghazi for constructing private homes in Oct. 2013 provides a telling example.
13. Despite its oil wealth, Libya faces serious short-term budget deficits due to high subsidies and public sector wages and the occupation of oil terminals in 2013, leaving relatively little money for badly needed development purposes.
14. For a concise overview of some of the challenges this entails, see Kane, Sean, 'The Libyan Rorschach', The Middle East Channel, 12 June 2012.
15. Berman, Sheri, 'The Promise of the Arab Spring: In Political Development, No Gain Without Pain', *Foreign Affairs*, 92, 1 (2013), pp. 64–74. Berman's argument must be considered with some caution: in the European context 'systemic pressure' kept democracy movements on track, which is lacking in the Middle East and North Africa.
16. Vandewalle, Dirk, 'Libya's Ikhwan After the Revolution' (unpublished paper). The best and most dispassionate discussion can be found in El Gomati, Anas, 'Al-Qaeda's Strategy Evolves in Libya', Sadeq Institute, 18 Oct. 2013.
17. First, Ruth, *Libya: The Elusive Revolution*, London: Penguin Africa Library, 1975.

2. THE CORRIDOR OF UNCERTAINTY: THE NATIONAL TRANSITIONAL COUNCIL'S BATTLE FOR LEGITIMACY AND RECOGNITION

1. The 'corridor of uncertainty' is a phrase used in the game of cricket to refer to a situation in which a batsman must immediately determine whether to play forward or back, or to leave the delivery, and in football when the ball lands between the last defender and the goalkeeper and both players have a split second to decide who will take the ball. In both cases indecision can spell doom.

2. Mustafa Abd al-Jalil was born in Baida, east Libya, in 1952. He graduated from the department of Shari'a and Law in the Arabic Language and Islamic Studies faculty of the University of Libya in 1975. He was appointed assistant to the secretary of the public prosecutor in Baida, and appointed a judge in 1978. In 2002, he was appointed president of the court of appeals and then president of the court in Baida, before being made minister of justice in 2007.

3. Al-Toraifi, Adel, 'Mustafa Abd al-Jalil on Libya's Revolution', *Asharq Al-Awsat*, 21 Oct. 2013.

4. Ahmad Gebreel, interview with Bartu, London, 2 Nov. 2012.

5. Zahi Mugharbi feels this was done because the government saw in Ghugha a potential leader and wanted him out of the way. Zahi Mugharbi, interview with Bartu, Skype, San Francisco–Benghazi, 16 Aug. 2013.

6. Full text of Saif al-Islam's speech, as transcribed and tweeted live by @SultanAlQassemi with screenshots from Al Jazeera, 20 Feb. 2011, http://www.uruknet.info/?p=m75191&hd&l=e&fb=1 last accessed 9 May 2013.

7. Mu'ammar al-Qadhafi speech, translated 22 Feb. 2011, http://www.youtube.com/watch?v=69wBG6ULNzQ last accessed 9 May 2013.

8. Schemm, Paul, 'Battle at Army Base Broke Gadhafi Hold in Benghazi', Associated Press, http://www.washingtonpost.com/wp-dyn/content/article/2011/02/25/AR2011022505021_3.html last accessed 26 Dec. 2013.

9. Mohamed Wefati, interview with Bartu, Skype, San Francisco–Tripoli, 26 July 2013.

10. Abd al-Karim Bazama, interview with Bartu, Skype, 6 Apr. 2013.

11. Bazama, interview with Cole, Tripoli, 15 Mar. 2013.

12. Ibid.

13. Hana al-Gallal, interview with Bartu, Skype, San Francisco–Amman, 26 Aug. 2013.

14. Bazama, interview, 15 Mar. 2013.

15. Gebreel, interview, 2 Nov. 2012. Media reports of the day featured Mustafa Abd al-Jalil mentioning this.

16. Ibrahim Dabbashi, interview with Bartu, Amman, 20 Apr. 2014.

17. See transcript of Libyan Ambassador Abd al-Rahman Shalgham's address to the UN Security Council, Inner City Press, 25 Feb. 2011, http://www.innercitypress.com/unuk4libya022511.html last accessed 20 Aug. 2013.

18. Dabbashi, interview, 20 Apr. 2014; Wefati, interview, 26 July 2013.

19. Saif al Islam mentioned this twice in his 20 Feb. 2011 speech. 'Remember my words. 200 billion dollars of projects are now underway, they won't be fin-

ished ... Even the leader Qadhafi said he wants a constitution. We can even have autonomous rule, with limited central government powers. Brothers there are 200 billion dollars of projects at stake now. We will agree to all these issues immediately.' Full text of Saif al-Islam al-Qadhafi's speech, as transcribed and tweeted live by @SultanAlQassemi with screenshots from Al Jazeera, 20 Feb. 2011, http://www.uruknet.info/?p=m75191&hd&l=e&fb=1 last accessed 9 May 2013.

20. See Kurt Debeuf's blog post, 'The untold story of Libya's Mahmud Gebril', euobserver.com, 18 May 2013, for a salutary account of how Jibril won critical recognition and assistance for the revolution in its critical first days: http://blogs.euobserver.com/debeuf/2013/05/18/the-untold-story-of-libyas-mahmud-gebril/ last accessed 25 July 2013.

21. Toraifi, 'Mustafa Abd al-Jalil on Libya's Revolution'.

22. A magicJack is a voice over internet protocol (VoIP) device that plugs into the USB port of a computer, allowing any standard landline telephone connection to be plugged into it.

23. Consultation and Support Group for the 17 February Revolution, 'Urgent Steps to Activate the Work of the Libyan Transitional Council', Benghazi, 28 Feb. 2011.

24. See National Transitional Council, 'Founding Statement of the Interim Transitional National Council', 5 Mar. 2011, http://www.mpil.de/files/pdf1/founding_statement_of_the_interim_transitional_national_council.pdf last accessed 10 May 2013. The original statement was completed by Zahi Mugharbi on 2 Mar. See also, 'The Libyan Republic Declaration of the Establishment of the National Transitional Temporary Council' (unofficial translation), 2 Mar. 2011, in Filiu, Jean-Pierre, *The Arab Revolution Ten Lessons from the Democratic Uprising*, New York: Oxford University Press, 2011, pp. 163–5.

25. Mugharbi, interview, 16 Aug. 2013.

26. National Transitional Council, 'Founding Statement'.

27. Wefati, interview, 26 July 2013.

28. Ahmad Gebreel, interview with Bartu, Skype, San Francisco–Baida, 10 May 2013.

29. Diplomatic source requesting anonymity, discussion with Bartu, Amman, 1 Nov. 2012.

30. According to Chorin, Abd al-Jalil had dispatched Jibril and Isawi to Paris following the surprise visit to Benghazi in early Mar by Bernard-Henri Lévy, who phoned President Nicolas Sarkozy directly and convinced him to receive a delegation. Abd al-Jalil agreed to this on the basis that France would recognise the NTC as the sole legitimate representative of the Libyan people, which it did. Chorin, Ethan, *Exit the Colonel: The Hidden History of the Libyan Revolution*, New York: Perseus, 2012, p. 219, quoting from Levy's Nov. 2011 Benghazi memoir, Lévy, Bernard-Henri, *La Guerre sans l'aimer*, Paris, France: Bernard Grasset, 2011, p. 81.

31. For a discussion of some of the personalities and issues see McGreal, Chris,

'Libyan Rebel Efforts Frustrated by Internal Disputes over Leadership', *The Guardian*, 3 Apr. 2011, http://www.theguardian.com/world/2011/apr/03/libya-rebel-leadership-split last accessed 16 Aug. 2013; and Urban, Mark, 'The Task of Forming a More Effective anti-Gaddafi army', BBC News, 15 Apr. 2011, http://www.bbc.co.uk/blogs/newsnight/markurban/2011/04/the_task_of_forming_a_more_eff.html last accessed 16 Aug. 2013.

32. National Transitional Council, 'A Roadmap for Libya', 29 Apr. 2011, pp. 2, 5.
33. National Transitional Council, 'A Vision of a Democratic Libya, 29 Mar. 2013', para. 8c.
34. Chorin, *Exit the Colonel*, pp. 196–7, notes an earlier statement crafted by Fathi al-Ba'ja, Muhammad al-Mufti, and Salih al-Ghazal in the first week after the revolution and passed by Abd al-Hafiz Ghugha to Al Jazeera via Mohammed Nabus. Chorin quotes from al-Ba'ja, Fathi, 'Libya ila Ayn? al-Maqala allati Kassafat Wahm al-Islah', *Miyadin*, 22 May 2011, pp. 4–5.
35. Wefati, interview, 26 July 2013.
36. The Roadmap said, 'We are not interested in perpetuating the same structures and processes of the Qadhafi regime.' National Transitional Council, 'A Roadmap for Libya', 29 Apr. 2011, p. 8.
37. On 30 May, with Decision No. 67, the Council renamed the armed forces as the 'National Liberation Army'.
38. Hana al-Jalal was initially appointed minister for education but resigned over the lack of transparency and preparedness in the NTC.
39. The minister for oil and finance was Ali Tarhuni; for defence, Jalal al-Dghaili; economics, Abdullah Shamia; health, Naji Barakat; justice and human rights, Muhammad al-Alaqi; culture and community affairs, Atiya al-Awjili; social welfare, Hania al-Guma'ti; reconstruction and infrastructure, Ahmad al-Jihani; transportation and communication, Anwar al-Fituri; Islamic affairs, Salim al-Shaikhi; environment, Bilqasim al-Numir; media, Mahmud Shammam; and interior; Ahmad Hussain al-Daraht.
40. Alamin Bilhajj, Abd al-Razzaq al-Aradi, Abd al-Razzaq Bu Hajar and Mohammad Harizi represented Tripoli in the early months.
41. Arif Ali Nayid, email communication with Bartu, 27 June 2013.
42. The UN mediator Abd al-Ilah al-Khatib travelled to the 9 June Abu Dhabi meeting with Jibril and Ghugha from Benghazi after having first met Abd al-Jalil. Khatib told Jibril he thought the government in Tripoli felt in a stronger position than before. Ahmad Gebreel, interview with Bartu, Skype, San Francisco–Baida, 11 May 2013.
43. PriceWaterhouseCooper, 'Report of the Independent External Examiner of the Temporary Financing Mechanism Quarter 1, Inception through 30 September 2011', 19 Jan. 2012, para. 7.5.
44. Nayid, email communication with Bartu, 26 June 2013.
45. See 'Meeting Outcomes of the Interim National Council held on 19 March 2011', http://www.ntclibya.org/english/meeting-on-19-march-2011/ last accessed 9 May 2013.
46. Salaries were normally paid on a staggered basis from the twenty-fifth to

thirtieth of each month. In the week beginning 21 Mar. the daily withdrawal limit was 1,000 LYD (US$800). The next week it was 750 LYD (US$600).

47. Statement from the conference chair, UK Foreign Secretary William Hague, 29 Mar. 2011.

48. PriceWaterhouseCooper, 'Report of the Independent External Examiner', para. 7.2.

49. The Vitol Group is the world's largest independent oil trader. See O'Keefe, Brian, with Doris Burke, 'The Unseen Hand that Moves the World's Oil', *Fortune*, 28 Feb. 2013.

50. Libya Contact Group, 'National Transitional Council—Libya, Report on Urgent Destabilising Factors', Abu Dhabi, UAE, 9 June 2011, p. 4.

51. Libya Contact Group, 'NTC Six Month Budget', Abu Dhabi, UAE, June 2011.

52. International Contact Group on Libya, 'Report on Urgent Destabilising Factors', Abu Dhabi, UAE, 9 June 2011, p. 4.

53. Gebreel, interview, 11 May 2013.

54. Abd al-Karim Bazama, email communication with Bartu, 20 Aug. 2013.

55. PriceWaterhouseCooper, 'Report of the Independent External Examiner', para. 6.4.

56. Libya Contact Group, 'Fourth Meeting of the Libya Contact Group Chair's Statement', Istanbul, 15 July 2011.

57. PriceWaterhouseCooper, 'Report of the Independent External Examiner', paras 3.2–3.4. The Canadian government would release 1 billion Canadian dollars against frozen funds on 30 Oct. to the Ministry of Finance and Oil to pay public sector salaries for Oct. via this method.

58. On 16 Dec. 2011, UN sanctions were lifted on the Central Bank of Libya and its foreign subsidiary, the Libyan Foreign Bank, allowing these bodies to access funds previously frozen. This decision allowed Libyan government ministries to utilise these frozen assets and receive funds from abroad, using the international banking system. Thereafter the TFM stopped receiving funds. PriceWaterhouseCooper, 'Report of the Independent External Examiner', paras 1.3–1.4.

59. PriceWaterhouseCooper, 'Report of the Independent External Examiner', para. 8.18.

60. Tariq al-Tumi, conversation with Bartu, London, 23 July 2013.

61. One source claims those who encouraged Isawi to bring Yunis in for questioning, at least on the day of his death, were Salim al-Shaikhi, the Islamic affairs minister and member of the Muslim Brotherhood, the head of the 17 February Battalion, Fawzi Bu Katif, and Minister of Defence Jalal al-Dghaili, who backed out later that day.

62. Author's notes at the time from sources close to Yunis's family.

63. 'NTC Confirms General Yunis Killed AFTER Interrogation', *Tripoli Post*, 31 July 2011, http://www.tripolipost.com/articledetail.asp?c=1&i=6540 last accessed 16 Aug. 2013.

64. The Provisional National Transitional Council 'The Constituent Covenant for the Transitional Period' dated 21 June 2012, copy in author's possession.

65. Gallal, interview, 26 Aug. 2013.
66. English-language copy in author's possession.
67. Wefati, interview, 26 July 2013.
68. Ibid.
69. Gallal, interview, 26 Aug. 2013.

3. THE FALL OF TRIPOLI: PART 1

1. This and the following chapter are based primarily on 'elite interviews' cross-referenced with the authors' eyewitness knowledge and conversations in Tripoli during and after the revolution. 'Elite interviewing' in the social sciences refers to sampling interviewees because of their knowledge, normally but not always because they have decision-making power or were participants in events. Elite interviewing has methodological limitations: the pool of interviewees is limited; interviews are generally semi- or unstructured; must accommodate interviewees' wishes on topics of discussion; interview time is limited and interviewees are sometimes not recontactable. Above all information provided is not bound to objectivity and may omit key facts. To address these issues, the authors triangulated where possible between interviewees without revealing confidential information, and attempted to portray all interviewees fairly while accounting for their political and personal backgrounds. Multiple drafts of the chapter were circulated for comment, with context and further information provided by Mary Fitzgerald, Peter Bartu, Frederic Wehrey, Brian McQuinn, Bill Wheeler, and Ahmed Labnouj. Interviewees for this chapter included (in alphabetical order): Abd al-Razzaq al-Aradi, Sadat al-Badri, Abd al-Karim Bazama, Abd al-Hakim Bilhajj, Alamin Bilhajj, Adil Bu Ghrain, Hisham Bu Hajar, Fawzi Bu Katif, Miftah al-Dhuwadi, Muhammad Ghazawi, Adnan Ghirwi, Imhammad Ghula, Mahdi al-Harati, General Abd al-Salam al-Hasi, Khalid Kara, Adil Khalil, Hisham Krikshi, Mahmud Jibril, Ed Marques, Khalid al-Misrati, Arif Ali Nayid, Mustafa Nuh, Abd al-Latif Qudur, Najm al-Din Ra'is, Nasir Ra'is, Wanis al-Sahli, Ali Sallabi, Muhammad Shaikh, Anis Sharif, Khalid Sharif, Ali Tarhuni, and Muhammad Umaish. Qatari officials who played direct roles in the revolution were also consulted.
2. Forces within the Katibat Fadil fired on a funeral procession on 18 Feb., provoking protesters to attack the base. On 20 Feb., the base was breached in a suicide car bomb attack by Mehdi Ziu, provoking its looting.
3. See Chorin, Ethan, *Exit Gaddafi: The Hidden Hand of the Libyan Revolution*, London: Saqi, 2012, p. 192. In this chapter, the phrase 'security brigades' refers to all the aforementioned entities.
4. Khan, observations in Tripoli, 17 Feb. 2011.
5. Chorin, *Exit Gaddafi*, p. 188.
6. General Abd al-Salam al-Hasi, interview with Cole, Nov. 2012. Radio interview available at 'Saadi Gaddafi radio interview', YouTube, http://www.youtube.com/watch?v=nNQLbGVOnY8, last accessed on 13 Dec. 2013.
7. Fathi al-Ba'ja, interview with Cole, Benghazi, 7 Nov. 2012.

8. Chorin, *Exit Gaddafi*, pp. 193–196 based on interviews with Fathi al-Ba'ja and Abd al-Salam al-Mismari.
9. Zahi Mugharbi, interview with Cole, Skype, Washington D.C.–Benghazi, 25 Aug. 2013.
10. The NFSL was atomised after a failed military putsch effort in the 1980s; the Muslim Brotherhood had accepted a deal in 2005 whereby its members were allowed to return to Libya.
11. Sadat al-Badri and Hisham Krikshi, interview with Cole and Khan, Tripoli, 13 June 2012.
12. Badri, interview with Cole and Khan, Tripoli, 27 July 2012.
13. Ali Sallabi, interview with Cole, Doha, 13 Dec. 2012.
14. Rashid, Muhammad, 'Ilaqatuhu bi-Saif al-Islam', Al Jazeera, http://www.aljazeera.net/programs/pages/421c1276–4d9b-4224-ac48–80f3bcd32a86, last accessed 15 Dec. 2013.
15. al-Huni, Muhammad, 'al-Zalim al-Mazlum', *Al Majalla*, http://almajalla.net/2011/07/article1867, last accessed 23 Dec. 2013.
16. Chorin, *Exit Gaddafi*, pp. 197–8, based on two eyewitness interviews.
17. The general assumption is that Saif was compelled by his family to toe their harder line. Journalist Lindsey Hilsum recounts the view of an anonymous source who spoke to Saif after the speech. '[It] went through several drafts. "Saif thought he could calm people down, but in the end he had to appear the most radical so his brothers couldn't blame him. It was because of the conflict within the family. That's why he was so angry."' Hilsum, Lindsey, *Sandstorm: Libya in the Time of Revolution*, London, Faber and Faber, 2013, p. 185.
18. Saif al-Islam's speech (Al Jazeera English translation of the live broadcast), accessible at http://www.uruknet.info/?p=m75191&hd&l=e&fb=1, last accessed 23 Dec. 2013.
19. Adil Bu Ghrain, interview with Khan, 24 July 2012; Khan's personal observations in Tripoli, 17 Feb. 2011.
20. Badri, interview, 27 July 2012.
21. Mohamed Wefati, conversation with Cole, Skype, Oxford–Washington, Nov. 2013.
22. Hisham Bu Hajar, interview with Khan, Tripoli, 25 July 2012. This is the consensus of most interviewees present in Tripoli including Sadat al-Badri, Adil Bu Ghrain, Imhammad Ghula and Adnan Ghirwi.
23. Badri, interview, 27 July 2012.
24. No 'official' figures exist, because the dead were sometimes removed by security brigades, and the wounded avoided official hospitals for fear of arrest. This figure is based on the consensus of I'tilaf members Sadat al-Badri, Hisham Bu Hajar, Adil Bu Ghrain, Imhammad Ghula, Adil Khalil, Adnan Ghirwi, and Umar Khan's interactions with participants in the protests.
25. Mu'tasim al-Qadhafi, Qadhafi's son, left Libya for Venezuela on 20 Feb.; an eyewitness account generated the rumour that Qadhafi himself had left. On 21 Feb. British Foreign Secretary William Hague reported the rumour.
26. Jawad, Rana, 'Tripoli Residents "Quiet but Confused"', *BBC News*, http://

www.bbc.co.uk/news/world-middle-east-12558846, 23 Feb. 2011, republished in *Tripoli Witness*, London: Gilgamesh Publishing, 2012.

27. 'Khitab al-Za'im Mu'ammar Qadhafi', Libyan Jamahiriyya Broadcasting Corporation/YouTube, accessed at http://www.youtube.com/watch?v=YCGNZ AeKRDA on 23 Dec. 2013.

28. The original outburst ran '*tathir Libia shibr shibr bait bait dar dar zinqa zinqa, fard fard hatta tatahhur al-balad min al-dans wal-najasa.*' The extract, with 'man antom', may be viewed at 'Mu'ammar al-Qadhafi Zinqa Zinqa', *Al Arabiyya*/ YouTube, accessed at http://www.youtube.com/watch?v=u4j8wr9te WE on 23 Dec. 2013.

29. 'Gaddafi Says Will Open Arsenals to Arm Libyans if Needed', *Reuters*, 25 Feb. 2011, accessed at http://www.reuters.com/article/2011/02/25/us-libya-gaddafi-arms-idUSTRE71O50420110225 on 23 Dec. 2013.

30. Badri, interview, 27 July 2012.

31. Bu Hajar, interview, 25 July 2012.

32. Ja'far al-Janzuri (a doctor serving in a hospital treating protestors), interview with Khan, Tripoli, 25 July 2012; Imhammad Ghula, interview with Khan, Tripoli, 23 July 2012; Krikshi, interview 13 June 2012.

33. Janzuri, interview, 25 July 2012.

34. Suq al-Jum'a neighbourhood coordinator, interview with Cole, Djerba, 20 Aug. 2011.

35. Muhammad Shaikh, interview with Cole, Tripoli, 13 Sep. 2011.

36. Mhani, interview with Cole, Tripoli, 15 May 2013; Khan personal observations in Tripoli. See also Hilsum, *Sandstorm*, pp. 220–5.

37. Information collected by Muhammad Basit al-Warfalli. Arif Ali Nayid, interview with Cole, Dubai, 8 Jan. 2014.

38. Nayid, interview, 8 Jan. 2014.

39. Ibid.

40. Najm al-Din Ra'is, interview with Cole and Khan, Tripoli, 12 May 2013.

41. Muhammad Ghazawi, interview with Cole and Khan, Tripoli, 23 May 2013.

42. Ra'is, interview, 12 May 2013. Shaikh, interview, 13 Sep. 2011; Shaikh, interview with Wheeler, Tripoli, 12 Oct. 2011.

43. Ra'is, interview, 12 May 2013; Shaikh, interview, 13 Sep. 2011.

44. Hisham Krikshi, interview with Cole and Khan, Tripoli, 25 July 2012.

45. Hisham Bu Hajar, interview, 25 July 2012.

46. Ibid.

47. Nizar Kawan, interview with Fitzgerald, Tripoli, Oct. 2012; Muhammad Umaish, interview with Cole and Khan, Tripoli, 14 July 2012.

48. Shaikh, interview, 13 Sep. 2011; Badri, interview, 27 July 2012; Ra'is, interview, 12 May 2013.

49. Badri, interview, 27 July 2012.

50. Mustafa Nuh, interview with Khan, Tripoli, 28 Oct. 2012.

51. Shaikh, interview, 12 Oct. 2011.

52. Usama Riyani, interview with Khan, Tripoli, 10 Aug. 2012; Nuh, interview, 28 October 2012.

53. *I'tilaf* documents viewed by Cole and Khan; Riyani, interview, 10 Aug. 2012.
54. Bu Hajar, interview, 25 July 2012.
55. Ibid.
56. Fawzi Bu Katif, interview with Cole, Tripoli, 18 May 2013; Hamid al-Hasi, interview with Cole, Benghazi, 11 Nov. 2012.
57. Bu Katif, interview,18 May 2013. See 'Libyan Rebel Fighters Claim NATO Airstrikes Hit Their Forces', *Associated Press*, 7 Apr. 2011, http://www.foxnews.com/world/2011/04/07/libyan-rebel-fighters-claim-nato-airstrikes-hit-forces/, last accessed on 11 Jan. 2014.
58. NTC security source based in al-Fadil hotel, confidential interview with Cole, Tripoli, 10 Nov. 2012.
59. Arif Nayid, interview with Cole, Dubai, 9 Jan. 2014. Photocopied 'Provisional NTC' document with NTC stamp, viewed by Cole, 9 Jan. 2014.
60. The shipment was supplemented with private business sources from Dubai. Nayid, interview, 9 Jan. 2014.
61. Source requesting anonymity, interview with Cole. See 'Libyan rebels receiving anti-tank weapons from Qatar', *The Guardian*, 14 Apr. 2011, http://www.the-guardian.com/world/2011/apr/14/libya-rebels-weapons-qatar, last accessed on 11 Jan. 2014.
62. The prime minister opened the meeting saying that Qatar aimed 'to help the Libyan people defend themselves.' Qatar's foreign minister clarified, 'To defend yourself, you need certain equipment to do that.' See 'Arming Libya's Rebels: A Debate in Doha', *TIME*, 13 Apr. 2013, http://content.time.com/time/world/article/0,8599,2065124,00.html, last accessed on 23 Dec. 2013.
63. See 'Libyan Rebels Say They're Being Sent Weapons', *New York Times*, 16 Apr. 2011, accessed online at http://www.nytimes.com/2011/04/17/world/africa/17libya.html on 14 Jan. 2014.
64. Mahmud Jibril, interview with Cole and Fitzgerald, Tripoli, 1 December 2012.
65. Ibid.
66. Ibid.
67. NTC security source, interview 10 Nov. 2012.
68. Members of the network, confidential group interview with Cole, Jan. 2014.
69. Nayid, interview, 9 Jan. 2014.
70. Ibid. Turkish and Qatari officials were later appended to the ISRT.
71. Ibid. For example, Nayid argued that the ISRT considered placing strategic institutions under foreign technocratic management.
72. Libyan security source working closely with Mustafa Abd al-Jalil requesting anonymity, interview with Cole, Benghazi, 12 May 2013.
73. From 2007–11 Jibril served as head of the National Planning Council of Libya and of the National Economic Development Board.
74. Sallabi, interview, 13 Dec. 2012.
75. Alamin Bilhajj, interview with Fitzgerald and Cole, Tripoli, 20 Nov. 2012.
76. Sallabi, interview, 13 Dec. 2012.
77. There was significant confusion at the time between meeting participants over travel schedules. The general agreement was to move to Benghazi, but each participant followed their personal schedules.

78. Nayid, interview, 9 Jan. 2014; Abd al-Razzaq al-Aradi, interview with Khan, Tripoli, 28 Nov. 2012.

79. Alamin Bilhajj, interview, 20 Nov. 2012.

80. Umaish, interview, 14 July 2012. The other nominees included Muhammad Huraizi, Sidiq al-Kabir, Abd al-Razzaq Mukhtar. Bilhajj was not I'tilaf's choice; he was nominated by the Brotherhood.

81. The group flew first to the UAE on 9 May on aircraft supplied by the UAE's Abdullah bin Zayid, then to Qatar on 11 May on Qatari government aircraft.

82. Nayid's proposed NTC candidates included the Tebu military leader Baraka Wardaku from Murzuq, the Tuareg commander Uthnait Koni, Ali Zaidan, Faisal Qirqab from Zuwara and Abd al-Majid Saif al-Nasr from Sebha.

83. Alamin Bilhajj, interview, 20 Nov. 2012. Nayid, interview, 9 Jan. 2014.

84. Abd al-Hakim Bilhajj, interview with Khan, Tripoli, 25 Nov. 2012; Miftah al-Dhuwadi, interview with Fitzgerald and Khan, Tripoli, Oct. 2012.

85. Dhuwadi, interview, Oct. 2012.

86. Sallabi, interview, 13 Dec. 2012.

87. Abd al-Hakim Bilhajj, interview, 25 Nov. 2012.

88. Sallabi, interview, 13 Dec. 2012.

89. Libyan member of an operations room requesting anonymity, interview with Cole, Tripoli, 10 May 2013; Sallabi, interview, 13 Dec. 2012.

90. Sallabi, interview, 13 Dec. 2012.

91. Abd al-Hakim Bilhajj, interview, 25 Nov. 2012.

92. Ibid.

93. Western diplomat, interview with Cole, Tripoli, 18 Sep. 2011.

94. Alamin Bilhajj, interview with Cole, and Khan, 1 Dec. 2012.

95. Nayid, interview, 9 Jan. 2014.

96. Abd al-Hakim Bilhajj, interview, 25 Nov. 2012.

97. Ibid.

98. Western diplomat, interview, 18 Sep. 2011.

99. Nayid, interview, 9 Jan. 2014.

100. Ibid.

101. Bu Katif, interview, 18 May 2013.

102. Head of administration of the Rafallah al-Sahati Companies, interview with Cole, Benghazi, 5 Nov. 2012; Nayid, interview, 9 Jan. 2014.

103. Sallabi, interview, 13 Dec. 2012.

104. The figure three comes from an author interview with a person knowledgable of the shipments. For the figure five, see Dagher, Sam, Charles Levinson and Margaret Coker, 'Tiny Kingdom's Huge Role in Libya Draws Concern', *Wall Street Journal*, 17 Oct. 2011, http://online.wsj.com/news/articles/SB1000142 4052970204002304576627000922764650 last accessed 23 Dec. 2013.

105. Misrati, interview, 22 May 2013.

106. Nayid, interview, 9 January 2014.

107. Western diplomat, interview, 18 Sep. 2011.

108. Senior Qatari official, interview with Cole, Doha, 16 Jan. 2013.

89. Jibril, interview, 1 Dec. 2012.
90. Alamin Bilhajj, interview, 1 Dec. 2012; Libyan security source, interview, 26 Mar 2013.
91. Tripoli battalion fighter, interview with Cole, Tripoli, 4 Sep. 2011; NTC defence spokesman, interview, 11 Sep. 2011.
92. Abd al-Hakim Bilhajj, interview with Khan, Tripoli, 25 Nov. 2012.
93. Both men went on to form the 'National Guard', a parallel militia entity. Khalid Sharif, interview with Khan, 20 Oct. 2012.
94. Ali Sallabi, interview with Cole, Doha, 13 Dec. 2012.
95. Western diplomat requesting anonymity.
96. Firnana, interview, 10 Sep. 2011. According to a member of one Islamist grouping to have travelled to Zintan in early October to exhort Zintani groups to remain in the capital for this purpose. Anis al-Sharif, interview with Cole, Tripoli, 20 November 2012.
97. Cole and Fitzgerald interview with Mahdi al-Harati, 5 Sep. 2011; Abd al-Hakim Bilhajj, interview, 25 Nov. 2012.
98. See 'Belhaj Arrested then Released at Tripoli Airport', *Tripoli Post*, 26 Nov. 2011, http://www.tripolipost.com/articledetail.asp?c=1&i=7368 last accessed 20 Apr. 2014.
99. Abd al-Hakim Bilhajj, interview, 25 Nov. 2012; Abd al-Wahhab al-Qa'id, interview with Khan, 22 June 2012.
100. Anis Sharif, interview, 20 November 2012.
101. Abd al-Hakim Bilhajj, interview, 25 Nov. 2012.
102. Tarhuni, interview, 9 May 2013.
103. Anis Sharif, interview, 20 November 2012.
104. Ibid.; Jibril, interview, 1 Dec. 2012.
105. Tarhuni, interview, 9 May 2013.
106. Hisham Bu Hajar, interview, 15 Sep. 2012; Firnana, interview, 10 Sep. 2011; Aradi, interview, 3 Mar 2013.
107. According to Bu Hajar, 'Jibril wrote the law ordering 13 people to form the Supreme Security Committee. It was headed by [former police officer] Mahmud Sharif, but the *thuwwar* resisted Sharif, so Tarhuni asked me to head it.' Hisham Bu Hajar, interview, 15 Sep. 2012.
108. Source requesting anonymity, interview with Cole.
109. Jibril, interview, 1 Dec. 2012.
110. Tarhuni, interview, 9 May 2013.
111. Ghula, interview, 23 July 2012.
112. For background see Dagher, Sam, Charles Levinson and Margaret Coker, 'Tiny Kingdom's Huge Role in Libya Draws Concern', *Wall Street Journal*, 17 Oct. 2011, http://online.wsj.com/news/articles/SB100014240529702040 02304576627000922764650 last accessed 23 Dec. 2013.
113. Dagher et al., 'Tiny Kingdom's Huge Role'; Abd al-Hakim Bilhajj, interview, 25 Nov. 2012.
114. Jibril, interview, 1 Dec. 2012.
115. Ali Tarhuni, interview, 9 May 2013.

116. Ali Tarhuni, interview, 9 May 2013; Hisham Bu Hajar, interview, 15 Sep. 2012; Aradi, interview, 3 Mar 2013.
117. Hisham Krikshi, interview, 25 July 2012.
118. Cole interview with former LIFG member, Tripoli, 15 Nov. 2012.
119. Western diplomat requesting anonymity.

5. NATO's INTERVENTION

1. Borghard, Erica D., and Constantino Pischedda, 'Allies and Airpower in Libya', *Parameters*, 42, 1 (2012), pp. 63–74; Wehrey, Frederic, 'The Hidden Story of Airpower in Libya (And What it Means for Syria)', Foreign Policy. com, 11 Feb. 2013; Barrie, Douglas, 'Libya's Lessons: The Air Campaign', *Survival*, 54, 6, (2012–13), pp. 57–65.
2. Chivvis, Christopher, 'Libya and the Future of Liberal Intervention', *Survival*, 54, 6, (2012–13), p. 69.
3. NATO used the terms 'Anti-Qadhafi Forces' (AQF) and 'Pro-Qadhafi Forces' (PQF) to refer to armed combatants in Libya during Operation Unified Protector. 'Anti-Qadhafi Forces' in this chapter refers to all Libyan armed actors fighting Qadhafi regardless of political or social affiliation.
4. Commanders such as Abd al-Fatah Yunis and Wanis Bu Hamada are from the Obaidat tribe.
5. Libyan Air Force officer who planned and led the air strikes, interview with Wehrey, Benghazi, Libya, 11–12 Mar. 2012; Libyan Mirage F-1 pilot, Tripoli, Libya, 7 Mar 2012.
6. Commander of Banina Air Base, interview with Wehrey, Benghazi, 12 Mar 2012.
7. Defected Libyan Air Force officers, interview with Wehrey, Banina Air Base, Benghazi, 11 Mar 2012.
8. Malta- and Misrata-based opposition coordinator, interview with Wehrey, Tripoli, 8 Mar 2012.
9. Misrata-based opposition planner and field commander, interview with Wehrey, Misrata, 13 Mar 2012.
10. Libyan Air Force officer and Zintan-based opposition commander, interview with Wehrey, Tripoli, Libya, 10 Mar, 2012; Misratans recalled the story of Ali Hadith al-Obeidi, an Air Force general who defected from Mitiga Air Base and walked for nearly two weeks to join the opposition in Misrata; he was later killed in the assault on Zlitan. Malta- and Misrata-based opposition coordinator, interview, 8 Mar. 2012.
11. Chief of Zintan Military Council, interview with Wehrey, Zintan, 15 Mar 2012.
12. Chivvis, 'Libya and the Future', p. 69.
13. Senior NATO air commander, telephone interview with Wehrey, 12 Dec. 2013.
14. Ibid.
15. Senior NATO planner, telephone interview with Wehrey, 13 Dec. 2013.

23. Human Rights Watch, 'Death of a Dictator: Bloody Vengeance in Sirte', 2012.
24. Chapter 11, p. 279.
25. Human Rights Council, A/HRC/19/68, p. 120.
26. Human Rights Council, A/HRC/19/68, pp. 122–30.
27. Amnesty International, 'The Battle for Libya', pp. 72–3.
28. Human Rights Council, A/HRC/19/68, pp. 155–7.
29. Human Rights Council, A/HRC/19/68, pp. 78–9.
30. Human Rights Council, A/HRC/17/44, p. 6.
31. Human Rights Council, A/HRC/19/68, pp. 136–7.
32. Iraq is however sometimes studied as an example. The Committee on Integrity and Patriotism said it studied Debaathification and rejected its blanket approach.
33. Human Rights Council, A/HRC/19/68, p. 42.
34. Human Rights Council, A/HRC/19/68, pp. 42–3. The agency reported directly to Qadhafi, and held jurisdiction over Abu Slim and Ain Zara prisons, which held political prisoners without trial.
35. The Revolutionary Guards were volunteers and were accepted for training through recommendations of other members. They underwent thorough security checks to ensure loyalty and were required to swear an oath to never betray Qadhafi. Human Rights Council, A/HRC/19/68, p. 43.
36. Human Rights Council, A/HRC/19/68, p. 41.
37. Office of the High Commissioner for Human Rights, 'Rule-of-Law Tools for Post-Conflict States: Vetting: An Operational Framework', 2006, p. 4.
38. United Nations Secretary-General, 'Rule of Law and Transitional Justice in Conflict and Post-conflict Societies', S/2004/616, para. 52.
39. See International Crisis Group, *Divided We Stand: Libya's Enduring Conflicts*, Brussels: International Crisis Group, vol. 130, 14 Sep. 2012.
40. See United Nations Support Mission in Libya, 'Torture and Deaths in Detention in Libya', 2013.
41. Ibid.
42. In 1971, the People's Court was established to try members of the former royal family and others accused of corruption, and conducted closed-door trials of political opponents. While it was abolished in 2005, a replacement court, the Supreme Security Court, was established in 2007. The trials of the court did not meet the minimum standards of fair trial, denying defendants the right to adequate defence, the right to be informed of charges, and the right to appeal. Lawyers were often denied access to political prisons such as Abu Slim. For further details see Human Rights Council, A/HRC/19/68, p. 39.
43. Article 35 of the Constitutional Declaration stated, 'All the provisions prescribed in the existing legislations shall continue to be effective in so far as they are not inconsistent with the provisions hereof until they are amended or repealed. Each reference in these legislations to the "People's Congresses", the "General People's Congress", shall be deemed as a reference to the Interim Transitional National Council or to the National Public Conference. Each reference to "General People's Committee" or the "People's Committees" shall

be deemed as a reference to the Executive Office, to the members of the Executive Office, to the interim government or to the members thereof each within its respective area of jurisdiction. Each reference to (Great Socialist People's Libyan Arab Jamahiriyya) shall be deemed as a reference to (Libya).'

44. Ahmetasevic, Nidzara, 'Sarajevo's Model under Threat', *International Justice Tribune*, 15 Feb. 2012. In 2010, prosecutors were involved in 365 cases against some 1,165 individuals. According to National War Crimes Strategy, prosecutions in Bosnia were expected to last another fifteen years.

45. Human Rights Council, A/HRC/17/44, p. 21.

46. It is insufficient to demonstrate that murder, torture, or disappearances took place; it is also necessary to show *how* senior members of the regime participated, even where they did not give direct orders. Much expertise exists at the international level on how to conduct such investigations, including on information technology, analysis capabilities, witness protection and evidence storage.

47. Public Redacted Decision on the Admissibility of the case against Saif al-Islam, *The Prosecutor v. Saif al-Islam Gaddafi and Abdullah Al-Sanusi*, 31 May 2013.

48. Prosecutor versus Saif al-Islam Gaddafi and Abdullah al-Sanusi, Public Redacted Decision on Admissibility of the Case Against Abdullah al-Sanusi, ICC-01/11–01/11, 11 Oct. 2013.

49. The first Additional Protocol to the Geneva Conventions provides that 'at the end of hostilities, the authorities in power shall endeavour to grant the broadest possible amnesty to persons who have participated in the armed conflict, or those deprived of their liberty for reasons related to the armed conflict, whether they are interned or detained'. See Additional Protocol I to the Geneva Conventions of 1949, Article 6 (5).

50. Wierda interviews with Libyan judiciary, Tripoli, Dec. 2012.

51. General National Congress Decision 59 refers to the creation of a committee to 'undertake the review and investigation of Abu Slim Massacre of 1996. It shall identify the number of missing persons and facilitate procedures pertaining to the proof of decease, as well as provide a proposal regarding compensations and privileges to be granted to their families and relatives.'

52. For an extensive discussion on these issues see United Nations High Commissioner for Refugees, 'Report on Housing, Land and Property Issues and the Response to Displacement in Libya', Geneva, 2012.

8. FINDING THEIR PLACE: LIBYA'S ISLAMISTS DURING
AND AFTER THE REVOLUTION

1. The information in this chapter is based on the author's personal observations and interviews in Libya from Feb. to Apr. and Aug. to Sep. 2011, followed by several months' fieldwork in Libya in 2012. Interviewees from the Muslim Brotherhood include Bashir al-Kubti, Alamin Bilhajj, Abdullah Shamia, Abd al-Latif Karmus, Nizar Kawan and Fawzi Bu Katif. From the LIFG/LIMC, Abd al-

Hakim Bilhajj, Sami al-Sa'adi, Miftah al-Dhuwadi, Abdullah Zway, Khalid al-Sharif, Anis al-Sharif, Abd al-Wahhab al-Qa'id and Isma'il Kamuka. Others interviewed for the chapter include Ali Sallabi, Muhammad Bu Sidra and Fathi al-Ba'ja.

2. On Islamism and the evolution of Islamist movements, see Roy, Olivier, *The Failure of Political Islam*, London: I. B. Tauris, 1994; Roy, Olivier, *Globalised Islam: The Search for a New Ummah*, London: Hurst, 2004; Kepel, Gilles, *Jihad: The Trail of Political Islam*, London: I.B. Tauris, 2004.
3. Alamin Bilhajj, interview with Fitzgerald, Tripoli, 12 Oct. 2012.
4. Fitzgerald observations in eastern Libya, Feb.–Apr. 2011.
5. Bashir al-Kubti, Alamin Bilhajj, Abdullah Shamia, Abd al-Latif Karmus, interviews with Fitzgerald, Tripoli, Oct.–Nov. 2012.
6. Abd al-Hakim Bilhajj, Sami al-Sa'adi, Miftah al-Dhuwadi, Abdullah Zway, Anis al-Sharif, interviews with Fitzgerald, Tripoli, Oct.–Nov. 2012.
7. Abdullah Shamia, interview with Fitzgerald, Tripoli, 10 Oct. 2012.
8. Ali Sallabi, Doha, interview with Cole, 13 Dec. 2012.
9. Fitzgerald interview, Benghazi, Feb. 2011.
10. Other Libyan opposition groups, interviews with Fitzgerald, Oct.–Nov. 2012.
11. Abd al-Latif Karmus, interview with Fitzgerald, Tripoli, 17 Oct. 2012.
12. Alamin Bilhajj, interview, 12 Oct. 2012.
13. Sulaiman Abd al-Qadir, general guide of the Libyan Muslim Brotherhood, interviewed by Sami Klaib. Liqa' Khas, Al-Jazeera Arabic, 30 May 2009.
14. Shamia, interview with Fitzgerald, Tripoli, 15 October, 2012.
15. Karmus, interview with Fitzgerald, 20 October, 2012.
16. Miftah al-Dhuwadi, interview with Fitzgerald, Tripoli, 1 Nov. 2012.
17. Alamin Bilhajj, interview, 12 Oct. 2012.
18. Fitzgerald observations and interviews in eastern Libya, Feb.–Apr. 2011.
19. Anis al-Sharif, interview with Fitzgerald, Tripoli, 20 Oct. 2012.
20. Alamin Bilhajj, interview, 12 Oct. 2012.
21. Ibid.
22. Ibid.
23. Fathi al-Ba'ja, Benghazi, interview with Fitzgerald, 5 Nov. 2012.
24. Alamin Bilhajj, interview, 12 Oct. 2012.
25. Ibid.
26. Ba'ja, interview, 5 Nov. 2012.
27. Benghazi-based aide to Mustafa Abd al-Jalil, telephone interview with Fitzgerald, 5 Oct. 2011.
28. Source requesting anonymity, interview with Fitzgerald, Tripoli, 22 Oct. 2012.
29. Ba'ja, interview, 5 Nov. 2012.
30. Stevens, Christopher, 'Die Hard in Derna: Report ID no. 08TRIPOLI430', Libya WikiLeaks cables, 6 Feb. 2008. Published in *The Daily Telegraph*, 31 Jan. 2011.
31. Felter, Joseph, and Brian Fishman, *Al-Qa'ida's Foreign Fighters in Iraq: A First Look at the Sinjar Records*, West Point, NY: Combating Terrorism Centre, 2007.

32. Robertson, Nic, and Paul Cruickshank, 'Al-Qaeda Send Veteran Jihadist to Establish Presence in Libya', *CNN*, 29 Dec. 2011.
33. Abd al-Basit Bu Hliqa, interview with Fitzgerald, Tripoli, 10 Nov. 2012.
34. Abd al-Mun'im al-Madhuni, interview with Fitzgerald, Ajdabiya, 21 Mar. 2011.
35. Ibid., Bu Hliqa, interview with Fitzgerald.
36. Source requesting anonymity, interview with Fitzgerald, Tripoli, 5 Nov. 2012.
37. Abd al-Hakim Bilhajj, interview with Fitzgerald, Tripoli, 20 Nov. 2012.
38. Bu Hliqa, interview 10 Nov. 2012.
39. Ibid., Bu Hliqa, interview with Fitzgerald.
40. Ibid., Bu Hliqa, interview with Fitzgerald.
41. Fawzi Bu Katif, interview with Fitzgerald, Benghazi, 20 Feb. 2012.
42. Badin became a prominent figure in the federalist movement that developed in eastern Libya within months of the fall of Gaddafi.
43. Bin Hamid later became a commander in the Libya Shield Forces, formed after the revolution and ostensibly under the control of the chief of staff.
44. Source requesting anonymity, interview with Fitzgerald, Benghazi, 29 Oct. 2012.
45. Bilhajj, Abd al-Hakim, 'The Revolution Belongs to All Libyans, Secular or Not', *The Guardian*, 27 Sep. 2011.
46. Source requesting anonymity, interview with Fitzgerald, Benghazi, 23 Sep. 2011.
47. Source requesting anonymity, interview with Fitzgerald, Tripoli, 2 Oct. 2012.
48. Ba'ja, interview, 5 Nov. 2012.
49. Ali Sallabi, interviews with Fitzgerald, Tripoli, Sep. 2011, and Benghazi, July 2012.
50. Shamia, interview, 10 Oct. 2012.
51. Ibid.
52. Alamin Bilhajj, interview, 12 Oct. 2012.
53. Source requesting anonymity, interview with Fitzgerald, Tripoli, 26 Feb. 2012.
54. Ba'ja, interview, 5 Nov. 2012.
55. Khalid al-Sharif, interview with Fitzgerald, Tripoli, 15 Nov. 2012.
56. Abd al-Hakim Bilhajj, interview, 20 Nov. 2012.
57. Bu Hliqa, interview 10 Nov. 2012.
58. Isma'il Kamuka, interview with Fitzgerald, Tripoli, 20 Nov. 2012.
59. Bu Hliqa, interview 10 Nov. 2012.
60. Ibid., Bu Hliqa, interview with Fitzgerald.
61. Fitzgerald observations at Abu Slim commemoration ceremony, Tripoli, June 2012.
62. Sami al-Sa'adi, interview with Fitzgerald, Tripoli, Mar. 2012.
63. Abd al-Hakim Bilhajj, interview with Fitzgerald, Tripoli, 5 Sep. 2011.
64. Sami al-Sa'adi, interview with Fitzgerald, Tripoli, 13 Oct. 2012.
65. The Arabic word *umma* can be translated as nation in the sense of the universal community—or nation—of Muslims.
66. Khalid al-Sharif, interview 15 Nov. 2012.
67. Pushed by the author to define what they meant by this, JCP, Homeland and

Moderate Nation members tended to explain it as meaning no law passed would contradict Islam.

68. Muhammad Bu Sidra, independent candidate for Benghazi, interview with Fitzgerald, 9 July 2012.
69. Muhammad Sawan, interview with Fitzgerald, Tripoli, 15 June 2012.
70. Source requesting anonymity, interview with Fitzgerald, Tripoli, 16 June 2012.
71. Muhammad al-Zahawi, interview with Fitzgerald, 17 Sep. 2012.
72. Fitzgerald interviews and observations, Benghazi, June 2012.
73. Zahawi, interview, 17 Sep. 2012.
74. Several Dirna residents, interviews with Fitzgerald during 2012 and 2013.
75. Source requesting anonymity, interview with Fitzgerald, Tripoli, 15 Nov. 2012.
76. Senior figures in JCP and Homeland Party, interviews with Fitzgerald, Tripoli and Benghazi, July 2012.
77. Bashir al-Kubti, interview with Fitzgerald, Benghazi, 9 July 2012.
78. Senior figures in JCP and Homeland Party, interviews, July 2012.
79. Anis al-Sharif, interview with Fitzgerald, Tripoli, 2 July 2012.
80. Imhammad Ghula, interview with Fitzgerald, Tripoli, 10 July 2012.

9. BARQA REBORN? EASTERN REGIONALISM AND LIBYA'S POLITICAL TRANSITION

1. The author was Benghazi representative for the Centre for Humanitarian Dialogue, an independent mediation organisation, from Nov. 2011 to June 2012. The author has subsequently worked with the United Nations; the views expressed are solely those of the author and do not represent the official views of the United Nations.
2. The statement listed eight cities in western and southern Libya that sent representatives to join the NTC and noted it was awaiting a Tripoli delegation. See 'Founding Statement of the Interim National Transitional Council', 5 Mar. 2011.
3. Qadhafi's second son and heir apparent, Saif al-Islam, hinted at this eventuality in his 20 Feb. 2011 televised speech where he indicated that a constitution could be prepared that 'even ... [has] ... autonomous rule, with limited central powers'.
4. Vandewalle, Dirk, *Libya since Independence: Oil and Statebuilding*, Ithaca: Cornell University Press, 1998, pp. 43–5.
5. Najem, Faraj, 'Tribe, Islam and State in Libya', unpublished PhD dissertation on file with the author, pp. 170–9.
6. Obeidi, Amal, *Political Culture in Libya*, Richmond: Curzon Press, 2001, p. 116.
7. The main Jibarna tribes are the Awaghir, the Magharba, the Abid and the Arafa. The major Harabi tribes are the Ubaida, the Hasa, the Fayid, the Bara'sa and the Dursa. The Sa'adi, at least according to their own origin story, see themselves as bound by blood lineage and common genealogical descent and as purely Arab Bedouin. This is as compared to the east's lesser client tribes, which are perceived as more mixed between Arabs and indigenous Berbers.

8. Khadduri, Majid, *Modern Libya: A Study in Political Development*, Baltimore: Johns Hopkins Press, 1963, p. 8.

9. Obeidi, *Political Culture in Libya*.

10. See Pelt, Adrian, *Libyan Independence and the United Nations. A Case of Planned Decolonization*, New Haven: Yale University Press, 1970, pp. 36–57.

11. Vandewalle, *Libya since Independence*, p. 49.

12. Vandewalle, Dirk, *A History of Modern Libya*, Cambridge: Cambridge University Press, pp. 47–8.

13. Obeidi, *Political Culture in Libya*, p. 116.

14. Vandewalle, *A History of Modern Libya*, p. 49. During the 1960s, wealthy and economically powerful Tripolitanian families such as the Fakini and Muntasir families (from the Western Mountains and Misrata, respectively) also entered the kingdom's formal and informal power structures. See Lacher, Wolfram, 'Families, Tribes and Cities in the Libyan Revolution', *Middle East Policy Council*, 18, 4 (2011).

15. Vandewalle, *A History of Modern Libya*, p. 50.

16. According to the US Government's Energy Information Agency, the Sirt Basin is still estimated to account for approximately 80 per cent of Libya's 44 billion barrels of proven oil reserves.

17. For a fuller exposition of this argument, see Wright, John, *A History of Libya*, London: Hurst Publishers, 2010, p. 187.

18. Full text of Saif al-Islam al-Qadhafi's speech on 20 Feb. 2011, transcribed by Sultan al-Qasimi and available at http://mylogicoftruth.wordpress.com/2011/02/20/full-text-of-saif-gaddafis-speech/

19. See Wehrey, Frederic, 'The Struggle for Security in Eastern Libya', Washington DC: Carnegie Endowment for International Peace, 2012.

20. See Lacher, 'Families, Tribes and Cities'.

21. Obeidi, *Political Culture in Libya*, p. 131.

22. St. John, Ronald Bruce, *Libya: From Colony to Revolution*, Oxford: OneWorld Publications, 2011, pp. 292–3.

23. Tarkowski Tempelhof, Susanne, and Manal Omar, 'Stakeholders of Libya's February 17 Revolution', Washington DC: United States Institute of Peace, Report No. 300, 2012, pp. 6–7. Upon the author's arrival in Benghazi in early Nov. 2011, internet service and domestic cellphone calls were still free of charge.

24. See NTC, 'Founding Statement'.

25. Tarkowski Tempelhof and Omar, 'Stakeholders'.

26. In the context of Libya's conservative and observant society it can be difficult to pinpoint what constitutes an 'Islamist'. Aside from listing specific groups, one useful classifier may be to consider Islamists as those actors whose leading goal and motivation for the revolution was to see Islam become the main legal and political reference point for the new Libyan state.

27. See for example, Husken, Thomas, 'The Neo-Tribal Competitive Order in the Borderland of Egypt and Libya', in Engel, Ulf and Paul Nugent, eds., *Respacing*

Africa, Boston: Brill, 2010, pp. 181–2. The author encountered significant antipathy towards the Muslim Brotherhood in the Ubaida stronghold of Tubruq, where residents indicated that the Brotherhood's Freedom and Justice Party would not be allowed to open a local representation office—Kane, meetings with Tubruq Local Council, Tubruq Youth Council, academics and the Tubruq Union of Revolutionary Phalanxes, Tubruq, 1 Feb. 2012.

28. The Arabian tribes that originally migrated to eastern Libya during the eleventh century also settled in Tripolitania, and some tribes in the city of Tripoli are said to directly descend from them. However, given the more extensive urbanisation, trade and intermixing that occurred in western Libya, the ability to trace lineage to a common ancestor is less prevalent. Tribes in western Libya therefore consist not just of traditional shared lineage associations but also geographic alliances that form large semi-tribal entities.

29. Kane notes of a public hearing on the draft Libyan electoral law held at the Da'wa Islamiya Conference Centre in Benghazi on 8 Jan. 2012. Professor Abd al-Qadir Qadura, Professor of Constitutional Law at Benghazi University, meeting with Kane, 20 Nov. 2011. Qadura is also a member of the influential Awaghir tribe, the second largest of the Sa'adi tribes.

31. Lacher, 'Families, Tribes and Cities'.

32. Ibid.

33. See International Republican Institute, 'Survey of Public Opinion in Eastern Libya: October 12–25, 2011', Washington DC, 2011.

34. Kane interviews, Dirna, 14–15 Apr. 2012. The regime reportedly cut off water and electricity to towns suspected of harbouring LIFG militants.

35. In late 2012 and 2013, the return of these institutions to Benghazi was to become a political demand of eastern federalists and in June 2013 the Libyan Government ordered the return of the National Oil Company, Libyan Airlines, and other companies to Benghazi. The move was welcomed locally and met with dancing in the street, but as of writing had yet to be implemented. See Ruhayem, Ahmed, 'Federalists Celebrate Return of NOC to Benghazi', *Libya Herald*, 7 June 2013.

36. Wehrey, 'Struggle for Security'.

37. Ubaida tribal notables from the eastern town of Tubruq, interviews with Kane, 14 Apr. 2012.

38. See 'Libyans protest against Jalil, NTC', AFP World News, 12 Dec. 2011.

39. See 'NTC Declares Benghazi Economic Capital after Demos', AFP World News, 12 Dec. 2011.

40. Dr Peter Bartu, UN political advisor, interview with Kane, Benghazi, Dec. 2012.

41. For further details on this process see Pelt, *Libyan Independence*.

42. Article 15 in the unofficial UNSMIL Translation of the 3 Jan. 2012 draft of the Libyan Electoral Law.

43. The author attended all three conferences.

44. Kane, notes of public hearings at Da'wa Islamiya Conference Centre on 8 Jan. 2012.

45. Kane, notes of public hearings attended at Benghazi International University on 5 Jan. 2012.

46. Kane, notes of public hearings at Benghazi University Faculty of Law on 9 Jan. 2012.

47. See 'Protesters Storm Grounds of Libya's Interim Government's Headquarters in Benghazi', Associated Press, 21 Jan. 2012.

48. NTC representatives attending the meeting on 21 Jan. 2012, interviews with Kane.

49. Article 4 of Libya's National Transitional Council's 'Law No. 4 of 2012 Concerning General National Conference Elections'.

50. See El Houni, Hind and Nadine Sherif, 'A Martyr in the Making—But for the Right Cause?', *Libya Herald*, 9 June 2012.

51. Wehrey, 'Struggle for Security'.

52. See Lacher, Wolfram, 'Fault Lines of the Revolution: Political Actors, Camps and Conflicts in the New Libya', Berlin: Stiftung Wissenschaft und Politik, 2013, p. 21.

53. See al-Shaheibi, Rami, 'Eastern Libya Declares Semiautonomous Region', Associated Press, 6 Mar. 2012.

54. Unofficial translation of 'The Conference of Barqa Citizens—Closing Statement', 6 Mar. 2012, on file with author.

55. See Shaheibi, 'Eastern Libya Declares'.

56. 'Libya Leader Claims Arabs Supporting "Sedition" in East', AFP, 7 Mar. 2012.

57. For example, the Muslim Brotherhood, the longtime opposition group the National Front for the Salvation of Libya, the Democratic National Party, the Free National Party, the Libya Revolutionists Union, the 17 of February Revolutionists and the Democratic Libyan Youth Society all released statements opposing federalism. See 'Creation of Cyrenaica Council sparks furious federalism row', *Libya Herald*, 7 Mar. 2012.

58. 'Libya to Open Government Offices in Benghazi, Sabha "to avert" federalism', Financial Times Agency, 14 Mar. 2012.

59. Constitutional Amendment No. 1 (2012) on 'Amendment of Certain Items of Article 30 of the Constitutional Declaration', 13 Mar. 2011. The caveat of the two-thirds majority plus one appears intended to avoid a repeat of the 1951 experience where two regions can simply disregard the views of a third.

60. 'Libya's Federalist Camp Clings to Autonomy Bid', AFP, 17 Apr. 2012.

61. The regional guard was reportedly a force of approximately 3,000 men headed by Abd al-Jawad Bidin and with strong representation from the Sa'adi Magharba tribe of Ajdabiya.

62. Khan, Umar, and George Grant, 'NTC Takes Responsibility for Constitution from National Conference', *Libya Herald*, 5 July 2012.

63. See International Republican Institute, 'Survey of Public Opinion in Eastern Libya'.

64. See 'Cyrenaica Council Rejected by Benghazi Council', *Libya Herald*, 7 Mar. 2012.

65. Sulaiman Khalifa of the National Democratic Alliance as quoted in Fetouri,

Issam, 'Update 2—Eastern Libya Defies Tripoli to Create Autonomous Council', Reuters, 6 Mar. 2012.

66. See Lacher, 'Families, Tribes and Cities'.

67. Workshops held in Benghazi, Ajdabiya, Baida, Dirna and Tubruq. For example, in Baida, when discussions of federalism began participants took the author to the memorial to the city's revolutionary martyrs and explained that some of city's youth had been killed after volunteering to help defend the besieged western city of Misrata against pro-Qadhafi troops. Emotional parents related that they had chosen for their sons' remains to stay in Misrata as a symbol of national unity.

68. The Ubaida hold Mustafa Abd al-Jalil partially to blame for the assassination of General Abd al-Fattah Yunis, a prominent member of the Ubaida.

69. The Zway are the largest of Barqa's approximately 25 client tribes (*marabtin*) and are historically affiliated with the Marghaba. See Najem, 'Tribe, Islam and State in Libya'.

70. Tribal elders from these towns, interviews with Kane, Ajdabiya, 24 Jan. 2012.

71. Remarks attributed to Abdullah bin Idris, member of the Jalu town council in eastern Libya's desert interior, in 'Freed of Gadhafi, Libya's Instability only Deepens', Associated Press, 3 Mar. 2012. The Sarir oilfield, Libya's largest, as well as the nearby Masila oil field are located on Zwaya tribal land and produce about 17 per cent of the country's total crude output, see Geographic Services, Inc., 'Geographical and Tribal Factors at Play in Kufrah, Libya', 22 Sep. 2011. The Zwaya also wielded this threat against the Qadhafi regime in the early weeks of the revolution.

72. Kane, interviews held in Dirna, 14–15 Apr. 2012.

73. See Pelt, *Libyan Independence*, p. 44.

74. See 'Creation of Cyrenaica Council Sparks Furious Federalism Row', *Libya Herald*, 7 Mar. 2012.

75. Tubruq Local Council, Tubruq Youth Council, academics and the Tubruq Union of Revolutionary Phalanxes, meetings with Kane, Tubruq, 1 Feb. 2012.

76. See Youssef, Nancy A., 'In Libya, Chaos is Taking a Toll on Freedom of Press, Speech', *McClatchy DC*, 18 June 2013.

77. 'NTC Spokesman Denies Chairman Threatens "Force of Weapons" against Federalism', WAL news agency, 7 Mar. 2012.

78. On 29 June 2012, *Al-Sharq Al-Awsat* quoted Abu Bakr Bu'airi, head of the political office for the Barqa Council, hinting that 'maybe' border closures between east and west Libya were signs that 'we will not permit electoral material to ... enter this region'. See also, Grant, George, 'Federalists Steal Ballot Papers in Ajdabiya and Brega; Delay Vote', *Libya Herald*, 7 July 2012.

79. Voter turnout figures provided by the Electoral Support of Office of UNSMIL via email on 27 Oct. 2013.

80. UNSMIL Media Report, 8 July 2012. For example, a post on the Al-Manara Media Group site entitled 'Residents of Benghazi Are an Example of Nationalism and a Slap to the Face of Those Calling for Boycotting Elections' received 120,000 'likes'.

81. See Doherty, Megan, '"Give us Change We Can See": Citizen's Views of

Libya's Political Process', National Democratic Institute findings from focus groups conducted from 28 Oct.–10 Nov. 2012.

82. Quoted in Laessing, Elf, and Ghaith Shennib, 'In Libya's East, a Former Rebel Commander Tests Tripoli', Reuters, 27 Oct. 2013.

83. See 'Mahmoud Jibril Warns against Division of Libya because of Centralisation', Libya al-Mustaqbal, 11 Aug. 2013.

84. See 'The Constitution We Want: The Nation-Wide Survey on the Constitution Technical Report and Survey Results', Research and Consulting Centre of the University of Benghazi, Feb.–Mar. 2013.

85. Ibid.

86. The Kufra reservoir in southeast Libya currently supplies 3.68 million cubic metres a day of drinking and agricultural water while by way of comparison the Murzuq basin in southwest Libya provides 1 million cubic metres a day. Qadhafi planned to ultimately use the Kufra system to help western Libya meet its rapidly growing water demand.

87. According to Benghazi University's 'The Constitution We Want' survey, conducted in Mar.–Apr. 2013, only 15 percent of easterners favoured the idea of a federal state.

88. In Oct. 2013, Sanusi denied any relationship with this group. See Mzioudet, Houda, 'Federalist Head Distances himself from Jadhran, Announces New Council of Cyrenaica', *Libya Herald*, 30 Oct. 2013.

89. See Coker, Margaret, 'Ex-Rebel, With Militia, Lays Claim to Libyan Oil Patch', *Wall Street Journal*, 5 Oct. 2010.

10. HISTORY'S WARRIORS: THE EMERGENCE OF REVOLUTIONARY BATTALIONS IN MISRATA

1. See terminology notes on p. ix.

2. Muhammad Amir, interview with McQuinn, Misrata, 17 Sept. 2011.

3. On the armaments of Misrata's revolutionary battalions, see McQuinn, Brian, 'After the Fall: Libya's Evolving Armed Groups', Geneva: Small Arms Survey, 2012.

4. A collective narrative is defined as a multivocal fictive history reflexively produced by individuals who perceive themselves as insiders to a differentiated organisation or group. See: Brown, Andrew D., 'A Narrative Approach to Collective Identities', *Journal of Management Studies* 43, 4 (2006), 731–53; Green, Melanie C., Jeffrey J. Strange, and Timothy C. Brock, eds, *Narrative Impact: Social and Cognitive Foundations*, London: Taylor and Francis, 2002. On collective memory see Halbwachs, Maurice, *On Collective Memory*, Ed. Lewis A. Coser, Chicago: University of Chicago Press, 1992.

5. Anderson, Lisa, 'The Tripoli Republic, 1918–1922' in *Social and Economic Development of Libya*, by E G H. Joffé and K. S. McLachlan, eds, Wisbech: Middle East and North African Studies Press, 1982, p. 44; Evans-Pritchard, E. E., 'The Sanusi of Cyrenaica', *Africa: Journal of the International African Institute*, 15, 2 (1945), p. 67.

6. The strategy included funding *Lion of the Desert*, a Hollywood movie directed by Moustapha Akkad and starting Anthony Quinn.

7. Ahmida, Ali Abdullatif, *The Making of Modern Libya*, Albany: State University of New York Press, 2009, p. 1; Anderson, 'The Tripoli Republic', p. 43; Evans-Pritchard, E E., 'Italy and the Sanusiya Order in Cyrenaica', *Bulletin of the School of Oriental and African Studies* 11, 4 (1946): p. 843.

8. Ahmida, *Making of Modern Libya*; Evans-Pritchard, 'Italy and the Sanusiya Order'.

9. St John, Ronald Bruce, *Libya From Colony to Revolution*, Oxford: Oneworld, 2011.

10. See, Davis, John, *Libyan Politics: Tribe and Revolution*, Berkeley: University of California Press, 1988; Evans-Pritchard, E. E. *The Sanusi of Cyernaica*, Oxford: Oxford University Press, 1949; Peters, Emrys L., Jack Goody, and Emanuel Marx, *The Bedouin of Cyrenaica: Studies in Personal and Corporate Power*, Cambridge: Cambridge University Press, 1990; Abu-Lughod, Lila, *Veiled Sentiments: Honour and Poetry in Bedouin Society*, Berkeley: University of California Press, 1986.

11. Kalyvas, Stathis, *The Logic of Violence in Civil Wars*, Cambridge: Cambridge University Press, 2006.

12. For more background on oral history theory, see Green, Anna, 'Individual Remembering and "Collective Memory": Theoretical Presuppositions and Contemporary Debates', *Oral History* 32, 2 (2004), pp. 35–44; Magnusson, Sigurdur Gylfi, '"The Singularization of History": Social History and Microhistory Within the Postmodern State of Knowledge', *Journal of Social History* 36, 3 (2003), pp. 701–35.

13. Amnesty International, *The Battle for Libya: Killings, Disappearances and Torture*, London: Amnesty International, 2011.

14. BBC News, 'Libya Revolt as It Happened: Monday', 2011; McQuinn, Brian. *Armed Groups in Libya: Typology and Roles*, Geneva: Small Arms Survey, 2012; Edwards, William, 'Violent Protests Rock Libyan City of Benghazi', France 24, 16 Feb. 2011.

15. Edwards, 'Violent Protests'.

16. 'Libyan Police Stations Torched', Al Jazeera, 16 Feb. 2011.

17. Al-Tuhami Bu Zian, interview with McQuinn, Misrata, 10 Mar. 2012.

18. Ibid.

19. Human Rights Watch, 'Libya: Governments Should Demand End to Unlawful Killings', New York: Human Rights Watch, 2011; Rice, Xan, 'Libyan Rebels Pay a Heavy Price for Resisting Gaddafi in Misrata', *The Guardian*, 21 Apr. 2011.

20. Usama Karami, interviews with McQuinn, Misrata, 24–27 Oct. 2011.

21. *Jihad* is often inaccurately translated as holy war. On this misconception see, Marranci, G., *Jihad beyond Islam*, Oxford: Berg, 2006.

22. Schemm, Paul, and Maggie Michael, 'Gadhafi Forces Strike Back at Revolt Near Tripoli', Associated Press, 24 Feb. 2011.

23. Rice, 'Libyan Rebels Pay a Heavy Price'.

24. Muhammad Amir, interview with McQuinn, Misrata, 2 Aug. 2011.

25. The Misratan Union of Revolutionaries was an umbrella organisation estab-
    lished in November falling the death of Qadhafi that brought together the
    majority of revolutionary battalions. The organisation would go on to play a
    prominent role in the establishment of the Libyan Shield and in organising
    Misratan battalions in the post-war transition. Salim Jawha became its leader,
    solidifying his role as one of the more prominent military commanders in
    Misrata.

26. Tahir Ba'ur, interviews with McQuinn, Misrata, Nov. 3–5, 2011.

27. United Nations Security Council, 'Briefing by Special Representative of the
    Secretary-General for Libya, Ian Martin to the Security Council', S/PV.6807:
    6807th Meeting, United Nations, 2012, p. 26.

28. Fighters present and the military council members who received the supplies
    once looted from the airport, Misrata, interviews with McQuinn, July 2011–
    Mar. 2012.

29. Salim Jawha, head of forces in Misrata by the end of the war, interviews with
    McQuinn, Misrata, Nov. 2011–Mar. 2012.

30. A generic term referring to any improvised incendiary device fashioned from
    glass bottles filled with gasoline and fitted with a cloth wick, which, when lit,
    ignites the gasoline when the bottle shatters on impact. The term originated in
    Finland during the Soviet Union's invasion in Nov. 1939; named in satirical
    honour of Soviet Foreign Minister Vyacheslav Molotov.

31. Salim Jawha, interviews with McQuinn, 28–29 Nov. 2011.

32. Four witnesses of the events at the Courthouse on 6 Mar 2011, interviews with
    McQuinn, Misrata, July–Dec. 2011.

33. Communication committee responsible for the negotiations, interviews with
    McQuinn, Misrata, Nov. 2011.

34. Schemm and Michael, 'Gadhafi Forces Strike Back'.

35. Ba'ur, interviews, Nov. 3–5, 2011.

36. Bashir al-Migrisi, interview with McQuinn, Misrata, 10 Nov. 2011.

37. United Nations Security Council, 'Resolution 1973 (2011)', New York: United
    Nations, S/RES/1973, 17 Mar 2011.

38. Jawha, interviews, Nov. 2011–Mar. 2012.

39. Ba'ur, interviews, Nov. 3–5, 2011.

40. McQuinn, Brian, 'Assessing (In)security after the Arab Spring: The Case of
    Libya', *PS: Political Science & Politics*, 46, 4 (2013), pp. 716–20.

41. NATO, 'NATO Takes Command in Libya Air Operations', Brussels: North
    Atlantic Treaty Organisation, 31 Mar 2011.

42. The figures for small arms in Misrata are averages of estimates provided by
    eight senior commanders and MMC members, including the MMC member
    responsible for organising weapon deliveries to Misrata.

43. *Takbir*, from the verb *kabbara* 'to confess the greatness of', is the practice of
    invoking the phrase *Allahu akbar*, 'God is greatest', in the prayer ritual, *adhan*
    (call to prayer), and in personal devotion. Bowker, John, *The Concise Oxford
    Dictionary of World Religions*, Oxford: Oxford University Press, 1997. On its
    use as it relates to *jihad* see Marranci, *Jihad Beyond Islam*.

44. United Nations Security Council, 'Letter dated 17 Feb. 2012 from the Panel of Experts on Libya Established Pursuant to Resolution 1973 (2011) Addressed to the President of the Security Council', S/2012/163, New York: United Nations, p. 26.

45. Chivers, C. J., 'Taking Airport, Rebels in Libya Loosen Noose', *The New York Times*, 11 May 2011.

46. Ba'ur, interviews, Nov. 3–5, 2011.

47. Unpublished MUR registration records as of 15 Nov. 2011.

48. Author's analysis based on random samples of fighter–auxiliary personnel ratios in fifteen battalions using a stratified sampling method to account for different group sizes.

49. Thompson, Edwina A., *Trust Is the Coin of the Realm*, Oxford: Oxford University Press, 2011.

50. Human Rights Watch, 'Death of a Dictator: Bloody Vengeance in Sirte', New York City: Human Rights Watch, 2012.

51. McQuinn, 'After the Fall'.

52. The MUR registered all members of the battalions in the months following Qadhafi's death. Each supplied the MMC and the MUR with a photocopy of each member's ID card with a form containing basic information such as birth date, previous job and intention to serve in the police or military.

53. Twelve battalions registered with the MUR without recording the number of their members. To estimate these, the 12 battalions were multiplied by the average number of members in the remaining 224 battalions.

54. *Jamahiriyya*, translated as 'state of the masses', articulated Qadhafi's vision of governance without a state. See, Vandewalle, Dirk, *Libya since Independence: Oil and State-building*, Ithaca: Cornell University Press, 1998, Chapter 4.

55. Ghashat, Hesham M., 'The Governance of Libyan Ports: Determining a Framework for Successful Devolution', PhD Thesis, Edinburgh Napier University, 2012; Joffé, George, 'Libya's Saharan Destiny', *The Journal of North African Studies* 10, 3–4 (2005), pp. 605–17.

56. Jawha, interview with McQuinn, Misrata, Nov. 2011. Jawha's assessment of NATO's role in the success of the revolution was as follows: 'Before May, NATO was 30 per cent responsible for our success, after May it was much higher.'

57. Whitehouse, Harvey, 'Human Rites: Rituals Bind Us, in Modern Societies and Prehistoric Tribes alike. But Can our Loyalties Stretch to All of Humankind?', *Aeon Magazine*, 2012.

58. Yusuf Amir, interview with McQuinn, 15 Nov. 2011.

11. FACTIONALISM RESURGENT: THE WAR IN THE JABAL NAFUSA

1. The authors would like to extend their gratitude to Ahmad Yarro, Usama Juwaili, Milad al-Amin and Mus'ab al-Qa'id for their help and assistance in making the research for this chapter possible.

2. This chapter preserves the use of 'Amazigh' as singular and adjectival term,

using 'Imazighen' as the group noun. For example, while incorrect to say 'the Amazigh' to denote a group of people, it is correct to say 'Amazigh towns'.

3. See terminology notes on p. viii.

4. The 'Hilalian invasion' was a migration of several tribes, most importantly the Bani Hilal and Bani Salim, from the Arabian peninsula into North Africa during the eleventh and twelfth centuries. Their migration contributed decisively to the region's Arabisation. See 'Hilaliens', *Encyclopédie berbère*, Aix-en-Provence: Edisud, 2000, pp. 3465–8; Poncet, Jean, 'Le mythe de la "catastrophe" hilalienne', *Civilisations*, 22, 5 (1967), pp. 1099–1120.

5. Zintan *Shura* Council Members, interviews with Lacher, Zintan, Nov. 2012; Milad al-Amin and Khalifa Dwaib Madghiu, interviews with Labnouj, Zintan, Dec. 2012; see also, Cauneille, Auguste, 'Le semi-nomadisme dans l'Ouest libyen (Fezzan, Tripolitaine)' in: UNESCO, *Nomades et Nomadismes au Sahara*, Paris: UNESCO, 1963.

6. Abdullatif Ahmida, Ali, *The Making of Modern Libya: State Formation, Colonization, and Resistance* (2nd ed.), New York: State University of New York, 2009, pp. 51–4; 117–32.

7. Cauneille, Auguste, 'Le Nomadisme des Zentân (Tripolitaine et Fezzân)', *Travaux de l'Institut de Recherches Sahariennes*, 16, 1957, pp. 73–99.

8. Del Boca, Angelo, *Naissance de la nation libyenne. A travers les mémoires de Mohammed Fekini*, Paris: Editions Milelli, 2008, pp. 67–83 and 117–48.

9. Graziani, Rodolfo, *Verso Il Fezzan*, Tripoli: Cacopardo, 1929.

10. Al-Kday, Umar, 'Tafkik al-Mandhumat al-Amniya wal-Askariya lil-Qadhafi', *Libya Watanona*, 7 Apr. 2013, www.libya-watanona.com/adab/omarkdey/ok070411a.htm last accessed 6 Jan. 2014.

11. Zintanis with experience in Qadhafi's military and security apparatus numbered close to a thousand. Usama Juwaili, interview with Labnouj, Zintan, Mar. 2013.

12. The same night the Warfalla officers were arrested, Zintan saw protests in which the local police station had been set on fire. Dozens were arrested. Though the protests appear to have been triggered by local tensions over the choice of the Basic People's Committee and Conference, Qadhafi's intelligence services suspected a link to the coup plot. Underlining Zintan's close ties, the families of four executed Warfalla officers were exiled from Bani Walid to Zintan in 1999. Dr Musa Graifa, email communication with Lacher, Tripoli, Oct. 2013. Also see Ouannes, Moncef, *Militaires, Elites et Modernisation dans la Libye Contemporaine*, Paris: L'Harmattan, 2009, pp. 310–12.

13. Madghiu, interview, Dec. 2012.

14. Chaker, Salem, and Masin Ferkal, 'Berbères de Libye: un Paramètre Méconnu, une Irruption Politique Inattendue', *Politique Africaine* 125 (2012), pp. 105–26.

15. 'Regime-Orchestrated Attacks against Berbers in Yefren', Diplomatic Cable, US Embassy Tripoli, 13 Jan. 2009, http://www.cablegatesearch.net/cable.php?id=09TRIPOLI22&q=amazigh last accessed 6 Jan. 2014.

16. Salim Madi and Fathi Yusef; Sulaiman Yahmad; Sifao Twawa; interviews with Lacher, Tripoli, Nalut and Yefren Jan.–Feb. 2014.

17. For background on the history of Popular Social Leadership Committees, see Chapter 12, p. 293.
18. Milad al-Amin, interview with Lacher, Zintan, Feb. 2014.
19. Amin and Madghiu, interviews with Labnouj, Zintan, Dec. 2012.
20. Madghiu, interview, Dec. 2012.
21. Bashir al-Tha'ailib and Amin, interviews with Lacher, Zintan, Feb. 2014.
22. See the account of Usama al-Tubbal's father, in al-Rummah, Ali, *Audha' ala thawrat 17 fibrayir min arshif al-thawra fi al-Zintan*, Vol. 1, Zintan: Centre for Historical Documentation, 2013, pp. 16–17
23. Musa Hakim and Yusef, interviews with Lacher, Jadu and Tripoli, Jan. 2014.
24. Muhammad al-Khamaisi, interviews with Lacher, Nalut, Feb. 2014.
25. Twawa and Muhammad al-Shumakhi, interviews with Lacher, Yefren, Jan. 2014.
26. Al-Khairi al-Talib, interview with Lacher, Nalut, Feb. 2014.
27. Jamal Abu Aziz, Ibrahim Madi and Yusef, interviews with Lacher, Nalut, Yefren and Tripoli, Jan.–Feb. 2014.
28. See al-Quti's account, in Bin Dilla, Muhammad, *Nalut al-jihad min al-ajdad ila al-ahfad*, Benghazi: Dar al-Kutub al-Wataniya, 2013, pp. 30–3.
29. Abu Aziz, Yusef and Hakim, interviews with Lacher, Nalut, Tripoli and Jadu, Jan.–Feb. 2014. See also Bin Dilla, *Nalut al-jihad*, p. 57.
30. Tariq al-Tayyib and Twawa, interviews with Lacher, Tripoli and Yefren, Jan. 2013; See also Rummah, *Audha'*, Vol. 1, pp. 147–80.
31. See Firnana's account, in Rummah, *Audha'*, Vol. 1, pp. 256–61.
32. Muhammad Umar, interview with Lacher, Yefren, Sep. 2013.
33. Khalid al-Azzabi and Khamaisi, interviews with Lacher, Nalut, Feb. 2014.
34. Col. Ahmad Yarro, interviews with Lacher, Nalut, Jan.–Feb. 2013.
35. Ufnait al-Koni, Tripoli, interview with Lacher, June 2012.
36. Khamis Barka, interview with Lacher, Tripoli, Sep. 2013; Graifa, email communication, Tripoli, Oct. 2013; Another episode of an arms deal between Zintanis and Tebu in the far south is recounted in Rummah, *Audha'*, Vol. 1, pp. 228–37.
37. Salim al-Qal'awi, interview with Lacher, Yefren, Jan. 2014.
38. Amin, interview Feb. 2014.
39. Khamaisi, interview, Feb. 2014.
40. Yusef, interview, Jan. 2014.
41. Mukhtar Said and Said Misbah Amir, interviews with Lacher, Tripoli, Feb. 2014.
42. See Shaaban Abu Sita's account, in Bin Dilla, *Nalut al-jihad*, pp. 49–50.
43. Mus'ab al-Qa'id and Umar, interviews with Lacher, Yefren, Sep. 2013.
44. From early Mar 2011 until the liberation of Tripoli, Qadhafi relied on the two mobile phone companies controlled by his son Muhammad to deliver SMS messages rallying loyalists to attack rebels in the mountains. Messages often named specific loyalist tribes, leading to their eventual stigmatisation after the revolution. Labnouj observations, Tripoli, July 2011.
45. Amin and Madghiu; Sasi Khzam, interviews with Labnouj, Zintan and al-Qal'a, Dec. 2012.

46. Shumakhi, interview Jan. 2014. Also see Bin Dilla, *Nalut al-jihad*, p. 78.

47. See the accounts of prisoners taken by Zintan in Rummah, *Audha'*, Vol. 2, pp. 23–8.

48. Ibrahim Madi and Yusef, interviews with Lacher, Yefren and Tripoli, Jan. 2014; See also Rummah, *Audha'*, Vol. 2, p. 13.

49. Umar, interview, Sep. 2013.

50. Qa'id, interview, Sep. 2013.

51. Umar, interview, Sep. 2013.

52. According to documents seized by Naluti revolutionaries and reproduced in Mas'ud al-Azzabi, *Ma'arik thuwwar 17 fibrayir: ma'arik Nalut numudhajan*, Benghazi: Dar al-Fadel, 2011, pp. 75–82.

53. Abu Aziz and Azzabi, interviews with Lacher, Nalut, Feb. 2014.

54. Yusef, interview Jan. 2014; Abu Aziz, interview, Feb. 2014; Tayyib, interview, Jan. 2013.

55. Abu Aziz, Khamaisi and Talib, interviews with Lacher, Nalut, Feb. 2014; Mustafa Hammadi, interview with Lacher, Tripoli, Apr. 2014.

56. Shaaban Mshayikh, Yahmad and Khamaisi, interviews with Lacher, Nalut, Feb. 2014.

57. Yusef, interview Jan. 2014.

58. Government forces briefly recaptured the area on 28 Apr. but were beaten back immediately afterwards.

59. Hakim, Tayyib, Talib and Azzabi, interviews with Lacher, Jadu, Tripoli and Nalut, Jan.-Feb. 2014.

60. Juwaili, interview, Mar. 2013.

61. Atif Barqiq, interview with Lacher, Nalut, Feb. 2014.

62. Ibrahim Madi, interview, Jan. 2014; Abu Aziz, interview, Feb. 2014; Barqiq, interview Feb. 2014.

63. Azzabi, interview, Feb. 2014.

64. The commanders of Zintan's initial seven battalions included Col. Mukhtar al-Akhdar (Zintan Martyrs Battalion), Col. Al-Ujmi al-Uthayri (Abtal al-Zintan Battalion), as well as the civilians al-Hadi al-Amyani, Bashir al-Tha'ailib (Jihad Battalion), Jum'a Ahsay (Nasr Battalion), Salama al-Mabruk, and Muhammad al-Madani's son Ibrahim. Amin and Tha'ailib, interviews with Lacher, Zintan, Feb. 2014.

65. Oman's historical connections with the town go back to Jadu-born Sulaiman al-Baruni (1870–1940), who spent the last sixteen years of his life in Oman.

66. Abu Aziz, interview, Feb. 2014.

67. Juwaili, interview, Mar. 2013.

68. Twawa, interview Jan. 2013; Ibrahim Madi, interview, Jan. 2014; Yusef, interview Jan. 2014; Talib, interview, Feb. 2014.

69. On the Chief of Staff's visit, see p. 77, Chapter 3.

70. Talib, interview, Feb. 2014; Abu Aziz, interview, Feb. 2014.

71. Yusef, interview Jan. 2014.

72. Tayyib, interview, Jan. 2013.

73. Nuri al-Din Shirwi, interview with Lacher, Yefren, Feb. 2014; Tayyib, interview, Jan. 2013; Yusef, interview Jan. 2014.

74. Umar, interview, Sep. 2013. Retreating government forces executed 34 boys and men from al-Qal'a whom they had held prisoner for weeks. *Full Report of the International Commission of Inquiry on Libya*, New York: UN Human Rights Council, 8 Mar. 2012.

75. Umar, interview, Sep. 2013.

76. 'Fighting in Libya pits neighbours against each other', Reuters, 16 May 2011.

77. Said and Amir, interviews, Feb. 2014; 'Libya: Opposition Forces Should Protect Civilians and Hospitals: Looting, Arson, and Some Beatings in Captured Western Towns', Human Rights Watch, 13 July 2011, www.hrw. org/news/2011/07/13/libya-opposition-forces-should-protect-civilians-and-hospitals; 'Voyage dans les villes fantômes du Djebel Nefousa en guerre', *Le Figaro*, 11 July 2011.

78. Khamaisi, interview, Feb. 2014; *Full Report of the International Commission of Inquiry on Libya*, New York: UN Human Rights Council, 8 Mar. 2012.

79. Tha'ailib, interview, Feb. 2014.

80. 'Ba'd arba' muhawalat lil-harab: Abdesselam Jalloud yanshaqq 'an al-Qadhafi w yasil al-Zintan mashuban bi-usratihi', *Libya al-Jadida*, 19 Aug. 2011, السلام-عيد-للهرب-محاولات-اربع-بعد-جلود last accessed 6 Jan. 2014.

81. 'Sarkozy says Gaddafi aide is in France', *Financial Times*, 1 May 2012; '"Gaddafi's banker" Bashir Saleh seen in South Africa', *The Guardian*, 2 June 2013.

82. Eyewitness requesting anonymity, interview with Lacher, Tripoli, Sep. 2013.

83. Yarro, interviews with Labnouj, Nalut, Apr.–Nov. 2012.

84. Koni, interview, June 2012; Hammadi, interview, Apr. 2014.

85. See al-Rummah, *Audha'*, Vol. 2, pp. 284–88.

86. See a joint letter by Zintanis and Imanghassaten leaders to Defence Minister Juwaili, dated 14 Nov. 2011, reproduced in Rummah, *Audha'*, Vol. 2, pp. 290–96. On the Maghawir brigade and relations between Sahelian Tuareg fighters and the tribal establishment of Libyan Tuareg communities, see Lacher, Wolfram, 'Libya's Fractious South and Regional Instability', Small Arms Survey, Security Assessment in North Africa Dispatch No. 3, Feb. 2014, www.smallarmssurvey.org/fileadmin/docs/R-SANA/SANA-Dispatch3-Libyas-Fractuous-South.pdf

87. Local observer from Ubari wishing to remain anonymous, interview with Lacher, Tripoli, Apr. 2014.

88. Majdi Abu Hanna, interviews with Lacher, Sabha, Sep. 2013; Qa'id, interview, Sep. 2013.

89. *Report of the Secretary-General on the United Nations Support Mission in Libya*, UN Security Council, 30 Aug. 2012, http://unsmil.unmissions.org/Portals/unsmil/Documents/SGReport30August2012.pdf; 'Several thousand displaced in Jebel Nafusa: ICRC claim', *Libya Herald*, 21 June 2012, www.libya-herald.com/2012/06/21/several-thousand-displaced-in-jebel-nafissa-icrc-claim

90. Said and Amir, interviews, Feb. 2014.

91. Land used by the Mashashiya in Awayniya is claimed by the Yefreni Khalayfa

tribe. Minor land disputes between the Mashashiya and Zintan do exist in Fassanu, west of Mizdah. Qa'id, interview, Sep. 2013; Qal'awi, interview, Jan. 2014; Amin, interview, Feb. 2014.

92. *Full Report of the International Commission of Inquiry on Libya*, New York: UN Human Rights Council, 8 Mar. 2012.

93. Khamaisi, interview, Feb. 2014.

94. 'Al-Ittifaq bain ahali al-Zintan wa-ahali mintaqat al-Riyayna al-Gharbiya', *Lana*, 18 Aug. 2013, http://www.lana-news.ly/ara/news/view/29072/

95. Amin, interview, Feb. 2014.

96. Tabib, Rafaa, *Effets de la frontière tuniso-libyenne sur les recompositions économiques et sociales des Werghemmas: de la possession à la réappropriation des territoires*, PhD thesis, Université de Tours, 2012, pp. 199–203.

97. Misrati businessman requesting anonymity, interviews with Lacher, Misrata, Apr. 2013; Qa'id, interview Sep. 2013.

98. Abu Aziz, interview, Feb. 2014; Khamaisi, interview, Feb. 2014; Talib, interview, Feb. 2014. Also see Kartas, Moncef, *On the Edge? Trafficking and Insecurity at the Tunisian–Libyan Border*, Small Arms Survey Working Paper, Geneva: Small Arms Survey, 2013, p. 44; and 'Thuwar Nalut ya'taridun 'ala fath manfadh barri jadid…', *Lana*, 20 Aug. 2013, http://www.lana-news.ly/ara/news/view/29252/

99. Local observer from Ubari wishing to remain anonymous, interview with Lacher, Tripoli, Apr. 2014.

100. Shaw, Mark, and Fiona Mangan, *Illicit Trafficking and Libya's Transition: Profits and Losses*. Washington, D.C.: United States Institute for Peace, 2014.

101. Local observer requesting anonymity, interview with Lacher, Bani Walid, Apr. 2014.

102. Hussain al-Wakwak, interviews with Lacher, Tripoli, Feb. 2014; Hammadi, interview, Apr. 2014.

103. Lacher, Wolfram, *Fault Lines of the Revolution: Political Actors, Camps and Conflicts in the New Libya*, SWP Research Paper, May 2013.

104. Wakwak, interview, Feb. 2014.

105. 'Suqut qatilin w arba'a jarha fi ishtibakat Salah ad-Din', *al-Tadhamon*, 25 June 2013.

106. Shirwi, interview, Sep. 2013; Amin, interview, Feb. 2014; A list of tribes that attended the forum is reproduced in Rummah, *Audha'*, Vol. 2, pp. 329–32.

107. Lacher interview with Umar Matuq, Zintan, Feb. 2014.

108. Chaker, Salem, and Masin Ferkal, 'Berbères de Libye: un Paramètre Méconnu, une Irruption Politique Inattendue', *Politique Africaine* 125 (Mar. 2012) pp. 105–26.

109. Mustafa Abd al-Jalil, telephone interview, Libya Awalan TV, 28 Nov. 2011.

110. Shirwi, interview, Sep. 2013.

111. Khalid al-Gallal, interview with Lacher, Nalut, July 2013; Talib, interview Feb. 2014.

112. While this primarily refers to oral history, several towns have begun documenting their experiences during the war. See Rummah, *Audha'*; Azzabi, interview, Feb. 2014.; and Bin Dilla, *Nalut al-jihad*.

September and October should be arrested—those people are not wanted.' Zintani leader of the reconciliation negotiations, interview, 16 Apr. 2012; The deputy head of the 28 May brigade also itemised those wanted: 'We want all those involved in attacking our headquarters on 25 Jan. and killing us on five separate occasions; on 28 May in Bani Walid, in Tarhuna when our supporters there were killed, in Khwarzin where seven were killed, and during the Suq al-Jum'a incident.' Tariq Durman, interview with Cole, Tripoli, 18 Mar 2012.

84. Bani Walid representative in the negotiations requesting anonymity, interview with Cole, 30 Jan. 2012.

85. Jadak, interview, 22 Feb. 2012.

86. According to one resident, al-Wa'ir was a member of the *Jamamla* branch of the Bani Walid, and in part was protecting the traditional important families of the *Sa'da* branch against the threat posed by the 28 May movement, which came from less traditionally important families.

87. Barghuti, interview 23 Feb. 2012; head of Bani Walid *Sa'dat* family, interview, 24 Feb. 2012.

88. Opinions canvassed from several family heads, Bani Walid, 21 Feb. 2012.

89. Head of Bani Walid *Jamamla* family, interview 21 Feb. 2012.

90. Warfalla family head, interview with Cole, Sabha, 10 May 2012; Warfalla Social Council members, Benghazi, 20 Feb. 2012.

13. LIBYA'S TEBU: LIVING IN THE MARGINS

1. Ibrahim Abu Bakr, interview with Murray, Awbari, Apr. 28, 2013.

2. 'Libya Says 147 Dead in Week of Southern Tribal Clashes', Reuters, 1 Apr. 2012; 'The Battle for the Kufra Oasis and the Ongoing war in Libya', Jamestown Foundation, 23 Feb. 2012.

3. Vandewalle, Dirk, *A History of Modern Libya* (2nd ed.), Cambridge: Cambridge University Press, 2012.

4. Wehrey, Frederic, 'The Struggle for Security in Eastern Libya', Washington DC: Carnegie Endowment for International Peace, 2012.

5. Isa Abd al-Majid Mansur, interview with Murray, Zuaila, 19 Sep. 2012; Ali Ramadan Sida, interview with Murray, Kufra, 22 Sep. 2012; Rami al-Shabiabi, interview with Murray, Tripoli, 1 Oct. 2012.

6. Ibid.

7. Ibid.

8. Blench, Roger, 'Why are there so many Pastoral Groups in Eastern Africa?', in Azarya, Victor, ed., *Pastoralists Under Pressure?: Fulbe Societies Confronting Change in West Africa*, Leiden: Brill, 1999.

9. See Capot-Rey, 'Le Nomadisme des Toubou', in UNESCO, *Nomades et Nomadismes au Sahara*, 1963, http://unesdoc.unesco.org/images/0006/000699/069980fo.pdf

10. Blench, 'Pastoral Groups'.

11. Cole, Peter, 'Borderline Chaos? Securing Libya's Borders', Carnegie Endowment for International Peace, 18 Oct. 2012.

12. Wehrey, 'The Struggle For Security'.
13. Cole, 'Borderline Chaos?'.
14. Muhammad Lino, interview with Murray, Tripoli, 15 Sep. 2012.
15. Adam Arami al-Tibawi, interview with Murray, Tripoli, 10 Sep. 2012.
16. Ibid.
17. Cole, 'Borderline Chaos?'.
18. Ibid.
19. International Crisis Group, 'Libya/Chad: Beyond Political Influence', *Africa Briefing*, 71, 23 Mar 2010.
20. Ibid.
21. Mansur, interview with Murray, Zuaila, 19 Sep. 2012.
22. International Crisis Group, 'Libya/Chad'.
23. Ali Ramadan Sida, interview with Murray, Kufra, 22 Sep. 2012.
24. Ibid.
25. International Crisis Group, 'Libya/Chad'.
26. Ibid.
27. Baraka Wardaku, interview with Murray, Tripoli, 9 Sep. 2012; Hussein Shakki, interview with Murray, Tripoli, 28 Sep. 2012.
28. Mansur, interview 19 Sep. 2012.
29. Bazinga Mawlami, Zuaila, interview with Murray, 20 Sep. 2012.
30. Lino, interview, 15 Sep. 2012; Cole, 'Borderline Chaos?'.
31. Salah Arzai, interview with Murray, Tripoli, 9 Sep. 2012.
32. Ibid.
33. Adam Ahmad, interview with Murray, Sabha, 6 July, 2012.
34. Murray visit to Tebu communities in Sabha, Kufra, Ribyana, Zuaila, Murzuq, Awbari, 2012 and 2013.
35. Wehrey, 'The Struggle for Security'.
36. Weinberg, Gerhard L. *A World at Arms: A Global History of World War II*, Cambridge: Cambridge University Press, 2005.
37. Ibid.
38. Yunis Isa, interview with Murray, Ribyana, 21 Sep. 2012; UN General Assembly, Human Rights Council report, 15 July 2010.
39. Ibid.
40. Isa, interview, 21 Sep. 2012; UN Human Rights Council, 'Report of the Special Rapporteur on the Situation of Human Rights and Fundamental Freedoms of Indigenous People, James Anaya', A/HRC/15/37, 19 July 2010.
41. Mansur, interview, 19 Sep. 2012.
42. Ibid.
43. Tibawi, interview, 10 Sep. 2012; Hasan Musa, interview with Murray, Tripoli, 18 Sep. 2012.
44. Tibawi, interview, 10 Sep. 2012.
45. Musa, interview, 18 Sep. 2012.
46. Rajab Ramadan, interview with Murray, Kufra, 23 Sep. 2012.
47. Tibawi, interview with Murry, 10 Sep. 2012.
48. Flint, Julie and Alex de Waal, *Darfur: A New History Of A Long War*, London: Zed Books, 2008.

49. Alex de Waal, Skype interview with Murray, 11 Jan. 2013.
50. Alhag, Esim, 'The Sudanese Role in Libya 2011', The World Peace Foundation, 17 Dec. 2012.
51. De Waal, interview, 11 Jan. 2013.
52. Lino, interview, 15 Sep. 2012.
53. Ibid.
54. Adam Sidi Abdullah, interview with Murray, Tripoli, 23 Apr. 2013.
55. Ibid.
56. Ali Ramadan Sida, interview with Murray, Kufra, 22 Sep. 2012.
57. Ibid.
58. Ibid.
59. Isa, interview, 21 Sep. 2012.
60. Sida, interview with Murry, 22 Sep. 2012.
61. Musa, interview, 18 Sep. 2012.
62. Tibawi, interview, 10 Sep. 2012.
63. Ibid.
64. Sida, interview, 22 Sep. 2012.
65. Fathi al-Ba'ja, interview with Murray, Tripoli, 18 Sep. 2012.
66. Ibid.
67. Sida, interview, 22 Sep. 2012.
68. Ibid.
69. Ibid.
70. Isa, interview, 21 Sep. 2012.
71. Muhammad Abu Sadana, interview with Murray, 10 Apr. 2012.
72. Ibid.
73. Isa, interview, 21 Sep. 2012.
74. Ramadan Sulaiman, interview with Murray, Awbari, 28 Apr. 2013.
75. Ibid.
76. De Waal, interview, 11 Jan. 2013.
77. Tahir Muhammad Makni, interview with Murray, Tripoli, 29 Sep. 2012.
78. Ibid.
79. Baraka Wardaku, interview with Murray, Tripoli, 9 Sep. 2012.
80. Ibid.
81. Wedeman, Ben, 'Government Forces Enter Libya's Sabha, to Cheers', CNN. com, 21 Sep. 2011.
82. Baraka Wardaku, interview, 9 Sep. 2012.
83. Sida, interview, 22 Sep. 2012.
84. See Scheele, Judith. *Smugglers and Saints of the Sahara*. Cambridge: Cambridge University Press, 2012.
85. Author's visit to Kufra, Apr. and Sep. 2012.
86. Sida, interview, 22 Sep. 2012.
87. Ibid.
88. Ibid.
89. Khadija Hamid Yusuf, interview with Murray, Kufra, 23 Sep. 2012.
90. Sida, interview, 22 Sep. 2012.

91. Rami al-Shahiabi, interview with Murray, Tripoli, 1 Oct. 2012.
92. Ibid.
93. ICRC staff, confidential interview with Murray, Tripoli, 28 Sep. 2012.
94. Sida, interview, 22 Sep. 2012.
95. Muhammad Sidi, interview with Murray, Tripoli, 27 Apr. 2013.
96. Author's observation, Tuyuri school, Sabha, 12 July 2012.
97. Waleed, Farah, 'Tripoli Conference Produces Sabha Peace Deal', *Libya Herald*, 20 Apr. 2012.
98. International Crisis Group, 'Divided We Stand: Libya's Enduring Conflicts', *Middle East/North Africa Report*, 130, 14 Sep. 2012.
99. Muhammad Ali, Sabha, interview with Murray, 6 July 2012.
100. Tibawi, interview, 10 Sep. 2012.
101. Ibid.
102. Makni, interview, 29 Sep. 2012.
103. 'GNC announces temporary closure of southern borders and declares south a "closed military zone"', *Libya Herald*, 17 Dec. 2012.
104. Musa, interview, 18 Sep. 2012.

14. TUAREG MILITANCY AND THE SAHELIAN SHOCKWAVES OF THE LIBYAN REVOLUTION

1. I am thankful to Peter Cole and Brian McQuinn for their comments and their patience in the elaboration of this work. I also wish to express my gratitude to Savannah de Tessieres for a careful reading of an earlier version of this chapter.
2. This paper focuses primarily on nomadic Tuareg originating from Niger and Mali, many of whom had settled in Libya, often relying on ties built with Libyan Tuareg in Ghat, Murzuq, Awbari or Ghadames.
3. Puhl, Jan, 'Sub-Saharan Africans Risk Everything to Flee Libya', Spiegel Online, 5 Apr. 2011; Midal, Assan, 'La Guerre constraint les Touaregs à retourner sur leurs terres', France 24, 18 Mar. 2011.
4. Prier, Pierre, 'Du cash pour les milliers de mercenaires de Kadhafi', *Le Figaro*, 4 Apr. 2011; RFI, 'Cris d'alarme d'élus maliens au sujet des Touaregs enrôlés dans l'armée de Kadhafi', RFI, 2 Mar. 2011.
5. According to the Tuareg separatists of the MNLA, the Azawad is the Malian territory roughly situated in the north of Mopti, comprising the provinces of Kidal, Gao and Timbuktu. However its geographic definition refers to a zone of pasture situated north of the Niger River bend. Sociologically, the Azawad mixes pastoralists as well as farmers and merchants from different ethnic backgrounds: Tuareg, Arab, Songhai, Fulani or Bellah. For further details on the political construction of Azawad, see, Lecocq, Baz, *That Desert Is Our Country*, PhD Thesis, University of Amsterdam, 2002.
6. Pellerin, Mathieu, 'Le Sahel et la contagion libyenne', *Politique Etrangère*, 4 (2012), pp. 835–47; Risen, James, Mark Mazzetti and Michael S. Schmidt, 'U.S.-Approved Arms for Libya Rebels Fell Into Jihadis' Hands', *The New York Times*, 5 Dec. 2012.

7. Niger security forces stopped a convoy carrying large amounts of cash as well as hundreds of kilos of explosives, supposedly to be delivered to al-Qa'ida in the Islamic Maghreb (see Diallo, Ibrahim Manzo, 'Reportage exclusif: Abta Hamidine s'apprêtait à livrer les quatre otages français au clan Kadhafi', *Aïr Info*, 29 June, (2011); United Nations Security Council, 'Final Report of the Panel of Experts established pursuant to Security Council resolution 1973 (2011) concerning Libya', S/2012/163, 2011.

8. International Crisis Group, 'Mali: Avoiding Escalation', *Africa Report*, 189, 18 July 2012.

9. See, Berry, Sarah, 'Hegemony on a Shoestring: Indirect Rule and Access to Agricultural Land', *Africa* 62, 3 (1992), pp. 327–55.

10. For the internal factors causing the collapse of the Malian state, see International Crisis Group, 'Mali: Avoiding Escalation'.

11. Moussa's real name is anonymised. All quotes are from daily conversations with the author over May 2009.

12. Scheele, Judith. *Smugglers and Saints of the Sahara*, Cambridge: Cambridge University Press, 2012.

13. For a detailed account on the social implications and perceptions of participating in drug trafficking in the Sahara see Scheele, *Smugglers and Saints*.

14. Bate, Felix and Nathalie Prevost, 'Crossing Desert from Libya to Niger Fraught with Danger', Reuters, 8 Sep. 2011.

15. Boisbouvier, Christophe, 'Libye : le récit exclusif de la cavale d'Abdallah Senoussi', *Jeune Afrique*, 2 Apr. 2012.

16. Lydon, Ghislaine, *On Trans-Saharan Trails: Islamic Law, Trade Networks, and Cross-Cultural Exchange in Nineteenth-Century Western Africa*, Cambridge: Cambridge University Press, 2009.

17. Boesen, Elisabeth and Laurence Marfaing (eds), *Les nouveaux urbains dans l'espace Sahara-Sahel. Un cosmopolitisme par le bas*, Paris: Karthala, 2007.

18. Even bandits have a code of conduct, as noted by Scheele, which is consistent with the Hobsbawm research. See Scheele, *Smugglers and Saints*; Hobsbawm, Eric, *Bandits*, New York: The New Press, 2000.

19. Brachet, Julien. *Un désert cosmopolite. Migrations de transit dans la région d'Agadez*, PhD Thesis, Paris: Université Panthéon-Sorbonne, 2007; Bensaâd, Ali, 'L'immigration en Libye: Une ressource et la diversité de ses usages', *Politique Africaine*, 125 (2012), pp. 83–102.

20. 'Gaddafi's Son "Flees to Niger"', Al Jazeera, 11 Sep. 2011. http://www.aljazeera.com/news/africa/2011/09/2011911215032843976.html last accessed 6 Jan. 2013.

21. On complicity between officials and narco-traffickers in the Sahel, particularly Mali, see Lacher, Wolfram, 'Organised Crime and Conflict in the Sahel-Sahara Region', Washington DC: Carnegie Endowment for International Peace, 2012. See also Guichaoua, Yvan, 'Mali: The Fallacy of Ungoverned Spaces', University of East Anglia DEV Blog, http://www.uea.ac.uk/international-development/dev-blog/home/-/asset_publisher/1I1JoAAhCZsR/blog/id/2506832 last accessed 14 Nov. 2013.

22. Triaud, Jean-Louis, 'Un mauvais départ: 1920, l'Aïr en ruines', in Bernus, Edmond, Paul Clauzel, Pierre Boilley and Jean-Louis Triaud (eds), *Nomades et commandants*, Paris: Karthala, 1993, pp. 93–100.

23. Brachet, Julien, 'Le négoce caravanier au Sahara central : histoire, évolution des pratiques et enjeux chez les Touaregs Kel Aïr (Niger)', *Les Cahiers d'Outre-Mer*, 226–7 (2004), 117–36; Grégoire, Emmanuel, *Touaregs du Niger, Le Destin d'un Mythe*, Paris: Karthala, 2001.

24. Notable scholarly references on the *ishumar* include: Ag Ahar, Elleli, 'L'initiation d'un ashamur', *Revue des Mondes Musulmans et de la Méditerranée* 57 (1990), pp. 141–52; Lecocq, Baz, 'Unemployed Intellectuals in the Sahara: The Teshumara Nationalist Movement and the Revolutions in Tuareg Society', *International Review of Social History*, 49 (2004), pp. 87–109; Kohl, Ines, 'Going "off road": With Toyota, Chech and E-Guitar through a Saharan Borderland', In Hahn, Hans Peter and Georg Klute (eds), *Cultures of Migration*, Berlin: LIT Verlag, 2007, pp. 89–106; Deycard, Frédéric, 'Political Cultures and Tuareg Mobilizations', in Guichaoua, Yvan (ed.), *Understanding Collective Political Violence*, Basingstoke: Palgrave-Macmillan, 2011, pp. 46–64; Grémont, Charles, André Marty, Rhissa Ag Mossa and Younoussa Hamara Toure, *Les liens sociaux au Nord-Mali*, Paris: Karthala, 2004.

25. For testimonies of Tuareg migrants, see Kohl, Ines, 'Libya, the "Europe of Ishumar": Between Losing and Reinventing Tradition', in Fischer, Anja and Ines Kohl (eds) *Tuareg Society within a Globalised World: Saharan Life in Transition*. London: I. B. Tauris, 2010, pp. 143–5.

26. Vallée, Olivier, 'Kadhafi: le dernier roi d'Afrique', *Politique Africaine*, 125 (2012), pp. 147–67.

27. For background on CEN-SAD, see Joffe, George, 'Libyan Saharan destiny', *The Journal of North African Studies*, 10, 3–4 (2005), pp. 605–17.

28. Brachet, *Un désert cosmopolite*; Bensaâd, 'L'immigration en Libye'.

29. Intervention by Libyan actors elsewhere in the continent included support to: Idi Amin in Uganda, Polisario Front in the Western Sahara, Goukouni Oueddei's short-lived government in Chad and to Charles Taylor in Liberia. See Joffe, 'Libyan Saharan destiny'.

30. Deycard, Frédéric, *Les rebellions touaregues du Niger: Combattants, mobilisations et culture politique*, PhD dissertation, Institut d'études politiques de Bordeaux, 2011.

31. Joffe, 'Libyan Saharan destiny'.

32. St John, Ronald Bruce, *Historical Dictionary of Libya*, 4th edition, Lanham, MD: Scarecrow Press, 2006.

33. See Grémont et al., *Les liens sociaux au Nord-Mali*.

34. Guichaoua interview with former rebel leader in Niger, Niamey, Aug. 2007.

35. Qadhafi behaved similarly in Chad (see International Crisis Group, 'Africa Without Qadhafi: The Case of Chad.', *Africa Report*, 180, 2011).

36. This insurgency is analysed in detail in Guichaoua, Yvan, 'Circumstantial Alliances and Loose Loyalties in Rebellion Making: The Case of Tuareg Insurgency in Northern Niger (2007–2009)', in Guichaoua (ed.), *Understand-*

ing Collective Political Violence, pp. 246–65. This section is based on dozens of interviews conducted in Paris, Niamey, Agadez and Tamanrasset between 2007 and 2012.

37. United Nations Development Programme, 'Consolidation de la paix dans l'Aïr et l'Azawak', http://www.pnud.ne/fich09_PCPAA.htm last accessed 30 Dec. 2012.

38. 'A propos des 500 ex-rebelles', *Le Républicain*, 18 Aug. 2005.

39. MNJ combatant, interview with Guichaoua, Niamey, Mar 2011.

40. Forestier, Patrick, 'La Chute du Guide: les révélations d'un proche de Kadhafi', *Paris-Match*, 11 Sep. 2011.

41. Interviews with MNJ ex-combatants, Niamey, Mar. 2012.

42. This vague figure was estimated by ex-combatants interviewed in Niamey in Mar 2012.

43. 'Libye: témoignages de "mercenaires" touareg de Kaddafi rentrés au Niger', *Jeune Afrique*, 4 Sep. 2011, http://www.jeuneafrique.com/Article/DEPAFP20 110904211545/ last accessed 30 Dec. 2012.

44. For the detailed calendar of successive arrivals in Niger in Sep. 2011 of pro-Qadhafi dignitaries, see United Nations Security Council, 'Security Council Authorizes Deployment of African-led International Support Mission in Mali for Initial Year-long Period', SC/10870, (2012).

45. Gueugneau, Christophe and Fabrice Arfi, 'Ziad Takieddine rattrapé par ses affaires libyennes', *Mediapart*, 6 Dec. 2012, http://www.mediapart.fr/journal/international/061212/ziad-takieddine-rattrape-par-ses-affaires-libyennes?page_article=4 last accessed 25 May 2013; Thiolay, Boris, 'Kadhafi-Sarkozy: L'encombrant Monsieur Bachir', *L'Express*, 15 May 2012, http://www.lexpress.fr/actualite/monde/afrique/kadhafi-sarkozy-l-encombrant-monsieur-bachir_1114915.html last accessed 30 Dec. 2012.

46. Humphreys, Macartan and H. Ag Mohamed, 'Senegal and Mali', in Collier, Paul and Nicholas Sambanis (eds), *Understanding Civil War. Evidence and Analysis: Africa*, Washington DC: WorldBank, 2005, pp. 247–302.

47. Ex-rebel leaders, interview with Guichaoua, Niamey, Mar 2012.

48. Morgan, Andy, 'The causes of the uprising in northern Mali', *Think Africa Press*, 6 Feb. 2012, http://thinkafricapress.com/mali/causes-uprising-northern-mali-tuareg, last accessed 30 Dec. 2012.

49. 'Nous devons resserrer les rangs et éviter toute confrontation qui diviserait le mouvement', *El Watan*, 9 Apr. 2012.

50. Pellerin, 'Le Sahel et la contagion libyenne'.

51. Security analyst, interview with Guichaoua, Niamey, Mar 2012.

INDEX

17 February Battalion: as member of GRC, 114, 191; members of, 77, 190–2, 201
17 February Coalition (*I'tilaf Sab'at Ashr Fibrayir*): 57, 64, 68–9, 82, 85, 87–91, 95, 98–9, 114, 206; as member of GRC, 114, 191; conflict with Stabilisation Committee, 82; 'Draft of a Constitutional Declaration', 51; formation of, 63, 68, 191; formation of Benghazi local council, 35; members of, 33, 38–9, 41, 51, 83, 90, 102, 191; Tripoli Local Council, 95–8
17 February Revolution (Libyan Civil War)(2011): 1, 8–10, 13, 19–21, 29–31, 36, 50, 53–4, 56–7, 143–4, 150, 153, 169–70, 172, 187, 189, 206, 211–13, 221, 224, 232, 254, 257, 294–5, 301, 307, 321–2, 324, 329, 332; Baida demonstrations, 33; Battle of Brega, 64, 66; Battle of Shakshuk, 275; civilian casualties during, 122; defection of Nalut and Zintan, 12; development of protests, 59–61; emergence of battalions in, 249–53; fall of Tripoli, 5, 31–2, 46–8, 50, 53, 67–8, 78–9, 82, 85, 88, 94, 99, 103–4, 128, 132, 137–8, 183, 193, 195, 197, 206, 232, 236, 243, 253, 257, 276, 278, 297, 315; fighters from/in, 7, 91, 95, 100–1, 125, 139, 146, 180, 247, 299; imposition of no-fly zone, 5, 54, 65, 111, 189, 295, 313; internally displaced persons (IDPs) during, 157, 244; NATO airstrikes during, 2, 5, 48, 54, 64, 66, 70, 75, 77, 81, 87, 105–6, 112, 116–19, 123–4, 138, 173, 229, 245, 251–2, 255, 271–2, 275; Operation Odyssey Dawn, 110, 116, 121; Operation Unified Protector, 110, 116, 121; plans for 'Day of Rage', 180–1, 233; pro-government rallies, 234; role of Sa'adi tribes in, 221; seizure of Gharyan and Zawiya, 88–9; Siege of Bab al-Azizyya, 93; Siege of Benghazi, 39, 105–6, 109–10, 124; Siege of Misrata, 11, 238–50, 253–5; Tibesti car bombing, 43; urban warfare in 245–50; use of sexual violence during, 156; use of social media and ICT during, 56, 61, 231, 241, 263; Zawiya Uprising, 236, 242

389

220, 307; demonstrations/riots in, 33, 234, 262–3; local governing council of, 221; NTC representatives from, 185

al-Ba'ja, Fathi: 33, 50, 53, 57, 64–5, 185–8, 192, 195, 313; author of 'Vision of a Democratic Libya', 39; drafting of 'Roadmap for Libya', 40; supporters of, 52, 185; visit to Washington DC (2011), 53

Bani Walid (city): 12–13, 82, 91, 97–8, 103, 137, 149–50, 160, 162, 186, 210, 237, 276, 282, 294–5, 298, 300–2; arrival of Saif al-Islam al-Qadhafi, 298–9; branches of, 292–3, 296; conflict with Misrata, 287, 289–90, 292, 297; failed coup d'état (1993), 12, 289–91, 296; local council of, 299–300; siege and sacking of, 279, 299; sheltering of loyalists, 296–7, 299; support for Qadhafi regime in, 12, 123, 295–6

Bani Walid Crisis Administration Committee: 296

al-Banna, Hasan: founder of Muslim Brotherhood, 178

Bannur, Jamal: 33

Bara'sa (tribe): 211, 218

al-Bara'si, Abdullah Hasan: death of, 127, 135–6

Barawi, Fawzi: background of, 201

Barqa Conference (see Cyrenaica): Barqa Declaration, 218–19; participants in, 218

Barqa Military Council: 218, 223; members of, 218

Barqa Regional Guard: 223

Barqa Youth Movement: 226–7; members of, 226

al-Baruni, Sulaiman: 232; forces led by, 260; opposition to, 260

Bashagha, Fathi: 109; position in Misratan network, 73, 108, 118

Bashir, General Abd al-Salam: forces led by, 270

Ba'ur, Tahir: 242, 244, 250–1; Secretary of MUR, 237

battalions, revolutionary (see militias): ix, 23, 91, 98, 101, 107–8, 121, 137, 139, 156, 245–7; 17 February Battalion (Benghazi); 114, 190–2, 201; 17 February Battalion (Bilhajj), 77; 28 May Battalion, 297,; Abu Slim Martyr's Battalion, 201–2; Abu Ubaida bin al-Jarrah, 201; Ahmad Sharif, 312, creation of, 107–8; entry into Tripoli; 91–4, fight against Bani Walid, 298–301; governance of; 98–104, 139–43; impact on NTC and GNC, 25, 49, 204; issues in transitional justice, 145–6, 156–7, 163, 165, 167, 300–1, members of, 123; Misratan, 85–6, 229, 232–55, 238–9, 246–9; Nur, 202; pro-federalist, 218, 221; Qa'qa', 282; Tripolitanan, 77, 89–93; Salafist, 201–2; Umar al-Mukhtar Battalion, 114, 190–2; western mountains (inc. Zintani), 273–8

Bay, General Nuri: forces led by, 231

Bazama, Abd al-Karim: meeting with Abd al-Salam al-Hasi (2011), 34

Bedouin: culture of, 232, 298; territory inhabited by, 209; tribal governance traditions of, 208

Belgium: 110; Brussels, 63–4; government of, 63

Benghazi (city): 1, 6, 19, 26, 35–7, 44, 49, 51, 57, 62, 68–70, 72, 74–5, 77–8, 82, 87, 91, 94, 97, 107, 113, 125, 127, 137, 144, 166, 179–81, 183–93, 195–6, 200–2, 205–6, 208–10, 213–19, 222–4, 227, 243, 245, 291,

Internal Security Service: ix, 277; offices of, 264; remit of, 158; revenge killings of, 157

internal state security infrastructure (*al-Amn al-Dakhili*): x, 60–1, 154, 289–90; extrajudicial executions, 156; imprisonment, 154–5; personnel of, 61; torture, 156

International Atomic Energy Authority (IAEA): 140–1

International Committee for Missing Persons: 172

International Committee of the Red Cross (ICRC): 97

International Court of Justice (ICJ): ruling on Ouzou Strip ownership (1994), 307

International Criminal Court (ICC): 154, 159, 164, 168; arrest warrants issued by, 166–7, 241; detaining of personnel of (2012), 167; jurisdiction of, 144; Office of Public Defence Counsel, 167; personnel of, 156, 167; Pre-Trial Chamber, 167–8; referral of Libya to (2011), 8, 32, 36

International Stabilisation Response Committee: support for Stabilisation Committee, 96

International Stabilisation Response Team (ISRT): formation of, 67

Iran: 189; Revolutionary Guard, 185

Iraq: 2, 67; 'Debaathification' policy of, 159–60; Operation Iraqi Freedom (2003–11), 6, 52, 105, 111, 158, 188; transitional justice process of, 158; UN Iraq-Kuwait Observation Mission (1991–2003), 130

al-Isawi, Ali: 38, 48–9; accusation of role in assassination of Abd al-Fattah Yusuf, 193; arrival of Benghazi, 37; resignation of (2011), 36–7; Vice Chair of NTC Executive Committee, 185

Ishkal, al-Barrani: commander of Imhammad Imgharyif Brigade, 56; defection of, 87

Islam: 10, 19, 29, 163, 184, 186, 195, 197, 202, 324–5, 334; Eid, 48, 224; Ibadi, 258; militant, 205; political, 41; Qur'an, 177, 202; Ramadan, 46, 48, 85, 119, 318; *sharia*, 10, 162, 177–9, 186–7, 200–2; Sufism, 66–7, 187, 207, 210; Sunni, 258

Islamic Legion: creation of (1979), 327–8; use in Niger and Mali rebellions, 328

Islamic Movement for Reform: formerly LIMC, 198–9

Islamism/Islamist(s): 5, 10–11, 14, 23–4, 51, 68, 79, 88, 99–100, 179, 184–6, 188, 192–5, 199–202, 204, 212–14, 219, 223–4, 275, 290, 322, 325, 334–5; agitation, 290; as victims of Abu Slim Massacre (1996), 179; cities associated with, 188; concept of, 10, 177–8; factions of NTC, 4, 53, 186; influence in formation of NTC, 4, 186; influence on fall of Tripoli, 67, 72–79; international movements, 196, 202, 204, 322, 325, 334; interpretation of *sharia*, 187, 202; militant, 187, 212; networks, 2, 5, 67, 71–3, 79, 222; nonaligned, 178, 193, 204; opposition to Barqa Declaration, 219, 223; political, 196, 203, 223; presence amongst fighting groups, 191, 200, 275; radical, 29; relationship with Qatar, 72–5, 77, 203, 275; secular opposition to, 194–5, 203; spectrum, 178, 191, 193–4, 203

Isma'il, Muhammad: 167

Israel: blockade of Gaza (2010), 77

al-Issawi, General Muhammad: 268

Italy: 36, 110; colonies of, 9, 12,

INDEX

Suwaihli, Ramadan: 9, 11, 231–2, 254; image of, 230
Sweden: 110
Switzerland: 181; Geneva, 44; Zurich, 181
Syria: 189; Civil War (2011–), 3; coup d'état (1949), 3; Homs, 236; Zwaitina, 43, 115

al-Tabib, Salim: 185
Tajura (prison): 307
Tajura (town): 55–6, 83–4, 91, 93, 185; arms/support sent from/to, 86; fighters from/in, 85, 89, 99–100; prison, 307; protests/riots in, 58, 60; withdrawal of security brigades from, 59
takfir: 178, 188, 193
Takut (town): 276
al-Tamtam, Muhammad: 265, 272
Tamzin (town): 268; volunteers from, 271
Tantush, Khalid: criminal charges brought against, 166
Tarhuni, Ali Abd al-Salam: 44, 94–5, 102–3, 274; attempt at unity discussion, 101; background of, 43; media appearances of, 94–5
Tarhuna (town): 290, 297, 299–302; fighters from/in, 281; military base in, 56, 82; recruitment of loyalists from, 291; sheltering of Mashashiya in, 276; weaponry sourced from, 82, 94
Tawergha (town): 124, 149, 156, 173–4, 237, 242, 250, 252; IDPs from, 136; Misratan assault on, 119, 157; razing of, 146; retributive justice targeting population of, 157; torture of detainees from, 146; use for loyalist artillery barrage deployment, 121
Taylor, Melinda: criminal charges brought against, 167
Tebu: 2, 9, 12, 70, 140, 150, 267, 278, 281, 303–11, 317–18, 321; conflict with Awlad Bu Saif and Awlad Shulaiman (2012), 318; culture of, 315; Daza, 305; guarding posts manned by, 282; networks of, 74; repression of education rights of, 310; territory controlled by, 98; territory inhabited by, 13, 305–9, 311–12, 313–17, 318–19; Tibetsi, 305
Tebu National Assembly: 306
thuwwar (see revolutionaries): 115, 121, 164; amnesties targeting, 169; backgrounds of, 10; concept of, 8; influence over implementation of transitional justice, 164; influence over state-building efforts, 22; internal conflicts of, 22; Misrata Conference (2011), 99; NFA targeting of, 302; opposition to Criminalisation of Torture, Enforced Disappearances, and Discrimination (Law 38)(2013), 169; opposition to reconciliation efforts, 163; reparations promised to, 171; refusal to disarm/disband, 22, 101; retributive justice conducted by, 156–7, 159; self-identification of persons as, 137; use of force to pass Political and Administrative Isolation Law, 26–7, 160
al-Tibawi, Adam Arami: 306; role in formation of Libya Change Movement, 310
Tiji (town): 271; capture of, 276, 280; loyalist presence in, 269
Timor-Leste: Indonesian Occupation of (1975–99), 130; UN Transitional Administration in East-Timor (1999–2002), 130
Tir, Mustafa: 62
Tirbil, Fathi: 192; arrest of (2011), 1, 33, 180, 234

412